Plotting
the reading
experience

Plotting the reading experience

theory / practice / politics

Paulette M. Rothbauer, Kjell Ivar Skjerdingstad,
Lynne (E.F.) McKechnie, and Knut Oterholm,
editors

WILFRID LAURIER
UNIVERSITY PRESS

Wilfrid Laurier University Press acknowledges the support of the Canada Council for the Arts for our publishing program. We acknowledge the financial support of the Government of Canada through the Canada Book Fund for our publishing activities. Funding provided by the Government of Ontario and the Ontario Arts Council. This work was supported by the Research Support Fund.

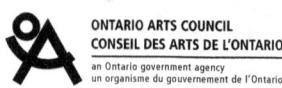

Library and Archives Canada Cataloguing in Publication
Title: Plotting the reading experience : theory, practice, politics / Paulette M. Rothbauer, Kjell Ivar Skjerdingstad, Lynne (E.F.) McKechnie, and Knut Oterholm, editors.
Names: Rothbauer, Paulette M., editor. | Skjerdingstad, Kjell Ivar, 1964- editor. | McKechnie, Lynne, editor. | Oterholm, Knut, 1966- editor.
Description: Published in hardcover in 2016. | Includes bibliographical references and index.
Identifiers: Canadiana 20230237878 | ISBN 9781771121736 (softcover)
Subjects: LCSH: Reading—Psychological aspects. | LCSH: Reading—Political aspects. | LCSH: Reading—Social aspects.
Classification: LCC BF456.R2 P56 2023 | DDC 418/.4019—dc23

Cover design by Svein Johan Reisang. Text design by Angela Booth Malleau.

Some material in chapter 9 is based on portions of *Reading Beyond the Book: The Social Practices of Contemporary Literary Culture*, by Danielle Fuller and DeNel Rehberg Sedo (New York: Routledge, 2013). Copyright © 2013 from *Reading Beyond the Book: The Social Practices of Contemporary Literary Culture* by Danielle Fuller and DeNel Rehberg Sedo. Reproduced by permission of Taylor and Francis Group, LLC, a division of Informa plc.

© 2016 Wilfrid Laurier University Press
Waterloo, Ontario, Canada
www.wlupress.wlu.ca

Every reasonable effort has been made to acquire permission for copyrighted material used in this text, and to acknowledge all such indebtedness accurately. Any errors and omissions called to the publisher's attention will be corrected in future printings.

No part of this publication may be reproduced, stored in a retrieval system, or transmitted, in any form or by any means, without the prior written consent of the publisher or a licence from the Canadian Copyright Licensing Agency (Access Copyright). For an Access Copyright licence, visit http://www.accesscopyright.ca or call toll free to 1-800-893-5777.

For their work on the reader's experience of reading, which continues to inform and inspire, we dedicate this volume to

Dr. Catherine Sheldrick Ross, Reading Scholar, Professor and Dean Emerita of the Faculty of Information and Media Studies, University of Western Ontario

and

Dr. Jofrid Karner Smidt, Scholar of Literature and Reception Theory, Professor Emerita of the Department of Archivistics, Library and Information Studies at Oslo and Akershus University College of Applied Sciences

Contents

List of Figures and Tables • ix

Acknowledgements • xi

1. Introduction: Plotting the Reading Experience • *Kjell Ivar Skjerdingstad and Paulette Rothbauer* • 1

PART 1 • THEORY

2. The Hidden Foundations of Critical Reading • *Magnus Persson* • 19

3. What Is a Reading Experience? The Development of a Theoretical and Empirical Understanding • *Gitte Balling* • 37

4. Reimagining Reading • *Gabrielle Cliff Hodges* • 55

5. Evidence of Reading? The Swedish Public's Letters to Selma Lagerlöf: Quantitative and Qualitative Approaches to the History of Reading • *Jenny Bergenmar and Maria Karlsson* • 73

6. Byatt versus Bloom: or, Reading by Patricide versus Reading by Love • *Marianne Børch* • 87

7. A Cognitive Poetic Approach to Researching the Reading Experience • *Sara Whiteley* • 99

8. Tempering Ambiguity – The Quality of the Reading Experience • *Kjell Ivar Skjerdingstad and Knut Oterholm* • 115

PART 2 • PRACTICE

9. Fun ... and Other Reasons for Sharing Reading with Strangers: Mass Reading Events and the Possibilities of Pleasure • *Danielle Fuller and DeNel Rehberg Sedo* • 133

10. The Once and Future Self: (Re)reading Personal Lists, Notes, and Calendars • *Pamela McKenzie and Elisabeth Davies* • 149

11. More Benefit from a Well-Stocked Library Than a Well-Stocked Pharmacy: How Do Readers Use Books as Therapy? • *Liz Brewster* • 167

12 Literary Reading as a Social Technology: An Exploratory Study on Shared Reading Groups • *Mette Steenberg* • 183

13 The Indescribable Described: Readers' Experiences When Reading about Tragic Loss • *Eva Maria (Emy) Koopman* • 199

14 When Comics Set the Pace: The Experience of Time and the Reading of Comics • *Lucia Cedeira Serantes* • 217

15 Reading Groups in Swedish Public Libraries • *Kerstin Rydbeck* • 233

PART 3 • POLITICS

16 "I readed it!" (Marissa, 4 years): The Experience of Reading from the Perspective of Children Themselves: A Cautionary Tale • *Lynne (E.F.) McKechnie* • 249

17 Reading the Readers: Tracking Visible Online Reading Audiences • *Marianne Martens* • 263

18 Literature in Common: Reading for Pleasure in School Reading Groups • *Teresa Cremin and Joan Swann* • 279

19 Desire and Becoming – Multilingual Pupils' Reading Experiences • *Joron Pihl and Kristin Skinstad van der Kooij* • 301

20 Experiencing the Social Melodrama in the Twenty-First Century: Approaches of Amateur and Professional Criticism • *Cecilie Naper* • 317

21 The Republic of Readers: Book Clubs in the United Kingdom of the Netherlands, 1815–1830 • *Arnold Lubbers* • 331

22 "Crazy Thirst for Knowledge": Chinese Readers and the 1980s "Book Series Fever" • *Shih-Wen Sue Chen* • 349

23 Enabling Testimonies and Producing Witnesses: Exploring Readers' Responses to Two Norwegian Post-Terror Blogs • *Tonje Vold* • 367

Notes on Contributors • 383

Index • 391

List of figures and tables

Figure 3.1   Characteristics of the Reading Experience – The Good Story • 46

Figure 3.2   Characteristics of the Reading Experience – Well-Written • 46

Figure 3.3   The Temporal Dimension of the Articulated Reading Experience • 47

Figure 7.1   A Text-World Diagram of the Three Worlds Cued by Lines 1–11 of "I'll Be There to Love and Comfort You" • 108

Figure 13.1   Main Reasons for Reading *Tonio* • 205

Figure 18.1   Seating arrangements, English classroom • 289

Figure 18.2   Seating arrangements, library reading group • 289

Figure 18.3   Eating in the Library: Group Website Extract • 290

Table 2.1   Critical Reading versus Ordinary Reading • 26

Table 7.1   Groups Recorded Discussing "I'll Be There to Love and Comfort You" • 102

Table 17.1   Twilight Fandom (from *TwilightSaga.com*) • 271

Table 17.2   Alyxandra Harvey's Q&A • 273

Table 20.1   Reader Interest in the Three Novels • 321

Acknowledgements

This book would not exist without the enthusiastic response to our call for papers for a one-off symposium on "Researching the Reading Experience" held in Oslo, Norway, 11–12 June 2013. Over two sunny days on the campus of Oslo and Akershus University College of Applied Sciences, we heard from more than sixty scholars with various perspectives on and approaches to the study of readers and reading. We are sincerely grateful for the generosity of all the participants at the symposium for contributing to this growing international conversation. We also acknowledge the financial support from the Norwegian Centre for International Cooperation in Education (SIU) for financing the collaboration between the Faculty of Information & Media Studies at the University of Western Ontario and the Department for Archivistics, Library and Information Sciences at Høgskolen i Oslo og Akershus. For their ongoing support we thank Dag Jenssen, Dean of the Faculty of Social Sciences, HiOA; Liv Gjestrum, Head of the Department for Archivistics, Library and Information Sciences, HiOA; and Tom Carmichael, Dean of the Faculty of Information and Media Studies, The University of Western Ontario.

The twenty-three papers in this volume were generated from the symposium and were selected for the extent to which the authors's work addressed one of the three distinct, yet overlapping, themes of Theory/Practice/Politics to emerge from the symposium. We thank all of the authors who agreed to work with us, over several long months, to bring this collection to fruition. We are grateful not only for their expertise but also for their responsiveness, patience, and, at times, kindly offered advice.

Finally, we acknowledge the generous financial support from the Research Foundation of Oslo and Akershus University College of Applied Sciences.

Introduction
Plotting the Reading Experience

Kjell Ivar Skjerdingstad and Paulette Rothbauer

The Ambiguity of the Reading Experience

In recent years we have seen a consolidation of interest relating to what could be broadly conceived of as the experience of reading – the affective, performative, material, embodied, and sensual aspects of reading have gained footing alongside more traditional cognitive and social perspectives on reader engagement. In putting the reader at the centre of the reading experience, this volume of scholarly essays provides a multidisciplinary and multivalent articulation of what it means to be a reader reading in and across various social, cultural, and political contexts. It provides insights regarding the relationships among readers, but also between readers and texts, between readers and the institutions of reading such as libraries, publishers, and bookstores, and between readers and the circumstances, contexts, and outcomes of reading.[1]

Targeting the experience of reading, however, is not easy. To experience and to read are both highly complex phenomena that involve body, sense, and affect; at the same time, they entail cognitive processes taking place in certain historical and geographical settings. As Derek Attridge puts it, "to experience something is to encounter or undergo it, to be exposed to and be transformed by it, without necessarily registering it – or all of it – as an emotional, physical or intellectual event" (2004, 19). Following from Attridge's definition, we address reading in this volume as both the experience and the learning that we draw from that which has been lived through, highlighting in turn both the ambiguity of the reading experience and the existential possibilities of reading for transforming people.

Just as experience is a notion hard to grasp fully in a definition, so too is reading. In his still influential work *The Psychology and Pedagogy of Reading*, E.B. Huey resists defining reading:

> Reading itself, as a psycho-physiological process, is almost as good as a miracle ... To completely analyze what we do when we read would almost be the acme of a psychologist's achievements, for it would be to describe very many

of the most intricate workings of the human mind, as well as to unravel the tangled story of the most remarkable specific performance that civilization has learned in all its history. (1908, 5–6)

Following Huey then, reading must still be understood as an open and uncertain phenomenon. Besides perceiving the mystery of reading, he laments that while humans have been busy engineering locomotives or telegraphy, they have forgotten to consider the act of reading with a similar fervour (421). However, paradoxically, Huey's two-mindedness might be read as a confirmation of an attitude that is profoundly uncertain of reading, although certain in observing its importance and impact on the development of modernity.

Starting out from *experience* and *reading*, this book underscores that the doubled openness of experiencing and reading is, following Hans-Georg Gadamer, "due not to a deficiency in reflection but to the essence of the historical being that we are" (1989, 302). Of course, the inability to grasp a phenomenon fully may be due to a lack of knowledge or effort, but it is also, as Gadamer points out, an indispensable condition of being, understanding, and reading. For Gadamer, reading means being embedded in contexts that can never be fully understood. As the father of modern hermeneutics, his point – which may be translated as the art of reading – is that even though understanding is always uneasy and unsettled, it is possible for the reader-subjects to reach a common or shared understanding that approaches a "true" reading achieved through articulation of and dialogues in language.

While subscribing to this argument, the overall strategy of this volume is also the opposite. More than searching for mutual agreement and consensus, we follow Ludwig Wittgenstein, who encourages us to seek the meaning of phenomena not through definition but by plotting significance in different *practices* where they are *in use*. Our investigation then is, as Wittgenstein has put it, "directed not towards phenomena, but, as one might say, towards the '*possibilities*' of phenomena" (1986, 42). So, while the authors of the different essays in this volume all explore the reading experience, we resist reducing the complexity of the phenomena under study to a least common denominator. Rather, we seek to investigate the possibilities of reading by plotting a variety of understandings. In other words, we give full play to the tension between a drive to define "the meaning" of the reading experience and a recognition of the futility of such foreclosure.

Although our point of departure here is an open understanding, to review some definitions of a reading experience may be valuable. In the chapter "The Reading Experience" in their book *Reading Matters*, Ross, McKechnie, and Rothbauer (2006) depart from the scarce information on "real" reading that survey data and statistical averages can offer. Without actually defining the term in a strict sense, they show that readers experience reading as living inside a situation, as deep enjoyment flowing through the book or in one's own mind, and as being enchanted. The homepage of the *Reading Experience Database* (RED), by contrast, states that "a 'reading experience' means a recorded engagement with a written or printed text – beyond the mere fact of possession" (Reading Experience Database 2014). Given RED's concern for collecting, maintaining or archiving materials, this definition is both precise and useful. For many of the essays in this volume it may be read as an orienting backdrop.

At the same time, however, such a definition reveals a more general methodological and theoretical problem: RED addresses testimonies of reading experiences rather than experiences of reading. It is precisely this "blind spot" that is the starting point of this book: a subject's understanding or articulation, written or oral, of a reading experience is different from the reading experience as such – or only a part of it is – as Gitte Balling argues in her theoretical chapter. The articulation of the experience is both separated in time from a presumed actual affective experience, and of a different character than cognition and language. Therefore, there is both a difference and an intimate connection between experiencing and articulating experience, between its corporeal, sensuous, and affective, and cognitive and linguistic dimensions.[2]

We are concerned with the possibilities of the reading experience and aim to disclose *a* – not *the* – heterogeneity of its functions, qualities, uses, and pleasures in a manner that should convey the ambiguity of our subject. By *plotting* the reading experience, we thus refer to an effort to see a wide range of characterizing features. As this volume has grown out of research and education in Library and Information Science – itself an interdisciplinary nexus of scholarship – it has been an editorial strategy to select essays from a variety of scholarly fields, theoretical positions, and methodological stances of divergent perspectives, some of which may even contradict one another. This diversity of voices of researchers and traditions corresponds to the collecting and mediating principles of the library itself and its constituent discipline. There is, we hope, a persuasive logic in describing this volume in the developing field of what we might term "reading studies"[3] as a small library, a community enlivened by the lack of consensus – an agora. In plotting the reading experience by way of numerous specific research contributions, and as each of these works situates itself in the surrounding landscape of research, we present a map of a select research front on the reading experience.

Setting the Coordinates

By addressing the experience of reading, we privilege reading both as a phenomenon pertaining to individuals and their subjectivity and as part of their practice as social and cultural beings. This understanding is reflected in how this volume is divided into three distinct yet imbricated sections – *Theory*, *Practice*, and *Politics*.

With Theory we want to highlight both the need for profound conceptual understanding of the phenomenon under study and the fact that reading is itself of first-order theory: theory is etymologically connected to discovering, seeing, revising – to *reading*, in other words. In this first section we are particularly concerned with representing some ways of conceptualizing the experience of reading.

As both a consequence and a prerequisite for the theoretical chapters, we set out in the second part, Practice, to represent some individual and social practices of reading. We emphasize that reading is also *doing* in that it is experienced and enacted in a variety of ways always situated – socially, historically, economically and so on. Furthermore, as a practice, reading must be thought of partly as realizing an intention, partly as an answer to a text read in context.

In Politics, a focus on the experience of reading allows us to see the necessity of an inclusive, broad conceptualization of reading that permits self-determined desire and independent choice along with recognition of the social structures of reading. Through the various chapters of the final section we argue that the experience of reading is political in the way that it supports the autonomy of readers that contributes to the discovery of unknown opportunities in readers' lives and reading cultures.

By dividing the book into three sections with forward slashes – *Theory/Practice/Politics* – we signal their strong interdependence. Rather than seeing these as three exclusive themes, we use them as a kind of analytical framework – as holding places for related concerns. However, each section leaks into the others, in this way allowing attention to be placed on the distinctiveness of the scholar's commitments to one area or another while at the same time allowing us to emphasize the sites of intersection and overlap. In other words, no one chapter, no one set of research problems or questions, no one set of philosophical concerns can reside with ease into any one of these categories. Yet such framing is necessary to hold the phenomena related to the reading experience in place long enough to tease out some of their ambiguities and implications.

Direction/Theory

Concepts, models, and theories should help us understand the world better (i.e., reality, our selves, and others). In this sense, theory is the opposite of myth or ideology – of conceptual structures that tend to blind us or at least to confirm the world as it is (Barthes [1957]1993). Theory is connected to attention, movement, and what Schopenhauer calls "*Selbstdenken*" (1851, §257). But theory is also about reading – in a certain sense, theory *is* reading, as reading *is* theory. Just as the link between theory and seeing is well known, so are the intimate connections between reading and seeing (e.g., Lindhé 2010, 5 ff.; Piper 2012, 26, 166; Stewart 2006; Manguel 2007). In the Germanic languages the word for reading – *lesen, lese, lesa* – literally means to gather together, which again presupposes both a working hand and an attentive look.

Reading – of poetry, of fiction, of reminders – precisely makes us see what we did not remember, know, or even could imagine. Read together, the chapters in the Theory section intend to show this: there is no singular way of understanding, no singular way of reading. Reading is about difference and displays the individual as well as his or her particular situation in place and time. Reading is about gaining knowledge of oneself and the world or just having a good time, it is a way of seeing oneself in the world and of creating images and visions of how things could or should be; and at the same time, reading opens windows to the past – or to the future – as things could have been or might be. Reading is a way of acting or withdrawing, of thinking and being-in-the-world. Although no theory can account fully for reading, different perspectives illuminate distinct aspects, and when taken together they more deeply inform us on the "nature" of reading. The Theory section of this book confirms the overall story of a phenomenon that is impossible to grasp fully and therefore demands composure and a good degree of self-effacement from researchers as well as from teachers, parents, politicians, and readers. In a certain sense we might claim that humility, in the sense of standing back with attentive patience (as Simone Weil has put it), is at the core of reading.

In his chapter "The Hidden Foundations of Critical Reading," Magnus Persson discusses how even critical reading among expert readers, acclaimed scholars of comparative literature, relies on invisible and unheard reading experiences. Persson describes and analyzes some of these hidden foundations of critical reading, looking for "emotional or phenomenological leaks that give us a clue as to what actually happens in the reading experience" (27). He argues that this does not mean that critical readings should be sent "off to the graveyard of long gone theories" but ought to be supplemented by an opening towards "the subjective and experience-oriented, the body, intimacy, warmth, emotion, and pleasure" (33).

In "What Is a Reading Experience? The Development of a Theoretical and Empirical Understanding," Gitte Balling relates the concept of experience to literature, aesthetics, and everyday life as she outlines its character and transformational power. She sketches the reading experience as a cluster of characteristics around "the well-written" and "the good story." Given that any reading is situated in space and history, she further understands the reading experience as a narrative by way of what happens *before* in expectations or motivations, *during* in the "here and now" and the subsequent moods that embed it, and *after* in traces, memories, and understandings.

While the reading experience, for Balling, is individually and temporally oriented, Gabrielle Cliff Hodges outlines a spatial theory of the reading experience by merging socio-cultural perspectives with cultural geography. She suggests that reading should be reimagined "as a space created by readers' trajectories meeting and interacting." She argues that "reading is not about some readers forging farther ahead faster than others, but about spaces created from the bundling together ... of different trajectories, constantly shifting and being reshaped" (58). By recounting biographies of parents and grandparents along with youth, she both creates theory and tells a story that makes it possible to "reach different conclusions about young readers' attainment and potential" (55).

In "The Swedish Public's Letters to Selma Lagerlöf," Jenny Bergenmar and Maria Karlsson discuss "the possibilities and challenges connected to letters from the public to an author as a source in the history of reading" (74). The authors implement a historical perspective to plot reading experiences culled from a database containing more than 40,000 letters written to the 1909 winner of the Nobel Prize for Literature, Selma Lagerlöf. Bergenmar and Karlsson's rich methodology opens towards a theory of reading that depicts the diversity of both the practices and the meanings of reading.

While Bergenmar and Karlsson write about letters to an author, Marianne Børch deals with letters in fiction. She shows how literature itself often represents ways of experiencing reading. In comparing a theory of the reading experience extracted from Harold Bloom with one based on representations of reading in A.S. Byatt's romance *Possession* (1990), she draws a distinction between reading by love and reading by patricide. She shows how the characters in Byatt's novel actually become better readers and better humans – when they read by love. Børch concludes that "the enigmatical process by which past and present, poet and poet, engage in passionate intercourse to beget originality upon an original is better conceptualized as love than as patricide" (95).

In the Chapter 7, Sara Whiteley offers a cognitive poetic perspective on the reading experience by connecting the language of a poem with its effects. She approaches the reading experience as a quality of mental life and thereby demonstrates that cognitive approaches are not "necessarily reductive and purely objective" (100). Following Leech and Short, her question concerns "how, when we read, we get from the words on the page to the meanings in our heads and effects in our hearts" (2007, 287). Whiteley discloses a theoretical perspective that allows access to the reading experience by asking how and why literature creates certain psychological effects and meanings.

In their chapter on literary criticism written by teenagers, Skjerdingstad and Oterholm theorize the *quality* of the reading experience as dwelling and tempering. Dwelling emphasizes the corporeal concreteness of reading as a practice that offers and constructs a place to be – to rest or orient oneself and continue in life as well as in fiction. While dwelling anchors the quality of the reading experience in literature, tempering refers to how a reader navigates between oppositions. In the context of reading, tempering is both a matter of judgment and a practical ability; when taken together, these can transcend reading. Tempering concerns the ability to read situations in a broader sense, to cope with that which is encountered. Through close readings, the authors show that by paying attention to traces of reading experiences, one may disclose important qualities in texts written by seemingly poor writers and readers – to detect something unanticipated.

Direction/Practice

Reading conveys words that enable us to refer to the world, to concepts that make us see at a distance, and to models that allow us to make connections. At the same time, reading is a way of doing. So in this section, we aim to plot practices of reading. This is a story about variety, complexity, and multitude. This accounts of course for the different practices revealed in the chapters, but also for the scientific practices embedded in style and writing as well as in the diversity of methods, theories, and research questions applied. Reading involves the cognitive processes of encoding and decoding text, but also touch, tangibility, embodiment, and action. Reading involves registration and reception, but it is also a *doing* in a corporeal dialectics – a practice. Reading is a craft strongly linked to the hands as well as to the position of the body and the surroundings in which it takes place.[4]

In our daily lives we are immersed in reading – not only in the strong and literal sense as a concentrated practice as when studying Montaigne or relaxing with a Scandinavian crime novel, but even as we look through the shelves of the pharmacy, watch a music video, drive through a crossroads, or turn on our cellphones or washing machine. Plotting all of these reading practices is an impossible task. Neither can we tell the complete tale of how reading plots everyday life or how reality demands and is formed by acts of reading, nor will we divide the reading landscape into distinct fields. Rather, this section presents research on just some of the ways reading is used and enacted by individuals and groups. Again, the goal is to enhance our understanding of the different ways reading is executed by different people according to their situations, needs, desires, and abilities.

In Chapter 9, Danielle Fuller and DeNel Rehberg Sedo investigate the experiences of readers taking part in mass reading events such as author readings and bus tours to the sites where a novel takes place. They explore reading as a practice that involves experiences that go "beyond the book," such as travelling to novels' locales and interacting with authors. They argue that "the social, emotional, intellectual, and aesthetic pleasures provided by reading events work together in various ways to inform what 'fun' means to contemporary readers" (134). They conclude that in "an era of technological transition from codex to e-book, readers are actively seeking the re-mediation of their reading experiences not only through different media, but also through other readers" (134).

While Fuller and Rehberg Sedo are concerned about "big reading" practices, McKenzie and Davies in Chapter 10 investigate the minor and ephemeral. They bring to the surface practices and experiences that tend to be overlooked both by researchers and by readers themselves. Paying attention to the rereading of texts and to the different ways a reader experiences a text over time, the authors explore a temporal dimension of reading that is often ignored in reading research. To that end, they analyze the experiences of rereading lists, notes, and calendars that people use to "keep track of things" in their everyday lives. McKenzie and Davies show how readers in the practice of rereading ephemeral texts produce both the texts and themselves – rereading and retelling their own lives. A banal note in a calendar can be transformed into an emotionally rich story.

In Chapter 11, Liz Brewster highlights that the meanings and aims of bibliotherapy are malleable. While service providers often focus on the type of text used, Brewster's research starts with users and their experiences. By focusing on the qualities of reading experiences and how these may in turn improve health and well-being, the chapter identifies four new user-centred models not previously discussed in the academic literature. These models synthesize readers' needs throughout their experiences of mental health problems in *emotive, escapist, social,* and *informational* bibliotherapy. Brewster explores motives for using reading as a therapy or coping mechanism.

She argues that building on these four concepts will help shape future bibliotherapy interventions in the public library, as well as enhance our understanding of the motives and benefits of reading for all readers.

In Chapter 12 on literary reading as "a social technology," Mette Steenberg explores bibliotherapeutic contexts and outcomes. Taking an ethnographic approach, she studies "shared reading" as a material practice that both motivates and constrains social interactions and that functions as a technology for interacting with co-readers and for building a common world. Steenberg addresses questions of how setting and place as well as voluntary engagement influence the outcomes of shared reading groups. She stresses the importance of the reading group as a "free space" with a skilled facilitator who does not have a therapeutic relationship with the patients, thus keeping the aesthetic purpose of the activity in sight. The reading group is a way of creating "in the words of the staff – 'human' and 'sane' relations not just between patients but between patients and staff alike" (187).

Chapter 13 is also written partly from a bibliotherapeutic context. In it, Emy Koopman examines the practices of reading Dutch author Van der Heijden's "requiem novel" *Tonio* (2011) as represented in online commentaries. She delves into the experiences of why people want to read about the death of the author's twenty-one-year-old son in a traffic accident and the aftermath of this loss. Treating the work as representative of a broad trend in Western countries of autobiographical and semi-autobiographical books about grave suffering – from depression or cancer to dealing with the death of one's child – Koopman depicts and discusses the feelings and thoughts that such literature about suffering may evoke. Her findings show that for readers who have suffered similar losses, such reading may bring comfort, but it may also provide perspectives on these experiences. For others, a sensible and productive curiosity is crucial, one that, as Koopman puts it, goes beyond pure voyeurism and reflects readers' hopes that the author will be able to articulate or give shape to his or her grief.

In Chapter 14, Lucia Cedeira Serantes defies stereotypes about the reading practices related to comics. She argues that a temporal approach to the experience of reading reveals a more complex understanding of what is often termed a "light" or "easy" read. Assigning particular importance to the experiences that surround the practices of reading, she shows how readers construct comics as complex narratives that have smoothly adapted to the temporal requirements connected to a current state of time scarcity. In a digital society that seems to be defined by acceleration, speed, and instantaneity, readers appreciate the specific quality of comics to allow for moments of contemplation. Comics seem to allow for or to enhance a specific temporal duality in the reading experience. The visual element of comics supports a quick immersion in the narrative, thus sustaining an effective and efficient use of the available time for reading.

In Chapter 15, in her study of reading groups in Swedish libraries, Kerstin Rydbeck offers a historical overview of this practice in contemporary Sweden. Reading groups emerged among the upper classes in the early nineteenth century and spread through pietism (which supported a specific reflective way of reading) as well as through the labour and Temperance movements. As study circles became a dominant venue for free education, reading groups developed a political role in the founding of social democracy. In contrast to this, Rydbeck shows that while a great many Swedes still participate in study circles, participation in book circles has decreased and the functions of those circles have changed. Today, she notes, most book circle participants are older, educated women. As groups that have lost their explicit political function, they now demand novels focusing on "life stories," "relations," "sorrow," and "reconciliation."

Direction/Politics

There is a common understanding that reading is a key element in political democracy and individual empowerment. It is a problem for democracy if the understanding of reading in kindergartens, schools, and other socializing institutions is reduced to reading for quantitatively measurable literacy skills or scholastic achievement.

In Canada and the United States as well as in Norway and Britain, we see reading skills garnering attention in schools, libraries, and research – and in politics. Although there are exceptions – like in Britain, for example, where the emphasis in curricula is on reading for pleasure (see Cremin and Swann in Chapter 18) – the predominant way of answering perceived literacy or reading crises seems to be approaches that connect reading to particular needs, qualifications, or levels of literacy.

The potential political power of the reading experience goes further, without contradicting this understanding of the relationship between reading skills and political participation. The works of French philosopher Jacques Rancière enable us to grasp this. At the core of Rancière's thinking on politics are two ideas of special relevance here. First *equality* is the universal and ahistorical foundation for all human being, thinking, and practice. Equality is therefore not a goal for politics, but its point of departure (Rockhill 2009, 2). For Rancière, politics has to do with policing, which again is connected to keeping – and of course suppressing – things, ideas, and subjects in the places they are assigned. "Politics revolves around what is seen and what can be said about it, around who has the ability to see and the talent to speak, around the properties of spaces and the possibilities of time" (Rancière 2009, 13). So inherent in the concept of politics is the ability to see, possess language, speak, *and* to be heard and seen. "There is thus an 'aesthetics' at the core of politics" (Rockhill 2009, 85). Second, aesthetics is understood as the "delimitation of spaces and times, of the visible and the invisible, of speech and noise, that simultaneously determines the place and the stakes of politics as a form of experience" (Rancière 2009, 13). This makes politics a question of what Rancière calls the distribution of the sensible, of what a person is able to see or is restricted from seeing, of what groups and individuals are able to perceive and to articulate, and of who is raising their voices and who is listened to. Politics, then, is the production of equality depending on everyday aesthetics that in turn depend *inter alia* on the reading experience.

This means that politics is only possible when groups or individuals perceive themselves clearly in relation to others as well as to the material world. Politics comes into play when those who have not spoken articulate inequalities so far unseen and begin to talk in contexts where others listen. Aesthetics therefore is inherently political for it allows new ways to perceive, talk, perform, and act. So in Rancière's thinking, which is partly founded in phenomenology and partly in deconstruction, politics, and aesthetics, body, mind, perception, language, and the field of possible actions are comprehended as interconnected and inseparable.

What we underscore in this section following from what we have learned by reading Rancière, is that the seemingly purposeless and most individual readings may well have a political outcome. This conviction has guided the selection of chapters in this section; it also underpins this entire book: Reading is politics.

Lynne McKechnie points this out in Chapter 16, "'I readed it!' (Marissa, 4 years): The Experience of Reading from the Perspective of Children Themselves: A Cautionary Tale." McKechnie shows that among small children, reading and even prereading makes an incontestable argument for the importance of actually experiencing reading. Her research reflects a certain scholarly irreverence and departure from entrenched positions on children's literacy practices.

In Chapter 17, Marianne Martens discusses how the reader has become visible in a new way through the online reading audiences of the digital society. She shows how a largely invisible "implied reader" has been replaced by a visible and vocal reading audience. By analyzing the reading audiences of popular fiction series for young readers, this chapter exposes how readers come to challenge the positions of traditional gatekeepers such as librarians, teachers, and critics. The new technologies provide rich evidence of reading experiences; they also provide publishers with a clear view of a population that was previously difficult to reach. As Martens writes, such audiences serve not only as readers but also as peer-to-peer reviewers, peer-to-peer marketers, and providers of free consumer research and of content.

Chapter 18 offers another perspective on shared reading as Teresa Cremin and Joan Swann consider the reading experiences of voluntary reading groups in schools. They argue that although such groups seem to occupy a liminal space on the fringes of education, they represent a kind of reading experience that extends young people's reading beyond popular fiction into contemporary literature outside the traditional literary canon. By identifying a number of features that characterize and construct such groups that forgo objectives-led approaches or assessment, Cremin and Swann show a way to increase participation in reading. They point to the potential of extracurricular reading groups and the potential of specific initiatives such as shadowing children's book awards to broaden reading opportunities for young people.

Framing the reading experience as "reading the world and self" (Masny and Cole, 2009), Joron Pihl and Kristin Skinstad van der Kooij in Chapter 19 ask what makes passionate readers and what the reading experience actually does. Through close readings of interviews with multilingual pupils, they disclose how *apparently* poor language and limited experiences of reading may have profound intellectual and emotional impact. Hence the reading experience becomes an ambiguous vehicle of children's ways of *becoming*. They argue that to enable this process of individual and political empowerment, teaching has to go beyond the mechanical provision of simple books to "poor readers," and that reading has to be liberated from assessments based on standardized tests.

In a similar vein, Cecilie Naper in Chapter 20 shows how the reception by amateur and professional critics of popular fiction that might be termed "social melodrama" operates in a political arena in which evaluation criteria are tested and contested. Relying on a varied tradition of scholarship concerning "literary fascination," Naper analyzes the assessments made of this popular genre by interrogating the cultural and symbolic influences reflected in the differing stances on what constitutes quality literature.

While Naper shows that the various threads of reception of reading materials are affected by the cultural and symbolic capital brought to critics' readings, Arnold Lubbers in Chapter 21, "The Republic of Readers: Book Clubs in the United Kingdom of the Netherlands, 1815–1830," goes further. He illustrates how regulated and shared reading practices in Dutch book clubs in the early 1800s contributed to national unity. Interestingly, he also argues that these widespread book clubs did this quite outside the influence of reading materials themselves, and that such political work occurred through the organization and conduct of the clubs, which harnessed "the widely shared discourse of reconciliation, from a collective desire for harmony and peace" (344–45).

Chapter 22 looks at the explosion of reading in China in the decade before the Tiananmen Square incident of 4 June 1989. In the context of China's increasing commodity culture, Shih-Wen Sue Chen observes a current trend towards idealizing the 1980s as a decade when the "youthful enthusiasm of a whole generation was released" and when the cultural aspirations of the Chinese people broadened as a result of the "open door" policy. By examining the "Crazy Thirst for Knowledge" in a period following strong cultural restraint, Shih-Wen Sue Chen sketches a backdrop for the Politics section: a documentation of the need to read and to experience reading as "opening an unknown door and seeing a different world" (360). In this way the author highlights the political aspect of the reading experience, regardless of what is being read.

In Chapter 23, the last in this book, "Enabling Testimonies and Producing Witnesses," Tonje Vold examines the blogs that were produced in the wake of the mass shooting that occurred in Norway on 22 July 2011, an unprecedented catastrophe. Twitter, text messages, and Facebook played a crucial role in mediating the catastrophic events there; later, blogs enabled survivors to offer testimonies. Vold shows how the traces of reading experiences left by readers display the readers' need for bloggers to "give terror a face" and actually came to enable these testimonies as witnesses in a "grid of trauma." In her reading of the blogs, Vold underscores how blogging is never "just" reading or writing; it is also a social, interactive, communicative textual practice in that both the invisible and the unbelievable are at least partly graspable, and therefore present a possible starting point for individual and common action through a reconfiguration of the sensible – to use Rancière's terms. Vold's study shows the reading experience to be part of a political practice linked to dialogue and to writing.

Taken together, the essays in this collection cohere around the concept of "reading experience," plotting diverse coordinates that help us, in the end, to navigate the ambiguous, contested, multiple, and intersecting terrains of reading practices, theories of reading, and the politics that are bound up within, throughout, and around reading and readers. This collection represents scholarship from across the disciplines and does not seek to resolve differences in perspectives and methodologies. Rather, we hope to leave a map without boundaries to inspire new journeys for fellow travellers.

Notes

1 The "Researching the Reading Experience" conference was held in Oslo in June 2013. It was organized by researchers in the Faculty of Information and Media Studies at the University of Western Ontario in London, Ontario, Canada, and the Department of Archivistics, Information, and Library Science at Oslo and Akershus University College of Applied Sciences in Norway. The chapters in this volume by Magnus Persson and Lynne McKechnie are based on keynote addresses presented by the authors at the conference.
2 This is a basic assumption in phenomenological as well as pragmatic philosophy. For an accessible argument for this position, see for example, Hans Ulrich Gumbrecht, *Production of Presence: What Meaning Cannot Convey*.
3 We have not included a literature review of related research on reading and readers here, but even a glance at the references in this volume points to the richness of scholarship in the field of contemporary reading studies.
4 See, for example, Julie Wilson, *Seen Reading*, partly a blog with related activities, partly a book of microfictions emerging from the author's observations of readers in public – her literary voyeurism, as she terms it. Julie Wilson, *Seen Reading* (Toronto: Freehand, 2012), http://www.seenreading.com.

References

Attridge, Derek. 2004. *The Singularity of Literature*. London: Routledge.
Barthes, Roland. [1957]1993. *Mythologies*. Translated by Annette Lavers. Reprint, London: Vintage.
Huey, Edward B. 1908. *The Psychology and Pedagogy of Reading*. Norwood: Norwood Press.
Gadamer, Hans-Georg. 1989. *Truth and Method*. London: Sheed & Ward, 1989.
Gumbrecht, Hans Ulrich. 2004. *Production of Presence: What Meaning Cannot Convey*. Stanford: Stanford University Press.
Leech, Geoffrey N., and Mick Short. 2007. *Style in Fiction*, 2nd ed. Harlow: Pearson Education.
Lindhé, Cecilia. 2010. ""Bildseendet föds ifingertopperna" Om en ekfras för den digitala tidsåldern." *Ekfrase: Nordisk tidsskrift for visuell kultur* 1: 4–16.
Manguel. Alberto. 2010. *A Reader on Reading*. New Haven: Yale University Press.
Masny, Diana, and David R. Cole, eds. 2009. *Multiple Literacies Theory: A Deleuzian Perspective*. Rotterdam: Sense Publishers.
Piper, Andrew. 2012. *Book Was There: Reading in Electronic Times*. Chicago: University of Chicago Press.
Rancière, Jacques. 2009. *The Politics of Aesthetics*. London: Continuum.
The Reading Experience Database. http://www.open.ac.uk/Arts/RED/experience.htm
Rockhill, Gabriel. 2009. "The Janus-Face of Politicized Art: Jacques Rancière in Interview with Gabriel Rockhill." In *The Politics of Aesthetics* by Jacques Rancière, 45–61. London: Continuum.
Ross, Catherine S., Lynne (E.F.) McKechnie, and Paulette Rothbauer. 2006. *Reading Matters: What the Research Reveals about Reading, Libraries, and Community*. Westport: Libraries Unlimited.
Schopenhauer, Arthur. 1851. "Selbstdenken." In *Parerga und Paralipomena II*. Berlin, Druck und Verlag von A. W. Hayn. http://aboq.org/schopenhauer/parerga2/selbstdenken.htm

Stewart, Garrett. 2006. *The Look of Reading: Book, Painting, Text.* Chicago: University of Chicago Press.
Wittgenstein, Ludwig. 2001. *Philosophical Investigations.* Oxford: Blackwell.

part 1
theory

The Hidden Foundations of Critical Reading

Magnus Persson

What actually constitutes a reading experience? Which are its necessary conditions? When does it begin, and when does it end? Naive questions perhaps, but certainly not so easy to answer. In this essay, I specifically address "the *critical* reading experience" and its often hidden assumptions. The chapter has three parts. In the first part, "Critical Reading in Theory," I highlight two influential works of new criticism that explicitly try to determine the character of critical reading. In the second part, "Critical Reading in Practice," I describe and analyze some of the hidden foundations of critical reading through examples taken from the works of cultural theorists Fredric Jameson and bell hooks. Both scholars take their point of departure from an agenda of radical political change, which implies that the tensions between the critical and the (politically) passionate ought to be especially interesting and revealing. Finally, I draw some conclusions and summarize some of the merits and blind spots of critical reading.

Critical Reading in Theory

Despite the growing academic interest in real readers, literary scholars are a category of readers whose reading experiences we know very little about. This is somewhat paradoxical both because of the importance and impact of scholarly writing on new generations of readers and teachers, and because of the massive documentation available containing interpretations, "readings," of literary works.

These readings present implicit models of how the reading of literature should be exercised. These models can look very different in terms of ideological and theoretical orientation, yet most of them are united by an ideal of *critical reading*. Furthermore, critical reading is often considered to be "owned" by the academy (Warner 2004) and is contrasted to ordinary readers' reading. Guillory (2000) claims, for example, that due to the boom in theory, the relation between these two categories of readers can be described as a gap that has increasingly widened since the 1960s. Professional critical reading is characterized by distance, requires hard work, and rejects pleasure as a motivation or goal for reading. Lay reading, by contrast, valorizes immersion, identification, and pleasure. Another way to describe the gap is as a difference between studying and *just* reading literature. However, such a dichotomy may obscure as much as it reveals (Persson 2011).

In light of the "affective turn" (Clough and Halley 2007) and the growing interest in the emotional, bodily, and sensual aspects of reading, the doxa of critical reading has, in its turn, been subject to critique by several scholars (e.g., Gallop 2004; Sedgwick 2003). But the outcome of these critiques should not be a simple inversion of the hierarchy between critical and pleasurable reading. Much more interesting is to try to get a grip on the underlying motives and assumptions of critical reading. This way of reading has indeed its own kinds of pleasure, as Rita Felski (2011) suggests.

There are, of course, many types of critical reading. A broad and useful division is made by John Hillis Miller (2002) when he proposes a distinction between rhetorical reading and cultural criticism. The foremost characteristic of rhetorical reading is the rigorous close reading of texts in terms of what linguistic devices are being used to create the magic of the text, or the illusion of transparency: figurative language, shifting points of view, irony, and so on. Cultural criticism strives to reveal how texts mediate ideological notions of class, gender, and race relations. The aim is to denaturalize what is represented as natural, commonsensical, or universal. Both Fredric Jameson and bell hooks belong to this category.

I will start with two examples taken from New Criticism, as it is an early and clear example of what Hillis Miller calls the rhetorical variant of critical reading. New Criticism is also frequently associated with a refutation of anything with the slightest air of subjectivity, naivety, and emotionality. Strong demands on objectivity prevail, along with an imperative to focus on the text itself rather than irrelevant external factors. The point of revisiting New Criticism is that this movement was fighting for close reading before it was institutionalized, so those foundations of critical reading that were later to become hidden, are here still visible. Then I will jump forward more than fifty years and try to summarize the critique of critical reading pursued by contemporary scholars such as Karin Littau, Rita Felski, and Michael Warner.

That New Criticism should have something *in principal* against emotions in literature and the reading of it is, however, a misconception – and a frequent one. The title of the sequel to Monroe C. Beardsley's and W.K. Wimsatt's famous essay "The Intentional Fallacy" – "The Affective Fallacy (1954) – leads the mind in such a direction, but its mission is not to banish emotions while reading poetry, but rather to question certain kinds of feelings and, more importantly, certain theories about the emotions. The authors turn against a number of historical and contemporary strands of what they call affective theories. One of these is the physiological form of affective criticism, which indulges in goose-flesh experiences, shivers down the spine, and strong gut feelings. Another variant is the theory of hallucination, which is characterized by a focus on reading experiences where the immersion is so strong that the difference between the literary work and reality is erased. At the time, Beardsley and Wimsatt noted, with slight relief, that such naive readerly reactions were found primarily among "the myriad audience of movie and radio" (1954, 31). A third form of affective criticism is the experimental one, which has "led them [the readers] into the dreary and antiseptic laboratory," asked them what colours that come to mind when reading a poem by Keats, and measured their "psychogalvanic reflexes" (1954, 31).

Beardsley and Wimsatt stress that the poetic discourse often is about emotions and that it probably is the case that "poets have been leading expositors of the laws of feeling" (1954, 39). But their main point is that the feelings activated in the reading experience are irrelevant if they do not correlate with the poem itself (cf. T.S. Eliot's objective correlative):

> The more specific the account of the emotion induced by a poem, the more nearly it will be an account of the reasons for emotion, the poem itself, and the more reliable it will be as an account of what the poem is likely to induce in other – sufficiently informed – readers. (1954, 34)

According to Beardsley and Wimsatt, the objective critic should simply not pay any attention to the reader's intense mental images or strong emotions. They cannot be falsified (how could they be?), and they are not relevant other than as, at best, a description of the meaning the poem already has. If affective criticism were given free scope, the result would be total relativism, or, in the dramatic words of the authors, "the sequence of licenses is endless" (1954, 27).

It is striking how the bodily dimensions of the reading experience come out badly in this article. An example:

> The emotions correlative to the objects of poetry become a part of the matter dealt with – not communicated to the reader like an infection or a disease, not inflicted mechanically like a bullet or knife wound, not administered like a poison, not simply expressed as by expletives or grimaces or rhythms, but presented in their objects and contemplated as a pattern of knowledge. Poetry is a way of fixing emotions. (1954, 38)

Reason is pitted against emotion, objectivity against subjectivity. Reading is a cold, cerebral activity, as when Beardsley and Wimsatt tell the following tale, with approval, and with an implicit gender coding: "Thomas Mann and a friend came out of a movie weeping copiously – but Mann narrates the incident in support of his view that movies are not art. 'Art is a *cold* sphere'" (1954, 31).

Nonetheless, the merit of the essay on the affective fallacy by Beardsley and Wimsatt is that the reading experience is put under explicit scrutiny, even though the conclusion is that in the long run it is of no particular interest for the field of serious criticism. And by this, they sanction the hidden assumptions of critical reading for future generations of literary scholars.

Let me give one more example from New Criticism. I.A. Richards was not only a central figure within New Criticism, but also a pioneer in empirical reception studies. His goals are similar to those of Beardsley and Wimsatt – to remove the obstacles for objective criticism – but he grants a larger significance for the reading experience and the role of emotions in it. In *Practical Criticism* (1929) he emphasizes how incredibly hard it is to describe and analyze feelings. He therefore sees a necessary relationship between literary studies and psychology. He writes that the reader's personal situation influences his or her reading, and that one is often drawn to poetry for a mirror of one's latest emotional crisis. Furthermore, this is nothing for which to apologize:

> Thus memories, whether of emotional crisis or of scenes visited or incidents observed, are not to be hastily excluded as mere personal intrusions. That they are personal is nothing against them – all experience is personal – the only conditions are that they must be genuine and relevant, and must respect the liberty and autonomy of the poem. (Richards [1929]1956, 227)

Nevertheless, his verdict on his students' ways of reading poetry is harsh. Richards, as you may recall, had a large number of students read and comment on poems. Most of the students obviously failed to obtain the "relevant mental condition" in their reading experiences. The list of the most common problems for the understanding of poetry becomes very long: difficulties in understanding both the literal and the symbolic levels; rhythm and other formal aspects; stock responses; general critical preconceptions. Also on the list are what are called "mnemonic irrelevances," and these include irrelevant associations, memories of events in one's own life, and emotional reactions that are not pertinent to the poem at hand ([1929]1956, 12–15). So despite a more open attitude towards the significance of personal experiences and the role of emotions, Richards stresses that it is paramount that relevance be tested in relation to the text itself. In an interesting passage, Richards discusses what can trigger the emotions, and he acknowledges that it can be all sorts of strange things, such as the weather, drugs, fatigue, and illness. Then the critic gives us an unusual glimpse of one of his own (unsuccessful) reading experiences:

> I reluctantly recall that the last time I had influenza a very stupid novel filled my eyes with tears again and again until I could not see the pages. Influenza is thought by many to be a disorder of the autonomic nervous system, and if this be so, there would be nothing surprising in this effect. All our emotional susceptibilities may be more or less affected, but the results are most marked with those which we can luxuriate in, those which do not obviously endanger our self-esteem. ([1929]1956, 243)

It is a moving scene, where Richards actually contradicts his colleagues Beardsley and Wimsatt: the feelings evoked by reading literature can spread like "an infection or a disease." Once again it is the body and the emotions that make a mess of things, becoming obstacles for achieving the "relevant mental condition." Thomas Mann crying at the movies, or Richards crying over a book, is obviously so inappropriate that the artworks in question cannot really be art. That these strong emotional responses could be relevant objective correlatives is never considered.

What can we learn from these examples of new critical discussions of the reading experience? By highlighting flaws and fallacies, and through the sharp dividing lines between emotions, experiences, and associations that are relevant and genuine and those that are not, we get a sample of everything that critical reading is *not*. But does not New Criticism belong to history? The belief in the absolute autonomy of the poem is long since gone, and the prominence attached to the reader's co-productive role in making meaning has become common sense within literary theory. My point here is that we get a very clear example of how the distinction between the reading experience and its result is constructed. The reading experience becomes a necessary detour to the finished, and preferably written, interpretation of the literary work. All distractions and digressions along the way, all blind spots and false steps, all personal associations and feelings, all of this is sorted away and buried in oblivion.

The privileging of analytical distance runs like a common thread through modern literary theory. To name just one example, which I have analyzed thoroughly in another context (Persson 2011), we find the same emphasis on overcoming the subjective and "irrelevant" in a reader-oriented theorist such as Jonathan Culler (1975). But Culler's reader is not a reader of flesh and blood, but an ideal reader who has internalized the interpretative conventions sanctioned by the literary institution. Actual reader behaviours are not interesting, according to Culler:

> For behaviour can be influenced by a host of irrelevant factors: I may not have been paying attention at a given moment, may have been led astray by purely personal associations, may have forgotten something important from an earlier part of the text, may have made what I would recognize as a mistake if it were pointed out to me. ([1975]2002, 143)

I claim that all of the factors that Culler mentions are happening all the time in every reading experience – and that they therefore cannot be irrelevant! The echo from New Criticism a couple of decades earlier can be heard loud and clear in Culler's text. And with very few exceptions this stance has been the dominant one. Karin Littau writes in her critical exposé of twentieth-century literary theory: "In this respect, dispassionate analysis, whether it takes the form of a text-centered formalism or a reader-oriented will-to-interpretation, has a regulatory function: to put the intellect into control so as to bypass the unruly passions" (2006, 156).

That the reading of literature within higher education should be critical is a statement that most professional literary scholars would agree with. Indeed, that statement is so deeply rooted in literary studies that it has acquired the status of doxa – an idea that is so seemingly self-evident that it requires neither motivation nor disputation. Karin Littau, Rita Felski, and Michael Warner are among those scholars who recently have questioned the consensus regarding the superiority of critical reading.

Felski recognizes that the idea of questioning critical reading can give an absurd impression. What should students of literature be taught, if not critical reading? Some kind of transgression of "ordinary" reading must take place, otherwise literary studies loses its reason and right to exist. When a teacher teaches a particular text, the starting point must be that "appearances deceive and that texts do not willingly surrender their secrets" (2009, 28). The reader thus has work to do (with the teacher as boss, of course). The prime mover must be suspicion, and the method consists of reading between the lines and against the grain. As Felski points out, suspicion is the primary value also in those cases where the demystifying activity does not have to be performed by the reader but is inscribed in the text itself – for instance, through various defamiliarizing devices, or deconstructions of ordinary beliefs and ideas. The result is a manoeuvre that distinguishes and differentiates the critical reader from the ordinary reader: "Critic and work are thus bound together in an alliance of mutual mistrust vis-à-vis congealed forms of language and thought. Suspicion sustains and reproduces itself in a reflexive distrust of common knowledge and an emphasis on the chasm that separates scholarly and lay interpretation" (2009, 29).

What Felski describes is, to put it simply, the construction of a critical position (cf. Persson 2012). The critical reader reveals and rejects "congealed forms of language and thought" as they materialize in three places: in certain literary texts, in certain ways of reading, and in certain people. If you switch the word "certain" in the last sentence to "ordinary," the value-laden distinguishing effect becomes clearer. The critical reader stands outside and above ordinary people's ordinary way of reading ordinary literature.

Like Felski, Warner (2004) stresses the unquestioned status of critical reading. For literary studies, it is hard even to imagine another form of reading as legitimate. Yet it is only within professionalized and institutionalized literary studies that critical reading is practised. The academy "owns" critical reading:

> We are here, we like to tell our students, to save you from habits of uncritical reading that are naive, immature, unexamined – or worse. Don't read like children, like vacation readers on the beach, like escapists, like fundamentalists, like nationalists, like antiquarians, like consumers, like ideologues, like sexists, like tourists, like yourselves. (2004, 15)

And, one could add following poor old Richards, don't read if you have the flu. As Warner writes, one could question whether critical reading actually is a way of *reading*. More correctly, it could perhaps be described as a kind of institutionally sanctioned practice of commentary – an interpretive activity that presupposes not only the disapproval of naive reading, but also the idea that the reader should be an active producer of discourse. In other words, the reading of texts should simply generate new texts (essays, articles, books) about the texts that have been read.

A prerequisite for critical reading is that it be possible to draw a sharp line between text and reader. Critical reading, writes Warner (2004, 20) can even be seen as an ideal of how to make the distance between them as large as possible. But how can such a practice legitimize itself in relation to non-professional readers? According to Warner, it is not enough to refer to the expertise of the professional reader, to his or her exceptional competences. The idea of critical reading can be generated from and be seen as an image of *critical reason* as such. Warner writes: "Because the techniques of distanciating knowledge are tied to a subjectivity-forming ascesis toward freedom and have come to define agency in modern culture, a discipline of critical reading can draw on the widest cultural-historical meanings of critical reason" (2004, 23f).

Warner refers to Kant's "An Answer to the Question: What Is Enlightenment?" (1784) and his distinction between immature reading and the public use of reason. Kant states early in his text: "It is so convenient to be immature! If I have a book to have understanding in place of me ... I need not make any efforts at all" ([1784]2009, 1). This passive, imitative, and uncritical reading is later contrasted to the following ideal type: "But by the public use of one's own reason I mean that use which anyone may make of it *as a man of learning* addressing the entire *reading public*" ([1784]2009, 4). From a class or gender perspective, the critical position is hardly neutral. The position is exclusive. It can be occupied by a man of learning, but hardly by women, as we are told at the beginning of the text: "The guardians who have kindly taken upon themselves the work of supervision will soon see to it that by far the largest part of mankind (including the entire fair sex) should consider the step forward to maturity not only as difficult but also as highly dangerous" (]1784]2009, 1f). Here the gender-coded nature of reason that has been a leitmotif in the history of Western philosophy (Lloyd 1984) is more than suggested; it is the same kind of coding that during the whole of modernity has created a link between irrational, bad reading and women (Felski 1995; Larsson 1989), but also with men from lower social classes and children (Thavenius 1991). The critical position is thus not ideologically neutral or disinterested, and in the struggle over who can and may occupy it, much is at stake.

Based on the examples from New Criticism and the contemporary critique of critical reading, a provisional map of what are considered to be the differences between critical and ordinary reading, of what constitutes the hidden foundations of critical reading, can be made. See Table 2.1. Note that several dichotomies overlap.

Table 2.1 Critical Reading versus Ordinary Reading

Critical Reading	Ordinary Reading
Reason	Emotion
Objective	Subjective
Analytical	Naive
Disembodied	Embodied
Distant	Close
Cold	Warm
Text-centred	Personal experiences
Reflexivity	Immersion
Work	Pleasure
Production	Consumption
Academic	Non-academic

Is there not something strangely familiar to all these dichotomies? Is it not so that there is a hidden deep structure that is all too familiar? The critical position is not ideologically neutral, and one could perhaps be so bold as to add the following more overarching and socially encoded dichotomies:

Male	**Female**
High (culture, class)	Low (culture, class)

It is now time to look more closely at critical reading in practice. The following examples are taken from the works of cultural theorists Fredric Jameson and bell hooks. Some of the questions I pose to their texts are: Are there any traces of the reading experience itself in the texts? Do the texts confirm the typology above, or are there openings for transgressions of its dichotomies? Is it possible to say something about the desires that motivate these critical readings?

Critical Reading in Practice

Jameson and hooks have been leading names within critical theory for the past couple of decades. Jameson is considered one of the most prominent Marxist theorists today, with a large number of works on literature, film, postmodernism, and aesthetic theory. hooks is a key figure in North American black feminism, and her research has, like Jameson's, an impressive breadth and a socialist vantage point. Here I give some examples from just a couple of their works: Jameson's magnum opus *The Political Unconscious* (1981) and his book on film, *Signatures of the Visible* (1992), and hooks's *Yearning: Race, Gender, and Cultural Politics* (1990). The examples concern not just literature but film as well. These theorists draw no sharp boundaries between the arts, and their critical readings follow a similar logic regardless of what medium their analyses focus on.

Are there any traces of the actual reading experience itself in their texts? Are there any emotional or phenomenological leaks that give us a clue as to what actually happens in the reading experience? The differences between Jameson and hooks are considerable. Overall, Jameson is much more formal and distanced in his writing. His prose is distinctly academic and philosophical, and if you are waiting for emotional confessions your waiting will be in vain. Nonetheless, the whole of *The Political Unconscious* is really about what characterizes critical reading. This work offers a complete hermeneutic and theory of interpretation:

> *The Political Unconscious* accordingly turns on the dynamics of the act of interpretation and presupposes, as its organizational fiction, that we never really confront a text immediately, in all its freshness as a thing-in-itself. Rather, texts come before us as the always-already-read; we apprehend them through sedimented layers of previous interpretations, or – if the text is brand new – through the sedimented reading habits and categories developed by those inherited interpretive traditions. This presupposition then dictates the use of a method (which I have elsewhere termed "the metacommentary") according to which our object of study is less the text itself than the interpretations through which we attempt to confront and to appropriate it. Interpretation is here construed as an essentially allegorical act, which consists in rewriting a given text in terms of a particular interpretive master code. ([1981]2002, x)

It is interesting to note how Jameson uses reading and interpretation as synonyms. Reading is interpretation, regardless of whether it concerns a "bad," "sedimented" reading or a "good," symptomatic one. Critical reading is a kind of meta-reading in a dual sense. It presupposes the reading of other readings/interpretations, as well as thorough rereadings of the primary text in order to penetrate the sediments of our own and others' previous readings with all their blind spots.

Are there any more personal accounts of what kinds of *experiences* critical reading can offer? At the beginning of his book on film, Jameson emphasizes that watching film first of all is a strong physical experience, which reading novels also can be "if the words are sensory enough" (1992, 2). All of the essays in the book "began in the senses, so to speak, and attempt to derive a historical, perhaps first of all a film-historical, dimension from that initial experience" (1992, 3). Yet immediately after this, Jameson claims that critical reading extinguishes the original reading experience: "I may also say that this kind of analysis resembles Freud's mainly in the way in which, when successful, it liquidates the experiences in question and dissolves them without a trace; I find I have no desire to see again a movie about which I have written well" (1992, 3f).

One could say that Jameson here lends unexpected support to a common assumption among students, namely, that textual analysis kills the experience. bell hooks takes a somewhat different stance on this issue:

> One issue that surfaces when teaching the skills of radical cultural critique to students is a sense of conflict between pleasure and analysis. Initially they often assume that if you are critiquing a subject it must mean that you do not like it. Since I have written critical essays on two Spike Lee films, students will often say "Hey, you're really down on Spike." Or even before they "get on my case," if I express a positive interest in Lee's work, they are surprised because they assume that the critical essays are an attack. In any liberatory

pedagogy, students should learn how to distinguish between hostile critique that is about "trashing" and critique that's about illuminating and enriching our understanding. (1990, 7)

But it is probably a mistake to see this difference as indicative of an absence of pleasure in Jameson's critical readings – for both the producer and the consumer of them. Critical reading has, as Felski (2009, 228) writes, its own pleasures: the satisfaction in finding hidden patterns in texts; the ability to connect seemingly disparate textual elements; making new meaning. A skillful critical reading presupposes an intimate knowledge of the text, as well as a deep exploration of all its details, if the secrets of the text are to be revealed. As Felski writes, "Suspicion, in other words, may not be so very far removed from love" (2009, 231). Nor so far removed from other strong feelings, such as suffering.

In *Yearning*, hooks begins by thanking colleagues, friends, and family members who have been important to her during the writing of the book. This is not an unusual convention in academic texts, yet the confession here is very strong: "Many of these essays were born in the heat of passionate dialogues, sometimes even at moments of intense emotional pain" (1990, n.p.). And hooks does not restrict her emotions to paratexts such as "Acknowledgments," as so many academic texts do; instead, she makes them heard throughout the book. Reading experiences and the circumstances surrounding them (memories that are triggered, personal experiences that are actualized) are a given place in hooks's original academic prose, and this is not arbitrary:

> I have been working to change the way I speak and write, to incorporate in the manner of telling a sense of place, of not just who I am in the present but where I am coming from, the multiple voices within me. I have confronted silence, inarticulateness. When I say, then, that these words emerge from suffering, I refer to that personal struggle to name that location from which I come to voice – that space of my theorizing. (1990, 146)

hooks's position challenges several of the foundations for critical reading. The reading experience as such becomes important. Emotions and personal experiences are not just affirmed but are seen as indispensable to the credibility and relevance of critical reading. Tears, for example, are not seen as symptoms of bad art and a lack of discipline, as they were for the new critics and Thomas Mann. Rather, tears call for deeper reflection. Once again, it is the movies that trigger the tears:

> Riding home from the movie theater after seeing Euzan Palcy's film *A Dry White Season* with my best buddy from childhood, I tried to describe the thoughts and feelings that welled up in me as I watched the film, yet found

> myself unable to articulate them clearly. After moments of violent weeping came a screaming rage about the way western contexts of covert censorship – white supremacy, the academy – make it hard to say what you really want to say ... Finally I found words to talk and write about this film, words lacking some of the fire I initially felt, though sparks remain. (1990, 11)

Here the desires and affective registers of the reading experience itself become visible, and the complicated bridge over to an academic discourse is highlighted. Equally important, according to hooks, is that critical reading not be considered an activity that only can be performed in academic settings. It is not at all the case that the academy "owns" critical reading (cf. Warner 2004). hooks remembers the lively debates in her childhood home, debates about black people in television dramas: "Participating in household discussions about these works, many of us developed critical consciousness about the politics of race. Responding to televised cultural production, black people could express rage about racism as it informed representation, the construction of images" (1990, 4). hooks also emphasizes the importance of critical academics turning to audiences outside the academy, with an awareness of the privileges that come from being able to occupy a critical position (1990, 9f, 29). Jameson never makes, as far as I know, any direct appeals for practical critical activism; rather, he discusses the material and institutional conditions for theoretical work (1992, 47).

I now attempt to describe and exemplify the rhetoric and logic of critical reading. I take as my starting point that spatial metaphor governs much of what happens, or is presumed to happen, in a critical reading: the metaphor about *the surface and depth of the text*. Critical reading will result in a revelation. This presupposes that there is something to reveal, something the text hides. This hidden something is typically not found on the surface of the text, but in its depths, and its visibility demands a vigilant and suspicious gaze.

Jameson's oeuvre abounds with metaphors trying to frame the hidden truths of texts. In a fascinating essay, cognitive theorist Mary Thomas Crane (2009) has discerned four main types of surface/depth metaphors in *The Political Unconscious*: sediment, disguise, shell, and (empty) centre. It is the critic's job to dig through the sediments, unveil the disguise, open the shell, and locate the centre – which may be empty! For critical reading, it is all about finding "the informing power of forces or contradictions, which the text seeks in vain wholly to control or master," or, to put it differently, it is about "revealing those logical and ideological centers a particular historical text fails to realize, or on the contrary seeks desperately to repress" (Jameson [1981]2002, 34). In the depth layer, the text's contradictions, ideologies, hidden values, and distortions of history become visible. The act of critical reading is portrayed as a struggle between a resistant text and an inexhaustible reader who seems predetermined to win. Moreover, the surface/depth metaphor requires a sharp distinction between conscious and unconscious:

> Interpretation proper [...] always presupposes, if not a conception of the unconscious itself, then at least some mechanism of mystification or repression in terms of which it would make sense to seek a latent meaning behind a manifest one, or to rewrite the surface categories of a text in the stronger language of a more fundamental interpretive code. This is perhaps the place to answer the objection by the ordinary reader, when confronted with elaborate and ingenious interpretations, that the text means just what it says. Unfortunately, no society has ever been quite so mystified in quite so many ways as our own, saturated as it is with messages and information, the very vehicles of mystification ... If everything were transparent, then no ideology would be possible, and no domination either: evidently that is not our case. ([1981]2002, 45f)

Here a number of really interesting things about critical reading turn up: not everyone can perform it; the naive/unconscious reader believes that the text is identical to its surface. Furthermore, the aims and rewards of critical reading are suggested: the critical reader sees things that others do not and is thereby granted power and agency. And as ideologies are revealed, domination is identified and challenged. Textual struggle draws closer to political struggle.

The surface/depth metaphor has far-reaching consequences for how one understands the purpose, use, effectiveness, and actors of critical reading. As queer theorist Eve Kosofsky Sedgwick has pointed out, demystifying variants of critical reading (she calls them paranoid readings) presuppose a strong faith in the significance of critical revelation:

> The paranoid trust in exposure seemingly depends, in addition, on an infinite reservoir of naïveté in those who make up the audience for these unveilings. What is the basis for assuming that it will surprise or disturb, never mind motivate, anyone to learn that a given social manifestation is artificial, self-contradictory, imitative, phantasmatic, or even violent? (2003, 141)

Unlike Jameson, hooks does not develop a fully fledged grand theory of interpretation, but she still shows many similarities with his symptomatic reading. The surface/depth metaphor is in place, and so are the consequences just mentioned. In her analysis of Wim Wenders's film *Wings of Desire*, she is surprised at the film's unanimous success among critics and moviegoers. Beneath the film's progressive surface lurks misogyny and ethnocentrism:

> To many audiences watching *Wings of Desire*, the reassuring story may be that narrative which promises the possibility of radical change in European history, in white culture ... Imperialist masculinity is negated, and the new

vision evoked by angelic style is of a world wherein the visionary white men exude divine presence and regard life as sacred. They do so as angels. They do so as men. (1990, 167)

Critical reading is concerned with the internal contradictions of texts, which come into the light if you confront the surface and deep layers. Consequently, hooks (1990, 171) writes that Wenders probably has good intentions, but that "he does not fulfill the promise of his own creative assertions." In the end, the film continues to naturalize whiteness and masculinity. Spike Lee's film *Do the Right Thing* gets a similar treatment:

> Despite Spike Lee's courageous attempt to mix politics and art, to use film as a vehicle for exploring racism, and a popular film genre at that, the movie graphically portrays the racism we know without suggesting what can be done to bring about change. The film does not challenge conventional understandings of racism; it reiterates old notions. Racism is not simply prejudice. It does not always take the form of *overt* discrimination. Often subtle and *covert* forms of racist domination determine the contemporary lot of black people. (1990, 183; emphasis added)

It is hardly a coincidence that the most serious allegation concerns the absence of critical depth. Lee is unable to leave the surface layer and drill to sufficient depth to say anything about the hidden manifestations and causes of racism.

In hooks (but not in any of the texts by Jameson here discussed), there are also examples of that form of critical alliance between interpreter and art work that Felski discusses and that I mentioned earlier. Here the critical reader and the text use the same kinds of denaturalizing strategies, and critical reading is, somewhat paradoxically, transformed into sympathetic reading. This happens in hooks's reading of Zora Neal Hurston as a blend of anthropologist and fiction writer, and it happens in her chapter on Isaac Julien's film on the black, possibly homosexual, poet Langston Hughes. Here is an example of how the critic and the film text are united in the same demystifying project:

> In a world terrified by the onslaught of incurable diseases, one where the threat of aids links death to sexuality, all forms of transgressive sexuality are represented as both horrific and deadly. In such a cultural context, homosexual desire is often made to appear ugly, unromantic, undesirable. Julien's film *critically disrupts and subverts this representation.* Here the homoerotic, homosexual desire that, like all sexual passions, culminates in recognition of the possibility of loss, of dying, is both tragic and full of wonder. (1990, 196; emphasis added)

The film uses the same deconstructive devices as critical reading and can thereby expose the repressive clichés of dominant ideology.

What happens when the surface/depth metaphor is turned into a narrative? Can critical reading be seen as a kind of story? According to Felski, critical reading has strong similarities to the detective story:

> The critic, like the detective, refuses to take surface meanings at face value; the text, like the criminal suspect, must be scrutinized, interrogated, and made to yield its hidden secrets. Interpretation pivots on a skeptical and adversarial relationship to its object; the text, in George Levine's memorable phrase, is treated "as a kind of enemy to be arrested." While ordinary readers, just like hapless Watson, are easily deceived by the evidence of their eyes, the professional reader, whether critic or detective, presses below distracting surfaces to the deeper meaning of signs. (2009, 224)

Felski mentions that there are also big differences between the detective story and the hermeneutics of suspicion. Normally, the detective story does not reveal the killer from the outset, but this can very well happen in a piece of critical reading. The critic gladly names the guilty one right from the beginning – for instance, patriarchy, racism, or capitalism (or why not all three of them?). In critical reading, the question becomes not so much who did it but *how* it was done.

Conclusions

Many of the hidden foundations of critical reading can be found at work in the texts by hooks and Jameson. The basic surface/depth metaphor and the primacy of suspicion are both in place. As a consequence, two types of readers are constructed: naive/unconscious and critical/conscious. In contrast to Jameson, hooks is a contemporary theorist who consistently tries to find ways to cross the border between critical and ordinary reading. This does not mean that she in any way abandons critical reading. She instead tries to enrich it by welcoming practices that ever since new criticism have been deemed irrelevant and unwelcome: the subjective and experience-oriented, the body, intimacy, warmth, emotion, and pleasure. But even as she attests to the value of immersive reading experiences (the tears and the rage), these must be articulated in ways that make them compatible with a form (albeit strongly modified) of critical reading. My comparison of hooks and Jameson may seem to end in favour of hooks, but that has not been my point. In many respects they perform completely different kinds of critical reading practices, and humanistic scholarship would be much poorer if either of them were ruled out. My point has not been to invalidate hardcore variants of critical reading à la Jameson. Instead I have been driven by a curiosity about, not so much critical theory per se, but the critical reading experience. I completely agree with Felski (2009) when she writes that it is not a matter of dumping critical theory in favour of strictly affective reading practices. Rather, it is about breaking up the hegemony of critical reading, about making it more self-reflexive, inclusive, and humble towards other ways of reading.

Critical reading is motivated by various desires and pleasures. In many ways (but certainly not all), they probably differ from the ordinary reader's pleasures. The critical reader values the interpretation of signs, advanced problem solving, unexpected connections, textual contradictions, and hidden patterns. For hooks and Jameson, critical desire often goes hand in hand with political desire – with the belief that demystifying readings can make a difference and that such readings can, however slightly, upset the status quo and have emancipative effects. Perhaps this partly explains both Jameson's and hooks's interest in popular culture – critical reading must not focus solely on high culture; to have relevance, it must also delve deep into the popular imaginary. You can of course always doubt, as Sedgwick does, that critical reading really has the wished-for outcomes.

The critique of critical reading – here represented by Felski, Littau, Warner, and Sedgwick – is important and valuable. But, once again, it is not about sending critical reading off to the graveyard of long-dead theories. In her latest book, media theorist N. Katherine Hayles describes what she calls a crisis for close reading. If one believes her, the crisis especially concerns symptomatic reading as practised by Jameson: "After more than two decades of symptomatic reading, however, many literary scholars are not finding it a productive practice, perhaps because (like many deconstructive readings) its results have begun to seem formulaic, leading to predictable conclusions rather than compelling insights" (2012, 59).

Felski strikes a similar note when she writes that the immense success of critical reading now risks making it banal. Critical reading is the new mainstream: "It no longer tells us what we do not know; it singularly fails to surprise" (2009, 231). The dangers of doxa and routine analysis must of course be met. But isn't there something else left unspoken here, something *hidden*, an underlying logic according to which theoretical work must constantly innovate? The academy is also a market, and the demand for new theoretical goods seems insatiable. For whom are symptomatic readings no longer surprising? The answer is: the theoretical avant-garde, or to put it differently, the entrepreneurs of theory. But as Jameson ([1981]2002, 46) writes, we do not live in a society where everything is transparent, because then "no ideology would be possible, and no domination either." As long as there is ideology, there is a need for ideology critique – that is, for critical reading. That the superstars of contemporary theory have grown tired of it does not mean that today's pupils and students in schools and universities have done so, or that they do not need to learn to master the techniques of this very special form of reading practice.

And there I end my meditation on critical reading. It is, of course, itself an example of critical reading, or rather, metacritical reading. It strikes me that this is clearly hinted already in the title of my chapter: "The *Hidden* Foundations of Critical Reading." And you my critical reader have of course long since located what I am alluding to there. It is therefore with great pleasure I leave the final words to one of the pioneers of critical reading, none other than Karl Marx:

> It is always the direct relation of the owners of the conditions of production to the direct producers which reveals the innermost secret, the hidden foundation of the entire social construction. (2007, 919)

References

Beardsley, Monroe C., and William K. Wimsatt. 1954. "The Affective Fallacy." In *The Verbal Icon: Studies in the Meaning of Poetry*, edited by William K. Wimsatt, 21–39. Lexington: University Press of Kentucky.
Clough, Patricia Ticineto, and Jean Halley. 2007. *The Affective Turn: Theorizing the Social*. Durham: Duke University Press.
Crane, Mary Thomas. 2009. "Surface, Depth, and the Spatial Imaginary: A Cognitive Reading of *The Political Unconscious*." *Representations* 108(1): 76–97.
Culler, Jonathan. [1975]2002. "Literary Competence." *Structuralist Poetics*. Reprint, London and New York: Routledge.
Felski, Rita. 1995. *The Gender of Modernity*. Cambridge, MA: Harvard University Press.
———. 2009. "After Suspicion." *Profession* 8: 28–35.
———. 2011. "Suspicious Minds." *Poetics Today* 32(2): 215–34.
Gallop, Jane. 2004. "Introduction." In *Polemic: Critical or Uncritical*, edited by Jane Gallop, 1–12. New York and London: Routledge.
Guillory, John. 2000. "The Ethical Practice of Modernity: The Example of Reading." In *The Turn to Ethics*, edited by Marjorie Garber, Beatrice Hanssen, and Rebecca L. Walkowitz, 29–46. New York and London: Routledge.
Hayles, N. Katherine. 2012. *How We Think: Digital Media and Contemporary Technogenesis*. Chicago: University of Chicago Press.
hooks, bell. 1990. *Yearning: Race, Gender, and Cultural Politics*. Boston: South End Press.
Jameson, Fredric. [1981]2002. *The Political Unconscious*. Reprint, London and New York: Routledge.
———. 1992. *Signatures of the Visible*. London and New York: Routledge.
Kant, Immanuel. [1784]2009. *An Answer to the Question: What Is Enlightenment?* Reprint, London: Penguin Books.

Larsson, Lisbeth. 1989. *En annan historia. Om kvinnors läsning och svensk veckopress.* [*Another Story: On Women's Reading and the Swedish Weekly Press*]. Stockholm and Stehag: Symposion.

Littau, Karin. 2006. *Theories of Reading: Books, Bodies, and Bibliomania.* Cambridge: Polity Press.

Lloyd, Genevieve. 1984. *The Man of Reason: "Male" and "Female" in Western Philosophy.* London: Methuen.

Marx, Karl. 2007. *Capital: A Critique of Political Economy*, vol. 3, pt. 2. New York: Cosimo Books.

Miller, J. Hillis. 2002. *On Literature.* London and New York: Routledge.

Persson, Magnus. 2011. "On the Differences between Reading and Studying Literature." In *Why Study Literature?*, edited by Jan Alber et al., 177–93. Aarhus and København: Aarhus University Press.

———. 2012. *Den goda boken. Samtida föreställningar om litteratur och läsning.* [*The Good Book: Contemporary Conceptions on Literature and Reading*]. Lund: Studentlitteratur.

Richards, I.A. [1929]1956. *Practical Criticism: A Study of Literary Judgement.* Reprint, San Diego and New York: Harcourt Brace.

Sedgwick, Eve Kosofsky. 2003. "Paranoid Reading and Reparative Reading, or, You're So Paranoid, You Probably Think This Essay Is about You." In *Touching Feeling: Affect, Pedagogy, Performativity*, 123–51. Durham: Duke University Press.

Thavenius, Jan. 1991. *Klassbildning och folkuppfostran. Om litteraturundervisningens traditioner* [*The Formation of Class and Popular Education: On the Traditions of Teaching Literature*]. Stockholm and Stehag: Symposion.

Warner, Michael. 2004. "Uncritical Reading." In *Polemic: Critical or Uncritical*, edited by Jane Gallop, 13–38. New York and London: Routledge.

What Is a Reading Experience?
The Development of a Theoretical and Empirical Understanding

Gitte Balling

There are abundant commonplace notions of the reading experience. For example, a reading experience is described as being absorbed in a good story, when we forget about time and place, forget to eat or even to go to bed. A good read is when we learn about the world, learn about the human mind, and learn about ourselves. It is pleasure and entertainment, excitement and having a good time, but it is also self-realization and mind expansion. While there has been growing empirical research on reading over the years (e.g., in a Nordic context: Hansson 1959; Noreng 1974; Hansson 1989; Berntsen and Larsen 1993; Furhammar 1996; Smidt 2002; Naper 2007), the concept of the reading experience remains understudied. In my effort to answer the question *"What is a reading experience?,"* I begin by framing my discussion of the reading experience using aesthetic theory to explore what I call a *literary aesthetic experience*. I then challenge this theoretical understanding by developing a definition of the reading experience as it is conceived and articulated by real readers in a qualitative interview study with adult readers.

The Concept of Experience

Experience was a key concept in German Romanticism, where the concept of *Erlebnis* was introduced as a reaction to the heavy emphasis on reason during the Enlightenment (Jantzen 2007; Stigel 2007). As an antithesis to the rationalistic and analytic approach to reality favoured during the age of Enlightenment, the concept of experience connected to a more holistic perspective of the world – a perspective related to subjective self-realization (Jantzen 2007). Experience, in this Romantic understanding, refers to an emotional and sensuous subjective event that relates to something authentic and meaningful and that transcends daily and ordinary life.

Erfahrung is the dialectic counterpart to *Erlebnis*. While the concept of experience in both English and French means *to have* an experience (i.e., to experience something out of the ordinary) and *to be* experienced (i.e., to possess knowledge and competences based on the situations we have been in and the life we have lived), the Scandinavian and German languages do not hold this duality. Since the concept in the latter traditions was developed in opposition to the rationalism of the Enlightenment, sense and sensibility are separated in a conceptual dualism instead of being united in one concept as in English and French.

Thus the concept of experience that emerged from German Romanticism separated sense from sensibility, *Erlebnis* from *Erfahrung*. As a consequence, the concept of experience in the German philosophical tradition is juxtaposed with an immediate sensation tied to the experienced moment. Several directions in modern philosophy, including hermeneutics, phenomenology, and deconstruction, have challenged this reduction of complex wholes (Tomlin 2008), and this has had a decisive impact on the present understanding of the concept of experience. Thus Hans-Georg Gadamer in *Wahrheit und Metode* (*Truth and Method*) emphasizes that "something becomes an 'experience' not only insofar as it is experienced, but insofar as its being experienced makes a special impression that gives it a lasting importance" (1989, 61). According to Gadamer, the concept of experience holds both the experience itself and its result. The concept of experience is thus related not only to the fleeting and immediate but also to that which leaves a lasting impression in memory.[1]

Can the duality between *Erlebnis* and *Erfahrung* be bridged? The Danish researcher Jørgen Stigel has proposed a *dialectic of experience* where human sensory perception and human reason unite in a dialectic harmony through an aesthetic approach to reality. Stigel writes: "Experiences as 'Erlebnis' is thus a dialectic consequence of the fact that there exists a counterpart in a more rationally conceived 'Erfahrung' that is the accumulation and processed synthesis of Erlebnis" (2007, 125; my translation). This dialectic that characterizes the concept of experience leads back to Alexander Baumgarten and the beginning of modern aesthetics in the eighteenth century (Raffnsøe 1996). Following Baumgarten, aesthetics as the science of sensuous cognition does not view sensuous cognition as opposed to rational cognition; rather, it understands the two modes of cognition as different yet complementary dimensions in human cognition (Balling 2009).

Aesthetic Experience

But what is the difference between an ordinary experience and an aesthetic experience? According to Gadamer, the aesthetic experience is not simply an experience alongside other experiences – it is the very essence of experience:

> As the work of art as such is a world for itself, so also what is experienced aesthetically is, as an Erlebnis, removed from all connections with actuality. The work of art would seem almost by definition to be an aesthetic experience: that means, however, that the power of the work of art suddenly tears the person experiencing it out of the context of his life, and yet relates him back to the whole of his existence. In the experience of art is present a fullness of meaning that belongs not only to this particular content or object but rather stands for the meaningful whole of life. An aesthetic Erlebnis always contains the experience of an infinite whole. Precisely because it does not combine with other experiences to make one open experiential flow, but immedialtely represents the whole, its significance is infinite. (1989, 70)

The American philosopher John Dewey (1859–1952) did not distinguish between experience and aesthetic experience. Rather, he examined ordinary experiences to determine the aesthetic characteristic they contain. Accordingly, he defined aesthetic experience not as experience in relation to an aesthetic object, but as a particular potential quality in any experience. In everyday life, that includes continuous interaction with other people and the surroundings we experience. But still there is a difference between "to experience something" and "to have an experience." An experience is characterized as a distinct whole separate from the rest of daily life. An experience contains its own individual quality and autonomy, with all elements losing their individual status and converging in a whole:

> An experience has a unity that gives it its name, that meal, that storm, that rupture of friendship. The existence of this unity is constituted by a single quality that pervades the entire experience in spite of the variation of its constituent parts. This unity is neither emotional, practical nor intellectual, for these terms name distinctions that reflection can make within them. (Dewey [1934]2005, 38)

In a subsequent description of the experience, we may need to point out some properties as opposed to others, or differentiate among emotional, practical, and intellectual elements of the experience; but in the moment of experience, these distinctions do not exist. All experiences comprising this unity are aesthetic experiences: "no experience of whatever sort is a unity unless it has esthetic quality" ([1934]2005, 42). Practical and intellectual experiences are also aesthetic experiences, according to Dewey: "Hence *an* experience of thinking has its own esthetic quality. It differs from those experiences that are acknowledged to be esthetic, but only in its materials ... Nevertheless, the experience itself has a satisfying emotional quality because it possesses internal integration and fulfilment reached through ordered and organized movement" ([1934]2005, 39–40). Accordingly, it is not the "what" at which the experience is directed that is important. By emphasizing the unity of the experience, Dewey is attempting to detach aesthetics from its close association with the arts. The essence and value of art is not in the artwork itself, but in dynamic engagement: "Art is a quality that permeates an experience; it is not, save by a figure of speech, the experience itself. Esthetic experience is always more than esthetic. In it a body of matters and meaning, not in themselves esthetic, *become* esthetic as they enter into an ordered rhythmic movement towards consummation" ([1934]2005, 337).

Richard Shusterman (1999, 30) builds on Dewey's definition in his analysis of the concept of aesthetic experience. Based on the history of the concept as it has been developed in the twentieth century, he highlights four dimensions that are central to the tradition of the concept:

1. Its evaluative dimension: The aesthetic experience is essentially valuable and pleasurable.
2. Its phenomenological dimension: The aesthetic experience is something vividly felt and subjectively savoured, affectively absorbing us and focusing our attention on its immediate presence and thus standing out from the ordinary flow of routine experience.
3. Its semantic dimension: The aesthetic experience is a meaningful experience, not mere sensation.
4. Its demarcational–definitional dimension: The aesthetic experience is a distinctive experience closely identified with the distinction of fine art and representing a defining aim of art.

These four dimensions diverge, and according to Shusterman, this is what creates confusion and generates discussion about how to apply the concept. He emphasizes that the combination of affective power and meaning explains how aesthetic experience can be so transfigurative. He also points out that Dewey's definition, which he sees as evaluative, phenomenological, and transformational, has been gradually supplanted by a purely descriptive semantic understanding of the concept, whose main task has been to support the demarcation of art from other human domains. In other words, the last two dimensions in particular are highlighted in discussions about aesthetic experience and tend to define the current concept of aesthetics. In his emphasis on both Baumgarten's understanding of aesthetics and Dewey's concept of aesthetic experience, Shusterman attempts to re-establish the full potential of the concept. In summary, following from Shusterman, one can say that the aesthetic experience is a broad concept that psychologically implicates emotional and cognitive, sensory and reflective processes, and temporally embraces the notions of having an experience and of being experienced – both the immediate event and the reflection that an experience creates in the subject.

Reading and Meaning Making – Literary Aesthetic Experience

The concept of aesthetic experience can be further developed as *literary aesthetic experience* and extended to literature through Czech theorist Jan Mukařovský's (1977) concepts of intentionality and unintentionality. Mukařovský proposes a very broad concept of aesthetics in which the aesthetic experience is potentially realizable in relation to any human interaction. Moreover, he has developed a theory of reception in which the concepts of intentionality and unintentionality are introduced.

Mukařovský's concepts of intentionality and unintentionality are based on the assumption that all human-made phenomena are intentional products, which affects our perception of them. Thus tools are perceived due to their intended practical use. This is also true for works of art, since a work of art is not just a thing; it is also an autonomous sign with no relation to reality, that is, without a referent. This does not mean that the work only refers to itself; rather, all references in the work are only ever potential. To be actualized, they must pass through the mind of the perceiver. Applied to literature, the reading process is an interaction between the work and the reader in which the work's potential references are defined depending on the perceiver and, at the same time, the perceiver's own reality is affected by his or her engagement with the work.

Mukařovský stresses that the activation of the perceiver's perception of reality and experience of the world does not lead to aesthetic subjectivism. Both the aesthetic sign (i.e., the work) and the subject are part of the social and historical contexts in which they exist (Mukařovský 1970). Thus, aesthetic perception depends on a particular text, but also on the reader and on the specific context that constitutes the reading moment. The latter refers to the reader's personal life and life situation and also to the society and the social contexts in which the reader takes part. A reading experience can thus be understood as a process that is consciously influenced by its cultural, psychological, and historical contexts.

Intentionality in a work of art is the force that binds the semantic aspects together into the unity that gives the work its meaning. It is not the artist but the perceiver who (consciously or unconsciously) decides which components of the work will become the basis of the semantic unification. Apparently not all interpretations are possible, since to some degree the meaning-making process is predetermined by the organization of the work. Intentionality (of the piece of art in question) can thus only be fully understood if observed from the perspective of the perceivers.

Any aspect of the work that resists this process of creating semantic unification is experienced as *unintentionality* by the perceiver. Unintentionality teases or irritates the perceiver by challenging the creation of meaning, thereby provoking the perceiver to draw on her own experiences and feelings to make meaning:

> Only unintentionality is capable of making the work as mysterious for the perceiver as is a mysterious object, the purpose of which we do not know; only unintentionality is able to exasperate the perceiver's activity by its resistance to semantic unification; only unintentionality, which paves the way to the most varied associations in its unregulated nature, can set into motion the perceiver's entire existential experience, all the conscious and subconscious tendencies of his personality, upon his contact with the work. (Mukařovský 1977, 121f)

According to Mukařovský, the reception process is a continuous movement between intentionality and unintentionality, since both are essential elements in the reception of a work, and the relationship between them is dialectical, creating pleasure and displeasure, respectively. On the one hand, the reader creates meaning and unity, which creates a sense of pleasure. On the other hand, the reader can also experience a collapse of the reception process: elements that challenge the understanding and require the reader to exert herself in order to establish meaning. This unintended part of the reception process is described as a process of displeasure, resistance, and even violation. The reception process appears to be like a battle being fought continuously during reading. At the same time, Mukařovský points out that it is the unintended elements that make a lasting impression on the perceiver:

> On the other hand, since a semantically unregulated thing (which the work is because of its unintentionality) acquires the capacity to attract to itself the most varied images and feelings, which need not to have anything in common with its own semantic charge, the work thus becomes capable of being closely connected to the entirely personal experiences, images, and feelings of any perceiver – capable of affecting not only his conscious mental life but even of setting into motion forces which govern his subconscious. (1977, 106–7)

This quote shows that unintentionality is an essential part of the reading process as it relates to the reading experience as a process of self-realization. The reading process is thus an activity that makes us aware of the work as fiction, as a work of art, as linguistic structure. However, the reading process also requires that we understand the work in relation to our own reality.

By comparing the aesthetic philosophical understanding of the concept of experience with Mukařovský's reception theory, we might conceive the reading experience as a complex and multifaceted phenomenon, one that potentially creates an expanded consciousness and awareness in the reader. The reading experience is not only "Erlebnis" understood as a pre-reflexive phenomenological experience, but also "Erfahrung," a meaning-making process, one that only takes place through the recruitment of the subject's inner emotional life and experiences. But how does a reading experience manifest self in an empirical context?

An Empirically Based Understanding of the Reading Experience: The Articulated Reading Experience

The empirical study of the reading experience reported here investigates *the articulated reading experience* with a particular focus on *what* readers highlight as essential to the reading experience and *how* this is verbalized. The foregoing theoretically based understanding of reading experiences is complemented by an empirical approach based on a series of qualitative interviews conducted in 2008 among adult readers (Balling, 2009). The empirical study revolves around two main questions: According to the informants, what characterizes the reading experience? And how is the reading experience articulated?

Reading can be seen as an individual activity, first because reading takes place silently, and second because how a text is received is influenced by the individual reader and his or her background, experience, life condition, and so on. Many reading experiences are rarely articulated and communicated to others, but stay with the reader as a silent subjective experience. To initiate an interview where articulation is emphasized can be a novel and unfamiliar situation for readers. The informants in this study were therefore selected from among readers who were believed to possess a certain ability to reflect and who had had experiences with communicating their own reading. The interviewees consisted of two focus groups – members of a reading group in Copenhagen, Denmark, and a group of students from the University of Copenhagen, Royal School of Library and Information Science.

Both group and individual interviews were conducted among the participants in each group. The reading group consisted of eight women between fifty-nine and sixty-eight years of age, all residents of Copenhagen and all retired. For the group interview, seven of the eight members were present. Of the seven women, three agreed to do an individual interview. The students from the Royal School of Library and Information Science consisted of four women and four men between the ages of twenty-seven and forty-four. Of the eight, three male informants agreed to do an individual interview. They were selected to obtain a gender balance among the informants.

The analysis of the transcribed interviews focused on how informants articulated their reading experiences, both in the sense of *what* they said (i.e., content) and *how* they said it (i.e., form). The analysis aimed for connections and patterns among the different informants, and also within their individual statements.

The overall results of the analysis show that reading and reading experiences are articulated in multiple ways. Nevertheless, general trends emerge that to a greater or lesser extent apply to all informants. In the words of my participants, a good reading experience allows readers to:

- gain knowledge about the world and oneself
- experience recognition and identification with the characters
- become emotionally involved
- forget time and place
- enjoy a book that is well written
- activate the reader's imagination. (Balling, 2009)

These findings are not surprising and confirm the results obtained from previous studies (e.g., Hansson 1989; Toyne and Usherwood 2001; Ross, McKechnie, and Rothbauer 2006). Of interest here, though, is *how* the interviewees talk about their reading experiences, as illustrated in the following two interview excerpts:

> Well, I will say that it is relaxing, in one way or another. I wouldn't call it escape, perhaps rather a journey. A reality journey – a journey into another reality. And through this journey one can perhaps gain insight into something else or into oneself; see something recognizable, so that one can better deal with it. (M, 34, S)[2]

> When I went to Iceland, I got a hold of a collection of poems from the Faroe Islands, and read it on the way up there. When I was there I read two Icelandic crime novels, which I by the way thought were really good and better than Stieg Larsson. In the Icelandic novels, I felt the authors described the local atmosphere, which I recognized up there. I probably would not have felt that if I hadn't read that book. It gave me a relationship to the place. I went to a wedding there, and I thought it was funny to have read about the open spaces and the solitude, you can feel by being so isolated. The gloomy atmosphere and the dystopian thoughts you could get in the dark winters. But I also read because it is entertaining. (M, 27, S)

These quotations indicate that reading is something that on the one hand is relaxing and entertaining and on the other hand creates knowledge and experience. This dual role of reading is articulated by other participants as well:

> There is peace and harmony and a feeling that you could learn something and maybe experience that feeling of 'ohhhh ... are they also thinking like that?' That's a good reading experience. (F, 66, S)
>
> But at the same time it creates some feelings in me, makes me able to relate to other people – an old man – what is he thinking? How does he live? Why did he end up alone on an island? And that is exactly what V. said at the beginning – that you ask yourself some questions afterwards. Am I living my life the right way? And at the same time you get answers on other issues, other life questions, and the existential state of it all. (M, 40, G)

Accordingly, the reading experience is characterized both by the mood and the feelings that reading evokes in the reader *while* reading and by the knowledge or insight into human relationships or into other eras or cultures that stays with the reader *after* reading. Relying on a theoretical understanding, we might conclude that the reading experience is articulated by the informants as containing both *Erlebnis* and *Erfahrung*.

However, a good reading experience is not just about the feelings and emotions the reader experiences during reading; it is also about how the reader experiences the book as an aesthetic and literary object:

> I guess the main thing for me is that the language is good. And I think that's why I believe that you can talk about good and bad writers. There are some writers who just know how to spell properly, use proper syntax, and use a metaphor. But it's not just about skills, good writing must also transcend good skills. That's what makes a good writer. (M, 42, S)
>
> For me good literature happens when an author is a master of the genre he writes in, masters the language he has chosen to use, and has control over the characters so that they don't take off on the reader, that they are well-grounded. They must be complex and trustworthy. (M, 27, G)

When a book is well written, it affects the reading experience and the reader's ability to become immersed in the story:

> A story is well-written if you can empathize with the characters to the degree that their feelings become your own. It's all about identification, right? So in terms of feelings, it depends on what you are supposed to feel – is there something special you should be feeling? I will say that I've read books without the big connections to feelings, but then it was something really funny. So you should also be able to laugh. (M, 34, S)

Based on the analysis of the informants' statements, a number of characteristics connected to the reading experience can be identified. Below I have grouped these characteristics around two main characteristics – namely, the *good story* that is *well-written*. These characteristics are visualized in two different figures. The figures suggest a perfectly symmetrical relationship between the characteristics, which is not necessarily the case. The figures are meant only to visualize the various expressions relating to the main characteristics of a good reading experience that emerged in the interviews:

Figure 3.1 Characteristics of the Reading Experience – the Good Story (Balling 2009, 133)

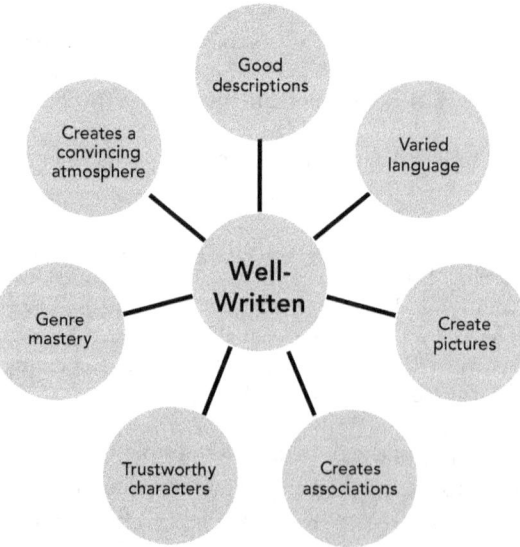

Figure 3.2 Characteristics of the Reading Experience – Well-Written (Balling 2009, 134)

As mentioned earlier, the articulated reading experience contains aspects related to the reading experience *while* reading and aspects related to the *result* of the reading experience. Expectations and motivation are additional important aspects of reading that may affect the reception and thus the experience. When asked about what expectations they have of a good book, two of the informants replied:

> There should be some action, and it should be written in a language I like to read ... If there's too much social realism and they use the worst kind of language, then I can't be bothered to read it. There's nothing for me there. I prefer something that leaves me with something. (F, 68, S)

> I guess it's about being challenged at some level. If you aren't challenged, then maybe you won't finish the book. You might get stuck or think it's poorly written. It has to touch something within you – hit on something personal to you. And it should hit on a wide range of one's emotions too, I suppose? (F, 40, G)

Thus, the articulated reading experience contains what we might refer to as a temporal dimension, where the articulation is linked partly to the motivations and expectations for reading (i.e., the *before* of the reading experience), partly to feelings and moods in the reader while reading (i.e., the *here and now* of the reading experience), and partly to the outcome of the reading (i.e., the *after* of the reading experience). Figure 3.3 illustrates the temporal dimension of the articulated reading experience.

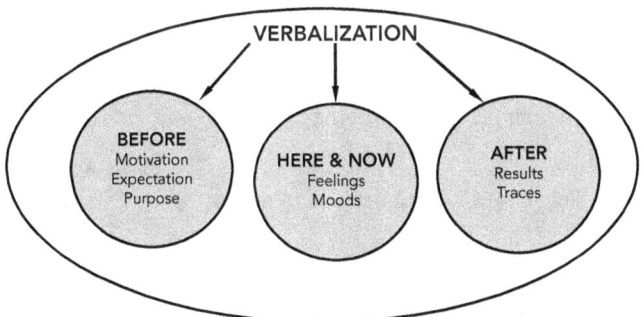

Figure 3.3 The Temporal Dimension of the Articulated Reading Experience – the Before, Here & Now and After of the Reading Experience (Balling 2009, 138)

Readers have expectations, motives, and preferences and perhaps even prejudices that affect them *before* reading. They have particular experiences *during* reading: they are entertained, are relaxed, thrilled, and so on, *while* they read. And they are left with knowledge or a feeling, an experience, *after* reading. When readers talk about their reading experiences, they talk not only about the reading moment but also about the entire culture and the mental process, which together constitute a reading experience.

The Challenging Reading Experiences

The above quotations point to the expectations that a reader brings to a reading experience, as well as the elements that may prevent or obstruct a good reading experience. In many cases the reading experience is obstructed by the same two main characteristics that are highlighted in the above figures: the *language* (i.e., well-written) and the *narrative* (i.e., the good story). Generally, a good reading experience is about whether the reader is able to penetrate the story; is able to build up and maintain the fictional space; and is able to be immersed in the story to a degree and at a level that is appropriate to the reader and reading situation.

> I think it's about finding it peaceful and letting go. It's so relaxing to read a book. (M, 27, S)

> There's this soft floating feeling of being lost in a good story, something you can imagine spatially. It gets your imagination going, right? It activates my picture-making ability. (M, 42, S)

Here the informants describe the enjoyment related to a story's meaning and coherence. Following Mukařovský, this touches on intentionality. Unintentionality arises when something is "sticking out" and damages the flow – for example, in the language or the themes:

> Why on earth was he so negative and why on earth was she so inflexible? Why was she feeling so bad? Why couldn't they meet? Somehow it was too negative for me. (F, 66, S)

> It was one metaphor built on top of the next metaphor built on top of the next metaphor. And in reality, all he was doing was walking through a garden, and that took up eight or ten pages. Not that I am the type that needs constant action, but this was just too much. (M, 27, S)

The experience of inconsistency or of elements with which the reader cannot come to terms may result in the reader putting the book down. But unintentionality can also be a challenge that can be overcome:

> It was the same when I started on Harry Potter. I had to start it three times because I thought it was so stupid. With Muggles and weird owls. I thought: Come on. This is nonsense. Then two of my colleagues told me I had to read the book. And I think six months went by before I got started because there were these characters and because it was just this garbage that didn't work. But then something snapped for me at some point, and I'm not sure exactly what it was, but that kind of is the funny thing about these books – you keep reading them, even if you think: What the hell is going on here? (F, 40, G)

The analysis of the empirical material confirms the theoretical understanding of the reading experience. A reading experience includes both *Erlebnis* and *Erfahrung*, and informants express both the enjoyment of intentionality and the resistance – and the rewards – of unintentionality. The empirical evidence further shows that the reading experience is to be understood as a temporal phenomenon, one that contains a *before* (expectations), a *now* (the feelings, thoughts, and moods that occur during reading) and an *after* (the imprint the reading leaves on the reader). The important finding is that readers do not describe the experience (*Erlebnis*) and the realization (*Erfahrung*) as separate phenomena, but as two sides of the same coin where the actual experience of reading and the result of reading merge.

The Problem of Articulating Reading Experiences

The interview study, in line with other empirical studies, represents the reading experience as a physical and mental phenomenon that is difficult to verbalize (Balling 2009; Escarpit 1991; Berntsen and Larsen 1993). Even readers with a high degree of reflexivity express difficulties with putting their reading experiences into words (Balling 2009). This also applies to the informants who try to overcome it by using words like "well," "in some way," and "maybe":

> Well, what does the story do to me? That's a good question, so ... [long pause]. I guess you could say that with a good crime novel, I just want to be entertained. It is a feeling of spending quality time with the characters that I am on a journey with. (M, 27, S)

> That's hard. You know it when you read it. But it's that combination of one's imagination being activated ... Hmmmmm, I think it's difficult to describe how a book character is not trustworthy. And it's maybe even harder with fantasy. (M, 34, S)

One reason for this difficulty with articulating the reading experience is that language can be characterized as *polyfunctional*: language exists and is used in all areas of life, and words and signs have a variety of meanings depending on the function, the context, and the receiver. Linguistic signs do not get their meaning through stable, objective references to universal phenomena; rather, they are given different meanings depending on the participants' language ability and the functional contexts and genres in which they are put in play:

> Expressed metaphorical language is not a tool made with a specific application in mind, such as e.g. a hammer, but is rather an instrument that can be used to "play" – conversation, sticky notes, textbooks, nursery rhymes, recipes, hymns, statute books, novels – and so on and so on and so forth. (Gammelgaard 2003, 31; my translation)

Another reason for the difficulty in verbalizing the reading experience is that the reading experience is not only a linguistic phenomenon but also a phenomenological and psychological phenomenon that besides cognitive, rational, conceived experiences includes sensuous and unconscious layers of meaning. According to literary scholar Jørgen Dines Johansen, this fact makes great demands on language: "The point is that language must be stretched far and used innovatively to convey sensuous experiences" (2007, 188; my translation).

What Is a Reading Experience?

At the beginning of this chapter I examined reading experiences from both theoretical and empirical perspectives in order to grasp the depth and complexity of the concept of reading experiences. The two perspectives have much to offer in terms of contributions towards expanding our understanding of reading experiences, especially when taken together. First and foremost, the aesthetic theoretical approach sharpens our understanding of the importance and potential that aesthetic experiences contribute to the life of the subject. The aesthetic experience can be seen as a mental room where different understandings and world views can be tested and experienced, thereby strengthening the subject's ability to orient himself or herself and to act in a changing society. The theoretical perspective further contributes to an understanding of the aesthetic experience as dependent upon the subject. The aesthetic experience is about the sensuous and cognitive response that happens in the subject when encountering the object. The aesthetic experience is thus not solely linked to the characteristics of the object, but relates to the subject. This can increase our understanding of why different readers receive the same text differently, and also why the same reader can receive the same text differently depending on his or her life and life stage.

Reception theory positions reading as an extremely complex activity influenced by a variety of factors. The reader creates meaning by drawing on his or her own experiences, associations, preferences and ideas. Further reading is affected by the historical, social and collective contexts in which the subject is situated. All of these factors are part of and affect reading and help determine whether the reader has a good reading experience.

The empirical approach contributes first and foremost to a concretization of the reading experience in terms of informants' statements. This articulation creates an understanding of the reading experience, its elements and characteristics, and its many different manifestations. Similarly, and certainly not unimportantly, it brings focus to elements that prevent the good reading experience, which to some degree can be identified as the same elements that create a good reading experience. Second, the empirical approach exposes that articulation of the reading experience that seems to pose a challenge to the reader. The empirical material further shows that the reading experience can be understood as a temporal (the before, here and now, and after of the reading experience) and a spatial (reader, text, and context) phenomenon. The analysis shows that readers do not distinguish between these temporal and spatial dimensions, but articulate them as part of a total reading experience. The analysis also shows that, despite differences in expectations of reading among informants, there are many common elements that cut across gender, age, and education levels.

Notes

1 The theoretical foundation of this article is aesthetic theory. In a psychological understanding, the concept of experience is seen as a whole, where the structure of the experience contains the psychological, physiological, meaning creational, cultural, and social relations in the individual's ways of experiencing (Jantzen, Vetner, and Bouchet 2011, 47).
2 Notation refers to: Male/Female, age, Single or Group interview.

References

Balling, Gitte. 2009. *Litterær æstetisk oplevelse. Læsning, læseoplevelser og læseundersøgelser: en diskussion af teoretiske og metodiske tilgange.* [*Literary Aesthetic Experience: Reading, Reading Experiences, and Reading Studies: A Discussion of Theoretical and Methodological Approaches*]. PhD diss., København: Danmarks Biblioteksskole.
Berntsen, Dorthe, and Steen Folke Larsen. 1993. *Læsningens former* [*Forms of Reading*]. København: Gyldendal.
Dewey, John. [1934]2005. *Art as Experience.* Reprint, New York: Perigee.
Escarpit, Robert. 1993. "Methods in Reading Research." In *Studies on Research in Reading and Libraries: Approaches and Results from Several Countries.* IFLA Round Table on Research in Reading, edited by Paul Kaegbein, Bryan Luckham and V.D. Stelmarc, 1–16. Munich: K.G. Saur.
Furhammar, Sten. 1996. *Varför läser du?* [*Why Are You Reading?*] Stockholm: CarlssonsBokförlag.
Gadamer, Hans-Georg. 1989. *Truth and Method.* London: Sheed & Ward.

Gammelgaard, Karen. 2003. *Tekstens mening – en introduktion til Pragerskolen*. [*The Meaning of the Text: An Introduction to the Prague School*]. København: Roskilde Universitetsforlag.

Hansson, Gunner. 1959. *Dikten och läsaren*. [*The Poem and the Reader*]. Stockholm: Bonniers.

———. 1989. *Inte en dag utan en bok. Om läsning av populärfiktion*. [*Not One Day Without a Book: On the Reading of Popular Fiction*]. Linköping: Tema Kommunikation.

Jantzen, Christian. 2007. "Mellem nydelse og skuffelse. Et neurofysiologisk perspektiv på oplevelser." [Between Enjoyment and Disappointment: A Neuro-Physiological Perspective on Experience]. In: *Oplevelsesøkonomi. Vinkler på forbrug* [*Experience Economy: Perspectives on Consumption*], edited by Christian Jantzen and Tove Arendt Rasmussen, 135–64. Ålborg: Aalborg universitetsforlag.

Jantzen, Christian, Mikael Vetner, and Julie Bouchet. 2011. *Oplevelsesdesign. Tilrettelæggelse af unikke oplevelseskoncepter* [*Experimential Design: Facilitating Unique Concepts of Experience*]. København: Samfundslitteratur.

Johansen, Jørgen Dines. 2007. *Litteratur og intersubjektivitet. Tegn, bevidsthed, litteratur* [*Literature and Inter Subjectivity: Sign, Consciousness, Literature*. Odense: Syddansk Universitetsforlag.

Mukařovský, Jan. 1977. *Structure, Sign, and Function: Selected Essays by Jan Mukařovský*. Translated and edited by John Burbank and Peter Steiner. New Haven: Yale University Press.

———. 1970. *Aesthetic Function, Norm, and Value as Social Facts*. Translated from Czech, with notes and afterword by Mark E. Suino. Ann Arbor: University of Michigan Press.

Naper, Cecilie. 2007. *Kvinner, lesning og fascinasjon. "Bestselgere" i bibliotek og kiosk*. [*Women, Reading, and Fascination:"Bestsellers" in Libraries and Kiosks*]. Oslo: Pax Forlag A/S.

Noreng, Øystein. 1974. *Lesere og lesing. Rapport om Den norske Bokklubbens lesersosiologiske undersøkelse* [*Readers and Reading: Report on the Reader Sociological Investigation by the Norwegian Book Club*]. Oslo: Den norske Bokklubben.

Raffnsøe, Sverre. 1996. *Filosofisk æstetik. Jagten på den svigefulde sandhed* [*Philosophical Aesthetics: Hunting for the Deceitful Truth*]. København, DK: Museum Tusculanums Forlag.

Ross, Catherine Sheldrick, Lynne (E.F.) McKechnie, and Paulette M. Rothbauer. 2006. *Reading Matters: What the Research Reveals about Reading, Libraries, and Community*. Westport: Libraries Unlimited.

Smidt, Jofrid Karner. 2002. *Mellom elite og publikum. Litterær smak og litteraturformidling blant bibliotekarer i norske folkebibliotek* [*Between Elite and Audience: Literary Taste among Librarians in Norwegian Public Libraries*]. Oslo: Det historisk-filosofiske fakultet, Universitet i Oslo.

Stigel, Jørgen. 2007. "Oplevelse og æstetik." In *Oplevelsesøkonomi. Vinkler på forbrug*. [*Experience Economy: Perspectives on Consumption*], edited by Christian Jantzen and Tove Arendt Rasmussen, 115–32. Ålborg: Aalborg Universitetsforlag.

Shusterman, Richard. 1999. "The End of Aesthetic Experience." *Journal of Aesthetics and Art Criticism* 55(1): 29–41.

Tomlin, Adele. 2008. "Introduction: Contemplating the Undefinable." In *Aesthetic Experience*, edited by Richard Shusterman and Adele Tomlin, 1–15. New York: Routledge.

Toyne, Jackie, and Bob Usherwood. 2001. *Checking the Books: The Value and Impact of Public Library Book Reading*. Report of research founded by the Arts and Humanities Research Board, Sheffield Centre for the Public Library and Information in Society. Department of Information Studies, University of Sheffield.

Reimagining Reading

Gabrielle Cliff Hodges

This chapter stems from a multifaceted qualitative study that aimed to deepen explicit understanding of young people's reading experiences. In it, I outline briefly the rationale for and design of the study in order to contextualize what follows. I then reflect on how bringing multiple theoretical perspectives to bear – the social, cultural, spatial, and historical – can lead to different ways of imagining the field (Massey 2003). I suggest that if we reimagine reading as a space created by readers' trajectories meeting and interacting, shaped by their histories and capable of future transformation as a result of such encounters, we may not only understand it in more depth but also reach different conclusions about young readers' attainment and potential.

Methodology – Plotting Reading Histories

Starting in 2007, I undertook a study over an eighteen-month period, initiated within a state secondary school in rural eastern England. The class I worked with was a group of thirty students being taught by an experienced English teacher, Rosa.[1] A keen reader herself, she knew that many of the students were what might be described as habitual and committed readers. I specifically wanted to work with young people who did read, rather than those who did not. Since the aim of the study was to explore how the readership of twelve- to thirteen-year-old readers is constructed, I needed to try and work with people who regularly read for a variety of purposes and pleasures. In order to generate richly textured data about these particular readers' experiences, I designed a research project that would bring them into relief by means of engaging, stimulating English classroom teaching so that the subject of reading was at the forefront of students' minds, not something they were coming to without prior notice. To that end, I liaised closely with Rosa to devise four activities that might motivate the students as readers while also serving as research methods to generate valuable data (Cliff Hodges 2012). However, although the research began in an English classroom, the main focus was the students' independent reading, within and beyond the school.

I was constantly mindful, therefore, of the complexity of the research process and very aware that the data would have to comprise representations of the reading process, rather than reading per se.

Although all the students in the class were expected to undertake the English work, their participation in the research was voluntary. Consent was sought from them and their parents or caregivers. Most students were willing to participate in most aspects of the research. I have written about the research methods in detail elsewhere and so will refer to each only briefly here. For the purposes of this chapter, however, I will also highlight how each research method provided opportunities to find out about other readers these young people encountered, especially parents or grandparents, as the historical aspect of the project was of particular interest from the outset.

First, the students created critical incidents collages that charted formative events in their personal reading histories as far back as they could remember, and even beyond as a result of consulting their parents (Cliff Hodges 2010). The collages frequently included mention of the role played by adult family members in the students' development as readers – for example, reading aloud to them regularly as they learned to read for themselves, providing books and comics for them, taking them to libraries, and so on. Next, the students were invited to participate in semi-structured interviews with me in small groups of four or five. These offered opportunities to explore in greater depth how they perceived their reading relationships with parents or grandparents and the adults' influence on them as readers. From my reading of the transcripts and working with the data, I was often able to gain a strong sense of students' reading interactions with adults close to them in their home lives. Next, the students undertook an English activity based on interviews with children's authors, focusing on the interview as a popular oral or written genre. Each student carried out an interview with a parent or grandparent about *their* experiences as a reader, based on a schedule of questions, some of which I had already asked in the semi-structured interviews but adding several more to probe the adults' memories and recollections (Cliff Hodges 2013). The students were invited to suggest additional questions themselves. Most students stuck fairly close to the schedule, however. Many of them audio-recorded the interviews and then transcribed them. A few hand-wrote the answers and typed or hand-wrote them up afterwards. The interview transcripts were – for me as researcher – an interesting source of data, a very small part of which I will explore in more detail below. The final activity was for the students to keep a reading journal to chart their ongoing responses to a self-selected book. Interestingly, the journals revealed a number of the students choosing to read books recommended to them by a parent, and several of those books were adult rather than young adult books, a measure of the extent to which these young people were keen to be developing their maturity as readers.

Four Theoretical Perspectives

As already hinted at in the brief outline above, the research methods generated extensive, rich data. I now turn to the four key theoretical perspectives that informed both the design of the project and its methods as well as the subsequent data analysis. The first two perspectives are familiar and often closely linked – namely, the social and the cultural. My own prior research and pedagogy – as a class teacher and subsequently a teacher educator – were (and still are) deeply influenced by the social and cultural perspectives of theorists such as Lev Vygotsky (1986) and Jerome Bruner (1996). Embedded, therefore, in my prior thinking were notions of students' reading as both a social and cultural practice, and of them becoming readers within the different social and cultural contexts of their upbringing and education. These notions, however, were not deterministic; that is to say, I did not presume that enthusiastic young readers necessarily had avid readers as parents. What I *was* interested to explore, though, was whether and how students' (and their parents') social and cultural contexts might affect some of the various ways in which they read and perceived themselves as readers. Ideas in Vygotskian theory about the relationship between thought and language, for example, led to a strong emphasis on conversation in three of the four research methods. Likewise, Bruner's concerns about how young people learn specifically within and from their cultural contexts lie behind some of the prompts the students were offered in the reading journal activity as well as the questions asked in both sets of interviews.

Although Louise Rosenblatt's long-standing theories about the transactional process of reading ([1978]1994) do not specifically draw on the work of either Vygotsky or Bruner (though it appears that she was aware of both), there are nevertheless some strong synergies between them. For example, Rosenblatt foregrounds the role of the reader, in particular the way a reader brings prior knowledge and experience to bear on whatever text he or she engages with in order to create an individual reading (or "poem," as Rosenblatt terms it). She calls this process a transaction because the concept encapsulates the kind of reciprocal engagement she is imagining, not entirely distinct from some of the kinds of reciprocity explored by Vygotsky and Bruner. The importance of the reader's prior knowledge and experience, not just in reading but in the cultural contexts of learning more broadly, has equally been stressed by Vygotskian researchers such as Norma González, Luis Moll, and Cathy Amanti (2005) in their "funds of knowledge" investigations. Pedagogically, too, my design was informed by literary theorists such as Robert Scholes (1985), whose arguments about readers gaining textual power through reading, interpretation, and criticism include readers producing their own texts, not just consuming other people's. For Scholes, therefore, reading necessarily also involves discussion, debate, and many other forms of conversational transactions between readers, texts, and readings. Nevertheless, while this particular mix of theorists may be specific to my research, the idea of bringing social and cultural perspectives to bear on reading was not. Two further perspectives, both stemming from very different sources, were also incorporated. I turn to them now.

The first additional perspective was the spatial, gleaned specifically from the work of the cultural geographer Doreen Massey (2005). Her suggestion that space is constructed from different trajectories – whether of animate or inanimate phenomena – jostling together over time proved particularly thought-provoking. Rather than perceiving space as an area to be covered, Massey argues that space is inextricably linked with time and is therefore dynamic, not static. There are significant political implications embedded in her ideas, not least the notion that trajectories are not fixed but dynamic and are capable of transformation as they make contact with other trajectories. Applying her ideas to the field of reading appeared to enable a way of imagining it differently (Massey 2003). Thus, readers might be viewed as having individual reading trajectories, distinguished by what and how they have read thus far, as well as the trajectories of other readers and/or texts with whom they have engaged, and will continue to engage. Reading is not about some readers forging further ahead faster than others, but about spaces created from the bundling together (to use Massey's term) of different trajectories that are constantly shifting and being reshaped. The argument about spaces being in a state of constant movement leads Massey to insist that space should always, therefore, be characterized as space-time, operating simultaneously in two dimensions – the spatial *and* the temporal. Space and time, she argues, must always be conceived of as mutually reinforcing each other and hence not susceptible to discrete analysis.

Massey's interconnections between space and time chimed with the fourth theoretical perspective informing my research – the historical. Although the temporal and the historical are closely related, the distinction I saw between them was that the temporal had to do with the *general* passage of time and the historical had to do with *human* past time. Here, I was influenced by the work of reading historians who have used autobiographies as data to investigate not just what readers in the past may have read or the differences between reading then and now, but – crucially – how certain people in the past actually read and what they thought about their reading and readership (Altick 1957; Vincent 1981; Flint 1993; Rose 2001). Robert Darnton, a key scholar researching the history of books, explains that it is exceptionally difficult to determine how readers assimilated their books: "Reading remains the most difficult stage to study in the circuit that books follow" (2009, 192). Jonathan Rose, too, in his major work, *The Intellectual Life of the British Working Classes* (2001), suggests the need to move away from reception theory and use reader response theory instead so that there is less focus on the text and more focus on the reader. Often, of course, in the process of attending closely to readers, we learn what it was they read; but furthermore, we learn how they perceived or assimilated it.

To exemplify the potential value of bringing these four theoretical perspectives to bear before moving on to discuss some fragments from my own data, I offer a vignette from one history of reading and analyze briefly how it enables us to imagine the field differently, bringing ideas about reading into multi-dimensional and dynamic relief. The vignette comes from an autobiography co-written by Lord and Lady Aberdeen and published in 1925. A snippet of Lady Aberdeen recalling her childhood in mid-nineteenth-century London is reproduced by Kate Flint in *The Woman Reader 1837–1914*:

> [Lady Aberdeen] learnt to read from the under-butler, sitting with him in the front hall where he waited to open the door to visitors. But when the discovery of her new-found ability was made, the fairy-story books which had first excited her curiosity were banished to a top shelf in the schoolroom, and she was "furnished with a 'Mavor's spelling book' and made to start in the proper fashion" letter by letter, rather than by recognizing words – "under my mother's personal superintendence.'" (1993, 196)

What Lady Aberdeen is remembering is a critical period in her own reading history when she *learned* to read before being formally *taught* to read. The memory is wrought with social, cultural, spatial, and historical implications. First, there is the juxtaposition of a very young, upper-class girl with a man of relatively low social standing, the under-butler (not even the butler), possibly quite young himself. The job of waiting to open the front door of the house to visitors suggests the potential for considerable time to spare on the part of the under-butler; the girl, too, may have experienced loneliness if he was her companion of choice. However, it appears that it was reading that brought them together: she wanting to learn, he willing to assist. The physical space occupied by the under-butler in the front hall of the house afforded the little girl aesthetic space for reading much-beloved fairy tales. The very same fairy tales were later inaccessible in what should have been a more enabling space, namely, the schoolroom. Historically, the status and relative power of the characters in this anecdote stem from a particular period in time, but their reading experiences nevertheless connect the past with the present. Children learning to read in England today may well experience similar dissonance between self-selected reading with a loved companion and the imposition of simplistic word-level work deemed to be a necessary prologue to the main task. Culturally, too, the anecdote is of interest, in terms of the texts involved in the girl's learning to read and the differing views of how reading should be taught. It was fairy tales that activated and engaged the girl's imagination as a reader; by contrast, her mother's approach was one of narrow decoding with letter- or word-recognition preceding more holistic pleasure in reading. Both the under-butler and Lady Aberdeen's mother, therefore, had their own reading trajectories with which the young girl's intersected. Bringing all four theoretical perspectives to bear on this excerpt highlights the complexity of the spaces in which reading occurs and is shaped, as well as the momentum such spaces afford for readers' onward progress. In the remaining sections of this chapter, I refer to excerpts from the data generated by the students' interviews with their parents and grandparents and discuss the extent to which a reconfiguration of readers and reading is achieved through research that encourages us to reimagine reading. I end with some recommendations about how the methodology as a whole might be replicated in other contexts.

Biography and Schooling

The grandparents of the students I worked with were born just before or during the Second World War in the 1930s and 1940s, their parents in the 1950s or 1960s. The opening interview questions were about where they grew up and their memories of what it was like as a young person living there. Their answers yield a range of interesting but very diverse memories. More than half the adults say they grew up in English villages, and most remember them as friendly places where they knew everyone and where there were plenty of other children to play with. Steph is not untypical when she recalls:

> Yes I grew up in a village, and it was lovely, I had lots of friends, I was able to play out in the garden and there was never any trouble ... [I] used to be out for [h]ours and, and, um it was lovely, it was a good childhood.[2]

Ahmet grew up in Turkey, where, he says:

> It was a different style of life compared to today ... Everything was very basic but we still enjoyed life as much as we could with passion, with love, with care, with good relations not high technology. Generally everything was made by hand, basic things.

Four say they grew up on modern housing estates, which two describe as apparently rough yet happy and enjoyable places to live. Christine says that where she grew up compares favourably with where she currently lives:

> It was a very working class area on the south coast of England and I (and my parents) knew most of the neighbours unlike where we live now. My happiest memories come from living here. I had a good life, though money was very tight and my parents were quite strict (compared to many of my friends).

When asked about their memories of secondary school, the interviewees are more ambivalent. It is not always clear precisely what kind of school they attended: ten refer merely to "secondary" schools, some of which were single-sex; two attended Cornford, the school where I was conducting the research; five say they went to a grammar school, two to a comprehensive, although the system was relatively new at the time ("So it was a little bit of an experiment," as Caroline suggests). Only one specifically says she attended a private school, one went to a convent, and one was sent to a "boarding grammar school" in Ireland. Jenny moved between two schools:

> One was a girls' grammar school for two years and that was very strict, a stern kind of place, I wasn't very happy there. Then I went to a comprehensive school, it was mixed and was great fun and I really enjoyed having boys in the class. I was encouraged to be a reader there, particularly when I did my O-level English Literature – we had a brilliant teacher.

They not only went to schools of varying kinds but also had mixed experiences. As Keith explains:

> I didn't find [secondary school] very good, erm, I was probably a bit undecided of what I wanted to do when I left school and, er, at that time there wasn't much emphasis on helping school leavers. The teachers weren't much help either.

Christine says, "My memories of school are not of the learning but of the socialising. Our school was well known for being one of the worse schools in the county." By contrast, others have fond memories of their schools. Lee's father, Matt, says that "secondary school was a great experience preparing me for the real world and it help[ed] as I had a very inspirational teacher as well." The only other parents to comment specifically on the quality of the teaching are Jenny, whose "brilliant" English Literature O-level teacher has already been referred to above, and Tony, who was influenced as a reader by his English teacher, remembering in particular studying John Steinbeck's *The Grapes of Wrath* with him.

Memories of being encouraged to read at secondary school are generally mixed. A few respondents are positive. Amanda, recalls at her grammar school: "we were given free periods where you were expected to go to the library choose a book and read it in the library." Many, however, say they have no memory of any encouragement. Instead, they remember practicalities. Angela was "forced to read out loud in front of the class, which made some people stutter and which I hated," and Siobhan says that she, too, "hated it when the class read aloud because it was often slow and painful," though she did enjoy discussing the book afterwards.

Catherine reports very positively on her experience, continuing with her study of English into the sixth form:

> At sixteen doing an English A level I read Tomas Hardy's "Return of the Native." This then led me to read the rest of his books and then when I was seventeen me and three friends went on a holiday in Dorset, where we went to see Hardy's cottage at Stinsford.

This contrasts starkly with Christine's very negative experience of English at O-level:

> I do not remember being encouraged to develop as a reader apart from when I took English Literature which I did not enjoy and thought many of the questions asked in relation to the texts I read like Midsummer Nights Dream, Man For All Seasons and A Day of the Triffids were pointless. I struggled with the work given in relation to the reading that we were supposed to read. My experience of this as an "O" level subject put me off reading until I left school.

Despite the adults' mixed memories of school reading, when asked how they would describe themselves currently as readers almost all of them indicate that they do like reading: James, Jenny, and Keith, for example, describe themselves as avid or voracious; Margaret and Maria say they enjoy it; Catherine and Christine are among several who define themselves as people who read as much as time permits but do not have as much time as they would ideally like; yet another group reply in terms of being fast, slow, or confident. All responses, however, indicate that they think reading is important. Only one or two do not appear to class it as a hobby or interest – for example, Tracey, who reads a lot of trade magazines for work but tends not to read for pleasure.

Historical Elements of Habitual and Committed Reading

Having offered a glimpse of the parents' and grandparents' biographical details, I next explore the responses triggered by questions encouraging slightly more critical recollections and offering different analytical opportunities. One such question that proved to be particularly interesting was whether anyone read to these adults when they were young. Five people reply that they cannot remember anyone reading aloud to them but add that they feel sure someone must have done so. Everyone else is able to recall being read to, and their answers are historically interesting in terms of who it was that did the reading and the fact that it was habitual. Amanda is one of three who remembers being read to by her grandparents: "my grandparents [or] anybody who was visiting the house would have a book thrust upon them and asked to read, it happened a lot."

When referring to their parents reading to them, many of the adults specifically mention whether it was their mother or father who did the reading, and it is worth noting that almost as many say it was their father as their mother. The phrasing they use to describe their memories conveys a sense of the habitual. Margaret recalls, "I also remember my mum and dad reading to me ... My mum used to read Just So Stories by Rudyard Kipling to me," while Olivia says that her father "always read to me when I was ill, I remember. And sometimes he'd read to us on a Sunday as well." Only Siobhan says she disliked being read to as a child; she preferred to read herself, even though she later enjoyed reading to her own children. More detail is sometimes offered. For example, Jenny's mother and father both read to her. She remembers "being read Rupert Bear annuals at night time, by my Dad. He used to read the rhyming couplets and we enjoyed those and I did the same for my children." If these data are set alongside data from the students' own collages, we see that reading aloud with children seems among this group of families to be an almost universal practice or at least an aspiration. The question and its various responses also offer students a brief insight into the practice from a historical perspective, as something that was happening when their parents were children that was then replicated in their own childhood experiences. It allows them a glimpse that they may or may not have had previously of their grandparents (and in some cases, their great-grandparents) engaging in this particular aspect of parenting. The fact that, for the most part, the practice is not gender specific, and was shared even two generations ago by mothers and fathers, is an additional point of illumination.

Another question that prompts memories of the adults' own parents and grandparents is "When you were young, who influenced you most as a reader or did you just discover things to read for yourself?" Although friends are mentioned by four respondents, teachers and schools likewise, parents and grandparents feature much more strongly, often with reasons for their influence. Kate thinks that the chief influence may have been her grandfather, "who told me about how wonderful books were. He left school when he was young and educated himself by reading good literature." Like several others,

Margaret feels it was her parents who influenced her, "since they were keen readers."

At least half the respondents remember enjoying discovering things to read for themselves. Sometimes this is as well as being given reading matter by other people, sometimes not. Amanda's and Keith's respective responses represent these extremes. Amanda clearly had a range of options:

> I was always bought books to read or given books to read but I think an awful lot of it I discovered myself, erm ... the picture of Matilda[3] springs to mind traipsing off to the library to find books on different information but it was never a problem whatever I got was always agreed to be appropriate for me to read so it was never as if I was reading stuff that I shouldn't have been.

Keith, meanwhile, says:

> I think I just discovered things for myself. Although I always have been a voracious reader, my parents have not and my sister was not. So, er, I just enjoyed reading and finding things for myself. It turned out that I had more books than anyone else in my family!

These contrasting responses are evidence that the trajectories of keen readers like Keith do not always originate in readerly surroundings. This complicates correlations between family or school background and developing the habit of reading.

Libraries and Books

It is also interesting to note the powerful influence of libraries in these older interviewees' responses. In the extract above, Amanda mentions the library explicitly as one of several options available to her. For Keith, however, the library plays a key role. He tells his daughter that there was a library in the village where he grew up so he used to go there to get books. More crucial was the fortuitous fact of *where* his daily registration at school took place:

> I actually got my love of reading from the fact that my tutor, well my tutor room, was the school library, so we had access to the books, well, any books we wanted to, so I was a very voracious reader at an early age; fact/fiction, you name it really.

For the majority of others, libraries formed part of the routine associated with reading. Steph, like many, remembers getting reading material "from the library, in the village, we used to go every week with my dad, and get books out." For Amanda, "it was a Saturday morning ritual to visit and change our books, it was something I looked forward to and relished." Audrey and Catherine both remember the library vividly. For Audrey, the supply of books fed her appetite for reading:

> I was an avid reader and I would go to the library in holiday times [every] week and I'd bring home about four, three, I think it was three books we were allowed and I'd read them, go back and get some more books.

Catherine tells her son:

> My most vivid memory is spending ages in the library choosing books ... My parents enjoyed reading and used the library too.

Here, choice and independence are critical, as they are for Christine, who enjoyed the freedom to choose "anything that I liked when I was old enough to go to the library by myself." Although for many getting books from the library was valuable since there was little spare money to buy them, the availability of libraries was equally important in fostering the agency young readers felt able to exercise within them.

Any books the adults did own were obviously precious to them, as evidenced in their answers to the question, "Have you still got any of your books, magazines or comics from your childhood? If so, why have you kept them?" Their reasons for keeping them fall into several broad categories. In some instances, it is because the books have been passed down to them or received as gifts. Siobhan has already handed some of hers on to her daughter "because I enjoyed the stories, or because they came from grandparents and parents." Indeed, Siobhan's daughter later wrote a long series of reading journal entries about one of them – Lucy Maud Montgomery's *The Story Girl*. Matt, Simon, and Ahmet all feel the books might help their children understand their past – as Matt puts it, "so my children can experience what it was like to read in my time." The most commonly given reason, though, is that they are treasured possessions, because they are remembered, as Margaret says, as being "such lovely books, I wanted to read them to my children." Caroline says she has kept her Secret Seven books, Rupert Bear annuals, and old wildlife books "because they were special to me, sentimental value and that." For Steph, they hold "fond memories" and for Diane, "I suppose they are a bit like an old friend really." All these adults are conveying to their children and grandchildren a combination of the ongoing affection they feel towards these books and, in many cases, a sense that the feelings as much as the books themselves are a form of inheritance to be passed on to their children. Young people themselves are often avid collectors of books and magazines, frequently rereading them. Although their collections are precious to them right now, the adults' comments may signal to them that this could continue to be the case long into the future.

Some of the adults say they do not have enough space to keep old books. Diane used to keep her books and "stock them up but they started to take up too much space and I handed them to friends." However, from some of her other answers in the interview it is clear that they were important to her and her parents:

> I remember buying books aged nine or ten. I used to go out with my mum, and I used to buy a book a month from my series and that was a big event for me. We didn't have that many books, we had a few Atlases and things like that which was what my dad used to read ... My mother read all the time you never saw my mother in the evenings without a book by her side.

With even greater feeling, Diane explains another way in which her childhood reading has remained with her – namely, in her memories of what was probably Malcolm Saville's Lone Pine series, which she absolutely adored:

> I still think about it sometimes, it was almost like the secret seven, it was about a group of children that went on holiday together around the lay mind [Long Mynd] in wales and down on the south coast. And I often think about those stories because they really conjured up the whole place and the whole environment. These places which I've never been to in my life but I bet you if I went there I could tell you every thing about it.

The memories, if not the actual books themselves, are for Diane what form the trajectory of her childhood reading, travelling with her over the years. Her vivid articulation of these reading memories may suggest something of what her son, too, can expect to carry forward with him from any of his own equally powerful reading experiences.

Across the Generations

When asked to compare and contrast their own young adult reading with their children's or grandchildren's, the adults gave thoughtful answers from which certain patterns begin to emerge. The question about whether they used to read much as a child and, if so, what they liked about it reveals quite a strong similarity among them in terms of some of the key texts they recall. Their remembered childhood reading revolved for the most part around various well-known series, with Enid Blyton's Secret Seven, Famous Five, and Malory Towers having been especially popular. Other remembered favourites are Rupert Bear annuals, Paddington Bear books, and Winnie-the-Pooh stories. Certain titles are also mentioned by more than one person, notably Arthur Ransome's *Swallows & Amazons* and Kenneth Grahame's *The Wind in the Willows*, along with Lewis Carroll's *Alice in Wonderland*, Rudyard Kipling's *Just So Stories*, and Edith Nesbit's *The Railway Children*. Perhaps not surprisingly, therefore, their answers to the question about similarities and differences between what they used to read when they were young and the sorts of things their (grand)children read now chime clearly with each other.

Steph definitely read quite a lot as a child. She recalls being read the *Just So Stories* and *The Hobbit* by her dad, who used to take her every week to the library in the village. Like many of the other parents and grandparents, she seems to feel that the younger generation of readers has a greater choice of reading material available to them. She introduces a notion shared by many others in the research, about growth in the teenage book market since she was young:

> When I was your age I think I would have read far more children's books whereas I think you're reading more adult books, and there's a lot more books for teenagers and young adults but when I was young I think it was either children's books or adult. I also think nowadays the books are a lot more explicit and graphic, basically a lot more adult in contrast.

Audrey agrees: "there wasn't the range of books for teenagers that there are now." Today's young readers still enjoy the same Enid Blyton books as their parents and grandparents, and sometimes the same comics too. As Nathan mentions in the group interview,

> My granddad used to read the *Dandy* and the *Beano* and stuff like that ... in the war and then he used to like, whenever he went out he thought "Hmm, maybe [Nathan] might like this" so I was given the *Dandy* first and I liked it and then he gave me the *Beano* ... Just whenever he really went into town.

However, the same cannot be said of some of the social realist magazines produced for young people. Irene mentions that she used to read a lot of comics such as the *School Friend* and *Girls' Crystal*, which bear little or no relation – in either substance or values – to magazines like *Bliss*, *Shout*, or *Mizz* enjoyed by young readers now.

Amanda says that when she was a child, reading was her way of escaping:

> I could get away from what was normal and mundane er I could be the characters I, I always wanted to be what they were, do what they were doing go where they've been, erm ... I was always keen to go exploring and I wanted something well, exciting ... it showed me how dull it was where I lived [laughs] which I suppose isn't a good thing ... My most favourite type of reading was things like the Malory Towers or the secret Seven, Famous Five all the escape type things that got you away from normal real life.

She goes on to suggest that the idea of reading as a form of escape still pertains for young people today, but with very different styles of writing and writers, a trend she attributes to "society being so different so the content of books are different." Jenny puts it slightly differently but makes the same point as Steph about the teenage book market:

> I think you read a lot more of what I would call "girly" books, you know teenage girl books. When I was a child there weren't books aimed at the teenage market. There were adult books and children's books, so nothing much in between.

Keith is another of the adults who cites comics as one of the main differences in reading matter between his generation and his daughter's, though he also appears to see gender as another difference:

> I especially liked Victor, which is like a war comic; then I got into Commando, which is again war stories ... I think we've talked in the past like at an early age I read you fairy tales whereas my dad probably read me war stories or stories for boys! Now you are changing your view about things that you like. You are quite into the war stories like Anne Frank's Diary. I was into war like I told you a few times but in a different way. I liked the stories about the fighting and flying.

The parents make different but equally interesting comments about their perceived influence on their children's reading. Here, though, the emphasis is as much on cultural values as on social relationships. Kate puts it simply: "You have always seen that Dad and I like to read for pleasure and for work." Keith says something similar: "I think you have grown up knowing that your mother and I have always read." What is also interesting about these parents' comments is that they are not judgmental. They simply state what their children already know; they do not tell them what to think about it.

Reconfiguring Readers and Reading

Adopting spatial and historical as well as socio-cultural perspectives towards reading allows us to view readers and reading in space and over time, noting their constantly changing dynamics. The implications are important: crucially, there is no point – from spatial and historical perspectives – either in making simple judgments about any individual reader on the basis of what they appear to be doing or able to do at any single moment in time or in drawing equally simplistic conclusions about their potential. Such practice would be as incoherent as making claims about the power and reach of a river from a single stretch in its entire course. Instead, space-time – as reconfigured by Massey (2005) – encapsulates the connection between past and present time and its integral relationship with space, and hence the impossibility of separating one from the other. Massey's ideas have much in common with socio-cultural theory with its notion that stories shape and are shaped in the process of interactions with others. However, she brings the temporal and historical into play as well and the open-ended, personal, and political possibilities for future pathways. The spatial and historical perspectives, therefore, acknowledge past achievements or pitfalls, tolerate unevenness and unpredictability, and reconceptualize habit or commitment, not as fixed and stable entities, but paradoxically as arising out of change and encounters with uncertainty. They also anticipate multiple possibilities for the future rather than settled certainties.

There are important implications for parents, teachers, researchers, and the students themselves of adopting spatial and historical perspectives on reading. In particular, the emphasis is not only on attending to what is evident in the here and now, but also on construing it in the light of its trajectory thus far, acknowledging unpredictability, and capitalizing on the potential such uncertainty allows. In the United Kingdom and in many other countries where such ideas may be of interest, the main barrier to their being taken on may be the short-termism of much political intervention in education, with its need for immediate outcomes. Constructing a more richly layered view of individual readers over longer periods than the terms of office of most politicians requires close attention to detail, tolerance of uncertainty, breadth of knowledge, capacity for understanding, and aspiration towards complexity. These are values and practices that are not compatible with the pressures currently faced by many English teachers and their students (and, indeed, by many educational researchers); they are, however, as I have argued in this chapter, conducive to the development of young readers, pedagogically sound, and productive of valid, reliable research. I would also argue that the research methods suggested above are replicable in many other educational contexts and, indeed, with younger students than the ones involved here, enabling others to deepen their understanding and broaden the scope of what they think being a reader might mean.

Notes

1 The names of all those involved in this research – the teacher, the students, the parents, the grandparents, and the school – have been changed to ensure anonymity.
2 The students' spelling and punctuation have been retained as far as possible in quotations from their writing.
3 Presumably Roald Dahl's eponymous heroine from his 1988 novel, *Matilda*.

References

Altick, Richard Daniel. 1957. *The English Common Reader: A Social History of the Mass Reading Public 1800–1900*. Chicago: University of Chicago Press.
Bruner, Jerome. 1996. *The Culture of Education*. Cambridge, MA: Harvard University Press.
Cliff Hodges, Gabrielle. 2010. "Rivers of Reading: Using Critical Incident Collages to Learn about Adolescent Readers and Their Readership." *English in Education* 44(3): 181–200.
———. 2012. "Research and the Teaching of English: Spaces Where Reading Histories Meet." *English Teaching: Practice and Critique* 11(1): 7–25.
———. 2013. "Reading within Families: Taking a Historical Perspective." *Changing English* 20(2): 182–93.
Darnton, Robert. 2009. *The Case for Books: Past, Present, and Future*. New York: Public Affairs.
Flint, Kate. 1993. *The Woman Reader 1837–1914*. Oxford: Oxford University Press.
González, Norma, Luis Moll, and Cathy Amanti, eds. 2005. *Funds of Knowledge: Theorizing Practices in Households, Communities, and Classrooms*. Mahwah, NJ: Lawrence Erlbaum Associates.
Massey, Doreen. 2003. "Imagining the Field." In *Using Social Theory: Thinking through Research*, edited by Michael Pryke, Gillian Rose, and Sarah Whatmore, 71–88. London: Sage.
———. 2005. *For Space*. London: Sage.
Rose, Jonathan. 2001. *The Intellectual Life of the British Working Classes*. New Haven: Yale University Press.
Rosenblatt, Louise M. [1978]1994. *The Reader, the Text, the Poem: The Transactional Theory of the Literary Work*. Reprint, Carbondale: Southern Illinois University Press.
Scholes, Robert. 1985. *Textual Power: Literary Theory and the Teaching of English*. New Haven: Yale University Press.
Vincent, David. 1981. *Bread, Knowledge, and Freedom: A Study of Nineteenth-Century Working Class Autobiography*. London: Routledge.
Vygotsky, Lev Semyonovich. 1986. *Thought and Language*. Cambridge, MA: Massachusetts Institute of Technology.

Reading and Viewing Referred to in the Chapter by Students, Parents, and Grandparents

Prose Fiction and Playscripts

Blyton, Enid. 1942. Famous Five series. London: Hodder and Stoughton.
Blyton, Enid. 1946. Malory Towers series. London: Hodder and Stoughton.
Blyton, Enid. 1950. Secret Seven series. London: Hodder and Stoughton.
Bolt, Robert. 1960. *A Man for All Seasons*. London: Heinemann.
Bond, Michael. 1959. Paddington Bear series. London: William Collins and Sons.
Carroll, Lewis. 1865. *Alice in Wonderland*. London: Macmillan.
Frank, Anne. 1952. *Anne Frank: The Diary of a Young Girl*. London: Valentine Mitchell.

Grahame, Kenneth. 1908. *The Wind in the Willows*. London: Methuen.
Hardy, Thomas. [1878]1999. *The Return of the Native*. Harmondsworth: Penguin Books.
Kipling, Rudyard. [1902)]1987. *Just So Stories*. Harmondsworth: Puffin Books.
Milne, Alan Alexander. 1926. *Winnie-the-Pooh*. London: Methuen.
Montgomery, Lucy Maud. [1911]2006. *The Story Girl*. Teddington: Echo Library.
Nesbit, Edith. 1906. *The Railway Children*. London: Fisher Unwin.
Ransome, Arthur. 1930. *Swallows and Amazons*. London: Jonathan Cape.
Saville, Malcolm. 1943. Lone Pine series. London: Newnes.
Shakespeare, William. 1967. *A Midsummer Night's Dream*. Harmondsworth: Penguin Books.
Steinbeck, John. 1939. *The Grapes of Wrath*. London: Heinemann.
Tolkien, John Ronald Reuel. 1937. *The Hobbit*. London: George Allen and Unwin.
Wyndham, John. 1951. *The Day of the Triffids*. London: Michael Joseph.

Comics, magazines, and annuals

Beano. Dundee: D.C. Thomson and Co.
Bliss. Tunbridge Wells: Panini UK.
Commando. Dundee: D.C. Thomson and Co.
Dandy. Dundee: D.C. Thomson and Co.
Girls' Crystal. London: Amalgamated Press.
Mizz. Tunbridge Wells: Panini UK.
School Friend. London: Amalgamated Press.
Shout. Dundee: D.C. Thomson and Co.
Tourtel, Mary. Rupert Bear Annuals. London: Daily Express, 1936.
Victor. Dundee: D.C. Thomson and Co.

Evidence of Reading? 5
The Swedish Public's Letters to Selma Lagerlöf: Quantitative and Qualitative Approaches to the History of Reading

Jenny Bergenmar and Maria Karlsson

How were literary works used in the past? Why, how, where, when, and by whom were they read? These questions, put forward by Robert Darnton as essential for taking the "first steps toward a history of reading" ([1986]2011), are possible to answer only by using a combination of different historical sources. Commonly used sources in book history are statistics from lending libraries and the book market, evidence of distribution and publication, and reading lists from schools and other institutions. You may also get information from analyzing depictions of reading in literature, art, reviews, and so on. But if we want to study the differing reading practices and what reading, literature, and particular authors meant to the actual readers – in Darnton's terms, the evasive *how* and *why* – we need to go beyond easily accessible numbers and the literature reception of the intellectual elites. To understand reading in the past we have to get access to sources from people's private lives, such as diaries, autobiographies, and, not least, letters.

Within the fields of history of the book and reception studies, it has often been repeated that such evidence is hard to find. Darnton writes: "If the experience of the great mass of readers lies beyond the range of historical research, historians should be able to capture something of what reading meant for the few persons who left a record of it" ([1986]2011, 31). It is also true that it is only during the last couple of decades that the reading of the public in a broader sense has gained attention. Jonathan Rose (1995) has argued for the need to search the archives for historical records of reading. A sign of this shift in perspective is the Reading Experience Database (RED), which is, according to the project's own homepage, "the largest resource recording the experience of readers of its kind anywhere" (RED website). The database has over 30,000 records of reading experiences written in English.

One argument for using these kinds of written records of reading is that library statistics and sales figures can prove to be unreliable empirical evidence. As Simon Eliot, the founder of RED, writes, "This leads us to the first and greatest caveat in the history of reading: to own, buy, borrow or steal a book is no proof of wishing to read it, let alone proof of having read it" (Eliot, para. 7).

This problematic aspect of the quantitative approach to the history of reading has also been pivotal in the critique of Franco Moretti's concept of distant reading. Moretti (2005) radically argues that literary history needs to shift from readings of individual works to mapping and charting large-scale material in different ways, as a means to access *"a specific form of knowledge"* (2005, 126). Rachel Serlen questions the interpretative basis of Moretti's studies: "Moretti emphasizes the transparency of analysis in the face of good data because he wants to extricate literary studies from interpretation, narrowly construed as the reading of an individual text to discover what that text 'means,' in favour of explanation, in which the scholar no longer makes meaning out of text, but rather looks at the data and explains how the information came to be what it is" (2010, 220). An empirical, quantitative approach is no escape from interpretation.

Moretti's suggestion that we shift from close to distant reading is above all a suggestion to move from the interpretation of literary texts to the reception and dissemination of them. On this more general level – to leave room for other research strategies besides those focused solely on the literary text itself – it is easy for researchers in the field of history of reading to agree. But how are we to make best use of, for example, individual historical readings? The many letters to the Swedish author Selma Lagerlöf (1858–1940) are no doubt the kind of material that scholars of book history call for in search of historical records of reading. The collection spans a long period of time and thus represents uses of literature over time. But to what extent are letters to an author a reliable source? Can they be taken as evidence of general patterns, or can they only represent themselves, as individual cases? What precautions must we take when they are studied? This chapter discusses the possibilities and challenges connected to letters from the public to an author as a source in the history of reading, using the Lagerlöf letter collection as an exemplary case.

The Letters from the Public to Selma Lagerlöf

When researching the letters in the project "Reading Lagerlöf: The Letters to Selma Lagerlöf from the Public 1891–1940," we have certainly not suffered from a lack of historically documented reading experiences. The National Library of Sweden holds over 42,000 letters sent to the author in a fifty-year time period (1891–1940). The more than 17,000 letter writers include friends, family, and colleagues, but the majority of senders are people whom the author did not know. The material is highly heterogeneous, written by diverse correspondents: men and women of different ages and social demographics, from cities and rural areas as well as several different countries. This diversity has many different reasons: the literacy rate, the overall habit of writing letters, the notion of a celebrity author as approachable, mail delivery services, postage rates, and so on. In addition, there is of course a factor that has to do with the letter writers' mediated image of the author herself.

Lagerlöf was one of the bestselling authors of her time in Sweden. Her works were exceptionally widespread – including internationally – and were read in cheap editions, serial stories in papers, and popular journals by people from all social classes. In a survey covering the years of 1928–1931, a number of pupils were asked to make lists of the books present in their homes. Lagerlöf's debut novel *Gösta Berlings Saga* (1891) was number five on the list after the Bible, the Swedish hymn book, the New Testament, and a medical manual given out for free for commercial purposes. Lagerlöf was number three on the list of most occurring authors, after Jack London and Victor Hugo – thus she was the most occurring Swedish author (Dolotkhah 2011, 47).

The fact that her work was distributed in many different ways and by different media promoted Selma Lagerlöf's popularity. She was read in schools, there were radio readings, and her works were eventually adapted to film, theatre, and even opera. The press named her "Sweden's most popular woman," and she was portrayed as a queen, being the Nobel Prize winner of 1909 and a member of the Swedish Academy. The view of Lagerlöf was also highly gendered. She was seen as an icon of motherly goodness, which made her attractive to the less fortunate, who often wrote to ask her for money, a job, or other kinds of help. These letters from help-seekers are abundant, and scholars have equated them with letters from the general public, which are then construed as mail from beggars. But an investigation of the "beggars' letters" reveals much more nuanced subjects of interest to several disciplines today. Each of those letters contains a small autobiography and responds to the media image of a celebrity author, providing us with direct information on how readers received both Lagerlöf's work and her celebrity.

Overall, requests for financial aid account for about one-third of the letters from the Swedish senders, leaving a wide range of other letters. People write about all sorts of things – from spiritual issues, politics, and religion to what is going on in their everyday lives.

Individual Stories about Reading

Letters to authors account for very specific feelings and circumstances, making it difficult to generalize. This problem arises when dealing with all sources of reading from private life; this has been discussed as a weakness of Jonathan Rose's study *The Intellectual Life of the British Working Classes* (2001), for which autobiographical material was used (Collini 2008, 248; Allington 2010). The Lagerlöf collection has the advantage of being of a considerable size and stretching, as mentioned above, over a fairly long period of time: fifty years, from her debut to the year of her death. We have organized the many thousands of letters in a database so as to be able to present analysis derived from this abundance of data points in our study, even concerning quite specific matters. But what significance do those numbers have? To what extent are the letters to Selma Lagerlöf evidence of reading practices in general, or rather individual and situated stories about reading?

An aspect that has to be taken into account is that the readers who write to an author are always in the minority. In the words of Simon Eliot, "any reading recorded in an historically recoverable way is, almost by definition, an uncharacteristic event by an untypical person" (n.d., para. 11). Therefore, when dealing with letters from readers, the notion of "a common reader" simply does not apply. As Stephen Colclough has argued, this does not mean that individual records of reading lack value as evidence, but rather that we must take into account facts of difference and diversity by focusing on "the historical reader," and not on an illusive, typical reader (2009, 52).

The fact that letters to an author may also be connected to specific situations and purposes – in the case of Lagerlöf, to requests for economic support or professional advice – affects how the letters can be valued as records of readings. A sender asking for help or advice is likely to express a positive view of Lagerlöf's work. In other words, the truthfulness of the stories of reading told in the letters cannot be taken for granted. Putting forward fan mail as a neglected source for the history of reading, Clarence Karr writes that "although only those readers who interacted most profoundly with the texts wrote such letters, they still constitute an important cross-section of audience reception" (2000, 154). Even so, a seemingly neutral statement, such as "My wife read it aloud," may be designed to portray oneself favourably since it was a well-known biographical fact – often repeated by the press and by Lagerlöf herself – that the author was influenced by being read to as a child and appreciated that way of reading for her works.

As Daniel Allington (2010) has pointed out, there is a distinction to be made between records of reading and writings about reading.[1] Considering that there are several reasons why someone writing to a famous author might adjust a story about reading – or refer to a reading that was never performed – the letters must be consciously interpreted with close attention to the position of the letter writer and his or her stated purpose of writing. The close reading strategy rejected by Moretti is therefore impossible to avoid. On the other hand, even a lie about reading, or a somewhat twisted description of it, points towards practices and experiences of reading that probably did exist or, at least, were possible to imagine at the time. And what if there are (as in the case of the letters to Lagerlöf) many letters presenting similar narratives of readings? High numbers may of course strengthen the value of such evidence, since it is not very likely that numerous letter writers tell the same false story. An oft repeated story, truthful or not, would still point to an imagined way of reading that was common to several people.

There are also cases where several letters present detailed remarks on the same episode or scene in one of Selma Lagerlöf's works. Detailed and specific descriptions make a probable instance of reading interpretation more convincing, and even more so if they are presented by several senders. In their responses to Lagerlöf's *The Emperor of Portugallia* (1914), for example, many senders describe how their heart pounded, throbbed, or ached while reading the book. It is probable that these people actually had read the book, since the pounding heart of one of the characters is central to an early episode in the novel. Whether these readers' hearts *actually* were affected in different ways by reading, or whether the letter writers had found the exact same way to please Selma Lagerlöf, is hard to say. That reading *could* involve the heart of a reader, though, was obviously something that people at the time considered possible.

General Patterns and Numbers

The letters thus may be regarded as anecdotal evidence in the case of each letter writer, and cannot be taken as literal accounts of an individual's reading; nevertheless, it is interesting to search for patterns of how people narrate their reading, and then to make those narratives the data source for qualitative analysis. Before we can discuss some results concerning patterns, we have to ask ourselves to what extent this corpus of letters really can provide information on a macro-analytical level.

The task of combining micro- and macro-analytical studies of reading is almost impossible. One reason for this is that very different sources are used. Teresa Gerrard has argued that there is one hitherto unexplored source of evidence of reading that offers a way to overcome this limitation – namely, the "Answers to Correspondents" in popular weekly journals (Gerrard 2011; see also Nord 2001). In this section of the journal, letters from readers on different topics – among them literature – are answered. Gerrard claims that these documents avoid the overspecialization and the overgeneralization of many other sources, for three reasons:

> Firstly, they allow a manageable group of common (as opposed to exceptional) readers to be defined for close examination. Secondly, they combine the specific reading experiences with insights into the general habits of the common reader. Thirdly, they make possible a history of reading that is neither limited by genre nor restricted to books of literary merit. (2011, 380)

Compared to Gerrard's corpus, the letters to Selma Lagerlöf (or to any author) are a weaker source of information on the macro-analytical level, in the sense that they are limited to a single authorship. Consequently, letters to one single author do not provide very much information on which authors and genres that were popular during the period in question. However, in an investigation of letters to an author, one deals with the primary sources – readers' own words, not their opinions chosen by and filtered through the pen of an editor. Equally, someone who writes to an author is not influenced by the hope of being published and thereby becoming exposed to a number of unknown readers.

Furthermore, it is likely that the letters to Lagerlöf represent a more complete cross-section of society. According to Gerrard, the readers of the journal she was investigating, *Family Herald*, belonged to the expanding lower-middle and working classes. Most of the letter writers in the Lagerlöf letter collection can be described in the same way. In the case of Lagerlöf, however, there is also the advantage of being able to compare factory workers' expressions of their reading experiences with those of people who were not typical *Family Herald* readers – for instance, the upper-middle class, the aristocracy, or, and not least, the very poorest – the homeless, the unemployed – who probably not did view themselves as in a position to express opinions publicly, but for whom it was possible to write a private letter to Selma Lagerlöf. The age segments might differ as well – people of all ages wrote to Lagerlöf. There is a separate collection of several thousand letters from children to the author, and a significant number of letters sent to the author from different organizations. The letters also provide an opportunity to compare the use of literature in different countries. Thousands of letters in the collection are from abroad, and they evidently indicate specific reception histories in different countries, but these are mainly from the upper and middle classes and do not show the same cross-section of society as the letters from Swedish senders. However, the letters provide data that enable us to map the dissemination of this particular authorship worldwide (but mainly in Europe and the United States). With the use of geographic information systems (GISs), these data could contribute to a "geography of the book," as suggested by Black, McDonald, and Black (1998). This would be a boon for researchers investigating transnational networks in the dissemination of literature.

Another study that has contributed to the history of reading by using letters to an author is Judith Lyon-Caen's *La lecture et la vie: Les usages du roman au temps de Balzac*. Lyon-Caen examines letters to Honoré de Balzac and Eugène Sue, with a specific focus on how readers used the authors' texts to create a sense of self. The source texts are 125 letters to Honoré de Balzac and 415 to Eugène Sue (2006, 22). The problems she grapples with are similar to ours: How are we to conceptualize reading experiences that to the scholar may seem naive, sentimental, and, perhaps, as we discussed earlier, untruthful?

Lyon-Caen identifies additional categories among the letters: readers who are writers themselves and who wish to gain support from the author; readers who identify with fictional characters; and readers who wish to discuss what the novels have to say about society. Such categories frequently are present in the letters to Selma Lagerlöf too. In fact, several aspects of the letters analyzed by Lyon-Caen correspond very well with the letters to Lagerlöf, regardless of the time and place separating the authorships and the letter writers. In addition to the categories mentioned above, in many of the letters to Balzac, Sue, and Lagerlöf, a romance plot is used to make sense of the letter writers' own lives. These letter writers also seem to imitate the author's style and language when they write their own stories. Lagerlöf's readers refer to her texts as they interpret their own lives. They experience Lagerlöf as someone with a capacity to understand various predicaments in life, often associated with social problems, and they seem to take her texts as proof of that understanding. There is also a tendency among the senders to write about their own lives in a literary manner. Most frequently, though, the letter writers tend towards autobiography or diary – genres that Lyon-Caen claims are present in the letters to Balzac and Sue as well (2006, 134–37).

A dominant theme in the letters from readers to Balzac and Sue is the new potential of the novel to promote social change. Readers, especially those writing in response to *Les Mystères de Paris*, seem to appreciate the depiction of reality. This is not surprising, given that these authors aimed to etch social reality onto the romance plot. The readers seem less interested in what the literary elites refer to as the complicated architecture of Balzac's literary universe, or Sue's labyrinthian composition of Paris. Instead, they concentrate on what they view as the novels as conveying – a truthful and recognizable depiction of the social reality (Lyon-Caen 2006, 146). However, unlike Balzac and Sue, Selma Lagerlöf was not considered to be a realistic writer. Her reputation was shaped by the high estimation of the fairy tale at the turn of the century, which her publishers – and to a certain extent herself – aptly used to market several of her works. Lagerlöf was seen as a "storyteller," a mediator of tradition and past culture that had been lost in modernity, and of specific national qualities. But in the letters from the readers another image of Selma Lagerlöf also appears: the guardian of the poor, of the outcast, of the ill and destitute. This interpretation contributes to what can be called the "biographical legend" of Selma Lagerlöf, such as it was told by the press and by Lagerlöf herself in interviews and speeches (Tomashevsky 1978, 47–55; Claésson 2002). But it is also true that many readers observed these aspects of her literary work. Although her stories could not entirely fit within the realistic paradigm established by contemporary literary authorities, her readers apparently read them as, at least partly, depictions of reality. Readers appreciated that she wrote on a variety of themes that constituted recognizable circumstances for many: prostitution, alcoholism, the social disgrace of an illegitimate child, unemployment, and illness. Like the readers in Lyon-Caen's study, Lagerlöf's readers often seemed to disregard the aesthetic form of the text and to concentrate on the characters and their destinies.

The focus on social reality, by the readers both in Lyon-Caen's study and in ours, suggests that this interpretation depends on something other than the author's aesthetics and cultural context. The common denominator is most likely that the readers of all three authors were distributed across a broad social spectrum and that socially disadvantaged readers tended to put forward the social themes as a reality with which to identify. Social class is of crucial importance in the letters to Selma Lagerlöf. One may classify letters commenting on the aesthetic experience as reflecting a different but still important aspect of reading. Such letters stand in opposition to those from the readers who use the text to reach other ends: to recognize themselves, to improve themselves morally, to educate themselves, or for religious contemplation. These different aspects of reading correspond to different reading communities. The problem, however, is that the categories overlap. Sometimes specific aesthetic qualities are mentioned in, for example, the letters of personal improvement, and the other way around.

Another difficulty is that the different reading practices in many cases correspond to different social segments of society. Reading practices emphasizing the aesthetic value of the text are extremely rare when the sender lacks education and economic means. Those senders may well comment on aesthetic aspects of the text, but usually they frame the aesthetic experience differently. For instance, the aesthetic is not valued in itself, but rather as a means of creating insight into society or understanding personal experiences. Social class may determine how the reader approaches Selma Lagerlöf, and what paratexts the reader has access to, and reflect a different understanding of the different elements of the biographical legend that seem appropriate to use in framing one's understanding of the narrative.

To understand social class in relation to the letters, a qualitative approach is needed. But we have also tried to let our database keywords reflect more quantifiable aspects, such as how many letters were written in certain years, which works were most often mentioned, how many requests for autographs or financial aid Selma Lagerlöf received, and the distribution among men and women. Those categories are generally unambiguous and do not require interpretation but rather a close reading of the many letters.

But there is also information about reading we wanted the keywords to capture that is not easily converted into graphs. When a letter writer informs Selma Lagerlöf about how a reading was performed, this has been coded as, for instance, "reading aloud" (i.e., "*högläsning*"). This means we can search the database and find the letter writer stating that he or she has read aloud (or has been read aloud to), but it does not allow us to draw any conclusions about how common it was to read aloud at the time – not among all readers and not even among all readers of Lagerlöf. Letter writers who have read Selma Lagerlöf texts in a reading club are a similar example – they provide clues regarding how common this situation of reading was. The documents can nevertheless serve as traces of reading practices in specific reading communities. One such example is letters from schoolteachers (often also signed by the pupils), which usually document the use and reception of Lagerlöf's geography schoolbook, *The Wonderful Adventures of Nils* (1906–7). These school classes can be seen as specific face-to-face reading communities, with the members sharing a reading experience. The letters from them would, when combined with institutional records, be an even more valuable source. Letters like these would be a useful complement in studies like Christine Pawley's (2001) of late-nineteenth-century Osage, Iowa. For her study, Pawley used records from churches, schools, fraternal and voluntary organizations, and the public library.

The gender of readers is another interesting aspect that could be quantifiable. It is a widespread notion that Lagerlöf was read mostly by women. But in our source material there are as many male as female letter writers. Obviously, this does not prove that men read Lagerlöf to the same extent as women – it may merely suggest that men were more eager than women to write letters to authors. However, the numbers indicate that men's reading of Lagerlöf *might* have been more common than assumed, and by extension, that the "feminization" of Selma Lagerlöf began after her own lifetime. In addition, we find no support for the idea that there are specific differences in the reading practices of men and women when it comes to engaging the intellect, emotions, and the body (Karlsson 2008). The tears, the shivers, the pounding hearts, and the feelings of compassion experienced by male readers are confessed without embarrassment; so is the sense of losing track of time and space while reading. The opposition between a detached, intellectual (i.e., male) approach to literature and a consuming, affective (i.e., female) way of reading is neither useful nor adequate when it comes to the readings manifested in the letters to Selma Lagerlöf (for more on gendered reading, see Tompkins 1980; Flint 1995; Littau 2011). The difference between male and female readers appears in the way the author is addressed: women tend to use a more humble rhetoric and a more intimate idiom as they put forward everyday experiences of their private lives and dreams, while men often use a more authoritative tone and are more demanding when it comes to asking for money or favours (Karlsson 2008).

Reading practices intended to be detached and analytical are more often found in reviews by professional readers, which are not the focus in our study (even though many critics show heated emotions when it comes to Selma Lagerlöf). In readers' letters to Lagerlöf, emotional reading practices dominate, even in the letters focusing on aesthetic aspects. Typically in those letters, Lagerlöf's style is esteemed for its beauty, and this aesthetic experience of beauty is itself described in affective terms.

Another somewhat surprising finding in this study is that past reading practices remain to a considerable extent. In chronological terms, Selma Lagerlöf's years of authorship came long after what Rolf Engelsing (1974) has called the reading revolution, which supposedly changed reading habits from intensive reading of a few texts, for the purpose of learning and improving oneself, to extensive reading of many texts for entertainment or aesthetic experience (cited in Colclough 2009, 57). The collection of letters to Selma Lagerlöf challenges Engelsing's notion of intensive/extensive reading. Both in the letters describing the reading of Lagerlöf's texts as a means for self-improvement, and in those expressing a religious reading, repetition constitutes an important part of the reading experience. The readers return to the text, reading the same passages over and over again, and often learn them by heart, suggesting an intensive reading practice.

In the religious letters, Selma Lagerlöf's status as a spiritual or even religious authority is foregrounded – an aspect of her authorship often overlooked today. This indicates a new role for literature in a society becoming more and more secular. The letter writers express that Selma Lagerlöf is able to "preach without preaching" and mention using her texts as a substitute for devotional books or religious teaching material (Bergenmar 2012).

Conclusion

With Selma Lagerlöf, we are dealing with an author of modern times. She benefited from the all the channels of literary markets – her texts were published as magazine serials, or as short stories with illustrations by well-known artists. Also, they were sold in cheap editions and marketed to working-class readers, with low prices and appealing illustrations and covers. Many letter writers claimed to have bought many of her books and used words such as "thrilling" to describe them (which seemingly supports a reading focused on entertainment), but not all of them did so. A considerable number of the letter writers described a reading practice that could be characterized as intensive; that is, they read the same book over and over again for religious contemplation or as a means to learn how to be a good person. In other words, intensive and extensive reading often seemed to coexist. This was sometimes dependent on economic means (e.g., a book by Lagerlöf might have been the only novel in they owned) as well as on education.

The letters to Selma Lagerlöf suggest that her audience was strongly influenced by the press. Many of the letter writers explicitly state that they have read her works in serial form or as short stories in newspapers and various journals; they also seem to have followed the information about her life and career closely. There are letters from people who claim that they have not read anything by her – or for whom it is impossible to tell whether they have or not – but who still refer to the same characteristics of the author as the letter writers who claim to have read her do. The number of letters increased when the press reported more frequently about her – at the time of the Nobel Prize, on special birthdays, and when widely distributed journals published articles focusing on, for instance, the author's generosity to the poor. Again, we cannot say with certainty that the press had an impact on how the audience viewed Selma Lagerlöf in general, but the many letters to her give evidence of its influence.

In light of all the scholarly precautions and rigorous analysis required when using letters to the author as a source for history of reading, one may be inclined to follow William St. Clair's recommendation and choose other, more reliable sources such as library catalogues and educational archives (2004, 5). But this would reinforce the tendency within reception studies to favour public records over private ones. The reading described by individuals writing to authors may be neither entirely reliable nor unambiguous; nevertheless, it tells stories that other sources cannot provide. In the case of Selma Lagerlöf, the high numbers of letters support some of these stories to a fairly high degree, perhaps higher than in most available studies dealing with fewer letters from readers. As more and more private sources of reading in history are investigated, their significance as evidence will increase, which will make it possible for us to see different patterns of reading.

Note

1 However, the example of James Hoggs that Allington uses does not exactly apply in our case. Hoggs's autobiographical record of reading, claiming the experience of reading Burns to be of crucial importance to his literary development, is more likely to be a literary construct than a private letter to an author from an unknown individual, not active in the literary field.

References

Allington, Daniel. 2010. "On the Use of Anecdotal Evidence in Reception Study and the History of Reading." In *Reading in History: New Methodologies from the Anglo-American Tradition*, edited by Bonnie Gunzenhauser, 11–28. London: Pickering and Chatto.

Bergenmar, Jenny. 2012. "Predika utan att predika. Allmänhetens religiösa läsningar av Selma Lagerlöfs författarskap" [To Preach without Preaching: Religious Reading Practices in the Public's Letters to Selma Lagerlöf 1891–1940]. *Kyrkohistorisk årsskrift*. Publications of the Swedish Society of Church History I, 112: 85–103.

Black, Fiona, Bertrum H. McDonald, and Malcolm W. Black. 1998. "Geographic Information Systems: A New Research Method for Book History." *Book History* 1(1): 11–31.

Claésson, Dick. 2002. "The Narratives of the Biographical Legend: The Early Works of William Beckford." PhD diss., University of Gothenberg.

Colclough, Stephen. 2009. "Readers: Books and Biography." In *A Companion to the History of the Book*, edited by Simon Eliot and Jonathan Rose, 50–62. Malden and Oxford: Wiley-Blackwell.

Collini, Stefan. 2008. *Common Reading: Critics, Historians, Publics*. Oxford: Oxford University Press.

Darnton, Robert. [1986]2011. "First Steps Towards a History of Reading." *Australian Journal of French Studies* 23 (1986): 5–30. Reprinted in *The History of Reading: A Reader*, edited by Shafquat Towheed, Rosemary Crone, and Kate Halsey, 23–35. London and New York: Routledge.

Dolatkhah, Mats. 2011. "Det läsande barnet: Minnen av läspraktiker 1900–1940 [The Reading Child: Memories of Reading Practices 1900–1949]." PhD diss., University of Borås.

Engelsing, Rolf. 1974. *Der Burger als Leser. Lesergeschichte in Deutschland 1500–1800*. [*The Citizen as Reader: Histories of Readers in Germany 1500–1800*]. Stuttgart: Metzler.

Eliot, Simon. n.d. "The Reading Experience Database, or, What Are We to Do about the History of Reading." http://www.open.ac.uk/Arts/RED/redback.htm

Flint, Kate. 1995. *The Woman Reader, 1837–1914*. Oxford and New York: Oxford University Press.

Gerrard, Teresa. 2011. "New Methods in the History of Reading: Answers to Correspondents in *The Family Herald*, 1860–1900." In *The History of Reading:*

A Reader, edited by Shafquat Towheed, Rosemary Crone, and Kate Halsey, 379–88. Abingdon: Routledge.

Karlsson, Maria. 2008. "Läsarnas Lagerlöf: kroppen och känslorna." [Reading Lagerlöf: The Body and the Emotions.] In *En ny sits. Humaniora i förvandling. Vänbok till Margaretha Fahlgren* [*A New Setting: Humanities in Transformation*], edited by E. Heggestad, 233–40. Uppsala: Acta universitatis Uppsaliensis.

———. 2011. "Den verkliga publikens Selma Lagerlöf. [The Audience's Selma Lagerlöf]." In *Spår och speglingar* [*Tracks and Reflections*], edited by Maria Karlsson and Louise Vinge, 185–215. Möklinta: Gidlunds.

Karr, Clarence. 2000. *Authors and Audiences: Popular Canadian Fiction in the Early Twentieth Century*. Montreal and Kingston: McGill–Queen's University Press.

Littau, Karin. 2011. *Theories of Reading: Books, Bodies, and Bibliomania*. Cambridge: Polity Press.

Lyon-Caen, Judith. 2006. *La lecture et la vie: Les usage du roman au temps de Balzac* [*Reading and Life: Uses of the Novel in Balzac's Time*]. Paris: Tallandier.

Moretti, Franco. 2005. *Graphs, Maps, Trees: Abstract Models for a Literary History*. London: Verso.

Nord, David Paul. 2001. *Communities of Journalism: A History of American Newspapers and Their Readers*. Urbana: University of Illinois Press.

Pawley, Christine. 2001. *Reading on the Middle Border: The Culture of Print in Late-Nineteenth-Century Osage, Iowa*. Amherst: University of Massachusetts Press.

The Reading Experience Database. http://www.open.ac.uk/Arts/RED/experience.htm

Rose, Jonathan. 1995. "How Historians Study Reader Response: or, What Did Jo think of *Bleak House*." In *Literature in the Market-Place: Nineteenth Century British Publishing and Reading Practices*, edited by J.O. Jordan and R.L. Patterson, 195–212. Cambridge: Cambridge University Press.

———. 2001. *The Intellectual Life of the British Working Classes*. Yale: Nota Bene.

Serlen, Rachel. 2010. "The Distant Future? Reading Franco Moretti." *Literature Compass* 7(3): 214–25.

St. Clair, William. 2004. *The Reading Nation in the Romantic Period*. Cambridge: Cambridge University Press.

Tomashevsky, Boris. 1978. "Literature and Biography." In *Readings in Russian Poetics: Formalist and Structuralist Views*, edited by Ladislav Matejka and Krystyna Pomorska, 47–55. Cambridge, MA: MIT Press.

Tompkins, Jane P. 1980. "The Reader in History." In *Reader-Response Criticism: From Formalism to Poststructuralism*, edited by Jane P. Tompkins, 201–2. Baltimore: Johns Hopkins University Press.

Byatt versus Bloom   6
or, Reading by Patricide versus Reading by Love

Marianne Børch

The Realm of the Reading Experience

Reading is pure natural magic: I look at dark smudges upon white paper, and applying my attention and an acquired competence, they transport me into another world, somewhere over the rainbow, beyond the galaxies or the end of the world. And not only may reading create and cross possible spaces: time, too, is charmed. I can travel from the twentieth century to the Stone Age with William Golding, even as Geoffrey Chaucer calls me across six centuries, making me experience now what life was like for fourteenth-century lovers, and what the fourteenth century thought about life and love in ancient Troy.

Reading's ability to move me about, and thus move me to experience all sorts of otherness as real, makes reading the best possible education in cultural adaptability. The experience of *reality* is the magical bit: science can show neurons lighting up, detect chemical reactions, and show what parts of the brain are affected as we read; but it can account neither for the images of which the little explosions of energy are the symptoms, nor for the strange sequences of images into narrative, or the places we enter with that narrative as we read.

In his extremely intriguing and certainly also incredibly weird book *Omens of the Millennium*, the controversial literary critic Harold Bloom has a word for the place where we are when we read: he calls it the *imaginal* (1996, 167ff). He refuses to use the term "the Imaginary" for this realm for he wishes to avoid the suggestion of unreality imparted by that word, and the place he contemplates is as real as anything, although it is virtual from an empirical or positivist point of view. The *imaginal*, says Bloom, is a place we know in other ways, too. We go there, for instance, during a near-death experience; it is the place where angels move; and, to return, we go there when we read: I may walk about my everyday life, drive to pick up children in the kindergarten, fly or sail to Oslo, but in every physical location, I may at any time abscond and visit *the imaginal* by the vehicle of a book: there, Sir Lancelot is always riding about on a quest, Adam and Eve are waiting to let me in on their plan to eat the forbidden fruit, or Søren Kierkegaard repeats for me his struggle with understanding the patriarch Abraham in his most terrible moment. The enchanted garden is there. I go to it.

The *imaginal* is particularly good for evoking what is no more, but has been. The past is famously known as "another country – they do things differently there," and so it is a favourite topic of writers who wish to study the present in a displaced mirror. The most cited passage by Nathaniel Hawthorne must surely be his preface to *The House of Seven Gables*, where he describes romance as against readerly expectations of a novel: "The point of view in which [a] tale comes under the Romantic definition lies in the attempt to connect a bygone time with the very present that is flitting away from us" (as cited in Byatt 1990, epigraph. Quotations below not otherwise identified are from this work).

Reading the past, we read ourselves, but ourselves as both strange and uncannily familiar. If the transfer of a reader into a strange time and place is magical, no less magical seems the process by which influence is mediated between an admired model and his or her brilliant admirer, whose own creative work carries clear marks of the precursor's influence yet is self-evidently "original." New and personal. In her romance *Possession* (1990) – which has Hawthorne for her epigraph – Antonia Byatt explores the way a past writer may equally inspire and inhibit, and how both past and present writers may ultimately be set free and rendered individually powerful through learning to read.

Rereading the Past

Byatt's exploration is itself creative; but theorists and critics, too, struggle to make sense of the process of poetic influence in the more limited format of discursive analysis, and they accept the limitations as the price for insights amenable to intellectual and rational debate. Even so, the subtle phenomenon slips through the mesh. How might we explain the process by which the most original voice is also in some sense derivative, the processing of some great original? Already, the very word "original" gives away the paradox we consider, for we describe a breakthrough to something new as "original"; yet we also apply the word to the first instance, or the source, of a momentous phenomenon: its origin, its "original" form.

T.S. Eliot, himself a creative writer, tackled as a theorist the paradoxical relation between the individual writer and his enabling inspiration in his famous essay, "Tradition and the Individual Talent" (1921), where he explained how what is most personal becomes impersonal in the process of reading the tradition and rereading it creatively in a new work. Harold Bloom, already mentioned, is possibly most famous for a similar attempt to place or define how a precursor determines its descendants: In *The Western Canon* (1994), he argues that Shakespeare created the whole Western world – and created it by speaking through each and every one of us, as a ventriloquist speaks through his dummy. I do not even need to read Shakespeare to speak Shakespearean, for he has, as it were, read me, made me speak the words, and speak in the way that he made possible for me to speak. Bloom hates all those "schools of resentment" that seek to reduce literature to channels for ideological propaganda. But although he hates cultural criticism, feminism, postcolonial criticism, et cetera, all of which seek to demystify literature as ideologically manipulated, his own theory resembles those schools in seeing us all as brainwashed by the genius – though certainly the impersonal genius – of Shakespeare. The determination is strong, but it is ideologically diverse, or disinterested.

Bloom's *Western Canon* traces the way readers were made by being read by Shakespeare. But Bloom has devoted another series of studies to the process of reading, focusing this time on a particular group of readers whom he characterizes as "strong poets," those readers whose reading awakens in them a passionate response where boundless admiration mingles with deep frustration that they did not get there first; the model is so overpowering in its originality that it prevents the young admirer from finding his own original voice (1975, 1987, 1997).[1] To explain the process by which the new poet learns to appropriate the model even in breaking through to his own voice, Bloom, not surprisingly, borrows from Freud his explanatory model and terminology. Freud, I say not surprisingly, because Bloom views Freud as one of Shakespeare's finest latter-day mouthpieces.[2]

Reading as Following: The Son Reading the Father

I have often been bemused by the fact that while Freud's use in psychiatry is today mediated and modified in multiple ways, literary critics continue to find Freud himself useful (although Lacan's and Kristeva's readings are also influential). Bloom might explain the continued usefulness of pure Freud in a literary context from the way Freud himself formed his theories from literature: thus, Hamlet and Oedipus are the two great forebears of his theory for explaining influence among people as among texts;[3] and, I might add, Robert Louis Stevenson had already invented, if not named, the *id*, the *superego*, and the *ego* in *Dr. Jekyll and Mr. Hyde*.

According to Bloom's theory, every poet is a reader, and a strong poet is a strong reader, who cannot help distorting what he reads in such a way that the original determines the disciple's or *ephebe*'s text, which is also, however, wrested out of shape.[4] The encounter with the precursor is so overpowering that the *ephebe* experiences an anxiety of influence that results in a text that is both determined by and bent away from the original, swerving in a different direction from the course laid out by the model.[5]

Andrew Marvell's daring poem on Milton's *Paradise Lost* mediated Bloom's idea of influence as an anxiety. Marvell here imagines Milton, wrestling with God's hard truth, as the Samson of the Old Testament who, in defeating the Philistines, brings down the temple upon his own head. The equation Milton–Samson is theologically disturbing, since it implies that the Philistines are God's truth, the truth that Milton comes close to questioning in *Paradise Lost*. Samson's *agon*[6] as applied to Milton's struggle, in other words, threatens to bring down the entire edifice of Biblical truth.

The metaphors Marvell uses – of ruining, groping ... in spite, revenge – fit hand in glove with Bloom's Freud-inspired Primal Scene, where the poet–Son, jealous over the Father's *coitus* with the muse, fights his father and "kills" him in the sense that the son achieves dominance, or *priority*; although later in time, his poetic achievement demotes the father to secondary importance; he comes, in fact, to be seen as merely preparing the way for the fulfillment achieved in the son. Thus time is reversed, and the son becomes the father (1997, 9, 37).

Freud has found many critics, who argue that his theories work for men but not for humanity as a whole. If we turn to Bloom's Freudian explanation of a poet's so-called anxiety of literary influence, the same criticism may be voiced with even greater weight. I might take Virginia Woolf to witness here, but my purpose today is different, and others have done for Woolf what I could not do nearly as well. To find a valuable direction for understanding the nexus between indebtedness and originality, I shall digress to take a look at the way poets themselves have described the relation.

Perhaps the most frequent metaphor for the model–follower situation is that between child and parent, or beloved teacher and devoted disciple. At the end of *Troilus and Criseyde*, Chaucer addresses his "litel tragedye," releasing it upon the world, free of his originating influence, but as he hopes, loyal to Horace, Statius, Homer, Ovid, and Lucan (1987, V, 1786–92). He knows his poem is personally generated, but also that it belongs in a transpersonal whole. The father–son relationship Chaucer describes here is well known and often invoked in literary discussion, and Chaucer himself is famously named the father of the English tradition, a status manifest in his tomb at the centre of Poet's Corner in Westminster Abbey.

The male terminology of father and son is typical of critical parlance, but the poets' vocabulary frequently suggests that the influence is experienced as androgynous rather than male: the very idea of a muse suggests that the male poem needs female inspiration, or in-breathing, even as it indicates that no text is self-begotten: nothing is born from nothing. Similarly, great ideas are both born *and* begotten: the English verb "conceive" both for having an idea and for becoming pregnant suggests how the two processes are closely involved. So, when Zeus gives birth to Athena out of his head, she may validly be called his brainchild, a term we normally apply to a passionately promoted stroke of genius. In *Paradise Lost* (I, 17–26) Satan, having conceived the sinful thought of rebellion, self-begets and gives birth to Sin from his brain. Satan's brainchild is a parodic analogue of the Son begotten by a Father. But God's begetting is not just male, for the Logos-dove is doubly gendered. Milton suggests as much when he explicitly asks his "Heav'nly Muse" to beget a child upon him, a world of words similar to one she has already begotten and born once before – or, in fact, twice. The muse – God's Logos – once created the world (the word speaking the physical world into existence); and later, she told the story of that Creation to Moses (providing the Words for the Biblical word). Now, even as the "dovelike" spirit both begot and hatched Creation, even so Milton is both male and female, father and mother of his poem.

The androgynous begetting of poetry had already been humorously explored in Sir Philip Sidney's opening sonnet of his *Astrophil and Stella* sequence. Here, the poet is a child, who wishes to learn from his forebears, but finds the schoolroom of the old masters a dry and dusty place, where the freshness of "others' leaves" fails to pour its showers upon his sunburnt brain. The poet is already pregnant with the poem somehow begotten upon him, only, "great with child to speak and helpless in [his] throes," he needs the midwifely attentions of Dame Nature.

Even today, creative and cultural connections are conceptualized as a process of generation, and the hovering between male and female that might seem strangely uncanny in evoking a physical analogue is now released into a more openly philosophical conception: Woolf, already mentioned, considers creativity androgynous, while others contemplate creativity as the result of a sexual impulse unmarked by specific orientation. Michel Foucault's (1993) influential idea of genealogies of ideas and customs might be cited as a case in point, and a writer like Jeanette Winterson may illustrate the way the poetic as well as every other creative tradition is viewed as a process of continuous procreation, by which one artist begets a unique baby work of art upon another artist.[7] The begetting described here is not male only; rather, the biological factor is passed by, inspiration flowing between male and female, female and male, male and male, or female and female: biological marking is irrelevant, although the process is always imagined as erotic; and both partners may be artists (getting rid of the priority of artist over muse).

Reading by Love

The positive aspect of inspiration as a process of biologically unmarked but erotically triggered generation suggests an alternative understanding of literary influence. Much energy and mutual exchange go into the process by which influence begets a new and original child upon the original. The struggle is there, but as an act of love in which personal fulfillment coincides with unreserved openness to another.

In *Possession* (1990), a work that echoes with the influence of Milton, Marvell, and Bloom, Byatt is fascinated with reading. Her protagonist, Roland, thus far – almost at the end of the work – much less heroic than his namesake and crushed by an anxiety of influence with respect to his nineteenth-century precursor, Randolph Ash, is here rereading, perhaps for "the twelfth or maybe even the twentieth time," Ash's "The Garden of Proserpina":

> [T]he writer wrote alone, and the reader read alone, and they were alone with each other. True, the writer may have been alone also with Spenser's golden apples in the *Fairie Queene* ... may have seen Paradise Lost, in the garden where Eve recalled Pomona and Proserpina. He was alone when he wrote and he was not alone, then, all these voices sang, the same words, golden apples, different words in different places, an Irish castle, an unseen cottage, elastic-walled and grey round blind eyes ... a sense that the text [appears] to be wholly new, never before seen, is followed, almost immediately, by a sense that it *was always there*, that we as readers, knew it was always there, and have *always known* it was as it was, though we have only now for the first time recognised, become fully cognizant of, our knowledge. (1990, 271–72)

The presence of the passage here defines the crucial moment when the young scholar and poet learns, for the first time, to truly read, a process that mingles intimate familiarity with pristine freshness. At this point, Byatt has listed and analyzed a whole range of valid readings, but now focuses upon the specific reading by which an aspiring poet achieves his breakthrough, one through which influence remains strong but ceases to be oppressive or threatening. Roland's previously "subjected imagination" (469) is finally set free, and the precursor's text achieves its own release from the subjection previously wrought by his reader's subjected imagination. In Byatt's treatment, the double release is achieved as the anxiety of influence originally suffered by Roland is transformed into an act of love. A breakthrough that happens through the experience of human love.

A bit of paraphrase is needed at this point: Roland seeks to recover every possible bit of information about Ash, an icon of Victorian poetic greatness, whose fame rests upon his ability to invest his personal genius in an impersonal evocation of past voices, male as well as female, earning him the label of the Great Ventriloquist. Roland, despite ambitions to become a poet like Ash, earns a modest living as a very small cog in the multi-wheel mechanism that systematically churns out Ash scholarship – a mechanism that is jokingly referred to among its members as the Ash Factory. Its work is impeccable but unimaginative philology, and Byatt evocatively links its setting to Dante's *Inferno* (26ff.), which in turn triggers associations of "Ashes to ashes."

The book's other central scholarly community (among a host of minor ones) is the much more modern, radically feminist establishment of Lincoln University. This is directed by the female protagonist, Maud, whose research investigates the poetry of another Victorian, Christabel LaMotte, with a view to showing how a lesbian relationship may have nourished female genius even in an environment where female worth could not receive its due. The book follows the resurrection of Ash – this "dead man. Who had a thing about dead people" (19) – into a vibrantly live voice, and LaMotte into a poet whose merit transcends the feminist mould into which she is squeezed, or into whose service she is pressed by the feminists, one of Bloom's "schools of resentment." The resurrection happens, first, by means of reading, and what is read is a previously undiscovered batch of letters.

Private letters "[envision] no outcome, no closure"; moreover, they are written "for *a* reader" (130–31). Faced with no closure and one specific reader, the scholars find themselves struggling. How can they impose the biases they bring to their reading upon the letters with their passionate directedness towards an unknown female addressee existing in a complete historical void? The addressee turns out, of course, to be LaMotte: so much for the lesbian angle; and so much for the Victorian icon of impersonal creativity. The rest of the book records a process by which the modern protagonists learn to read well as their personal and scholarly biases are resisted and finally destroyed by those intransigent texts, the letters that refuse to obey their readers' desire for confirmation.

The enigmatic letters lead into a quest – *Possession*'s subtitle is *A Romance* – and we follow the quest for the true, or at least truer, Ash and LaMotte[8] by diffident male bottom-of-the-scholarly-hierarchy Roland, and brilliant but severely inhibited Maud. Although an ill-matched couple, they do, as the subtitle virtually promises, discover how their possessive quest for the equally odd nineteenth-century pair of poets gradually becomes an increasingly passionate possession with each other. As their love and their personalities develop, they become better readers – less anxious and defensive, precisely, and so, more open. At first they read possessively, in their own image, as it were. But as long they seek to find (only) what they look for, a confirmation of the rightness of their preconceptions and their own brilliance, they are obstructed by the letters, which refuse to make sense within the framework of their respective biases; gradually, the letters' strange voices force the protagonists to relax, to open themselves, and attend to something beyond their own desires and need for self-affirmation. They learn to read the letters, and they even begin to find things that are not even in them: there are things between the lines, there are pregnant silences, evasions, and omissions, even in new and other letters, whose writers come alive in their own right. Ash's wife Ellen and Christabel's housemate Blanche become more than muses and satellites of the great man and woman and turn out to have fascinating personalities and obliquely embedded information to impart to posterity. By means of achieved reading, a dead past and dead people encounter, matter to, and influence, people in the present.

The opening up towards good reading in *Possession* develops analogously with a passionate love between the protagonists, which overcomes the self-love that is shown to dominate the typically insecure modern scholar. Love is itself a frightening experience, threatening to throw down the barricades by which men as well as women protect the *personae* that impersonate their timid selves: the image of comfort and safety turns out, for both Roland and Maud, to be that of an egg, while the image of a broken eggshell and whipped-up egg white renders an experience where Maud has nearly lost her "circumscribed little independence" (159). These words quoted are Christabel's in an early, defensive letter to Ash, and what the modern scholars discover is that for all their liberation into modernity, they have their own self-protective blocks. In fact, the protective tower in which Lacan places the ego[9] is not just that in which females guard their "circumscribed little independence," but is shared by men and women alike.

Once love breaks down the barriers of the self, energies flow out in a painful loss of control, which is, however, necessary for the external influence to flow back in. A process of mutuality is thus suggested to be the true nature of the influence that unites lovers in one flesh even as they find their own independent selves (and not circumscribed little independences, but fully achieved ones). Analogously, mutuality characterizes the readerly encounter through which the *ephebe* and the precursor are both possessed and liberated.

Rereading the Reading

I should admit that in demonstrating Byatt's revision of Bloom, I am somewhat diffident about my own reading of Bloom himself. Bloom goes on and on about misprision, *agon*, struggle, patricide, *askesis*, and aggression, borrows from the Australian poet A.D. Hope "the argument of arms," which "holds that the struggle for supreme power is central to both poetry and to warfare" (in Bloom 1997, xxxiii) and cites Nietzsche, who declares that "Every talent must unfold itself in fighting" (in Bloom 1997, 52). However, the more I ponder his deliberately elusive text,[10] the more I feel that the process Bloom describes is not entirely different from the one Byatt evokes. Bloom's concept of *kenosis* resembles her idea of opening up through love. His *separation* is achieved the way lovers release each other's full personhood. On two occasions, he explicitly analogizes poetic influence and love, and there are hints in the Preface to the second edition (written twenty-four years after the first one) that Bloom is aware of a need of a swerve from his agnostic Freudian–Lucretian model towards a vocabulary of love.[11] Nevertheless, Byatt's metaphors and representations are markedly different from his, and surely we need to remember that metaphors and representations matter. Byatt thus re-encodes the process of influence as analyzed by Bloom; we might even see her as a "strong reader" of Bloom, who – in insisting that love is a better way of conceptualizing the miracle by which two entities become fully separate even as they become one – enforces a "swerve" from her admired model. Furthermore, Byatt modifies Bloom's understanding of poetic creation in her critique of the male orientation taken over from Freud. Bloom is not overtly talking about gender, but his discourse is. Even though Byatt uses a male and a female meeting in love's embrace as the narrative illustration of the meeting of souls, her description of her protagonists' education into better readers transcends gender differences. We no longer need to gender creativity as do Freud and Bloom.

But then, and to conclude, circumstances for understanding the process have changed. Byatt's nineteenth-century poet Christabel remarks on her loyalty to tradition in one of her fairy tales: "one day we will write it otherwise (155)." Things have changed between Ash/Lamotte and Roland/Maud, and despite their contemporaneity, the circumstances that determine Bloom's views are quite different from those that influence Byatt. These differences enable her to modify Bloom's theory, resulting in two central points: first, the enigmatic process by which past and present, poet and poet, engage in passionate intercourse to beget originality upon an original is better conceptualized as love than as patricide; and second, the theory of poetic influence should be valid for male and female *ephebes* alike.

Notes

1. In the following, Bloom's title *The Anxiety of Influence: A Theory of Poetry* will be abbreviated to *Anxiety*. Practical criticism is, essentially, the "endless quest of 'how to read'" (Bloom 1987, 69). On the poet as a special kind of reader, however, see *Anxiety*, 30–31, and also 43, where Bloom's overall intention is to "pursue the quest of learning to read any poem as its poet's deliberate misinterpretation ... of a precursor poem or poetry in general."
2. For example, "Shakespeare invented the domain of those metaphors of willing that Freud named the drives of Love and Death" (1997, viii). Bloom also claims, however, to be "a deliberate revisionist of some of the Freudian ideas" (1997, 8).
3. According to Bloom, the Oedipus complex should rightly be called the Hamlet complex (1997, xxii).
4. Bloom uses the word *ephebe* for a young and aspiring Athenian poet (1997, 10).
5. Bloom uses "swerve" to translate his concept of one step of the creative process named after Lucretius's "clinamen" (1997, 42–45).
6. Bloom defines *agon* as "the contest for aesthetic supremacy" (1997, xxiv). Marvell's identification of Milton with Samson refers to Milton's closet drama *Samson Agonistes*.
7. *Art & Lies* follows Picasso, a female painter, Handel, a male singer/musician, and Sappho (female poet), tracing the genealogy by which their art forms cross-fertilize through erotic but biologically unmarked interaction.
8. The quest never ends, for the full truth is never possessed, ensuring that longing for more knowledge that feeds quests. Byatt makes sure the reader gets this point by means of a "Postscript 1868" (508–10), in which the reader is given information about Ash that never becomes available to the protagonists.
9. Byatt inscribes all the relevant theory in her own work: the relevance of the Lacanian ego can be consulted in a letter written by the scholar Fergus Woolf (138).
10. Bloom asks that his theory be "judged" as "argument," but indirectly concedes that it may be difficult to respond to a text that "presents itself as a severe poem, reliant upon aphorism, apothegm, and a quite personal (though thoroughly traditional) mythic pattern" (1997, 13).
11. In a preface to his revised edition, Bloom deplores the way in which *Anxiety* has been "weakly misread," and seeks to correct earlier mistaken readings of himself by describing "strong misreading" as "a kind of falling in love" (1997, xxiii). In the following, original text of 1973, he notes that "Lichtenberg implies that Poetic Influence is an oxymoron. But then, so is Romantic Love an oxymoron, and Romantic Love is the closest analogue to Poetic Influence" (31).

References

Bloom, Harold. 1975. *A Map of Misreading*. New York: Oxford University Press.
———. 1987. *Ruin the Sacred Truths*. Cambridge, MA: Harvard University Press.
———. 1994. *The Western Canon*. New York: Harcourt Brace.
———. 1996. *Omens of the Millennium: The Gnosis of Angels, Dreams, and Resurrection*. New York: Riverhead Books.
———. 1997. *The Anxiety of Influence: A Theory of Poetry*. New York: Oxford University Press.
Byatt, A.S. 1990. *Possession*. London: Vintage.
Chaucer, Geoffrey. 1987. *Troilus and Criseyde* (c. 1383–85). The Riverside Chaucer. Oxford: Oxford University Press.

Eliot, T.S. 1921. "Tradition and the Individual Talent," In *The Sacred Wood*. New York: Knopf; Bartleby.com, 1996. http://www.bartleby.com/200/sw4.html

Foucault, Michel. 1993. "About the Beginnings of the Hermeneutics of the Self: Two Lectures at Dartmouth." *Political Theory* 21(2): 198–227.

Marvell, Andrew. 1674. "On Mr. Milton's 'Paradise Lost.'" http://classiclit.about.com/library/bl-etexts/amarvell/bl-amar-onmil.htm

Sidney, Philip 1580. *Astrophil and Stella 1: Loving in truth, and fain in verse my love to show.* Poetry Foundation. http://www.poetryfoundation.org/poem/174419

Winterson, Jeanette. 1990. *Art & Lies*. London: Vintage.

A Cognitive Poetic Approach to Researching the Reading Experience

7

Sara Whiteley

This essay investigates the experience of reading a particular poem: "I'll Be There to Love and Comfort You" (Armitage 2010) by making connections between the poem's language and its experiential effects. My analysis uses the cognitive poetic Text World Theory framework (Werth 1999; Gavins 2007) to consider the mental representations that are prompted by the language of the poem. I also draw on recordings of readers discussing the poem to gain a sense of the salient experiential features associated with the text. I argue that cognitive poetic analysis, which models the interaction between text and mind, can offer some explanation for a number of the experiential effects discussed by readers. In the first section I introduce some of the central principles behind the cognitive poetic perspective on the reading experience, provide some background information about the reader response data I refer to, and introduce the poem under discussion. My analysis in the second section centres on areas of similarity across the readers' discussions and relates these common responses to aspects of the language of the text.

Cognitive Poetics and Text World Theory

Cognitive poetics is an approach to literary study that is informed by research in the fields of cognitive linguistics, cognitive psychology, and the cognitive sciences. It suggests that readings of literary texts (and other texts, too) may be explained with reference to general human principles of linguistic and cognitive processing (Gavins and Steen 2003, 2). There are several variants of cognitive poetics; for instance, Stockwell (2005) distinguishes between a predominantly North American tradition that emerges more from psychology and linguistics departments, and a predominantly European tradition more associated with stylistics or literary linguistics (see also Brône and Vandaele 2009). The approach in this chapter is most closely aligned with the European, stylistically influenced strand of cognitive poetics. Stylistic analysis is underpinned by the assumption that "the primary interpretative procedures used in the reading of a literary text are *linguistic* procedures" (Carter 1982, 4). Leech and Short characterize the concerns of mainstream contemporary stylisticians to be "how, when we read, we get from the words on the page to the meanings in our heads and effects in our hearts" (2007, 287). These summaries reflect stylisticians' interest in the experience of reading, and also their belief that the language of the text or "words on the page" have a significant role to play in this experience. Because of its focus on the human mind, cognitive poetics places extra emphasis on the role of the reader in literary interpretation, representing a major evolution in stylistics (Carter and Stockwell 2008, 298).

The central feature of cognitive poetic analysis is the relation of the structure of literary texts to their presumed or observed psychological effects on a reader (Gavins and Steen 2001, 1). A common misconception is that cognitive poetics is necessarily reductive and purely objective in its approach to literature because of its focus on cognitive processes. But, as Brône and Vandaele point out, it is the "felt qualities of mental life" that cognitive poetics seeks to address, rather than "mere 'computation' or 'processing'" (2009, 2). Cognitive poetics is strongly influenced by the experientialism of cognitive linguistics and is fundamentally concerned with context – that is, it regards human minds as embodied and embedded in complex physical, social, and cultural situations. Analysts are interested in exploring *how* and *why* particular texts create particular interpretations or effects (Semino and Culpeper 2002, x) and in both the similarities and differences between different reading experiences (e.g., Stockwell 2002, 1–12).

In cognitive poetics, reading experiences are studied through a variety of methods. Brône and Vandaele (2009) make a useful distinction between the use of "first-person introspection" on the part of the analyst and "third-person observation" through more empirical means (2009, 6). First-person introspection involves the analyst explicating his or her own interpretation or experience of a text (for example, see Semino and Culpeper 2002; Gavins and Steen 2003). Brône and Vandaele describe first-person introspection as "indirectly empirical" (2009, 7), because analysts draw upon generalizable, empirically researched principles from linguistics and cognitive science in the articulation of their analysis. "Third-person observation" is more directly empirical, meaning (in its widest sense) that it involves the investigation of the responses of other readers in addition to or instead of those of the analysts themselves. Third-person empirical methods range from the use of informal or anecdotal observations regarding other readers through to more formal qualitative and quantitative studies of reader response. These third-person approaches are becoming increasingly common as cognitive poeticists seek to test and develop their claims about literary effect (for example, see Burke

2010; Gavins, 2013; Stockwell 2009; van Peer 1986; Whiteley 2010). This essay draws on both first- and third-person methods in order to investigate the experience of reading "I'll Be There to Love and Comfort You," in that I include both consideration of my own reading of the text and the interpretations and experiences that readers shared during recorded discussions about the poems.

The cognitive poetic framework that underpins my analysis is Text World Theory. Text World Theory is a cognitive-linguistic discourse-processing framework that combines a detailed focus on the linguistic features of a text with consideration of the conscious participation of a reader (for a comprehensive introduction, see Gavins 2007; Werth 1999). Text World Theory conceives of discourses (meaning instances of linguistic communication) as operating at two fundamental levels. First, they occur within a situational context, which is called the "discourse-world." And second, they involve a conceptual domain of understanding which is jointly constructed by the producer and recipient(s), known as a "text-world" (Werth 1999, 17). The discourse world involves two or more human participants engaged in linguistic communication, and also incorporates all the perceptual, linguistic, experiential, and cultural knowledge that these participants draw upon during discourse processing. Text-worlds are the mental representations that participants form in order to comprehend the discourse. They are constructed through the interaction between linguistic cues in the text and a discourse participant's knowledge stores and inferences (Werth 1999, 7). These two levels and their interaction form the foundation of text world analysis. Most discourses require participants to imagine multiple text-worlds, which can be richly detailed or fleeting and undeveloped, and switch between them as the discourse progresses. Text World Theory is interested in the relationship between the text-worlds created during discourse and the discourse's experiential effect.

Reader Discussion Data

The reader discussion data were collected during the University of Sheffield's "Creative Writing in the Community" project in 2010–11. My strand of the project was informed by the cognitive poetic interest in context and aimed to study how groups of readers in different contexts in Sheffield responded to the same literary texts (e.g., see Whiteley 2011a). I asked groups of students, academics, and local reading groups to read three poems by contemporary British poet Simon Armitage. The six groups that took part in the project are summarized in Table 7.1.

Table 7.1 Groups Recorded Discussing "I'll Be There to Love and Comfort You"

Reading group name	No. of participants	Gender	Age range	Highest qualification in English	Location of discussion	Length of discussion
Researchers'	8	Mixed	20–45	PhD/MA	Domestic (researcher present)	55 min.
Michael's	8	All male	56–75	A-level/O-level	Domestic	33 min.
Susan's	8	All female	46–75	Degree/O-level	Domestic	29 min.
Jane's	5	All female	56–75	Degree/A-level	Domestic	30 min.
Student group 1	4	Mixed	18–19	A-level	University room	23 min.
Student group 2	5	All female	18–19	A-level	University room	15 min.

The top four groups are established reading groups whose members regularly meet in one another's homes. They agreed to talk about poetry for this project, though they usually discuss academic papers (in the case of the researchers' group), or novels (in the case of Michael's, Susan's, and Jane's groups). The student groups were comprised of first-year undergraduates studying English at the University of Sheffield who responded to an email asking for volunteers. The table indicates the age range and gender of the groups, the length and location of their discussions, and also their members' highest formal educational qualification in English (A-levels refer to college education at ages 16–18, O-levels to high school education at ages 11–16).

When groups of people meet to talk about literary texts, their discussion typically involves negotiating interpretations and accounts of the text's effects (e.g., Peplow 2011; Swann and Allington 2009). Such discussions provide an interesting window onto literary reception that cognitive poeticists can use to "broaden [their] conception of what responses need to be explained by textual analysis" (Myers 2009; see also Whiteley 2011a, 2011b, 2014). Verbal interaction of this kind does not, of course, provide any privileged insight into the experiences or cognitive processes of readers as they read the poem, but no method of data collection fully enables this (Steen 1991). What it does provide is a "third-person" insight into the salient experiential features associated with the text in each particular interactional context, for which cognitive poetic analysis can attempt to account.

I found that despite the different academic contexts, there were often clear parallels between the way the poems were discussed and the types of responses that participants negotiated (see below and Whiteley 2011a). Short notes that, from a stylistic perspective, "the fascinating thing that needs to be explained is that we often agree on our understanding of poems, plays and novels *in spite* of the fact that we are all different" (1996, xi). In this chapter, my focus will be on some of the broad similarities between the responses to the poem across the different discussions.

The Poem

"I'll Be There to Love and Comfort You" by Simon Armitage is one of three poems that I asked the groups to discuss. Armitage is a well-known contemporary literary figure in the UK, whose work is both critically acclaimed and popular. The poem comes from his collection *Seeing Stars* (2010), which is widely regarded as an experimental departure from his established style. In terms of form, the poems blur the boundaries between prose and poetry through their unconventional lineation. In terms of content, reviewers often remark upon "how strange Armitage dares to be" (Noel-Tod 2010), describing the poems as "surreal" and "absurd" (Ruddock 2011; Noel-Tod 2010; Beddow 2010). From a cognitive poetic perspective, these poems were interesting because they seemed to evoke particularly distinctive reading experiences. I was interested to see how readers engaged with their more challenging or surprising aspects.

"I'll Be There to Love and Comfort You" initially represents a domestic scene involving the narrator and his wife overhearing their neighbours arguing:

> The couple next door were testing the structural fabric of the house with their difference of opinion. "I can't take much more of this," I said to Mimi my wife. Right then there was another almighty crash, as if every pan in the kitchen had clattered to the tiled floor. Mimi said, "Try to relax. Take one of your tablets." She brewed a pot of camomile tea and we retired to bed. (ll. 1–7)

The narrator and his wife go to bed and fall asleep, and the narrator is dreaming of an asteroid hitting planet Earth, when "unbelievably a fist came thumping through the / bedroom wall" (11–12). The knuckles of the fist are bloody, his wife still sleeping, covered in dust and debris, resembling a body pulled from the rubble of an earthquake. The narrator peers through the wall into a dark space "with just occasional flashes of purple or green / light, like those weird electrically-powered life forms / zipping around in the ocean depths" (21–23). Both are now awake as a voice is heard crying for help, recognized by the wife: "'It's her,' she said. I / said, 'Don't be crazy, Mimi, she'd be twenty-four by / now.'" (26–28). As the wife panics, the narrator pushes his arm through the hole in the wall to the other side, trying to pull back the crying creature, sensing a foggy "nineteenth- / century London street in late November" (33–34). The poem ends with the narrator opening his fist as "out of the void, slowly but slowly it / came: the pulsing starfish of a child's hand, swimming / and swimming and coming to settle on my upturned / palm" (36–40).

In the next section I review some of the interpretations and effects discussed by readers of the poem. This is followed by an analysis using the Text World Theory framework to consider how the poem's language may have influenced the reading experiences that readers shared and constructed in their discussions.

Analysis of "I'll Be There to Love and Comfort You"

Reader Responses

Across the group discussions,[1] participants were in broad agreement regarding a central interpretation of the poem as being about a couple who have lost a child, and in particular the narrator's emotions in relation to this loss. The negotiation of this interpretation in Michael's group is shown below:

> A: ... the thing comes crashing through the wall and he's back to something he's forgotten maybe and this is his child, maybe a dead child I think
>
> B: dead child
>
> C: I think it's a dead child and it's about loss and how loss is – how the trauma of loss surfaces in strange ways off beat ways
>
> A: in dreams maybe
>
> (Michael's Group)

However, the discussion groups also negotiated a range of possible interpretative variations regarding the age of the child and the nature of its death. Participants seemed more willing to accept diversity in interpretation here, and in many cases referred to sections of the text in order to support various deductions. Some of this range is illustrated in the excerpt from Susan's group:

> A: I don't know if the child was lost it was a miscarriage or a still born or died very young
>
> B: or stolen or something [...]

> K: I thought it was a slightly older child [...] I think with the first it's a sort of violent thing – it's tattooed and horrible and sinister [...] I think that might be symbolic of some kind of act of violence that the child had died [...]
> C: to me all that about ocean depths and the starfish of the child's hand swimming and swimming I think it's a miscarriage
> D: unless it's a child who drowned
> (Susan's Group)

In addition to this interpretative ambiguity, participants also noted the complexity of the poem. It was described as "puzzling" (Jane's Group), and several participants across the groups described reading it several times in order to make more sense of it.

> A: I was <u>confused, I was confused</u>, I didn't get it until I read it three times
> B: three times?
> C: yeah
> A: yeah I read it two or three times
> D: me too
> E: mmm
> F: its quite <u>disorientating</u> at first isn't it? I think
> (Researchers' Group)

Several groups made reference to the sense that the poem has two contrasting parts and that there is a sense of disjunction between them. For instance, a participant in Michael's Group said: "It's in two parts isn't it an everyday domestic going on next door and a surreal second half," while Susan's group said: "You think the two things are related but actually they're totally unrelated." In the student and public reading groups, this contrast was discussed in emotional and evaluative terms. For instance, Susan's group described feeling surprised or unsettled by this disjunction:

> [when] the poem starts off <u>you feel quite comfortable</u>, telling a little story and then all of a sudden something happens and <u>you feel uncomfortable</u> you know its very odd.
> (Susan's Group)

> When I first read it <u>I thought "oh!", it really was a shock</u> because I wasn't expecting that second paragraph, I was expecting a continuation of the first
> (Susan's Group)

Participants in other groups perceived a lack of connection between the two sections as an unsuccessful aspect of the text:

> [I]t didn't kind of work for me [...] it was just a sort of one way trip into this sci-fi fantasy place
>
> (Student Group 1)

> I couldn't see what the relationship of the first half was to the second half, I think each half in its own terms is good condensed descriptive stuff but I mean did anyone else see a link between the first and second part?
>
> (Michael's Group)

Below, I examine the mental representations (text-worlds) cued by the language of the poem, and relate this conceptual structure to the experiences that readers describe.

The Text-Worlds of the Poem

Like many poems, "I'll Be There to Love and Comfort You" constructs a narrative voice that is distinct from the discourse-world author's. The poem is written in the first-person, which establishes the existence of a narrator who is creating the text-worlds of the poem (see Gavins 2007, 131–35). Text-worlds are created by two types of linguistic features known as "world-builders" and "function-advancers" (Gavins 2007, 36, 54). World-builders establish the temporal and spatial parameters of the world and specify the entities and objects it contains. Function advancers are propositions that propel the narrative or dynamic within the text-world forward (Stockwell 2002, 137). The most significant text-world created in the first nine lines of the poem relates to an event in the past, indicated by the use of past-tense verbs such as "were" and "said." Temporal locatives in lines 1–9 of the poem also indicate the progression of time from the evening ("Right then") to the early hours of the morning ("the small hours"). The spatial location is indicated by noun phrases specifying place such as "the house," "the kitchen," and "bed" and by locative prepositions such as "next door." Entities (or "enactors") in this world are nominated by pronouns and noun phrases: "I," "Mimi," and "the couple next door." Noun phrases also nominate objects present in the text-world, such as "a pot of camomile tea" and "the tiled floor." Function-advancers are often verb phrases that indicate actions, events, or descriptive relations (analogous to Halliday's [1985, 1994] notion of transitivity processes). In lines 1 to 9, the narrative of the poem is advanced with verb phrases describing the actions of the couple next door, the verbalization and action processes of Mimi and the narrator, and events such as the clattering pans and the pounding and caterwauling.

In addition to establishing the parameters and events of the text-world, world-builders and function-advancers activate fields of knowledge that are relevant to the text's interpretation. Because each reader's text-world will be fleshed out with aspects of his or her own personal, experiential, and cultural knowledge, Text World Theory recognizes that our individual mental representations will be somewhat unique (Gavins 2007, 18–33). For instance, readers will need to activate their knowledge of marital relationships ("Mimi my wife") and domestic locations ("the house," "the kitchen," "bed") to form a text-world representation of the opening lines of the poem. My cultural and experiential knowledge about marriage and English houses led me to imagine that the narrator is male, that the couple live in a terraced or semi-detached house (which shares an internal wall with the neighbouring property), and that when the characters "retired to bed" they went upstairs to do so. But readers with different cultural knowledge about marriage, or who imagine a bungalow when they think of a house for example, may well enhance their text-worlds with different inferential information.

Inferencing is a central process in text-world construction, and the overarching interpretation of the poem as about child loss is also clearly a product of inferencing rather than explicit textual description. A number of features of the text combine to activate our knowledge about the loss of loved ones, in particular the behaviour of the central characters. For instance, both characters immediately know who the pronoun "her" refers to in line 26. Mimi has a strong emotional and possessive relationship to this character ("Get her back," ll. 28–29), and the narrator has specific knowledge about the person's age (l. 27). This young age and the final image of a "child's hand" (l. 38) provide further input to suggest that the lost person is a missing child.

As noted above, however, readers in the discussion groups seemed quite willing to accept variation regarding the specific age of the child and the nature of their loss. Obviously, one explanation for this variation in interpretation must be the different personal and experiential discourse-world knowledge that readers bring to their understanding of the discourse. But I would argue that other aspects of the text also work to permit and promote such variation. Text World Theory enables deeper investigation of the other linguistic cues that are important in creating this effect.

One such cue is the world-switching that is involved in conceptualizing the poem. It is common for discourses to create multiple text-worlds. Linguistic cues such as hypotheticals and modal expressions are one type of trigger for the construction of specialized text-worlds known as "modal-worlds" (Gavins 2007, 91–125). Text World Theory posits that we conceptualize the relationship between different types of worlds spatially in a manner that is intimately connected to our spatial conceptualization of knowledge more generally (Gavins 2007, 82). Modal-worlds are conceived as being more remote or distant mental constructs existing at a different ontological level, because they represent unrealized events or the (unverifiable) attitudes of a narrator. Three worlds that are central to the poem's effect are shown in Figure 7.1. In line 9 of the poem, a modal-world is created by the line "I was dreaming ..." (shown in Figure 7.1 as 'modal-world 2'). This expression indicates that the world-building and function-advancing information that follows it (the asteroid on a collision course with planet Earth) is not part of the ontological reality of the original text-world, so this world is formed at a greater conceptual distance.

Something particularly interesting happens in relation to the ontological structure of the poem's text-worlds with the use of the phrase "when unbelievably" in line 11. The modal adverb "unbelievably" cues the construction of another modal-world (shown as "modal-world 3" in Figure 7.1), in which a fist thumps through a wall. However, the ontological status of that world in relation to the existing text-worlds is ambiguous. The prefix "un-" indicates that the contents of this world are *less* believable than the dream and should be held at greater conceptual distance.

But this modal can also be used to express surprise over something that *did* happen, for example, in an expression like "unbelievably, they gave me

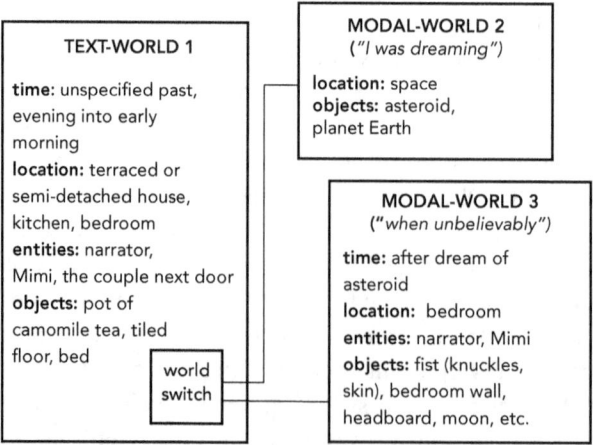

Figure 7.1 A Text-World Diagram of the Three Worlds Cued by Lines 1 to 11 of "I'll Be There to Love and Comfort You." World-builders are indicated. See Gavins (2007) for full diagram conventions.

my money back." This interpretation would decrease the conceptual distance at which modal-world 3 is constructed and make the narrator's voice appear more reliable. The content of modal-world 3 also contributes to the ambiguity here. There is a similarity between the world-building elements in worlds 1 and 3: both contain the enactors Mimi and the narrator, and both are set in the bedroom of the house. But there is also a similarity between the function-advancing elements in worlds 2 and 3: both involve a collision between a moving and a static object (the asteroid and planet earth, the fist and the wall).

In my reading of the poem, the similarities between the world-building features of worlds 1 and 3 were the most compelling, and I inferred a connection between these worlds, assuming that the text had switched from the dream in modal-world 2 back to the initial text-world. So when the fist is described as punching through the wall in lines 11 and 12, I expected that it belonged to one of "the couple next door," previously mentioned. Later, in line 20, when the narrator peers through the hole in the wall, one would expect the adjoining house to be visible. However, the couple next door are never mentioned again, and by the end of the poem they fade from attention. Instead, from line 15 onward, occurrences in modal-world 3 become increasingly unusual. Mimi is woken not by a loud crash, but by a quiet voice; the hole leads not to a house but to a void seemingly filled with liquid and air. As the poem progresses, these illogical world-building elements mark modal-world 3 as being more ontologically remote than previous worlds. Readers who assume that modal-world 3 is a version of the initial text-world are likely to have to reassess this connection.

In terms of conceptual structure, "I'll Be There to Love and Comfort You" establishes a trajectory into text-worlds that are increasingly ontologically ambiguous and remote. This kind of play with conceptual structure is common in absurd and surreal literary texts (Gavins 2000, 2013; Stockwell 2000) and is likely to be one of the reasons behind the confusion and sense of disjunction that readers discussed in the data. Discourse participants are usually motivated to construct a coherent representation of the discourse at hand, so when readers become aware of inconsistencies or illogicalities that may have arisen in their mental representations, action is normally taken to correct them (Gavin 2007, 142). In the discussion group data, readers demonstrate a number of approaches to establishing coherence. One option is to engage in "world repair" in which an aspect of the existing text-worlds is reconceptualized (Gavins 2007, 142). For instance, some participants reconceptualize modal-world 3 as a continuation of the dream, or an account of the supernatural, as this extract from Susan's group shows:

> A: you feel from a certain point that it became a dream [...]
> B: it is isn't it?
> C: depends
> D: it depends whether you want to see it as a ghost story or it as a dream or
> Many: mmm
> B: oh I never thought of that, I never thought of it as a ghost story
> F: oh I didn't think of it like that, no
> C: I thought of it as a ghost story
> B: // did you? I thought it was a dream
> D: // did you I thought it was something supernatural
> C: something supernatural yes – but yes a dream is more convincing
>
> (Susan's Group)

A second, more drastic, option is "world replacement," in which existing worlds are abandoned and reconstructed anew (Gavins 2007, 142). This kind of strategy is demonstrated in this comment from Student Group 1:

> I thought that the couple next door were this couple [Mimi and the narrator] in the past, because when the hand comes punching through the wall it's as if the past is coming back, and then when he [the narrator] reaches back [it's] as if he is reaching back into the past for a child.

World-replacement involves a significant reorganization of the text-worlds, and here the participant disregards linguistic cues in order to split the text into two spatio-temporal zones. Aspects of the poem are reinterpreted metaphorically, so that the wall between the houses becomes a division between past and present, and the couple next door become versions of Mimi and the narrator. Although the text-worlds of the poem require at least some world-repair in order to appear coherent, readers will respond differently to this requirement. Some of the readers quoted above felt that the poem "didn't work" for them. Their evaluative comments demonstrate a third option, which is to reject world-repair as being too arduous, or symptomatic of bad rather than artful writing on the part of the author.

Processes of world-replacement are not the only forms of metaphorical processing prompted by the poem. The language of the poem itself is highly metaphorical, which also contributes to the complexity of its text-worlds and its experiential effect. In the discussion data, several groups made explicit connections between the metaphors in the poem and different ideas about the child's age and loss (see for instance the extract from Susan's group). I would suggest that the rich knowledge domains activated by the metaphors in the poem are another significant factor in the interpretative variety in the discussions.

A new understanding of the conceptual basis of metaphor was one of the most significant developments in the rise of cognitive linguistics in the 1980s (e.g., Lakoff and Johnson 1980) and more recently conceptual integration has added further sophistication to earlier models (e.g., Faucconier and Turner 2002). Metaphor is now generally understood as a process of blending two conceptual domains or "input spaces" so that particular features of those domains are combined to produce a new and unique mental representation. Gavins (2007, 146–64) describes a metaphor's input spaces as fleeting text-worlds that represent the conceptual domains cued by the metaphor. These representations are then selectively combined to form a "blended-world." She argues that metaphors create a sense of "double vision," as readers conceptualize both the text-world of the discourse and the blended-world of the metaphor at the same time, making associations between the two.

In the opening line of the poem a metaphor is established when the couple next door are described as using an abstract phenomenon (a "difference of opinion") to test the physical properties of a building ("testing the structural fabric of the house"). One of the input spaces created by this metaphor is the notion of testing the structure of a building, which to my mind is something usually carried out by builders or engineers on bricks, mortar, or steel, using some kind of instrument, with the aim of establishing whether a construction has a secure and safe structure. The second input space is the notion of arguing, which is something carried out by two or more people, using gesture and language, with the purpose of reflecting and perhaps settling their disagreements. In the process of interpreting this metaphor, readers construct a blended-world in which certain aspects of these domains are combined and reconciled. Blended-worlds have an "emergent structure," meaning that new features that do not appear in either of the original input spaces can be generated (Gavins 2007, 148). In my blended-world, the couple, like builders or engineers, are somehow acting on the bricks and mortar of the house. But their instrument is their argument – which by implication is loud, emotional, and physical enough to have a tangible effect on the bricks and mortar. In my interpretation of this metaphor, the constructive aims of the builders are replaced by destructive aims. So the couple seem to be trying to destroy the house with their loud argument. In the "double vision" created by this metaphor, the contrast between the understated "difference of opinion" described by the narrator and the earth-shattering row in the blended-world creates humour.

Text World Theory is interested in both the relatively isolated blending processes cued by sentence-level "micrometaphors" and the more extensive "megametaphors" that are maintained and developed across entire texts (Gavins 2007, 146–64). At the level of individual metaphors, there is an interesting shift in their conceptual scope as the poem progresses. The metaphors that form part of text-world 1 (ll. 1–2, 4–5) have domestic input spaces that contain similar elements to the text-world they supplement: the walls of a house and a kitchen. From line 15 onward, however, once modal-world 3 is established, the metaphors begin to involve more remote input spaces that are temporally or spatially distant from the target in the text world: a faraway country afflicted by an earthquake (ll. 16–19), the ocean depths (ll. 23–24), or a nineteenth-century London street (ll. 32–33). Everything the narrator sees, feels, or hears through the hole in the wall in stanza two is described metaphorically. As the text-worlds of the poem become more conceptually remote, the metaphors incorporate increasingly novel input domains, which serves to amplify the inferencing processes involved in reading the text.

Several metaphorical elements in the text also share broad semantic connections. These semantic fields can act as input spaces for more extensive megametaphors that "feed intricate inferential information into the processing of the entire text" (Gavins 2007, 155). For instance, the destruction present in the blended-world I describe above resurfaces throughout the first stanza: in the pans falling to the floor (ll. 4–5) and the rubble caused by the fist / earthquake (ll. 11–19). Another megametaphor has water-related input spaces, such as the "life forms ... in the ocean depths" (l. 23), the foggy river (ll. 32–34), and the "pulsing starfish ... swimming" (ll. 38–39). These water-related metaphors seemed particularly influential in some readers' perception of the child as neonatal, as indicated by the first quotation from Susan's group above. During the discussions I recorded, further connections between these megametaphors were negotiated and developed by participants. For example, Jane's group linked the domain of destruction with the watery, neonatal imagery, with one participant remarking: "Birth is quite violent, like something smashing through into existence." When interpreting the poem, megametaphors can be combined and weighted differently to produce different effects, both at the moment of reading and during discussions about the text. The multiple blended-worlds that are formed during the reading of this poem exist alongside the text-worlds and contribute to variations in readers' interpretative responses.

Conclusions

Text World Theory analyses seek to account for the experience of reading through close attention to the linguistic cues and mental representations involved in processing a particular discourse. I have argued that the experience of reading "I'll Be There to Love and Comfort You" is particularly influenced by the text's trajectory into more conceptually remote text-worlds, the way it disrupts connections between those worlds prompting world-repair, and the rich, interconnecting metaphors that amplify the complexity of readers' mental representations. By relating my analysis of the text's language to the interpretative accounts that arose in readers' discussions about the poem, I hope to have shown that Text World Theory has the explanatory power to consider both convergent and divergent responses to a text. While it has not been possible here to do full justice to the complexity of the poem or to readers' discussions of it, I hope to have demonstrated some of the central principles of cognitive poetics as an approach to studying the reading experience.

Note

I am grateful to the Higher Education Innovation Fund at the University of Sheffield for funding this research as part of the "Creative Writing in the Community" project. Thanks also to Joe Bray, Sam Browse, Alison Gibbons, and David Peplow for their helpful input with earlier versions of my analysis.

1. Discussion extracts have been transcribed as prose for ease of reading. Inverted commas are used to show reported speech and question marks to indicate questions. Double slashes (//) indicate overlapping utterances. Ellipses in square brackets ([...]) indicate sections omitted for brevity. Comments in square brackets and underlining are my additions to aid clarity.

References

Armitage, Simon. 2010. *Seeing Stars*. London: Faber and Faber.
Beddow, Alastair. 2010."Review of *Seeing Stars* by Simon Armitage." *The Literateur*, 1 May. http://literateur.com/seeing-stars-by-simon-armitage
Brône, Geert, and Jeroen Vandaele. 2009. *Cognitive Poetics: Goals, Gains, and Gaps*, Berlin: Mouton de Gruyter.
Burke, Michael. 2010. *Literary Reading, Cognition, and Emotion: An Exploration of the Oceanic Mind*. London: Routledge.
Carter, Ronald. 1982. *Language and Literature*. London: George Allen Unwin.
Carter, Ronald, and Peter Stockwell. 2008. "Stylistics: Retrospect and Prospect." In *The Language and Literature Reader*, edited by Ronald Carter and Peter Stockwell, 291–302. London: Routledge.
Fauconnier, Gilles, and Mark Turner. 2002. *The Way We Think: Conceptual Blending and the Mind's Hidden Complexities*. Plymouth: Basic Books.
Gavins, Joanna. 2000. "Absurd Tricks with Bicycle Frames in the Text Worlds of *The Third Policeman*." *Nottingham Linguistic Circular* 15: 17–33.
———. 2007. *Text World Theory: An Introduction*. Edinburgh: Edinburgh University Press.
———. 2013. *Reading the Absurd*. Edinburgh: Edinburgh University Press.
Gavins, Joanna, and Gerard J. Steen, eds. 2003. *Cognitive Poetics in Practice*. London: Routledge.

Halliday, M.A.K. 1985. *An Introduction to Functional Grammar*. London: Arnold.
———. 1994. *An Introduction to Functional Grammar*. 2nd ed. London: Arnold.
Lakoff, George, and Mark Johnson. 1980. *Metaphors We Live By*. Chicago: University of Chicago Press.
Leech, Geoffrey N., and Mick Short. 2007 *Style in Fiction*, 2nd ed. Harlow: Pearson Education.
Myers, Greg. 2009. "Stylistics and 'Reading in Talk.'" *Language and Literature* 18(3): 338–44.
Noel-Tod, Jeremy. 2010. Review of *Seeing Stars* by Simon Armitage. *The Telegraph*, 24 June. http://www.telegraph.co.uk/culture/books/bookreviews/7851863/Seeing-Stars-by-Simon-Armitage-review.html
Peplow, David. 2011. "'Oh, I've Known a Lot of Irish People': Reading Groups and the Negotiation of Literary Interpretation." *Language and Literature* 20(4): 295–315.
Ruddock, Sam. 2011. Review of *Seeing Stars*, by Simon Armitage. Writers' Centre Norwich. http://www.writerscentrenorwich.org.uk/bookreviewseeingstarsbysimonarmitage.aspx
Semino, Elena, and Jonathan Culpeper, eds. 2002. *Cognitive Stylistics: Language and Cognition in Text Analysis*. Amsterdam: John Benjamins.
Short, Mick. 1996. *Exploring the Language of Poems, Plays, and Prose*. Harlow: Longman.
Steen, Gerard J. 1991. "The Empirical Study of Literary Reading: Methods of Data Collection." *Poetics* 20: 559–75.
Stockwell, Peter. 2000. "(Sur)real Stylistics: From Text to Contextualizing." In *Contextualized Stylistics*, edited by Tony Bex, Michael Burke, and Peter Stockwell, 15–42. Amsterdam: Rodopi.
———. 2002. *Cognitive Poetics*. London: Routledge.
———. 2005. "On Cognitive Poetics and Sylistics." In *Cognition and Literary Interpretation in Practice*, edited by Harri Veivo, Bo Pettersson, and Merja Polvinen, 267–82. Helsinki: Helsinki University Press.
———. 2009. *Texture: A Cognitive Aesthetics of Reading*. Edinburgh: Edinburgh University Press.
Swann, Joan, and Daniel Allington. 2009. "Reading Groups and the Language of Literary Texts: A Case Study in Social Reading." *Language and Literature* 18(3): 247–64.
van Peer, Willie. 1986. *Stylistics and Psychology: Investigations of Foregrounding*. London: Croom Helm.
Werth, Paul. 1999. *Text Worlds: Representing Conceptual Space in Discourse*. Harlow: Longman.
Whiteley, Sara. 2010. "Text World Theory and the Emotional Experience of Literary Discourse." PhD diss., University of Sheffield, UK.
———. 2011a. "Talking about 'An Accommodation': The Implications of Discussion Group Data for Community Engagement and Pedagogy." *Language and Literature* 20(3): 236–56.
———. 2011b. "Text World Theory, Real Readers and Emotional Responses to *The Remains of the Day*." *Language and Literature* 20(1): 23–42.
———. 2014. "Ethics." In *The Cambridge Handbook of Stylistics*, edited by Peter Stockwell and Sara Whiteley, 393–407. Cambridge: Cambridge University Press.

Tempering Ambiguity – The Quality of the Reading Experience

Kjell Ivar Skjerdingstad and Knut Oterholm

I'm a dweller on the threshold
– Van Morrison

This chapter reports on a project studying 640 literary reviews written by pupils between fourteen and sixteen years of age. In 2013, more than four hundred students in sixteen ordinary secondary schools (grades seven through nine) reviewed all fifty-four Norwegian youth books published the preceding year (*Foreningen !les* 2014). These reviews are the basis for *Uprisen* – the *UPrize* – an annual prize awarded the best youth book. The project is organized by *Foreningen !les* – the *Association !Read* – an independent organization working to enhance and promote literature and reading.

Between Book and Life-World

Our study of these reviews grew from an interest in how young people assess literature – their evaluation criteria for books as well as their reading preferences. We looked for notions of literary quality to compare with the perspectives of professional critics, librarians, publishers, and editors. However, we soon discovered that the assessments intertwined with what seemed to be miniature biographies or portraits of the readers. On the one hand, the youth reviewers concluded clearly that "this is a good book," or "this is not," referring to conventional criteria such as the degree of excitement or identification experienced and thus upholding a distance from the text. On the other hand, the reviews described reading experiences where an ambiguous multi-dimensional space between the book, the reader, and the world that surrounded her (i.e., the *Lebenswelt* or life-world) stood out. Even when books were judged as bad or rejected as morally reprehensible, there were strong traces of "rich" reading experiences. This made us shift our attention from the quality of the book to the quality of the reading experience. Subsequently our interest in mapping qualities changed to an exploration of the quality *of* quality. The material therefore is limited to a case study of five short reviews of three of the nominated books.

Reader response theory, at least since the 1970s, has shown us that readers adopt and transform the text according to their own desires, needs, and capacities. And as is well known, already in 1938 Louise Rosenblatt argued that the "relation between the reader and the signs on the page proceeds in a to-and-fro spiral in which each is continually being affected by what the other has contributed" (Rosenblatt [1938]1995, 26). What came to interest us, however, is *how* young people handle this spiral or execute this work of reading, assessing literature, and negotiating experience. In exploring this quality of the reading experience, we may even illuminate the matter of literary quality.

However, as current thinking in schools tends to approach reading within instrumental paradigms that ignore the literary as well as the experience (see McKechnie, Cliff Hodges, and Pihl and van der Kooij in this volume), attention to the quality of the reading experience could also contribute to the practices of literary mediation (i.e., *Vermittlung*). As we look more closely at reviews written by readers/writers with an apparently low formal competence, we will be examining how complex and/or important their reading experiences may have been; in other words, a reader is always more than a poor or good reader.[1]

The aim of this essay, then, is to disclose the quality of the reading experience. Through an inductive methodology, we highlight essential features of this phenomenon. We then conclude with a tentative conceptualization based on the core terms *dwelling* and *tempering*. Before moving on to our analysis of student reviews, we outline four facets of our framework.

The Invisibility of the Reading Experience

First, readers are reminded of the essential invisibility of the reading experience. As pointed out in the introduction to this book, and as amplified by Balling's chapter, no reading experience can be seen (or researched) except through an articulation. The reading experience is a corporeal phenomenon that we can never fully understand. Any articulation of any reading introduces dimensions of ambiguity. As empirical researchers on reading experiences, we can only bear witness to other readers' testimony of their readings. This also holds true for readers who write about their experiences – as is the case in our material. In one sense, their writings only express their individual experience. We as researchers witness their witnessing, even as the reader of this essay adds another layer of witnessing. However, in each layer the witness observes his own witnessing.

Second, there is an inevitable objection: The school context filters and distorts the (written) experiences in such a way that they are barely recognizable compared to the "real" experience. We are writing about reviews written as part of compulsory work in school settings – and as Gabrielle Cliff Hodges confirms in her chapter, the classroom is not the best site for enhancing the reading experience. Yet it is possible that a reading experience can be evoked, strengthened, and even constructed through the mandatory work of writing on a theme or a subject. In this sense, we could say that the reviews produce reading experiences. To support such a view, we could revisit phenomenology as well as deconstruction or even psychoanalysis, or the reflections of authors such as France's Maurice Blanchot or the Norwegian playwright Jon Fosse. The consequence of thinking an experience to be part of an unavailable unconsciousness, a pre-verbal perceptual layer or an ungraspable trace, is to recognize that articulation discloses and transforms experience – that the reading experience is also part of and not separate from the articulation. The experience continues to live as an active germ enabling and transforming the articulation on which it depends. A review therefore answers to, conveys, and elaborates the experience of reading: the articulation points back to and transforms the recollection of the experience – which in that sense remains silent.

As background, we suggest, third, that these reviews point to reading experiences that are emblematic rather than different from other reading experiences (say, of the romance reader). They are emblematic precisely in the sense that no experience can be grasped except through some kind of articulation. The pleasure of absorption or flow is important, but understanding it as such is impossible even through neurocognitive experiments as they do not allow for the inclusion of contextual influences from the surroundings, and the personal histories of readers. So we emphasize that this is not a matter of reconfiguring a division between cognitive highbrow reading and lowbrow affective escapism.

Fourth, our emphasis on quality should function, if not as a guarantee, then at least as a precaution against dualistic understandings of genres or modes of consciousness or between book, language, mind, and so on. We use the term "quality" as an attempt to avoid an entirely subjective and ultimately private understanding of the reading experience. Complementary to this, talking about the *quality* of something directs the attention towards an understanding of how the material matters. Quality can mediate between subject and object, reader and literature. Literally, quality refers to the character or condition of material, but only with regard to how matter is used. The quality of a fabric depends on whether it is part of a work outfit or a wedding dress. Talking about quality implies deciding, "What's in it for me?"

The quality of a book relates to the possibilities it evokes and to how a subject/reader grasps it from within her everyday reality. In everyday parlance, we use the concept of quality both to designate the nature of an object or a tool and to judge whether it answers our needs in the situation at hand. Thus, as Aristotle (*Categories*) wrote, quality is a hylomorphic term, meaning that form is matter and matter is form. Therefore, we cannot separate aesthetic quality from ethical or political values, the pleasures of reading from working through a text, emotional or affective response from cognitive reflections. Thinking is of course also a corporeal process: reading involves seeing, reflecting, departing, concentrating, feeling, wanting. In addressing the quality of the reading experience, we will be assuming that books are reviewed as part of a reading involving a variety of other realms of everyday life. To look for quality in reading experiences is to look for links between books and readers, past and present, body and surroundings – for the subject-reader's continuous work on understanding him/herself in a broader personal, social, cultural, historical, political, and economic context.

Settling Down and Seeing a Way Out

Basic to the quality of the reading experience, as represented in our material, is how readers conceive literature as a place to be. This is hardly surprising. In everyday language, we talk about the fictional world or the fantasy universe. Several contributors in this book refer to the notion of being transported to somewhere else, and Marianne Børch in her chapter refers to Harold Bloom's concept of the *imaginal* as an experience of being transported by reading into an ambiguous sphere of otherness and sameness (see Bloom 1996, 167ff.). A more recent example is Philip Davis's discussion in *Reading and the Reader* about how readers depend on textual places to create what he calls a holding-ground (2013). Martin Heidegger's concept of dwelling (2001) contributes to this conceptual work in both underscoring the ambiguity and emphasizing the concrete tangibility of the reading experience. A student review[2] of Ellen Fjestad's *Together We Shall Hold the Heavens* is typical for our material:

> The best book I ever read! Luka and Gard meet each other with a bang. Both live alone in their own dilapidated and dark place, but together they manage to create a light full of love and warmth. With a good story that is constructed in a simple and understandable manner, writer Ellen Fjestad has managed to write the best book I ever have come upon.
>
> The content is structured in a way that makes the book easy to read and easy to understand. Although the book looks thick and long, it is fast to read because the font is large and the pages are thick.

There is no first person in the book, only he and she. I myself found that this was very good, you sort of feel like the first person yourself. The only low spot of this book was when I realized that I was done with it.

Should I throw the dice it is six clearly. This is a book that I highly recommend to young people between 13 and 16. For this, it is a book that really is worth reading and in my opinion it really deserves to win the U-Prize.

Do you recommend the book Yes

The energy in this writing reveals how the book has done something to the reader. The first paragraph paraphrases the book as an encounter during which two people move from dark loneliness to a common space of warmth and love. Yet this observation runs counter to the other eight reviews of this book, all of which emphasize how the two characters are different: one has a rural background, the other an urban one, and so on. Even though the text suggests a student who does not fully master the grammar of writing, reading it has clearly been a meaningful event. Thus the introductory paraphrase seems to repeat this reader's particular reading experience in a factual and sober way.

The second paragraph emphasizes that the content is accessible because of the book's large fonts and thick pages, making it easier to understand and faster to read. It is not as long as a reader might fear. The reviewer sees and points out the palpable, material, and tangible features that make it possible to enter this book and thus enable it to hold quality for her.[3] The paragraph explains how the "content" of the book, the story of the loners, becomes accessible to the reader.

In the third paragraph, this reader states that the *lack* of a first-person narrator allows her to enter the story herself as the first-person character. She seems to be searching not for identification but for a world she can enter, where she can *be*. Because of its specific features, the book offers this reader a place that enables her to be more herself than common external "reality" does. Reading opens a space where she can perceive another world from the inside; this enables her to enter *as herself* and look with her gaze, feelings, and being at another world as she is. We might consider whether this actually transforms the reader into a seer or simply confirms the intimate connection between reading and seeing (Lindhé 2010, 5ff.; Piper 2012, 26, 166; Stewart 2006).

This review, then, tells a story of a reader coming to the book and finding it a place where she wants to be. Her only negative comment relates to how she is not allowed to be there anymore – the end throws her out. In this way, the review retells a story of an experience where the reading subject in the book finds a place to be in a manner that the outer world may not offer. In seeing the connection and not the difference, she is saying something about what she is looking for, and this opens up a possible reading of her reading as a touching miniature biography of the reader. Following Merleau-Ponty (2000), we can say that behind every observation there is a personal history.

Emblematically, this review perceives the book as a palpable construction that opens up a literary world in which literature becomes an accessible place: a place where the reading "I" can enter and *from* which he or she can unfold his or her being. This is what we mean when we refer to the core quality of the reading experience as *dwelling*: both settling down and recognizing that it is possible to move on.

Everyday Reality

The above review stresses how the reading experience displaces the reader into another world she can inhabit. By contrast, a very short review of *Ghost Hunters: Book One* by Magne Hovden (a fantasy that three out of eighteen reviews reject as a poor knock-off of *Harry Potter*) illustrates the importance of a tangible connection as a precondition for entering a literary world:

> My book review This book was simply impossible to put down! The imagination stretches to the impossible and the book is really good! If you are interested in fantasy books, I really recommend this. The author portray good and gives all the characters differents characteristics. The book is like a brick in the hand after reading a few pages. Do you recommend the book? Yes

As suggested by the reading selection and the style of the review, one might assume that this writer is a more reluctant or less-practised reader. Nevertheless, the review exhibits a strong commitment to reading *this* book, and it points out three strongly interconnected aspects. First, it highlights a fantasy that stretches itself to the impossible. Here it is the *stretching* that is emphasized, not what the fantastic actually *is*. Second, the portrayal of the characters as different from one another is underlined. Third, to express his appreciation, the reader uses an interesting metaphor – perhaps a metonymy. In Norwegian, to compare a book to a brick is the conventional way to call it inaccessible. Here, the opposite is the case. We might of course interpret this as an example of faulty Norwegian. But we might also read it literally, as holding the book. Alternatively, the book is holding on to the reader, keeping him in place, stabilizing him in this particular position through a strong and literally haptic and sensual connection. The book then, seems to enable the reader to stretch out and get in touch with its different characters. Of course we know that one of the main virtues of literature is that it connects the reader to other people; what is noteworthy here is how the concrete connection is emphasized as valuable.

Considering that *Ghost Hunters* is a fantasy book, the emphasis on the book being an anchor in everyday reality may seem surprising. Though of course it cannot be ignored that fantasy is appraised for the fantastic, it is remarkable how the eighteen reviewers in our sample appreciate it for enabling or staging the quotidian and ordinary.

> Ghost Hunters
> Three children with the same birth date. What's the worst that can happen? Eirik from Norway, Gunther from Berlin and American Lizzy from New York complete thirteen at the same day and wake up in a void full of darkness and a fear of where they are and how they got there. A door opens and they are told to be on a mission, they will save lives, take over powers and must prepare themselves for things they did not imagine that could be possible.
> The language in this book is good. Magne Hovden manages to portray the different youngsters. I easily manage to imagine the types in this way as Magne Hovden writes and express it. There are also some curse words in this book, which is pertaining to the various people and at the same time expresses how the persons are.
> The plot curve is good. It starts flat across and rises slowly up until it suddenly becomes a notch steeper (where it gets even more exciting) and bends horizontally across a small piece and going slightly downwards and horizontally to the side again. A perfect plot curve to me.
> This is a "fantasy-book" and among all fantasy books I've read this is the best. But I'm not very excited about fantastic literature. I also read one of the "Harry Potter" books. It was a huge success and a lot of popularity around the series. I would say that the Ghost Hunters is better.
> I recommend this book to those who like the fantasy-genre. And if you like this, you can always look forward to Book 2 too!
> Do you recommend the book? Yes

Most reviews of this book begin with a description of the scene where three characters find themselves in an unknown place, left alone by their respective parents and friends and not knowing how they got there. Because they have been cut off from their stories, their identity is not as accessible as narrative thinking on identity assumes: "We know what we are because we can say where we are, and we know this because we can say where we came from" (Brooks 1984, 276). The reviewer, though, describes this situation both as a catastrophe and as an opening of new possibilities – an echo of the modern dilemma of man as free, but also doomed to be alone and dependent solely on oneself.

As a fantasy, *Ghost Hunters* is appreciated for being "exciting." Yet *none* of the reviews that emphasize excitement, using this or similar terms, relates the excitement exclusively to an external plot driven by "action." The above reviewer describes the plot without describing *what* is exciting. By giving the plot attention and space in the review, but without grounding it in the literary text, the reader seems to be suggesting that she *expects* external excitement. Without exception, however, the reviewers tightly link external perspectives on excitement to what the conflict does to the protagonists and their ways of being, feeling, and behaving. Even a review that strongly emphasizes external action dedicates more than half its length to the initial situation of being lost and having to resolve the conflict together. Another devotes six lines out of seventeen to saying that the protagonists are told they will never ever meet their parents again, while still another underlines that "everything is unclear in their heads."

As far as the readers appreciate the texts for external action, this corresponds highly to observations on the development of characters and their relations.

> Together they [the protagonists] learn to fight against evil ghosts, but do they manage to stay together to fight the evil ghosts. I think the moral of this book is about sticking together and that it really is about friendship, love and cooperation.

Here the reviewer underscores that there are exciting actions, but their appeal is that they make it possible to show how the group manages *together* to meet challenges and solve problems. One review, titled "This book must be nominated!," does not mention excitement or plot at all. Two-thirds of this text highlights the individual problems faced by each character. Thus, the drama in and between the characters is what seems to make the book noteworthy to this reader: "The protagonists behaved as young people use to, they showed off, quarreled and fell in love."

Reviewers of fantasy often praise adventure and excitement. Our study, however, shows that this is primarily an armature or a background enabling the different personae to emerge, along with the interplay between them. Perhaps it is precisely because of its unrealistic qualities that fantasy allows realistic, recognizable everyday conflicts to stand out more clearly – hyperbolically. Fantasy permits a particularly distinct portrayal of characters and the relations between them that readers find relevant for understanding or negotiating themselves aswell as their questions, needs, and so on. The readings in our sample pay heed to friendship and the need to stand together to solve problems. The virtue of fantasy, then, seems to be that it confronts its characters with *real* existential problems – *real* of course within the realm depicted in the story. Fantasy reflects the problems of readers in their everyday reality and enables an existential realism, for it is not measured against depictions of an everyday reality. Fantasy is lauded because it throws recognizable and important everyday problems and relations into relief.

Construction Work

One review of Lars Mæhle's book *Fuck Off I Love You* (recommended by ten of twelve reviewers) rejects the book because it seems badly constructed and randomly composed:

> The book is about a leader of a gang called Two Face, a person who is deeply feared. He chooses the future for the people around him, deciding their destiny by tossing a coin. One side of the coin has the inscription "Fuck off" the other "I love you". If the coin shows up "I love you" the choice is good and it will end up good. If the coin turns out with "Fuck off" the action is bad. The book is a lot about family, love and friends.
>
> The book itself is not so good, it happen a lot of thing that does not add up and make sense. In the story the main character breaks up with his girlfriend because she throws up after eating a bad sausage. Such things happen a lot in the book; it looks like the author has written down the most random things he could think of. The book's ending is extremely disappointing, you start to realize why Two Face did what he did, but then the author ruins the story by telling a little too much. The book may often be confusing and the book is often quite boring. The book is made ten times worse because it is written in New Norwegian. I do not recommend this book, but to you who likes books written in New Norwegian so maybe this is the right book for you. (F5)

This book is written in Nynorsk – a second Norwegian language that high school students are obliged to learn but generally are reluctant to learn. This review makes it clear that the writer has not fully absorbed the codes of syntax and orthography. Her claim that the protagonist breaks up because the girl throws up strikes ones as a misreading; the feeling of confusion may well be a consequence of lack of comprehension. One might therefore claim that she is both a poor reader and a poor writer. In the reviewer's rejection of the book, however, it is more interesting to see *how* she reads. The review first identifies a mythological trope well known in popular culture: the powerful group leader everybody fears, he who *unpredictably* decides the future like a God. The paraphrase is to the point in foregrounding this as *one* important perspective on the story.

But the reviewer's fundamental critique is that the novel is chaotic and randomly constructed. She reads the protagonist's breakup as a response that is out of proportion to poorly motivated actions. Then, the ending is described as "extremely disappointing" because it tells too much. The novel becomes boring or predictable. The reviewer criticizes the author both for holding back and for telling too much, for constructing the work badly and for not taking the reader seriously. (This points to an observation valid for the entire sample of reviews: a strong resistance towards any kind of patronizing attitude.) Thus, the reviewer actually criticizes the author for behaving like a dark god himself – the reading space created through the text is, for this reviewer, both chaotic and desultory. The book gives both too much information and too little; it suffers from redundancy as well as entropy. It fails to construct a space that enables this reader/reviewer to dwell and find his way.

The affinity between how the reviewer sees the novel through the paraphrase, and her criticism of the author for scattering chaos everywhere, may not be intentional. Nevertheless, it discloses an experience of something essential though perhaps not articulated. Further work by the reader on articulating this would definitively thicken, deepen, or enhance the quality of the reading experience. One way of reading is reading between the lines – looking, for example, for psychological motivations – and this reader is perhaps not very good at that. Another less heralded competence is providing an overview of a work such as a novel from *one* consistent perspective. To convey a specific perspective in a paraphrase is a step towards seeing both one's own reading, thinking or seeing from the outside, and seeing other possible perspectives (Egeberg and Skjerdingstad 2011).

Dwelling

In what Mai and Ringgaard (2010, 12) claim is his main article on place, "Building Dwelling Thinking," Martin Heidegger states that "to dwell, to be set at peace, means to remain at peace within the free sphere that safeguards each thing in its nature. The fundamental character of dwelling is this sparing and preserving" (2001, 147). In a reading of Heidegger's article, the Norwegian architect Christian Norberg-Schulz emphasizes that

> "existential foothold" and "dwelling" are synonyms; ... "dwelling," in an existential sense, is the purpose of architecture. Man dwells when he can orientate himself within and identifies himself with an environment, or, in short, when he experiences the environment as meaningful. Dwelling therefore implies something more than "shelter." It implies that the spaces where life occurs are *places*, in the true sense of the word. A place is a space which has a distinct character. Since ancient times *a genius locus, or "spirit of place,"* has been recognized as the concrete reality man has to face and come to terms with in his daily life. Architecture means to visualize the *genius loci*, and the task of the architect is to create meaningful places, whereby he helps man to dwell. (1980, s. 5)

According to Norberg-Schultz, dwelling is the purpose of architecture because it empowers humankind in connecting meaningfully to its surroundings. Dwelling transforms the unlimited and abstract space into a concrete delimited place; it is about settling down and being at ease within a place, to feel at home.

There is however, another side to Heidegger's dwelling that tends to go unseen (Mai and Ringgaard 2010, 12–13). Dwelling – or finding a place to dwell – presupposes a moving and observant subject that through perception and language takes possession of a part of the world. Consequently, dwelling is also about being able to move on – to see that there is a way out. This, of course is in accordance with the fundamentals of Heidegger's thinking. Dwelling, as being, is to appropriate the things of the world, to transform the being-there of existence in transcending acts, words, consciousness. Norberg-Schultz suggests that by forwarding the notion of foothold, dwelling is also pausing to push off. Thus, he reminds us that even though dwelling is about place, it also implies temporality and movement, before and after. Time is remembering what was and therefore opening the fringe of what could be. To go beyond Heidegger's own text, perhaps it is not coincidental that the word "dwelling" in Old English means "lead astray," "hinder," "delay." These definitions traverse and linger between place and temporality: dwelling as something where you are led astray; not knowing where you are seems to be the opposite of home or a place as "having a distinct character." Then again, what comes to the surface is the ambiguity of the reading experience – arriving and departing, settling and breaking up, delimited openness and unambiguous diversity. The reader, of course, is sitting in his chair, but is also decentred and moved into literature, thus suggesting placement and timing.

For the architect, place is a space where everyday reality may occur. For the reader it is somewhere to move around, provided that the place is constructed by the author in a way that fits her – that is, her needs or desires. So while immersion or absorption may evoke associations of loss, decay, and passivity, and transportation presupposes a notion of division between the transporter and the transported, *dwelling* underscores the starting point of empowerment as taking into possession what is given or situated. Dwelling is more than shelter. It makes one able to oversee to navigate further. The paraphrases in the reviews quoted are representations of such overviews, which make it possible to go farther in this or that direction.

Working through Subjectivization

When assessing the quality of a book, reviewers must talk about themselves reading and determine a direction in their reading that is translatable into writing. This is a question not just of discovering and then writing, but also of inventing and seeing through the disclosure that may happen in the act of writing. The readers we have studied here dwell in an unfamiliar universe, experience a stretching of themselves towards or even all the way *to* – literally *touching on* – another world. As Tonje Vold shows in her essay in this book about the aftermath of the 22 July 2011 terror in Norway, the readers behind our reviews do not read "to put things in place." Quite the opposite, they are forced into reading and writing and are not terribly familiar with writing or literary culture. Despite all this, their reviews give evidence of important reading experiences. Therefore, if we were to identify a common denominator in these reviews, it would be that the readers try hard to come to terms with their own experience of reading. Subsequently, what they actually do is illustrate their own negotiations of whether a reading makes sense in relation to their own everyday reality. More specifically, we see how they stage a process of subjectivization by attempting to establish and re-establish an identity. Above we quoted *en passant* Peter Brooks on the necessary connection between history and identity. In the reviews, especially on fantasy, it is obvious that this connection is important to our readers. On the other hand, the notions of reading and subsequently of being and identity are shown to be more complex. It could definitely be relevant to discuss the meaning of place and dwelling in relation to a presumed turn from conceptualizing identity in terms of temporal development to doing so in terms of spatial involvement (see for example Tygstrup 2000). But we will instead underscore an assumption concerning how a literary universe is appropriated or inhabited through a reading experience where the intimate connection to the reader's (temporally constructed) background and everyday reality is basic. In other words, while dwelling anchors the quality of the reading experience in literature, we lack a complementary metaphor to anchor it in the reader.

Before turning to Montaigne and his concept of tempering, which is our reply to this challenge, we need to clarify how our material suggests a stretched or decentred notion of the subject as both "actor and agent, a free subjectivity that does things" and is "subjected, determined" and therefore also "subjected to various regimes (psycho-social, sexual, linguistic)" (Culler [1975]2000, 109). The subject, as Jonathan Culler here summarizes it, is inter-subjective, relational, and open-ended. To become a subject is, as Kant put it in "Thoughts on Education," to work oneself out from nature by means of others: "Animals are by their instinct all that they ever can be; some other reason has provided everything for them at the outset. But man needs a reason of his own. Having no instinct, he has to work out a plan of conduct for himself. Since, however, he is not able to do this all at once, but comes into the world undeveloped; others have to do it for him" ([1803]1900, 11).

In this context, Kant sets the scene: no individual can be *entirely* individual. To become human is to enter and connect to a world of history, language, and symbols that are already there. Freud's famous sentence "Where Id was, there Ego shall be" (1964, 80) implies that every individual must situate herself in relation to a symbolic Other – God or the Father. This implies a relation of interdependence and power *within* the subject as stretched out and influenced by symbolic powers. As Dany-Robert Dufour puts it: "Given that the 'subject' is *subiectus*, or one who has been *subjected*, we can say that history is a series of subjections to great figures placed at the centre of symbolic configurations" (2008, 26). Dufour's point is that in our time, commodities offer the easiest and therefore dominant way for late-modern subjects to perform this necessary connection. While pre-modern subjects more or less were defined by the Father God (or his various representations), the late modern subject is, as Dufour argues, far more vulnerable in being subjected to a never-ending economy of circulation that forces him or her to "fit in with never-ending flows of circulating commodities" (2008, 6).

Our point, however, is that our material confirms that *reading* – not reading this or that, but the *act* of reading as linking qualities of a literary place with the reader's own situation – offers a way of working oneself further out through subjectivity. A book is a map; by reading it, you can plot a way or a plan to get at least a little clearer on whether to continue or turn in another direction. The work of subjectivization, of the *one* becoming *human*, which Freud pinpoints in the sentence following the citation above, but which Dufour omits, "is a work of culture – not unlike the draining of the Zuyder Zee" (Freud 1964, 80). For Freud, then, figuring oneself out is a massive work of engineering – of draining, controlling, and disciplining the powers of nature. As John Hillis Miller states *The Ethics of Reading*: "Reading itself is extraordinary hard work. It does not occur that often. Clearheaded reflection on what really happens in an act of reading is even more difficult and rare" (1987, 3–4). Thus, Miller helps us restate how thinking about reading is both different from the reading experience and an indispensable part of it. The reading experience is an ongoing work of recollection, and traces of reading reshape the reader if only in the sense of getting older while reading and not being occupied with something else.

As the subject is inter-subjective, relational, and subject to something outside him- or herself, the quality of reading unfolds in the magnitude of this multi-dimensional stretching even *out of* oneself between body and text, between sentiments, cognitions, and articulation, between the reading situation and the imagination of the author writing, between the "I" and the Other. In reading and assessing literature even (or especially) when it is mandatory, when being forced to write about experience, we (pupils or researchers) write about not them/ourselves/that, but perform how we can be both subjected and subject, be and not be shut off, relate to and not dissolve. In the reading/writing practices we have looked at here, we depict a double sense of freedom *from* restraints and *of* connection. This ambiguity again is reflected in our material, in readings *off* the record, in a rejection of being spoken down to, in an appreciation of the book's stability – its capacity to connect.

Tempering Ambiguity

Reading is about coping with a complex ambiguity disclosed both in the sense of being and sensing the world (ontology), and in knowledge acquisition and questions of what may be said to be true (epistemology). This work or practice is the opposite of "headshrinking," both because it entails an expansion of the *I* and because it is an intellectual as well as a corporeal and practical process. "Tempering" is one term for these efforts to cope with oneself in reading, with the text, with the world, with others, and with subjectivity as it is disclosed in these intermediary or multi-dimensional zones.

Tempering (French: *temperer*) is, as mentioned, a word borrowed from Michel de Montaigne and refers to the art of navigating through life and death in a balanced or attuned way (Bale 2003, 10). Kjersti Bale quotes a passage from Montaigne's *Essais* "That to philosophize is to learn to die," where Mother Nature explains life as tempering:

> If you had not death, you would eternally curse me for having deprived you of it; I have mixed a little bitterness with it, to the end, that seeing of what convenience it is, you might not too greedily and indiscreetly seek and embrace it: and that you might be so established in this moderation, as neither to nauseate life, nor have any antipathy for dying, which I have decreed you shall once do, I have tempered the one and the other betwixt pleasure and pain. (Montaigne 1877, Ch. XIX)

In her reading of Montaigne, Bale stresses that tempering is a practical ability to combine properly, moderate, and keep in line. Tempering therefore is a matter of judgment. It is about finding one's way through a life that continuously changes, and being able to adapt to these changes. Bale describes Montaigne's way of writing as a movement *between* – between examples and universal laws, being and nothingness, sign and referent. Consequently, a zone of subtle scales of grey is highlighted: the in-between categories of established truths, assumed knowledge, stable sentences, safe positions. Reading, then, is judging others as well as events and aesthetic expressions, keeping in mind that judgments are based on premises that are possible illusions (responsibility) (Bale 2003, 262).

Bale distils the concept of tempering the text to address the intermediary zone between arts as an expression of lived life and her own efforts to understand and interpret the other, and further, to emphasize that this meeting conveys ethical reflection (Bale 2003, 10). While Bale initially demonstrates how an ethical reflection on guilt is evoked in her own reading of Gerhard Richter's photo painting *Onkel Rudi*, we would like to emphasize that an ethical reflection is inherent in all reading as reading per se. The idea of tempering therefore is a way to designate the quality of reading. Tempering is a strategy to read oneself in relation to the world and others, a capacity to manoeuvre within this multifold ambiguity, to cope with that which is encountered in reading the actual work in which the reader is literally involved. Tempering concerns the ability to read situations in the broadest sense and continuously change in accordance with how the situation changes and is changed. Thus, from yet another angle, tempering is getting at the unknown through one's own right words. Of course, our students, the readers in this study, may not have found the ultimate words – the best-tempered utterances. But that is not the point. The point is that they are on their way – "they are about to." All of them reveal words that disclose a direction towards an improvement in tempering the text, themselves, and the world.

Notes

1 This chapter should be read as an apology for close readings (see, for example, Franco Moretti's (2013) *Distant Reading* as a method for sharpening the gaze and increasing hermeneutical and phenomenological sensitivity). Through close readings, one may discover hidden aspects that can serve as footholds for students as well as for teachers, librarians, and researchers.
2 All cited passages from reviews are translated by the chapter authors. In spite of obvious problems, texts are transcribed as faithfully as possible to convey the imperfection of the original reviews.
3 The reviews are not signed; we alternate male and female pronouns for each reviewer.

References

Aristotle. *Categories*. 2009. Translated by E.M. Edghill. http://classics.mit.edu/Aristotle/categories.html
Bale, Kjersti. 2003. *Tekstens temperering. Michel de Montaignes essayistiske fremstillingsmåte* [*Tempering the Text: Michel de Montaigne's Essayistic Mode of Expression*]. Oslo: Pax.
Balling, Gitte. 2009. "Litterær æstetisk oplevelse. Læsning, læseoplevelser og læseundersøgelser: en diskussion af teoretiske og metodiske tilgange. [Literary Esthetic Experience: Reading, Reading Experiences, and Reading Studies: A Discussion of Theoretical and Methodological Approaches]." PhD diss., Danmarks Biblioteksskole [Royal School of Library and Information science].
Bloom, Harold. 1996. *Omens of the Millennium: The Gnosis of Angels, Dreams, and Resurrection*. London: Fourth Estate.
Brooks, Peter. 1984. *Reading for the Plot: Design and Intention in Narrative*. Cambridge, MA: Harvard University Press.

Culler, Jonathan. 2000. *Literary Theory: A Very Short Introduction*. Oxford: Oxford University Press.

Davis, Philip. 2013. *Reading and the Reader: The Literary Agenda*. Oxford: Oxford University Press.

Dufour, Dany-Robert. 2008. *The Art of Shrinking Heads: On the New Servitude of the Liberated in the Age of Total Capitalism*. Cambridge: Polity.

Egeberg, Ole, and Kjell Ivar Skjerdingstad. 2011. *Tanken sitter i øyet*. [*Thinking with the Eye*]. Oslo: Novus Forlag.

Foreningen !les. 18 July 2014. http://foreningenles.no/ungdom

Fjestad, Ellen. 2012. *Sammen skal vi holde himmelen* [*Together We Shall Hold the Heavens*]. Oslo: Schibsted.

Freud, Sigmund. 1964. "The Dissection of the Psychical Personality," In *New Introductory Lectures on Psychoanalysis*, vol. 22, Complete Works, Standard Edition, edited by James Strachey and Anna Freud, 57–80. London: Hogarth Press.

Heidegger, Martin. 2001. "Building Dwelling Thinking," In *Poetry, Language, Thought*, collected and translated by Alfred Hofstader, 13–61. New York: Harper Perennial.

Hovden, Magne. 2012. *Åndejegerne. Bok 1* [*Ghost Hunters: Book 1*]. Oslo: Aschehoug.

Kant, Immanuel. [1803]1900. *Kant on Education (über Pädagogik)*, edited by Annette Churton. Boston: D.C. Heath. http://files.libertyfund.org/files/356/0235_Bk.pdf

Lindhé, Cecilia. 2010. "'Bildseendet föds ifingertopperna" Om en ekfras för den digitala tidsåldern. [The Search for the Visual Is Born in the Fingertips: On an Ekphrasis for the Digital Age]." *Ekfrase: Nordisk tidsskrift for visuelle kultur* 1: 4–16.

Mai, Anne-Marie, and Dan Ringgaard. 2010. *Sted* [*Place*]. Aarhus: Aarhus Universitetsforlag.

Merleau-Ponty, Maurice. 2000. *Phenomenology of Perception*. London: Routledge and Kegan Paul.

Miller, J. Hillis. 1987. *The Ethics of Reading: Kant, de Man, Eliot, Trollope, James, and Benjamin*. New York: Columbia University Press.

Montaigne, Michel de. 1877. *Essays of Michel de Montaigne – Complete*. Project Gutenberg, 2012. http://www.gutenberg.org/files/3600/3600-h/3600-h.htm

Moretti, Franco. 2013. *Distant Reading*. London: Verso.

Mæhle, Lars. 2012. *Fuck Off I Love You*. Oslo: Samlaget.

Norberg-Schulz, Christian. 1980. *Genius Loci: Towards a Phenomenology of Architecture*. New York: Rizzoli.

Piper, Andrew. 2012. *Book Was There: Reading in Electronic Times*. Chicago: University of Chicago Press.

Rosenblatt, Louise. [1938]1995. *Literature as Exploration*. Reprint, New York: Modern Language Association of America.

Stewart, Garrett. 2006. *The Look of Reading: Book, Painting, and Text*. Chicago: University of Chicago Press.

Tygstrup, Frederik. 2000. "Kronotopisk identitet: A propos Morten Søndergaards Ubestemmelsessteder. [Chronotopic Identity: Apropos Morten Søndergaards' Indecisive Places.]" *Kritik* 14: 39–47.

Fun ... and Other Reasons for Sharing Reading with Strangers
Mass Reading Events and the Possibilities of Pleasure

Danielle Fuller and DeNel Rehberg Sedo

Any twenty-first-century analysis of book cultures necessarily involves investigating the social and cultural importance of print texts and what we call shared reading. Our contribution to this body of knowledge has been pursued through a collaborative, interdisciplinary research investigation of eleven different mass reading events (MREs) – the name we have decided to give to large-scale events that actively encourage readers to engage with selected books and with other readers (Fuller and Rehberg Sedo, 2013). The events we selected for the Beyond the Book study took place in three nation-states: Great Britain, Canada, and the United States. They were part of One Book, One Community programs (OBOCs) in which one book is selected for citizens of a city, state, province, or country to read at the same time. Our methods, which combined qualitative and quantitative approaches, generated more than seventy interviews with event organizers. We also held fifty-seven face-to-face focus groups with two hundred readers, conducted participant observation of more than sixty event activities, and disseminated an online questionnaire in each location that brought in more than 3,500 responses from readers. Many compelling stories and ideas about books, reading, book events, and community emerged from the vast amount of data the team gathered. This essay explores the various pleasures readers derive from their participation in some of the "live" events that form part of many mass reading programs. In particular, we consider the social, cultural, and emotional "uses" that readers make of face-to-face events such as author readings and literary bus tours.

One Book, One Community program organizers often harbour grand ideals for MREs. They may imagine them as forces for social change and individual transformation, or as opportunities to build bridges across different cultural groups in a city, or as "civilizing" projects that will produce more civically engaged citizens (Fuller and Rehberg Sedo 2013, 19–20; Griswold

2008, 58). More pragmatically, some organizers – in common with the directors of book festivals, for example – hope that events will generate revenue, encourage cultural tourism, and help brand their town, city, or region as a creative hub – that is, as an investment opportunity for cultural and creative industries and a lure for the kinds of professional people who Richard Florida (2002, 2005) argues will contribute to the regeneration of post-industrial wastelands (McGuigan 2010, 117). Such ideals and the ideologies, cultural policies, and economics that inform them are worth investigating and critiquing (Fuller and Rehberg Sedo 2013, 122–63). But in many ways, these idealistic goals and commercial aims are easier to access than the experiences and opinions of readers. For that reason, then, our focus in this article falls on the perspectives of those people who enjoy taking part in MREs, and, in particular, on the types of reading pleasures that "live" events provide. We suggest that in an era of technological transition from codex to e-book, readers are actively seeking the re-mediation of their reading experiences not only through different media but also through other readers.

We begin by introducing MREs, using two broadcast shows as examples of the cross-media reach that contemporary technologies make possible. We discuss why ideas about intimacy and entertainment are important aspects of MREs, before turning to consider some of the various pleasures that readers in our study derived from their participation in "live" events. The article ends with an argument that the social, emotional, intellectual, and aesthetic pleasures provided by reading events work together in various ways to inform what "fun" means to contemporary readers.

"Super-Sizing" Shared Reading: Mass Reading Events

As early as 2002, we began to notice the emergence of a "new" cultural formation of shared reading on both sides of the Atlantic. As researchers interested in popular culture, reading communities, cultural production, and mass media, we were intrigued by broadcast book programs such as the radio series *Canada Reads* (http://www.cbc.ca/books/canadareads) and by televised book clubs such as the Richard & Judy Book Club (http://www.richardandjudy.co.uk/home) in Britain. The phenomenal success of Oprah's Book Club, the first series of which aired in 1996, was a direct inspiration for both shows and also for the inception of the OBOC model. Nancy Pearl and Chris Higashi, professional librarians working at the Center for the Book in Seattle, Washington, launched the first city-wide reading program of this type in 1998. As the name suggests, a book – often but not always a work of literary fiction – is selected as the focus for a series of activities in which the citizens of a community, city, region, or even nation are invited to participate. Some activities, such as book discussions, assume that participants will read the book, but others, such as author events, craft workshops, and even camp-outs, canoe trips, and pub crawls, do not. Theatrical dramatizations, screenings of film adaptations, and staged readings of extracts from the book by professional actors or local celebrities are common to various iterations of the model. The opportunity to participate online is offered by most programs, but, in the mid-2000s, when we were investigating events, interactivity was often limited by budget constraints. The OBOC model has been widely replicated and adapted, not only in the United States and Canada but also in Britain, continental Europe, Singapore, and Australia.[1] Although it is impossible to provide an exact figure, we estimate that more than five hundred OBOC programs take place annually around the world.

When we began to research OBOCs, we were particularly fascinated by the ways these contemporary versions of shared reading took the concept of people reading and talking about a book, "super-sized" it, and transported it into public places and spaces. Significantly, these spaces were not confined to those where the meanings of reading have traditionally been made within northern industrialized societies like the United States, Canada, and Britain – spaces such as public libraries, schools, and city halls. While these locations were, and remain, common places to hold activities associated with city-wide reading programs, workplaces (e.g., offices) and leisure spaces such as pubs, ice rinks, and parks have also become temporary sites for shared book cultures. Sometimes these sites host activities such as singing, acting, making art, debating, or even eating a picnic or listening to a talk about Italian wine, none of which depend upon anyone reading a book.

What, we wondered, was going on? Why did people come together for these events? What cultural meanings about books and reading were being promoted and negotiated by the organizers and by the participants? Who were these events for, whose interests did they serve, and were they capable of generating any kind of social change, as some organizers claimed they could? These were among the questions that quickly sprang to mind as we identified more and more examples of initiatives for sharing reading. What we chose to reference through the term "mass reading event" was not only scale ("mass") and spectacle ("event") but also the idea that an event promoting reading and the sharing of reading usually engages with one or more aspects of the mass media, be it in print, broadcast, or digital form.

Two of the case studies that we subsequently chose to investigate depended on broadcast media for their primary delivery. Britain's Richard & Judy Book Club was broadcast as a segment on the couple's daytime television show on Channel 4 from 2004 to 2008. After that, the club ran for one season on a cable channel before becoming an online review show in partnership with the book retailer WHSmith.

The other broadcast MRE that we investigated has had a longer life, but, like the Richard & Judy Book Club, has existed on multiple platforms. *Canada Reads* is an annual five-day "battle of the books" radio show aired on the Canadian Broadcast Corporation's Radio 1. It completed its fourteenth series in March 2015. Apart from the 2012 series, which was the first *Canada Reads* to focus exclusively on works of non-fiction, the contest usually features a mix of novels, poetry, and short stories. The on-air show often follows a set format: five celebrities each champion a Canadian book, voting off one title per day until only one book is left. The *Survivor*-type format provokes some heated discussion and – as Fuller's students from her "Reading and Popular Culture" classes have noted – passionate defences of a book's subject, style, and capacity to emotionally engage the reader. The discussion makes for lively radio even though it is not in fact a "live" show (although many Canadians believe it is). Recorded on a single day, *Canada Reads* is edited into five 23-minute segments. But the producers of *Canada Reads* never intended to stop at radio (Fuller and Rehberg Sedo, 2006). After early attempts to produce a television show alongside the radio debates failed quite spectacularly, the production team focused on developing the *Canada Reads* website instead. Over the past fourteen years, they have been quick to embrace social media and evolving digital technologies. As a result of this responsiveness, the team has created a slickly produced website that currently incorporates vidcasts, audio podcasts, a Twitter feed, the work of a professional blogger, bulletin boards, discussion fora, and promotional material about the featured books and their celebrity champions (http://www.cbc.ca/books/canadareads). Via the website, the producers of *Canada Reads* have been able to offer Canadians different types of interactivity: the facility to comment on the books, to suggest their own choices, to respond to the on-air discussions, and to vote for a "People's Choice" winner. In a country that spans five time zones, these opportunities to connect directly with the content of a "national" radio program are significant ways of getting "up close and personal" with books, celebrities, authors and – crucially – other readers.

We introduce these two shows because their success depended, in part, on the co-extensive relationship between books and other media as it played out during the first decade of the twenty-first century. These mass-mediated reading events were also entertainment products of their time, not only in terms of their formats and genres but also in terms of their engagement with celebrity culture and their ability to generate substantial book sales (Allen 2009; Dugdale 2006; Farndale 2007; Fuller and Rehberg Sedo 2013). They thus help highlight the ways that shared reading has become part of popular culture. The success of these shows as popular entertainments depended on the ability of television and radio producers to exploit the communicative strategies of their primary medium of delivery to create intimacy with their viewers and listeners (Fuller and Rehberg Sedo 2006; Fuller 2007; Rehberg Sedo 2008). Significantly, too, in terms of the experiences of emotional intensification that many readers seek from books, both shows were produced by women who had a self-declared "passion for reading." Talin Vartanian, the producer of *Canada Reads*, told us, however, "I'm not a literary maven" (Fuller 2007, 13). Like Amanda Ross, the producer of the Richard & Judy Book Club, Vartanian does not claim to be a literary–cultural authority, but she loves books and she understood how to make them work in a non-print medium. In Ross's words: "If a book is entertaining to read, it's going to make entertaining TV, and vice versa, so that is the key – the key is to make sure the book's entertaining in the first place and then you're home and dry. It's gonna work" (pers. comm., 2006). In common with all MREs, regardless of how much celebrity sparkle and multimedia interactivity the organizers can afford to produce, making shared reading fun and pleasurable is, in fact, "the key." What that pleasure might involve for *participants* in MREs is our concern for the remainder of this article.

Fun and Other Reasons for Sharing Reading with Strangers

> It's so nice to be with other people who are appreciating the same thing. And then we went to the brewery. [laughs]
> —Anna, Kitchener/Waterloo/Cambridge focus group participant

At face value, Anna's comment appears to have nothing whatsoever to do with reading or book events. What is clear is that she went on an outing with a group of people, enjoyed the company and the sharing of some kind of experience or object, and then rounded off a fun day with a brewery tour and (presumably) a beer. Anna, a middle-aged white woman who lives in southern Ontario, Canada, is actually reflecting on her participation in a literary bus tour around sites associated with Jane Urquhart's novel *The Stone Carvers* (2001). Urquhart's novel was the 2003 selection for the OBOC program in the three neighbouring cities of Kitchener, Waterloo, and Cambridge. Taking Anna's words out of context, as we have done here, underlines what we believe to be a factor that does much to explain the popularity of contemporary MREs: they are a form of entertainment, well-suited to the time-pressured environment of twenty-first-century everyday life. What is on offer is a selection of encounters with books that do not involve the long-term time commitment of a private book group, nor do they necessarily depend on having read the selected book.

Within each MRE, a variety of events stage different kinds of engagement with elements of a book's content and its extra-textual aspects. These may include author appearances that explore the writer's biography or writing process, or films, discussion panels, and talks by experts that explore topical and contemporary issues raised by the selected book. Other types of activities we have come across include those that foreground the local connections between the book and the location of the event/s, such as camp-outs, canoe trips, walking tours of particular city neighbourhoods, pub crawls, picnics at sites described in the book, and, of course, the literary bus tour like the one Anna went on. Like other readers whom we met, Anna chose an aspect of her local OBOC program that appealed to her, and she clearly enjoyed both the content of the day and the experience of sharing it.

The most successful MREs – from Oprah's Book Club to *Canada Reads* to long-running OBOC programs in Chicago and Kitchener–Waterloo–Cambridge – exploit the opportunities offered by the co-extensive relationships among media to produce multiple encounters with books. Equally significant to their success as entertainments, MREs extend the possibility for multiple encounters with other *people*. They provide opportunities for human interaction via a socially networked event that can be engaged on- and off-line, once or repeatedly. These encounters may well be ephemeral, but as our research has demonstrated, they are capable of producing significant moments of identification or affective connection among participants (Fuller and Rehberg Sedo 2013, 232–35).

Like Anna, many people who take part in an MRE activity enjoy having their experience mediated through the presence and pleasures of other people. Re-experiencing a book through other readers, the author, various media, and visits to physical places enables reading to be a social and shared activity as well as an intellectual and somatic one. For readers who enjoy MREs, the pleasure of connection they experience combines with other kinds of pleasure, including the enjoyment of knowledge acquisition or an aesthetic engagement with the selected text. These latter pleasures coincide with the reasons why readers who engage in "recreational reading" do so. As library and information science scholar Vivian Howard illustrates, various contemporary studies of adult readers in Britain and North America nominate "escapism, relaxation, practical knowledge, self-development, self-knowledge, and aesthetic pleasure" (2011, 48) as reasons for reading. Readers who participate in MREs can redouble these pleasures while deriving further enjoyment from the framing of an event and the way a text is performed or re-presented. Such complex pleasures depend on the successful staging of a series of mediations between cultural workers, readers, authors, and texts that may lead to the production of various kinds of intimacy. These forms of intimacy include the social relations among readers, reader–text transactions, and the para-social relationships of reader–author encounters. We will discuss each of these forms of intimacy, but it is to these "reader–author" mediations that we turn first.

"The 'Why' behind the Book": The Pleasure of Author–Reader Mediations

Author events bring writers literally face to face with readers' various desires, including a desire for intimacy with the person behind the text. Such encounters offer readers an "embodied" version of the para-social relationship that can arise from a reader's engagement with the author's books and, perhaps, from following media coverage of their career (Fuller and Rehberg Sedo 2013, 214–34). As one reader from the Kitchener–Waterloo–Cambridge area eloquently stated in a survey response: "The event puts me in touch with the real person behind the book. I like to know more about the author and the 'why' behind the book." As this comment indicates, a desire to connect with an author in person may be coupled with an urge to authenticate the text via knowledge of the writer's life. Or, readers may wish to authorize and recontextualize the text as a culturally valuable object for themselves, for a particular cultural group, or for their local community. Readers may achieve this through the types of questions they ask of the writer about their life or about the content of the book, especially its themes and settings. The physical appearance of the author at various venues makes a significant contribution to some readers' urge to reinvest both the book (the commodity-text) and the author (the celebrity-text) with local-cultural meaning. These processes are at once psychological and material.

The psychological projection of the text onto the author and the identification of the author as a text is a process that Wenche Ommundsen posits as a common way in which readers handle print texts in contemporary Western cultural contexts (2007, 249). Our survey suggests that many keen readers seek out opportunities for encounters with authors, perhaps as a way of mediating or enhancing these projections and identifications. When we asked about the types of book events people attended in the course of a year, 37.6 percent of those who responded across the different sites nominated author readings ($n = 3,067$), while library events (29.3 percent) and book festivals (17.4 percent) ranked as the second and third most popular options. Since many events held in libraries or featured as part of book festivals also include talks, readings, and appearances by writers, it seems that author events are popular with readers who have the time, money, cultural literacy, and information to locate and attend book-related leisure activities.

Our observations of OBOC author events suggest that these occasions offer readers the opportunity to visually align the material book with the actual bodily presence of its original producer or his or her representative (such as a biographer), and, in turn, with their own bodies. At many sites, but especially in Kitchener–Waterloo–Cambridge and in Huntsville, Alabama, we observed that up to half the members of an audience would listen to the author while touching, clutching, flicking through, or following along in their own copy of the book. Of course, many readers bring along their copy of the featured book so that they can obtain the author's signature in it. This is one way of authenticating the link between the material text and its originator, while also creating a material trace or evidence of a meeting between writer and reader. Readers' handling of their copy during a live event also reminds us that, for many keen readers, the physical form of the codex is extremely familiar: it is an everyday object, albeit a cultural artifact that may hold all kinds of social and emotional associations for an individual reader. The physiological aspects of reading a printed book (the smell of paper, the feel of the spine, turning the pages by hand) can be an especially pleasurable part of the reading experience for some readers.

When readers take along their copy of a book to an author event they may be deriving a sense of security from taking a familiar object into a public place, or displaying their identity as an owner or collector of books. They may also be exhibiting their good taste in choosing a book that has been legitimated by the organizers, or subconsciously wishing to show that they are part of a community that is sharing the same book. Whatever motivations are involved, it appears that for some readers who attend author events, holding and handling their copy of the text is one means of participating in the entertainment that does not depend on having the confidence to speak in public. The sense of being both physically and psychologically connected to the material book and its author may also enhance the physical and emotional pleasure of taking part in a "live" event.

OBOC participants who attended our focus groups told us that the events can enhance or deepen their cognitive and intellectual engagement with a book. The temporal span of the OBOC model is partly responsible for this opportunity to undertake a type of intensive reading. OBOC programs usually extend over three or more months, enabling readers to develop their knowledge of the text across time and through a series of different activities that engage and re-engage with the book and its contexts. Not surprisingly, participants in OBOC programs tend to be information-seekers who enjoy learning about the writer's inspirations and their research and writing process. They also enjoy hearing other people's interpretations of and ideas about the text, and the author's own explanations of characters, imagery, and stylistic features.

Sylvia is a Chinese Canadian woman who was in her mid-twenties in 2006 when we met her. She works as a financial adviser and piano teacher in Vancouver. She vividly expressed the effect – and affect – of gaining a "deeper understanding" of an OBOC selection. She is talking below about taking part in an event featuring the writer Joy Kogawa, author of the 2005 OBOC Vancouver selection, *Obasan* (1981):

> I think it's – I think it gave me a greater understanding, like, you know, with seeing her presence and then to hear her. She – you know, the way she talked. You can sort of kind of imagine what it's really like, you know, kind of her personality into the book. You probably read it once, but you just don't know, you don't quite get it. It's a story. But with some people actually ... there and then they tell you the story, like, people asked about the background – you know, what does ... the house and trees and stuff symbolize, and you realize you get deeper, you gain a deeper understanding of the book. There's more *feeling* to it ... Well, just seeing that interaction between the people, like, you know, the readers and the author: it's actually quite interesting. Like, everything becomes alive! That's what I felt. (pers. comm., 2006)

Sylvia believes that her comprehension of the novel's meaning became "deeper" through a combination of factors: Kogawa's self-presentation and vocal performance, which enhanced her ability to "imagine" the setting and world of the book; the clarification of the plot that audience members articulated; and the decoding of imagery that was elucidated via the questions that people posed to Kogawa. In common with other readers whose responses to events we have analyzed, Sylvia values the *intensification of emotion* that the author event produces, as much as the intellectual knowledge she gains about the text. For her, the "live" dynamic of the event created by the mediation of the book among readers and author is both informative and thrilling in the way it animates and dramatizes the novel. "Everything becomes alive!," as Sylvia memorably put it. But what exactly "comes alive" for readers sometimes refers as much to the world outside the book as to the world depicted between the covers. In the next section we focus on the ways that locality, spectacle, and sociability combine at live events to make the local into a social experience.

"Everything Becomes Alive!": Making the Local Social

The promotion or representation of a regional or local community through the book selected for MREs or via the activities themselves is important to the readers in our study. Canadians in our study were especially motivated by the local and regional aspects of programming to participate in OBOC. This response may be underscored by the fact that several Canadian adaptations of the program deliberately focus on the connections between the selected book and the local area. Sometimes the local is brought out in terms of biographical associations that the author has with a particular place; at other times, the association may be more thematic or issue-based. The appeal of local or regional relevance is often inspired by readers' interest in learning more about their area and its history, but it is also shaped by the opportunities that activities such as the literary bus tour around places depicted in a novel offer for various kinds of social interaction with other readers.

One way that OBOC programs help readers make the local social, then, is by taking events outside of institutional spaces such as libraries to specific locations associated with local histories and communities. Readers themselves make local places meaningful in various ways, of course. Trudy, a professional administrator from the Kitchener–Waterloo area who is in her late fifties, offered a provocative and enthusiastic account of her participation in the literary bus tour around sites depicted in Jane Urquhart's novel *The Stone Carvers* (2001):

> I really enjoyed [*The Stone Carvers*] and the bus tour really bought that book alive ... because you went to places that were described that were part of the book and somehow it seems real, you know – I know it was a novel, but just, you know you could see the characters, you see the places ... You felt that what was described could have happened and you were where it, you were where these places were.

For Trudy, the tour offered a pleasurable opportunity to construct a mimetic identification between textual representation and the physical environment. Her sense of having stepped into the world of the book in both an imaginative and a physical way, moved her from an abstract textual world to a more material – in the sense of visceral – relationship with the text. Trudy's embodied and sensory experience prompts a form of identity work in which she "feels" (and by implication comes to know) the events of the novel both emotionally and physiologically. Although Trudy's experience is profoundly personal in one sense, her switch between first person and second person pronouns recalls the presence and participation of her friends and bus mates ("you were where these places were") as well as her desire to convince us as her listeners ("you know") that "the bus tour really bought that book alive." The shared aspect of the experience is, she infers, partly constitutive of the almost magical sensation of being in a place that is at once materially present and inscribed by a fictional narrative. That magical aspect, and Trudy's self-conscious account of it – "I know it was a novel, but ... you could see the characters" – breathes life into Rita Felski's (2008) conceptualization of contemporary aesthetic experiences of reading and film viewing as enchantments. Felski argues that "modern enchantments are those in which we are immersed but not submerged, bewitched but not beguiled, suspensions of disbelief that do not lose sight of the fictiveness of those fictions that enthrall us" (2008, 75). Immersed but not alone, Trudy can, it seems, be at once profoundly within herself yet outside her everyday self during this state of enchantment. The bus tour dramatizes the text for her but certainly does not simplify its meaning, its effects or its affects.

Visiting local places can also promote expressions of cultural and familial affiliation. Jill, a librarian in her late forties, grew up in Leamington, Ontario, which was the destination for the 2004 bus tour connected to Nino Ricci's novel *Lives of the Saints*. The trip included a visit to a tomato farm run by Ricci's sister and father. Jill talked about how she went on the tour because "I just wanted to see how others saw my community" (pers. comm., 2004). Jill curated her home-place and re-created part of the tour for us when she explained: "It's a very small community, but it's one of the most multicultural for communities that size and when you went on the tour you ... saw the Lebanese Club, and we did see, um, the German Club as well." Re-encountering her local place and its histories through the eyes and comments of the other participants and the Ricci family lent a different tenor to the notion of making the local social. For Jill, her "place" became new: "I must admit I learned a lot of things on the trip that I didn't think of," she told us.

For some participants, however, the pleasure of making the local social is less about how the setting, themes, and content of the book connect to their immediate physical environment or cultural group, and more about the idea or reality of people coming together to share reading as a community. Readers whom we met articulated different notions of community. As a fifteen-year-old member of the predominantly African American Kenwood Academy High School Teen Book Club in Chicago remarked: "It makes me feel good to be part of a city that is all reading the same book" (pers. comm., 2005). She speaks for many other reader-participants whom we met in various geographic locations who enjoyed being part of an imagined community of readers. But for many people, being able to share thoughts about the selected book face to face was also a crucial social practice and experience of community. For some readers this occurred within a regular book club, while for others it was more fleeting as they become part of one of the many stand-alone book discussions that pepper the programs of virtually all iterations of the OBOC model.

Thus, shared reading events can offer readers different notions of community and different modes of belonging. This is an important pleasure. In turn, these modes of belonging to the different communities that constitute a person's everyday life can satisfy a desire for a range of relationships with people, places, and creative texts. Lynn, a woman in her fifties from Waterloo, Ontario, eloquently described and contrasted the different experiences of community that she encounters through her membership in a series of arts-centred groups:

> I think some communities are intimate and I consider my book club to be intimate and I consider the small group that I go to the movies with to be intimate. And I reveal myself to them. But this One Book One Community gives me a whole other social network that is part of the warp and the woof of holding a community together. I can carry that book with me into a restaurant or to have a cup of coffee and somebody will stop and say, I read that book. (pers. comm., 2004)

Lynn's commentary articulates the added social and public dimension that a shared reading event can bring to the experiences of and possibilities for belonging. What Lynn appears to enjoy is the contrast between her "intimate" communities where she is prepared to "reveal" her private self, and the sensation of a more public self moving through the "whole other social network" that constitutes her wider community.

Lynn's sense of connecting with others – with strangers as well as friends – via a book featured in a mass reading event was echoed time and again by other readers. "Just seeing someone on the bus holding the book made me smile" was a comment we heard several times, for instance. One of the great surprises of the research for us was how many readers were satisfied by ephemeral experiences of community like these. Even those who participated in events not by reading the book but by attending a different activity could derive a feeling of pleasure from belonging – however tenuously – to a community of readers.

The fantasy of connection between people who are at once private and public persons, can, however fleetingly, become realized as a book becomes subject to a rereading or the point of departure for the sharing of emotional knowledge. Julie, a white woman in her thirties from Liverpool, England, articulated her pleasure in hearing a culturally diverse group of readers compare their own lived experiences about immigration to those portrayed in Andrea Levy's novel *Small Island* (2004). This public sharing of personal histories occurred in a large public library during a headline author event as part of 2007's Liverpool Reads:

> Some people talked about when they were growing up in Ireland ... People talked about growing up as a black person in Liverpool ... It was just lovely to see that, that people with different experiences were all bringing them to

this book event, this reading and then sharing in the enjoyment and then being able to relate to this book, but in their own ways, everyone obviously related to it in different ways. (pers. comm., 2007)

Julie enjoys the sense of being part of a community of readers and seeing her local community temporarily transformed from an imagined into an actual physical formation.

Like many contemporary readers, Julie is clearly also interested in hearing about other people's interpretations of texts. Indeed, a desire to learn is often braided with the sociability that both private book groups and larger-scale reading events offer. In our online survey, as a way of illustration, 34 percent (1,194) of respondents were either currently a member of a book club or had been in the past. Of those survey respondents who participated in OBOC events, 30 percent (442) felt that the main achievement of the program was "private enrichment" for the individual reader, but our qualitative data, including Julie's comments and those mentioned above, complicate that. Self-improvement coexists with the pleasure of sharing reading in a communal setting that realizes aspects of local history and contemporary realities, suggesting that readers like Julie may enjoy knowledge production as a relational activity. Re-experiencing a book through the medium of other people's narratives can certainly be heightened by the "spectacle" aspects of large events. The Liverpool Reads event that Julie attended, for example, incorporated Caribbean food and music as well as a high level of interaction between the author and the four-hundred-strong audience. Such a multisensory experience combined with Andrea Levy's skill at reading aloud to bring the book "to life again."

Another Liverpudlian, Suzanne, noted that "the music set an atmosphere ... It was quite evocative." In the same focus group, Anne explained how Levy's performance "made me want to read [the novel] again for the third time. Because when she did her bit, and she, you know, she can do the accents. When we read ... you don't say it out loud, do you? I don't read out loud, not any more anyway" (pers.comm., 2007). Hearing Levy's voice and the information that the author shared about her family history brought *Small Island* "alive" in a multi-dimensional way for these Liverpudlians. As Tracey, an Afro-Caribbean woman in her early forties, put it, "her experiences come through and you can see how she ... kind of portrayed the personalities and that came out in the way she spoke and their ... personalities came out through her, the way she was speaking and I thought that was, uh, that was really good."

The "live" vocal performance of an author was a consistent highlight for readers in our study, who often found it "wonderfully entertaining," as one reader expressed it. A Seattle reader, Meg, who was in her late twenties, also described the "thrill" of seeing a "celebrity" writer in person (pers. comm., 2007). What "comes alive" for readers then is not confined to the plot or characterization in a novel; it goes beyond the book to encompass extra-textual matters concerned with the production of texts and the value attached to contemporary celebrity. The author does not have to be a Pulitzer Prize winner or bestselling author to achieve this intimacy effect, but he or she must be open to taking part in a series of fairly intensive events and be prepared to mediate their own public persona with some honesty.

Conclusions

Listening to readers' experiences of and perceptions about mass reading events suggests why and how this particular form of shared reading is meaningful to some people. Reading events are a form of entertainment located within the contemporary media environment, and, as we have demonstrated, participants are attracted to events by the combination of social, emotional, intellectual and aesthetic pleasures on offer.

Investigating the complexity of reading pleasures mandates that multiple investigative measures be employed in order to account for the various reading practices of individual readers within shared reading environments. Readers engage in the various practices that are available to them and will create their own when necessary. However, while our research illustrates the multiple modes of reader engagement and shared reading that MREs make possible, we became acutely aware that our data were collected during a period of intense technological change. The introduction of devices such as e-readers and smartphones emphasized that, for some readers who could afford the hardware, the shift from codex to digital text had picked up speed. Online opportunities for sharing reading with others also increased rapidly during the first decade of the twenty-first century. Meanwhile, older media such as television and radio, and traditional modes of shared reading such as face-to-face book clubs, existed alongside newer platforms for book cultures and the social practices they inspire. Future research might explore how and why readers move among the various media modalities, with whom, and to what effect – and affect.

We suggest that in an era of technological transition from codex to e-book, readers are actively seeking the re-mediation of their reading experiences not only through different media but also through other readers. The pleasures of performance in the context of mass reading events, then, are predominantly about the sociability of shared reading. These contemporary forms of reading as a social practice produce moments of intimacy, affect, and belonging for readers for whom having fun with a bunch of strangers is all part of the desire to go beyond the book.

Note

Parts of this chapter are republished with permission of Taylor and Francis Group, LLC, a division of Informa plc, from *Reading Beyond the Book: The Social Practices of Contemporary Literary Culture*, by Danielle Fuller and DeNel Rehberg Sedo, 2013. Permission conveyed through Copyright Clearance Center, Inc.

1 See Fuller and Rehberg Sedo 2013, 309n1. Also see http://www.nederlandleest.nl.

References

Allen, Katie. 2009. "Ross Confident of Book Club Future." *The Book Seller*, 17 May. http://www.thebookseller.com/news/ross-confident-book-club-future.html
Dugdale, John. 2006. "Sofa, So Good: Many of This Year's Top Selling Authors Owe Their Fortunes to Richard and Judy." *Saturday Guardian*, 30 December 30, 18–19. http://www.guardian.co.uk/books/2006/dec/30/bestbooksoftheyear.bestbooks2
Farndale, Nigel. 2007. "The Best Seller." *Daily Telegraph*, 25 March. http://www.telegraph.co.uk/culture/3664052/The-best-seller.html
Felski, Rita. 2008. *Uses of Literature*. Malden and Oxford: Blackwell Publishing.
Florida, Richard. 2002. *The Rise of the Creative Class: And How It's Transforming Work, Leisure, Community, and Everyday Life*. New York: Basic Books.
———. 2005. *Cities and the Creative Class*. New York and London: Routledge.
Fuller, Danielle. 2007. "Listening to the Readers of 'Canada Reads.'" *Canadian Literature* 193 (Summer): 11–34.
Fuller, Danielle, and DeNel Rehberg Sedo. 2010. "A Reading Spectacle for the Nation: The CBC and 'Canada Reads.'" *Journal of Canadian Studies* 40(1): 5–36.
———. 2013. *Reading Beyond the Book: The Social Practices of Contemporary Literary Culture*. New York: Routledge.
Griswold, Wendy. 2008. *Regionalism and the Reading Class*. Chicago: University of Chicago Press.
Howard, Vivian. 2011. "The Importance of Pleasure Reading in the Lives of Young Teens: Self-Identification, Self-Construction, and Self-awareness." *Journal of Librarianship and Information Science* 43(1): 46–55.
McGuigan, Jim. 2010. *Cultural Analysis*. London: Sage.
Ommundsen, Wenche. 2007. "From the Altar to the Market-Place and Back Again: Understanding Literary Celebrity." In *Stardom and Celebrity: A Reader*, edited by Sean Redmond and Su Holmes, 244–55. London: Sage.
Rehberg Sedo, DeNel. 2008. "Richard & Judy's Book Club and 'Canada Reads': Readers, Books and Cultural Programming in a Digital Era." *Information, Communication, and Society* 11(2): 188–206.

The Once and Future Self
(Re)reading Personal Lists, Notes, and Calendars

Pamela McKenzie and Elisabeth Davies

Studies of the reader's experience have often ignored the temporal dimension of reading, with little attention to the rereading of texts and to the different ways a reader experiences a text over time. This paper analyzes the experience of (re)reading texts, such as lists, notes, and calendars, that individuals create and use to "keep track of things" in their everyday lives. We deliberately focus on texts written by and for the reader/authors themselves. These texts may be highly personal and are often created to be ephemeral; there is no need to keep the shopping list once the shopping is done. However, these texts may be kept: inadvertently, to be rediscovered, or deliberately, as mementos. We argue that in (re)reading these texts, participants are also rereading – and retelling – their own lives. Through these insignificant and ephemeral documents, readers ongoingly produce both the texts and themselves.

Reading and Rereading

Calinescu (1998) and Galef (1998) observe that "the vast majority of literary critics or theorists do not distinguish between reading and rereading" (Calinescu 1998, 51). Apart from a small number of reflections on the author's experience of rereading familiar literary works (e.g., Lesser 2002; Spacks 2011), there have as yet been few scholarly analyses of rereading (e.g., Calinescu 1993; Galef 1998).

Birkerts (1998, 340–41) and Galef (1998, 25) each identify two reasons that a reader may return to a text. First, one may reread to achieve a greater discernment of and mastery over the text. Davies (2007, 2008) interviewed theatre production professionals (e.g., sound, lighting, and costume designer, director, stage manager, actor) about the ways they interacted over time with the script of a single play they were producing. Davies argued that initial and subsequent readings differed and that each kind of professional read and reread the script differently according to his or her role. She likens the initial individual, silent readings to auditions for the script, as theatre professionals evaluate both the work experience the script represents for them and the artistic or literary quality of the story. As the time of the production approaches, theatre professionals read the script many times both individually and silently and orally and collectively. Subsequent readings of the script focus on analyzing the play in order to understand it better. Different professionals seek different kinds of mastery of the text: actors read for clues about the characters they will play; stage managers read to understand the work of the entire production. During the rehearsal period, the actors go "off-book," embodying the memorized script so that there is no longer a need to read from the physical text. Davies's study shows how a sense of mastery over the text varies both according to the roles individual readers have with respect to the production and, for each reader, over time.

A second reason to reread a text, particularly one read for pleasure, is that often, "we recall not so much the contents of a novel but our reactions to it" (Birkerts 1998, 341). According to David Galef, rereading therefore enables a form of time travel, "not just as excursion to the world and era of the text, but a near repetition of the reader's experience of earlier feelings" (Galef 1998, 25). Birkerts (1998, 341) likens rereading a novel to an encounter with an old lover. Whereas one may anticipate that the former lover has changed, one expects the words on the page to have stood still. A rereading forces us to recognize that it is we who have in fact changed since the initial reading: "When we return to a book, we encounter more than just the author's words – we simultaneously tour the picturesque ruins of our former selves" (Birkerts 1998, 341–42).

Calinescu (1993, 39) proposes that the notion of rereading addresses "a metaphorically circular time and a consciousness that (re)reading can be described, and indeed must be described, in both linear and circular terms." However, the notion of rereading as a circular experience is not without its challenges. On the one hand, the case may be made that a person reading a text is fundamentally different from the same person rereading the same text. "They are, in fact, experientially different, and if one follows the logical implications of this point, one reaches an absurdity: rereading is impossible, at least in the sense of the same reader picking up the text for a second time" (Galef 1998, 24). On the other hand, Galef (1998, 3) cites Nabokov's contention that every reading is in some sense a rereading. A reader brings to a new text the conventions of previously read texts (Bakhtin 1981): a truly novel reading is impossible.

We argue that rereading requires both revisiting the text and encountering it anew, and that in rereading a text, the reader is simultaneously revisiting and encountering him- or herself. Rereading is therefore tied in with identity as well as with time.

Burgess and Ivanič (2010) theorized the construction of writer identity across multiple timescales and showed how the act of reading is implicated in the ongoing development and adjustment of writer identity. Socially available possibilities for selfhood, or subject positions, exist on a sociocultural timescale of decades and centuries. From this set of possibilities, writers and readers construct autobiographical selves, which exist within the lifespan of the individual and develop and adapt over weeks, months, and years. Individual acts of writing and reading occur on a timescale of seconds, minutes, or hours. Through the act of writing, the writer constructs discoursal and authorial selves to be interpreted by the reader. The act of constructing these selves through the text in turn shapes the development of the writer's autobiographical self over a longer timescale. Through the act of reading, the reader constructs the "perceived writer," an identity for the writer that may persist throughout the lifetime of the reader and may change over multiple readings of the document. The act of reading and interpreting the identity of the writer likewise shapes the development of the reader's own autobiographical self over his or her lifetime. Finally, both the "perceived writer" and the reader's autobiographical self are constructed in relation to the possibilities for selfhood socially available to the reader at the time of reading. In reconfiguring their autobiographical selves, writers and readers are also contributing in small ways to the reshaping of the socially available possibilities from which they might draw in future. Whereas Calinescu, Galef, and Birkerts provide insight into how rereading enables a revisiting of one's identity as a reader, Burgess and Ivanič's analysis suggests that in rereading what we have written to and for ourselves we also reread ourselves as writers.

Genre and Method

We will build on these analyses to study the rereading of a form of text that has received little attention from reading researchers. Galef (1998, 27) notes that "to put it bluntly, not all texts repay rereading. It depends on the avowed purpose of the text: most newspapers are thrown out the day after they are read. It depends on the presumed simplicity of the text: most people do not reread the STOP sign their car is approaching." However, it is precisely the kinds of texts whose purpose is both simple and ephemeral that we have chosen to study:

Calendars: wall calendars and pocket agendas, online calendaring systems.

  Lists: ordered enumerations of things to do, items to acquire, or a combination of the two.

> Notes: reminders to oneself about something to be done or remembered. These take a variety of forms, including textual notes-to-self on small slips of paper (such as self-adhesive "stickies")," emails-to-self marked as "unread" to stand out in an inbox, and ongoing logs and notebooks.

We argue that these texts have particular characteristics that make their (re)reading meaningful. First, they are action-oriented (Whittaker 2011, 15) – that is, they contain details of tasks the reader is expected to do. They serve as external memory aids (Block and Morwitz 1999, 36), or tools for prospective remembering (Payne 1993), and therefore operate both forward and backward in time. The second characteristic of these texts is that they are written by and for the authors themselves – the intended reader is the future self.

These texts may be highly personal, "at times opaque and cryptic, their translation not always a straightforward practice" (Crewe 2011, 31). Because they are associated with an action, they must be kept accessible as reminders of the task to be done, but they are often ephemeral, discarded once the obligation has been fulfilled. However, they may be kept as future records of household transactions or as mementos of significant events or relationships (Marshall 2007). Their meaning may therefore change over time. We argue that lists, notes, and calendars do more than simply identify tasks to do, events to attend, or items to purchase. Calendars serve both administrative and social functions – thus, our participants recorded important personal and family details like birthdays and milestones; with the same calendars, they showed themselves and others what time slots were committed to what tasks or activities. Bassett, Beagan, and Chapman (2008, 215) found that in using knowledge of individual food preferences to develop and use lists for grocery shopping, "family members are involved in creating 'home.'" As Crewe (2011, 30) observes: "Lists narrate practice and desire ... For the list, this seemingly most humble and transitory fragment holds clues about objects and possessions, about love and loss, about meaning and memory." Lists, calendars, and notes "tell us more than we might imagine about ourselves, our connections to objects, and our social relations with others" (2011, 44).

In analyzing the meanings and transformations of these texts for the reader over time, we draw on Miller's (1994) conception of genre as social action. Miller advocated an ethnomethodological classification of genre, based on rhetorical practice and organized around situated actions. When we consider the development, reading, and writing of texts over time, it is evident that the genre initially written is not necessarily the same as the genre read. The passage of time renders the prospective retrospective. What was written as fact may be reread as historical fiction, and what was written as a plan may be read as a log. Miller argued for a focus on genre as a rhetorical means of connecting private intentions and public requirements: for connecting Burgess and Ivanič's (2010) "perceived writer" and reader's autobiographical self with socially available possibilities for selfhood. Although lists, calendars, and notes may ostensibly be created for instrumental purposes, we show the ways in which our participants also experienced the reading of these texts over time as a reading of their own identities.

Our analysis draws from interviews with ten participants living in two Canadian provinces, and from observation and photographs of the documents and other tools they used in their households for keeping track (McKenzie, Davies, and Wong 2010). Data collection for our larger study is ongoing. We selected our first ten participants (eight women and two men) purposively to represent a wide variety of household situations (living alone, with partner and/or children, in a university residence with other students), work characteristics (home-based businesses, work that requires travel, shiftwork), and the multiple roles they occupied in their paid and unpaid work (elite athlete, hairdresser, editor, labour activist, musician, producer, salesperson, student, teacher, writer, volunteer, manager of a chronic illness, full-time caregiver).

Our data set consists of over twelve hours of interviews, 330 photographs, and 500 pages of interview transcripts.[1] Data analysis for this study began with the identification of 143 passages of participants' talk about reading texts they had written for themselves. Nine of our ten participants mentioned all three kinds of texts (i.e., calendars, notes, and lists); the tenth mentioned calendars and notes but not lists.

Data analysis itself involved multiple rereadings, using the principles of open coding and constant comparison (Strauss and Corbin 1990). We read both within and across transcripts and attended to similarities and differences in (re)reading practices and to the metaphors (Ross 1987) participants used when talking about their writing and (re)reading of these texts. For this paper we have chosen examples that best illustrate the themes we identified.

Practices of (Re)reading

The interview transcripts[2] contain two kinds of rereading: one that took place in real time as respondents reread and discussed their texts with the interviewers, and the other that appeared in their retrospective accounts of how they have read and reread these texts over time. Our first excerpt is a performative rereading of the January page of a participant's calendar from an interview that took place in August.

> P: And then it just starts, you know, appointments, meetings, [brief hesitation] coyotes at seven-thirty ...
>
> I1: Climate change at seven-thirty. [I2 laughs in the background]
>
> P: Right. Ooh, I know what that was, that was the, uh, the, the Nature of [City Name] series that they do at the library downtown ...
>
> I1: Okay, and so, then, climate change is probably the same thing ...
>
> P: ... so they'll be, yeah, they'll be a couple of, yeah, [local river name] chickadees, [local] Woods, see, it all comes together.
>
> I2: [laughing] Coyotes ... [Everyone starts laughing]
>
> I1: [laughing] Coyotes and climate change.
>
> P: That was like, "What the hell?" [laughing]
>
> I2: Do they come at seven-thirty?
>
> P: They do! Seven-thirty sharp [howls like a coyote, I1 and I2 laughing].

The participant's hesitation over the unusual calendar entry indicates both a lack of recognition ("That was like, 'What the hell?'") and an effort to remember ("Ooh, I know what that was"), and a sense of obligation to demystify the calendar for the interviewers. The fact that participants were performing rereadings for us became evident when they reread and reframed their documents explicitly as research evidence:

> P: I haven't been flipping through this too much to kind find you guys some better examples ... um ...I'm trying to [flips through schedule book] ...

Although our participants were the primary authors of the texts they described, many of their calendars and notebooks existed prior to and independent of their own writing. These blank tools had particular affordances and embedded slots for the intended reader/writer.[3] Calendars structure time in particular ways, and the size of the lines and squares constrains what the user may write; they also contain images with potential meaning to users (Zalot 2001).

Our participants provided some readings of the blank documents that identified both the affordances of the tools for reading and writing, and the ways that the images and text that accompanied the tool were personally meaningful. One participant explained how a calendar reflected and supported a particular political position:

> P: And it's a good, it's a social justice calendar.
> I: Ohhh, so it's …
> P: It's got all kinds of history of union and social justice events, and
> I: [inaudible]
> P: It's good, eh?
> I: Yeah. OK.
> P: Not that I've memorized it all or anything.

Although this participant could not claim to know all of the information presented in the calendar, the fact that she could present herself as the owner and user of such a document was clearly important to the identity she chose to present to us.

As they described writing in their calendars, lists, and notes, participants attended to their future selves as readers. A musician with complex scheduling considerations explained the use of pencil rather than pen to facilitate future reading and editing:

> I: Okay, now you just said "pencilled in" and I noticed that this is literally pencilled in. This is not … you don't write in pen.
> P: Because it's all subject to change.
> I: Aha!
> P: [...] Sometimes concerts get cancelled. So let's say they don't sell enough tickets. It hasn't happened with these groups but um … it's happened in the past. Like, or if someone … a few people get sick, like "sorry, the show's cancelled" [...]
> I: Yeah.
> P: Um … so, I kind of … yeah, that's why I use pencil; just in case I need to erase it and let's say someone else calls me, or then I can just maybe do a few makeup lessons with students that I missed…
> I: Yeah.
> P: … like a couple weeks earlier. So that lets me at least manage it a little bit better.

Participants also described using codes, abbreviations, symbols, or shorthand that would be accessible to them as future readers, but not necessarily to others:

> P: So they're just kind of written in my own … random shorthand. That's the date. What it is. Yeah, that makes perfect sense to me but it might not sense to …

Because they were skilled readers of these documents they themselves had written, participants talked about their decisions to leave details out of their texts and their ability to read these absences:

> P: So, then I'll have things like, um ... I had a lunch with [colleague] on Thursday. I don't have my work in there because it's just a given. Um ...
>
> I: So there are a lot of things that are a given in your calendars.
>
> P: Yes, 'cause I do work Thursdays, so they're just a given, they're just understood.

Another participant, who worked variable shifts while her partner worked more regular hours, explained that she had recorded her hours in the calendar; her partner had not, and the absence of his work hours warranted no explanation:

> P: So you can see, work, you know, work schedule ... in there.
>
> I: Okay. So, your wor – The work schedule bit, is you ... the-these little, like 2:30, 9:30 ... 5:30, 12:30 things?
>
> P: Yeah ... 5:30, yeah.

Tools like lists developed meaning over time as participants took them up in different ways. A rereading of a text was commonly a step in rewriting or revising that text, and participants described revising to-do lists over time as they added or deleted items. (Re)reading one document also contributed to the creation and revision of other documents. A common example of documents paired in this way was the meal plan and the shopping list:

> P: I like flipping through the magazines or my cookbooks and figuring it out, and then I write my little lists of possible meals for the week, and then I write my grocery shopping list to what I want to make plus whatever regular stuff we end up with [...]
>
> I: So you've got your list of potential menus and I see your recipe for the sweet potatoes that you're going to have tonight ...
>
> P: Yep. All the recipes for whatever, like if I'm using any recipes, get stacked behind the meal list. So, presumably, if I was busy [at work] and [partner] was gonna cook and he's going "So what am I making?" I can say, "Well pick something off the thing [ie, meal plan] and all the books are behind it" [...] These are all fully compatible meals that could happen [laughs]. So there's not going to be a "but we don't have this [ingredient]!"

Genre transformations happened in a number of ways. Texts not initially created by the reader could be transformed by his or her inscription into personalized records. For example, writing a payment confirmation number onto a bill transformed it from an actionable invoice into something that would hereafter be read as a personally authored record of payment:

> P: Often what I'll do is I'll write the little number or I'll write on the bill the day I paid it, from what account, and the number, and also I'll print off the thing and staple it, so I can go back and say, "Hey, you know what, no, I paid this bill, on this date, from this account" or whatever.
>
> I: Yeah.
>
> P: Again, it's just to double-check so you can go back and look at the history.

A participant reread a plan as a work of historical fiction:

> I: And are there things that you do with [baby] during the week that are regular things?
>
> P: Uh, yeah. It's actually on here [moves over to chalkboard mounted on kitchen wall] … what is it, um … Tuesdays, but I didn't go today cause we had to go to the produce farm anyway …
>
> I: Okay
>
> P: Um … for my sister in law. And Friday … [name written on board] is actually like kind of a hippie momma center here in town
>
> I: Oh, okay!
>
> P: And so, I put it on there, and I don't always go both times and some weeks I don't go at all, but I keep it on there because that's something I do with [baby].

As did the actors in Davies's (2007, 2008) study, our participants described occasions when they went "off-book" – memorizing the relevant contents of a document to such an extent that a physical rereading was no longer necessary. Several participants described the act of writing itself as a memory aid:

> P: Often, since I did write it down I'll remember anyways.
>
> P: So. I kind of, often I put stuff in there [phone] and I don't need to check it ever again, just the … the same as writing things down … just the act of having made it exist somewhere will stick it in my brain enough that I'll remember it. But … I like to refer back.
>
> P: If things are far out [in time] I have a day planner
>
> I: Yeah.
>
> P: I write them in there. But I tend to remember.

Metaphors of (Re)reading

In describing their (re)reading to us, participants used a number of metaphors (Ross 1987). The most common treated the texts as though they were a faithful and transparent representation of reality (Law and Lynch 1988). These descriptions rendered the processes of writing and reading completely invisible. Participants described reading as

a) **seeing and knowing "what's happening":**

   P: Currently it has my work schedule on it, but it also has events, birthdays, if we're going out, stuff like that, which day is it compost out or recycling out, kind of like, all the stuff that is day-to-day stuff that has to happen every day shows up there [...] So I can see, well I've got clients, like this is blah blah blah, this is what's happening.

b) **remembering:**

   P: There's a little list on the side here of ... food that's in the freezer.
   I: Oh! What's that for? Well ...
   P: Just to remember what food is in the freezer.

c) **prioritizing:**

   Participants represented an item's position on a physical to-do list as equivalent to its priority in their lives and its placement on a calendar as parallel to its temporal and spatial location. Moving a word up or down on a list or to another square on a calendar was taken as equivalent to changing the priority for a task or the date and time for an event.

   P: I have my list of priorities and some things at the top of the list, um, then it gets my attention, and I can have, I can have people email me and say, well, why are, you know, ask me, why are you not responding and blah-blah-blah. Until I move it up to the top, I can pretty much just, you know, because, I just can't do it.

   I: Has your system ever failed you? Have you sort of missed something or forgotten a lesson or ...?

   P: Yeah. I mean a couple times I might have accidentally moved two [clients] at the same time, because the arrow went to the wrong spot.

d) **fulfilling an obligation, attending an event, or completing a task:**

   Destroying a to-do list was often presented as evidence that the list had been fulfilled. Accounts posited a direct relationship between the text and the world.

   P: I know that things have to get done and will get done, they need to be written down. Especially very, very small things. You know, they have to be written down [...] I will write down "vacuum" so

> that on a Saturday, if I'm at home or whatever, the damn vacuuming gets done.
>
> P: I should add [at work], particularly for things that require an action, like phoning a [client], photocopying some specific things, things to twig myself, um, I will use sticky notes at work ...
>
> I: Okay.
>
> P: ... on my desk, yeah. And then when I've finished a task, then I get rid of the ...
>
> I: ... sticky ...
>
> P: ... the sticky note, yeah.

Although these were common representations, participants did acknowledge texts as negotiated and rereadings as contingent:

> P: We're re-negotiating our mortgage right now so we were talking about interest rates and I had to make a sticky to look at interest rates. [laughs]
>
> I: Yeah, yeah.
>
> P: Umm, and we had to email our mortgage broker, so I had to make a sticky about that. Umm. We, we do stickies all the time.
>
> I: Yeah!
>
> P: Umm, and then as soon as I have to destroy it because I don't know if I've done it or not.
>
> I: Okay. And it, and you've crossed it out? And you've put a checkmark.
>
> P: Meaning I did it. Right.
>
> I: Okay. So, is that typical that you write something and then cross it out when it's done?
>
> P: Yeah, umm ... yeah. So ... I've done most of my physics homework. I did my German homework [quieter] for once.
>
> I: Okay.
>
> P2: I ... yeah. [flips through planner] Yeah, mostly, like, a lot of times I cross out, but if it's the *last* thing I need to do I don't often go back and cross it out.

Reading, Writing, and Identity

Other descriptions and performances of rereading showed that the rereading and writing of participant-authored texts were tightly bound up with the reading of the participants' identities. Several participants described attitudes towards reading and writing as fundamental elements of their own identities:

P: I'm a very like, written reminder sort of person.

P: I like the satisfaction of crossing something out.

I: Okay, so you're a crosser offer.

P: So that might be part of the motivation for the system.

I: So, it's a reward, essentially.

P: There's absolute ... there's satisfaction in it. To go "It is done."

P: I've been a list maker forever. Probably started when I was in school, and my mother was a list maker, too.

One question we asked all of our participants was whether their systems for keeping track had ever failed them. When describing failures, either in response to this question or spontaneously, participants represented their (re)reading and writing practices as accountable to themselves, to members of their households and workplaces, to formal organizations, and to assumptions that we as researchers might make about the socially available possibilities for identity. Although participants attributed some system failures to their failure to write something down properly, they also attributed failures to their failure to read either at all or in a particular way. An account of rereading therefore became an account of personal success or failure, and the text, regardless of its genre at the time of creation, became a performance evaluation.

P: And then I will use scraps of paper too. I have one here from before you came and I threw it out [opens drawer] which I should keep out because it still has stuff [laughs] that has to be done.

I: You haven't done it but you threw out the little piece of paper?

P: Yes I just threw it out to make myself feel good I guess. Yes. [laughs] [...]

I: Okay.

P: And then, so that eventually should go on – See really, it should go on here.

I: Onto your calendar on your computer.

P: Yeah.

I: Okay.

P: Sometimes I'm hopeful. I think "Well, I'll do it right away it doesn't have to be on the list" but ... And then, um ... [laughing] This is really making me feel like a failure.

P: Sometimes I ... forget about the note. Forget to do something. Forget to bring a note to remember to do it.

I: Yeah.

P: So, ummm ... Yeah. [pause] But ... [tsk noise] ... Or I just forget to write the note in the first place.

P: I actually showed up the wrong day one time.

I: Okay.

P: Because I put it in my day timer on the wrong day. [laughs]

I: Okay. Okay.

P: So it was right on the card. I just put it in my day timer wrong.

I: Okay.

P: So, that was hugely embarrassing.

Reading Relationships

Finally, participants described their reading of their lists, notes, and calendars as rereadings of their intimate relationships. One participant described how notes she created with a roommate served as "motivation in the mirror every day" and as an ongoing reflection of a supportive relationship.

I1: Let's go see ... Let's go see the bathroom mirror ... [All enter the bathroom, where mirror is covered with colourful sticky notes all along the frame with inspirational quotes and affirmations.]

P: We were feeling really down with exams.

I1: Ohhhh! Oh, this is so cute!

P: So, my roommate and I, like ... Originally all these were handwritten, but my roommate got really bored one day and typed them all out.

I1: Yeah.

P: Most of them ... I added some, but [I1 & I2 read the various notes.] Yeah ... Yeah, we had lots of fun with that.

I2: That's awesome.

P: I started with a couple and, I'm like, "We've gotta cheer up."

I1: Oh yeah.

P: So, now I can see my motivation in the mirror every day.

I1: That's – So –

P: Oh! I'm looking at ... "If you try, you might get exactly what you want. If you don't, you don't." Okay. So I'll try! I'll try today!

Another participant spoke directly of the storytelling potential of calendars from years past. While this participant described being able to re-create instrumental information from other sources, it was the experiential and relational information, the story of the family itself, that a rereading of the calendar afforded.

I: So how, how far back would you, like, have you ever felt that since you, since you get rid of a current calendar at the end of a year, if you've ever found yourself going back and saying, "Oh, damn, I threw out that calendar, when I had my last dentist appointment, and I can't remember how long it's been, or ..."

P: No, it's more, more sort of personal stuff, like, oh, I wonder when it was, like, you know, what year did we rent the cottage at such-and-such a place?

I: Yeah, okay.

P: Or, you know, what year did we go to, you know, and this is the sort of thing my mother would keep track of, where we went for Christmas every year, this sort of stuff, and, that's the sort of stuff that, me, because I can't remember things, you know, you start to – I mean, photographs help, of course, yeah, it's more that sort of ...

I: Okay.

P: Because I know I can *call* a dentist and say, when was my last, or hair appointment or the doctor or whatever, and theoretically, *they* keep track of things for me! [laughs] So, yeah, it's more sort of, it's more sort of those personal kind of storytelling things ...

Our analysis shows that the paired concepts we identified in our introduction: past and future, reading for mastery and reading to re-experience emotion, text and identity, are all deeply intertwined in the act of rereading. Our participants reread both for mastery (of the text and of the items on their lists and tasks on their calendars) and to recapture emotional response. They also experienced their mastery (or not) of the texts as a reflection of their identities.

Genres displayed fluidity over time as texts evolved from prospective to retrospective, from speculative fiction to historical fiction, from plan to evaluation. Texts written with instrumental goals, such as a calendar documenting when and where to get on an airplane, were transformed over time into emotionally rich stories of one's own past and the past of one's nearest and dearest.

In these actionable texts, writing is future-oriented and rereading is largely oriented towards the past. However, rereading is also future-oriented when it contributes to rewriting, through the revision of existing texts – for example, by adding items to or crossing them off a list, and by the creation of new and related texts, such as shopping lists to accompany menu plans. Writing of these texts was hopeful, determined, or optimistic, whereas rereading was associated with a wider variety of responses: bemused, nostalgic, critical.

Participants used a variety of metaphors to describe their (re)reading, but by far the most common metaphors collapsed the textual forms into the reader's actual experiences, rendering the acts of reading and writing invisible. In these descriptions, the text became a faithful representation of their identities. Our participants read themselves as the "perceived writer" in and through the text, and made the link between the perceived writer and the autobiographical self of the reader. These readings of themselves drew from the past in referring to socially available possibilities for selfhood, but extended into the future as they used their text/identity relationship to predict their own futures.

Finally, although we began our analysis by distinguishing between performative and descriptive rereading, it is important to acknowledge that both kinds of rereadings are in fact narrations of the past and present self to another audience: the researcher. The performative nature of rereading in the research interview means that these very personal documents become both available and accountable to someone else. The acts of performing and describing rereading therefore became in a very vivid way acts of performing the reader's identity.

Notes

This study was funded by the Social Sciences and Humanities Research Council of Canada.

1 Data collection and analysis conform to ethical guidelines on research on human subjects of the Social Sciences and Humanities Research Council of Canada (Canadian Institutes of Health Research et al. 2010). To maintain confidentiality, we identify participants by a generic initial.
2 Transcription conventions:
   I: Conversational turns are prefaced by an initial identifying the speaker (Participant, Interviewer), and a colon.
   //   Marks overlapping talk.
   (( )) Inaudible.
   []   Nonverbal elements such as laughter, physical gestures, changes in tone, or to indicate the removal or identifying details or the editing of the excerpt.
   ? !   Punctuation indicates both grammatical sentence-ends and emphatic or interrogative intonation.
3 See Coyle and Grodin 1993; Law and Lynch 1998; and McKenzie and Davies 2010 and 2012 for the ways that other kinds of texts position their readers in time – as novices in need of instruction to learn socially accepted ways of reading and of seeing and being.

References

Bakhtin, Mikhail M. 1981. *The Dialogic Imagination: Four Essays*. Austin: University of Texas Press.

Bassett, Raewyn, Brenda Beagan, and Gwen E. Chapman. 2008. "Grocery Lists: Connecting Family, Household, and Grocery Store." *British Food Journal* 110(3): 206–17.

Birkerts, Sven. 1998. "Some Thoughts on Rereading." In *Second Thoughts: A Focus on Rereading*, edited by David Galef, 340–43. Detroit: Wayne State University Press.

Block, Lauren G., and Vicki G. Morwitz. 1999. "Shopping Lists as an External Memory Aid for Grocery Shopping: Influences on List Writing and List Fulfilment." *Journal of Consumer Psychology* 8(4): 343–73.

Burgess, Amy, and Roz Ivanič. 2010. "Writing and Being Written: Issues of Identity across Timescales." *Written Communication* 27(2): 228–55.

Calinescu, Matei. 1993. *Rereading*. New Haven: Yale University Press.

———. 1998. "Orality in Literacy: Some Historical Paradoxes of Reading and Rereading." In *Second Thoughts: A Focus on Rereading*, edited by David Galef, 51–74. Detroit: Wayne State University Press.

Canadian Institutes of Health Research, Natural Sciences and Engineering Research Council of Canada and Social Sciences and Humanities Research Council of Canada. 2010. *Tri-Council Policy Statement: Ethical Conduct for Research Involving Humans*.

Coyle, Kelly, and Deborah Grodin. 1993. "Self-Help Books and the Construction of Reading: Readers and Reading in Textual Representation." *Text and Performance Quarterly* 13(1): 61–78.

Crewe, Louise. 2011. "Life Itemised: Lists, Loss, Unexpected Significance, and the Enduring Geographies of Discard." *Environment and Planning D: Society and Space* 29(1): 27–46.

Davies, Elisabeth. 2007. "Epistemic Practices of Theatre Production Professionals: An Activity Theory Approach." PhD diss., University of Western Ontario.

———. 2008. "The Script as Mediating Artifact in Professional Theater Production." *Archival Science* 8(3): 181–98.

Galef, David. 1998. "Observations on Rereading." In *Second Thoughts: A Focus on Rereading*, edited by David Galef, 17–33. Detroit: Wayne State University Press.

Iser, Wolfgang. 1994. "Interaction between Text and Reader." In *Readers and Reading*, edited by Andrew Bennett, 20–31. New York: Longman.

Law, John, and Michael Lynch. 1988. "Lists, Field Guides, and the Descriptive Organization of Seeing: Birdwatching as an Exemplary Observational Activity." In *Representation in Scientific Practice*, edited by Michael Lynch and Steve Woolgar, 267–99. Cambridge, MA: MIT Press.

Lesser, Wendy. 2002. *Nothing Remains the Same: Rereading and Remembering*. Boston: Houghton Mifflin.

Marshall, Catherine C. 2007. "How People Manage Personal Information over a Lifetime." In *Personal Information Management*, edited by William Jones and Jaime Teevan, 57–75. Seattle: University of Washington Press.

McKenzie, Pamela J., and Elisabeth Davies. 2010. "Documentary Tools in Everyday Life: The Wedding Planner." *Journal of Documentation* 66(6): 788–806.

———. 2012. "Genre Systems and 'Keeping Track' in Everyday Life." *Archival Science* 12(4): 437–60.

McKenzie, Pamela J., Elisabeth Davies, and Lola Wong. 2012. "Methodological Strategies for Studying Documentary Planning Work." In *Information Science:*

Synergy through Diversity: Proceedings of the Annual Conference of the Canadian Association for Information Science Conference, edited by Elaine Ménard, Valerie Nesset, and Sabine Mas. http://www.cais-acsi.ca/ojs/index.php/cais/article/view/387/119

Miller, Carolyn R. 1994. "Genre as Social Action." In *Genre and the New Rhetoric*, edited by Aviva Freedman and Peter Medway, 23–42. New York: Taylor and Francis.

Payne, Stephen J. 1993. "Understanding Calendar Use." *Human–Computer Interaction* 8(2): 83–100.

Ross, Catherine. 1987. "Metaphors of Reading." *Journal of Library History* 22(2): 147–63.

Spacks, Patricia Meyer. 2011. *On Rereading*. Cambridge, MA: Belknap Press of Harvard University Press.

Strauss, Anselm, and Juliet Corbin. 1990. *Basics of Qualitative Research: Grounded Theory Procedures and Techniques*. Newbury Park: Sage.

Whittaker, Steve. 2011. "Personal Information Management: From Information Consumption to Curation." In *Annual Review of Information Science and Technology*, edited by Blaise Cronin, vol. 45. Medford: Information Today.

Zalot, Michael. 2001."Wall Calendars: Structured Time, Mundane Memories, and Disposable Images." *Journal of Mundane Behavior* 2(3): 379–91.

More Benefit from a Well-Stocked Library Than a Well-Stocked Pharmacy

11

How Do Readers Use Books as Therapy?

Liz Brewster

Bibliotherapy is a psychosocial or psycho-educational intervention for mental health problems, centred on the use of reading to provide insight. Here, the aim is to examine the use of bibliotherapy for mental health and well-being, taking a reflexive approach to conceptualize bibliotherapy and therapeutic reading. I present findings from a doctoral study that analyzed and contrasted current bibliotherapy service provision in the UK with individual reading experiences. Of primary importance in this wider project was the finding that current models of bibliotherapy do not meet all the needs of people with mental health problems; thus, there is a gap between current service provision and reading experiences (Brewster 2013).

Readers who considered their experience to be "bibliotherapy" understood the concept differently when compared with the perspective of those providing bibliotherapy services. Service providers were often more focused on the type of text used, while readers were concerned about the outcome of the intervention. For readers, outcomes of the reading experience included emotional engagement, distraction and escapism, social support, and locating useful information to help them cope. Using data gathered from interviews and observations, the focus in this chapter is on the experiences of readers, who shared their personal, diverse understandings of bibliotherapy. The findings about current service provision and policy analysis are reported elsewhere; they conclude that the evidence-based practice discourse has previously legitimized the exclusion of the readers' voices in understandings of bibliotherapy (Brewster, Sen, and Cox 2012). Evidence of the effectiveness of bibliotherapy as an intervention is also presented elsewhere (Brewster 2011).

Bibliotherapy schemes like *Books on Prescription*, *Get into Reading*, and the *Reading and You Service (RAYS)* have operated in British public libraries since 2000, but there has been little evaluation of their impact and effectiveness (Frude 2005; Duffy et al. 2009; Davis et al. 2005).[1] More recent studies have started to add to the body of work exploring the experience of reading to maintain or improve mental health (Billington et al. 2010; Dowrick et al. 2012). The need to explore the experience of reading for well-being was identified following a study exploring the implementation of bibliotherapy schemes in British public libraries, in which librarians shared a wider problem with the evaluation of bibliotherapy schemes (Brewster 2007). Public library staff commented that in-depth evaluation of these cost-effective schemes was too expensive to conduct and that the "soft outcomes" of improved mental health were difficult to measure (Brewster 2007). Thus, while they had anecdotal evidence of the effectiveness of bibliotherapy, it was considered too sensitive to ask readers what they felt and experienced while reading. Public librarians found that while it is easy to measure how many books were being borrowed from the public library, it was not easy to understand what these books meant to people. Thus, if twenty people borrowed a book called *Overcoming Depression* as part of a *Books on Prescription* scheme, there was no way to measure how many of them actually improved their mental health because of it and what they thought of the experience. As Markless and Streatfield note, "no amount of monitoring of book loans will tell you whether the items borrowed were actually read, let alone whether the targeted users were in any way affected by what they read" (2006, 22).

Thus, the aim in this chapter is to provide the in-depth reader-led perspective missing from current research and practice: *How do people with mental health problems use reading as therapy, both in formal bibliotherapy schemes and independent of these schemes?* Following extensive qualitative research, I outline at four new user-centred models of bibliotherapy – emotive, escapist, social, and informational – that explore motivations for using reading as a therapy or coping mechanism.

Theorizing Reading as Therapy

Significant research has been conducted on Reader Response Theory, with implications for therapeutic interaction with literature. Such research does not engage with concepts of mental health and well-being directly; it does, however, present a useful theoretical framework. Several key concepts have been identified, including the positioning of the reader as the creator of meaning in the text, rather than the author (Rosenblatt [1938]1970). Reading is seen as a process of exploration; literature increases comprehension and understanding (Rosenblatt [1938]1970). The perspective of the reader is paramount, in that readers interpret texts in the context of their personal experiences. Interaction with the text is always a "transaction" in which the reader approaches the text from his or her own personal standpoint (Rosenblatt

[1938]1970). Reading is seen as an active phenomenon, not a passive one, and literature is the "process, not [the] product" (Atkinson and Coffey 1997; Leitch 1995). The exchange between the text and the reader relies on the biography of the reader as much as on the content of the text (Atkinson and Coffey 1997). For these reasons, reading the same text at different times in life may encourage a reinterpretation of the content (Rosenblatt [1938]1970). These principles underpin the understanding of reading that is presented here.

Emotive Bibliotherapy

Literature has been theorized as having four conceptual effects on the reader: identification, projection, catharsis (or abreaction), and insight (Shrodes 1949). Shrodes's work was influential in initial explorations of the psychological impact of literature, and her work has contributed to modern models of bibliotherapy in practice. More recent research, again not engaging with concepts of mental health, has established that in literature, readers find confirmation of thoughts and beliefs; reassurance; comfort; and acceptance of their views (Cohen 1992; Usherwood and Toyne 2002). Readers feel a connection between their experiences and those of characters in books, and this creates a sense of connection that validates their emotions (Usherwood and Toyne 2002). Thus, "reading imaginative literature is regarded as a special activity which serves to satisfy a wide variety of needs" (2002, 33). Ideas of reading serving a need summarize the perceived effects of emotive bibliotherapy.

Psychotherapeutic notions, such as catharsis, are also useful in exploring emotional engagement with literature (Gold 1990). Catharsis, an Aristotelian concept, contains notions of emotional expression, suspense, and thrill seeking, which combine to produce an emotional reaction in the audience of a text (Scheff 1979). Catharsis is regarded as a form of clarification of emotions and can be seen as a technique for resolving earlier painful experiences (Oatley 1995; Scheff 1979). Those experiencing the resolution of emotional trauma via catharsis may find that the vicarious experience (i.e., reading) may not be as overwhelming; reading literature or watching a play can bring a distance to remembered experience that enables the reader/audience to process their feelings (Scheff 1979). Catharsis is thus a significant concept in the use of reading as emotive bibliotherapy.

Escapist Bibliotherapy

Many pejorative judgments have been made about reading and literature; in particular, the concept of escapism, with its connections to fantasy and avoiding responsibility, has been seen in a negative light (Nell 1988). Escapism is connected to other qualities ascribed to literature, including absorption in or entrancement by a story – the idea of being *wrapped up* in what you are reading. Such qualities are viewed more positively (Nell 1988). Moving forward from the negative connotations of escapism, Usherwood and Toyne (2002) emphasize that reading is "more than merely a denial or retreat"; they see it as emancipatory, making a contribution to knowledge and coping techniques. Escapist bibliotherapy has not been widely theorized or discussed in the academic literature, though it is sure to be familiar to many readers.

Social Bibliotherapy

Reading has long been a social practice; the idea of individual reading emerged late in the eighteenth century (Manguel 1996). The recent popularity of discussing literature in book clubs shows that there is still a desire for reading in a social environment (Hartley 2002; Jacobsohn 1998).[2] There is some commonality in responses to literature, explained in part by Fish's (1976) notion of the interpretive community, in which a basic customary response to a work of literature is adopted by the reader; the creative aim of the writer is also included within an interpretive community. Criticisms of Fish's (1976) interpretive communities include that they lack attention to wider socio-cultural factors and that members of the constructed community lose their sense of self and identity (Leitch 1995). Situating the reader's response to a text in a personal history and the socio-cultural environment has been a fundamental aspect of critical engagement with Reader Response Theory (Iser 1995; Leitch 1995). Research with thirty readers responding to the same short story found both individuality and "orderliness-within-diversity" in responses, suggesting some commonality of interpretation (Miall and Kuiken 2002). Discussion of dialogue and reading communities often encompasses the idea that reading and interpreting a text – particularly in a group situation – is "the full act," with the writing of a narrative as just "half an act" (Oatley 1999). The concept of shared reading forms the basis of one of the models of bibliotherapy discussed here – social bibliotherapy.

Recent evaluations of bibliotherapy schemes like *Get into Reading* and *RAYS* has focused on observations in the group environment (Billington et al. 2010; Dowrick et al. 2012). An exploratory study focused on the "non-specified" benefits of reading literature in a social setting, commenting that the interaction between literature and group members mirrored previously established theoretical interpretations (Hodge, Robinson, and Davis 2007; Oatley 1999). Such work begins to build on the work of theorists like Fish (1976), applying ideas of interpretative communities to conclude that the mix of literature, group facilitator, and group environment was essential to a successful therapeutic interaction, which focused on the "telling [of] a new story about oneself" (Billington et al. 2010).

Informational Bibliotherapy

Information that helps people cope can be found in many sources, from fiction to self-help texts specifically designed to help people manage their mental health problems. Research exploring information seeking in works of fiction, and notions of information encountering, emphasize the potential positive experience of finding information in unexpected places, such as literature (Ross 1999; Erdelez 1999). One reported outcome of avid reading is serendipitously finding information that can be used to improve a life situation (Ross 1999). These conclusions are supported by Usherwood and Toyne's (2002) work, which found that fiction books can be used for problem solving and information gathering. Readers in Cohen (1992), Ross (1999), and Usherwood and Toyne's (2002) research all reported finding new knowledge about the world via reading, which encouraged them to change their perspectives.

Research highlights that people with mental health problems may prefer non-pharmacological, self-help strategies such as bibliotherapy to more traditionally allocated care (Priest et al. 1996). For example, barriers to traditional care such as people feeling stigmatized by seeking treatment from health providers can be removed by self-help (Clarke et al. 2006). The use of books might thus be a less stigmatizing method of accessing therapy (Cuijpers 1997). A preference for independent self-improvement – the "do-it-yourself" option – has also been established (Clarke et al. 2006). The large number and varied subject matter of self-help books is indicative of high consumer demand for – and thus potential acceptability of – self-help (Mains and Scogin 2003). However, there is a need for the application of empirical evidence and clinical judgment when considering whether to recommend these many and diverse titles, which vary in quality quite dramatically.

Life Narratives and Mental Health

To explore the experience of reading as a form of supportive therapy for mental health problems, the most appropriate approach was a narrative one whose aim was to understand the personal perspectives of readers on reading in relation to their lives. There were a number of reasons for this approach, including previous academic work taking a quantitative focus; not wanting to make presumptions about people's personal understandings of mental health (which surveys have shown varies; see, e.g., Priest et al. 1996); and not wanting to undervalue symptoms and contextual factors. Mental health is often a disputed concept with biological, social, and psychological explanations; gathering in-depth, personal perspectives was seen as a priority in this study. Beliefs about what causes depression can affect what treatment people think is appropriate. The medicalization of mental health problems has been seen to "create a dichotomy between the individual's experience of distress and the wider social context that underpins it" (Shaw and Taplin 2007). A holistic approach, one that takes account of all of these diverse perspectives, is often accepted as an explanation by people who have been diagnosed with mental health problems, for it mirrors their personal understanding (Kangas 2001).

Personal narratives of depression acknowledge an accumulation of long-term factors, such as a difficult relationship with family members or a genetic predisposition to mental health problems, combined with a specific event, as the causal factors. Explanatory narratives are sense-making exercises, and their purpose is often linked more closely to a need for meaningful explanations than to factual accuracy (Bentall 2009). People often engage pragmatically with various medical and non-medical discourses. Broom (2009, 1053) has observed that there is "a process of bricolage" whereby people construct explanations as a process of sense-making to understand their own health and well-being.

An understanding of the need to quantify and measure in health care also forms an essential element of the justification for taking a narrative approach here (Mol 2002). The mental health diagnostic interview and use of quantified scales are valued in health care, but they are also criticized for discounting contextual factors affecting mental health (Pilgrim 2002). There is a contrast between the requirement to record symptoms and a need to be aware of the context:

> Once numbers are scribbled in the patient's file, they come to have an independent existence as "indicators," and possible errors of translation are no longer retrievable. Nor is the tone of voice (confident, hesitant, pleading). Thus some complexities are left out; but something is also gained as numbers are easy to handle. (Mol 2002, 221)

While standardized mental health scales enable doctors to diagnose and treat, they do not take into account life circumstances. Thus, the qualitative methods described below were used to gather in-depth data about the reading experience.

Using Qualitative Methods to Explore the Reading Experience

Exploring the personal experiences of using bibliotherapy to manage mental health problems provides a counterpoint to the quantitative, randomized, controlled trials that are already in existence. I used a qualitative set of methods based on ethnographic principles, with the aim of describing and interpreting the way people use bibliotherapy and their reasons for reading. From this emic framework, an in-depth study of readers' experiences could emerge.

Participants were recruited via bibliotherapy groups operating in British public libraries. Some participants volunteered after seeing posters in public libraries or advertisements in a mental health service user magazine. Twenty-seven semi-structured interviews with readers were conducted. Topics included participants' understandings of the term bibliotherapy; the books that they viewed as having a therapeutic influence; and events in their lives connected with specific titles. All interviews were audio recorded and fully transcribed.

Participant observation, an ethnographic technique for working closely with groups, was also conducted, using the observer-as-participant method (Adler and Adler 1994). Sixteen observations of seven different bibliotherapy groups in public libraries and community locations throughout Britain were conducted, allowing for interaction with sixty-seven group members. Observations were recorded in detailed field notes; to avoid adversely affecting group behaviour, it was decided not to record group sessions. To maintain the integrity of the data, interviews with facilitators and some group members were conducted to confirm the data gathered as part of the observation process. These interviews also confirmed that the presence of a participant observer had not had a noticeable effect on group interaction.

Observation notes and interview transcripts were imported into QSR NVivo software for analysis. Two main approaches to coding the interview and observational data were used: one holistic, and one thematic, both emerging from the data using the constant comparison method (Saldaña 2009; Charmaz 2006). A full description of the coding process and framework is available elsewhere (Brewster 2011).

Participants in five areas of Britain were recruited, leading to a diverse sample of readers with a range of ages, diagnoses, and ethnicities. Of the twenty-seven interview participants, fifteen were also members of bibliotherapy groups. There was an equal mix of male and female participants, with thirteen women and fourteen men. This is quite unusual in light of the demographics of mental health, in that more women than men are typically diagnosed with mental health problems, and studies often struggle to recruit men. The youngest participant interviewed was in her mid-twenties, the oldest in her mid-seventies. The majority of participants were in their forties and fifties. Most interview participants came from a white British background. Length of diagnosis varied: some participants regarded themselves as newly diagnosed (one to three months since diagnosis); others had longer-term problems (forty-plus years). Reading habits and non-therapeutic reading experience were also wide-ranging.

Exploring the Reading-as-Therapy Experience

Bibliotherapy was understood differently by readers and library and mental health professionals. Themes emerging from the analysis of readers' experiences centred on their interaction with the texts either alone or in a group environment. Data from interviews and observations has generated four user-centred models of bibliotherapy: emotive, escapist, informational, and social. To summarize these models, bibliotherapy was variously understood as:

- an individual emotional connection with a work of imaginative literature;
- the use of reading as a distraction or the reading of escapist literature to help manage mental health problems;
- the social discussion of texts in a group environment;
- a quest for self-education and understanding about mental health problems.

Readers were asked to define bibliotherapy. All who provided a definition were very clear that therapeutic effect could be found in any text that a person found useful when experiencing distress; their definitions were not limited to a specific therapeutic approach such as cognitive behavioural therapy (CBT).

> It's in the eye of the beholder … my understanding of it is using books, short stories, either on your own or with the help of a therapist, to gain some insight into your mental, emotional state. Maybe get some inspiration, motivation, therapy from the actual use of the books themselves. (Winston)

The breadth and depth of titles read was immense. Therapeutic books were not limited in terms of type, genre, length, or subject. While one might expect some correlation regarding specific titles that readers found helpful, the diversity of books read produced a list of over two hundred titles (Brewster 2011). Readers also found that they read different types of book at different points in their lives and that having access to a variety of titles was important.

Over the years, the underlying support and help has actually come much more from books than medication. I think I've had much more benefit from a well-stocked library than a well-stocked pharmacy. (Winston)

Emotive Bibliotherapy

Emotive bibliotherapy contributed to the reading experience by allowing people to connect with literature. Emotional engagement with literature was valuable to many participants: eight of the twenty-seven interviewees mentioned an individual emotional connection to a text. There were three strands to this engagement: the use of literature for catharsis; empathy with characters' experiences; and emotional validation. As discussed, catharsis is widely recognized as the use of literature, art, theatre, or music to provide relief through learning about difficult subjects.

> A friend told me that after her mum died, she read an awful lot of literature which revolved around the death, as a way of processing it. (Olivia)

"Processing" emotions using literary depictions is at the heart of the concept of catharsis. Another participant (Julia) repeatedly returned to a text exploring the grief felt following the death of a child, thus presenting another example of using literature for cathartic purposes. She repeatedly reread the book in low periods; she felt that reading about someone who had gone through a similar traumatic experience helped put her own loss into perspective.

The experience of mental health problems can be isolating and lonely; similarly, many participants reported that life-changing events such as bereavement or retirement had made them feel alone. Literature was used as a coping mechanism to deal with these difficult situations. Emotive bibliotherapy was a form of normalization, with people finding comfort in recognizing their emotions. Milly found solace in reading for this reason. "I think because they make you feel less alone in a way, that you feel that that's your experience there on the page."

Experiencing empathy in relation to characters' narratives and identifying their own emotions in the texts made participants feel less alone, besides legitimizing their own reactions to experiences. While most participants found their experiences represented in fiction, some also spoke of self-help literature providing this validation: "I'm not unique in feeling this way, because for there to be a book written about [anxiety], it's got to be fairly commonplace. So it's reassuring. It validates the way that I'm feeling" (Louis).

Vivienne, who had experienced depression following the suicide of her husband, spoke of the way that reading about people who had undergone similar experiences, albeit fictional ones, helped her cope with her own emotions and grief. "Because grief is a bit like a madness, you do kind of think – 'I'm going crazy.' In that time, it was a mood thing, it was a coping mechanism."

Vivienne felt that the power of literature to articulate inexpressible emotions was of immense value and helped her understand her own feelings. She discussed her recognition of feelings of grief and loss in indirectly related literature. When talking of *The Lovely Bones* by Alice Sebold, she commented: "you feel almost validated. The emotions and feelings you had ... that wasn't just me. It's there and it's real." She recognized the importance of reading about other's situations and reflecting on them in light of her own circumstances.

Escapist Bibliotherapy

Escapism is often seen negatively, but the emphasis here rests on the perceived therapeutic nature of the escape, which progresses beyond relaxation and relates to some participants' inability to engage with emotionally challenging texts when depressed. "When I have been in a very severe depressive state, I read children's books. Sometimes I just go [to the library] and look at the pictures" (Amelia).

Participants discussed escapist literature as a safe world. Ten of them mentioned the escapist capacities of literature, using terms like "otherworldliness," "a very safe world," and "to go on a little journey" to describe the way that literature distracted them from their mental health symptoms. Connor stated that "there's a sense of being able to enter into a world that's possibly different to the real world." Children's books, crime fiction, and popular narrative non-fiction titles (e.g., history, science) – texts identified by participants as having a strong narrative – were all mentioned as having a positive impact on mental health. Crime fiction performed an important role for some participants, providing escapism through its predictable outcome. The familiar outcomes of genre fiction, such as crime fiction, has previously been viewed as a positive reason for reading it (Ross 1995; 2009). The narrative conventions of crime fiction – the familiar journey from discovery of the crime to its solution – provide reassurance. "I read detective stories ... I think I wanted reassurance that there were boundaries. Despite the fact that somebody's been hideously murdered in the study, there is a safe boundary all around it and someone's going to come along and solve it" (Nathan).

Escapism could also be found in different settings in literature. Science fiction and fantasy were also popular forms of escapist reading. Winston mentioned Evelyn Waugh's *Brideshead Revisited* and P.G. Wodehouse's *Jeeves and Wooster* stories, both of which are set in the 1930s, as having a value in their distance from the modern world. Reading texts set in bygone eras was mentioned as escapist by several participants; this may be because these texts exemplify the disconnection from daily life and the perceived safety of other worlds.

Social Bibliotherapy

Social bibliotherapy was identified as a concept through attendance at bibliotherapy groups in public libraries. Fifteen of the participants interviewed were identified as using this form of bibliotherapy. Participants benefited from the combination of reading and social interaction. Isaac had suffered from a loss of confidence after a breakdown and saw joining a reading group as an opportunity to continue to address this, getting used to being with people and improving his state of mind. "You don't have to pretend to be anything you're not, everybody's got their own opinions. It has helped build my confidence back. It's just total relaxation, enjoyment" (Isaac).

Three interacting elements were identified as vital to the implementation of these groups – the group environment, the group facilitator, and the literature itself. Sharing views about reading was considered to be one of the most important aspects. "It gets me out, mixing with people who love reading like I do. And I like discussing it and listening to other people's opinions especially the poetry, because I think everybody finds different things in poetry" (Virginia).

Several different group models (e.g., literature read aloud, reading and writing poetry, novels taken away to read individually and then discussed) were used, and various kinds of books were read as part of the social bibliotherapy experience. The opportunity to read material that participants had not chosen, and might not otherwise have read, was one reason cited for enjoying the groups. The atmosphere created by the communal reading of the book meant that there was implicit encouragement to continue to read even if a person did not initially enjoy the book. The findings presented here are supported by work conducted separately but simultaneously that examined one bibliotherapy scheme in Liverpool (Dowrick et al. 2012). Social bibliotherapy also represented a change for many participants, who were not in the habit of reading outside the group environment. The shift from close reading of texts to discussion of wider experiences was common to all the bibliotherapy groups I attended and observed.

Informational Bibliotherapy

Seven participants mentioned using texts as part of an informational bibliotherapy experience. While some participants used traditional CBT-based bibliotherapy materials to benefit, others found texts from the anti-psychiatry movement, those on mindfulness, and autobiographical works written by other mental health service users to be useful.

Readers used bibliotherapy to provide themselves with information and as a form of self-help or access to psychotherapy. One participant, Serena, was very vocal on the importance of this use of bibliotherapy for her. Serena's self-education can be seen as having therapeutic benefit, besides providing information. She referred to her use of books as "a quest for knowledge and understanding," and she was very aware that self-education helped her understand and cope with her condition. "The thing I like about a lot of the books I've been reading is that they're fairly practical."

Another participant, Silas, felt that reading helped him see a variety of ways out of his depression. *"It's given me some insight into trying to get over my depression ... The more insight I can get into how I can sort of help myself, the better."*

Louis discussed self-help books as a "do-it-yourself" option, viewing improving one's mental health as something that could be achieved by following a step-by-step guide. "If you want to learn about playing an instrument, you can get a guide on that, so if you want to learn about tuning your mind up then why should that be any different?"

Defining the Reading-as-Therapy Experience

Readers identified four previously undefined types of bibliotherapy – emotive, escapist, social, and informational – that they found beneficial for treating their mental health problems or for helping them maintain good mental health. These user-centred models demonstrate that there are methods of engaging readers using bibliotherapy that are not currently used in professional practice. The four models indicate that some of the benefits of bibliotherapy have not been recognized and point to a need for changes in practice to harness them.

Bibliotherapy can be experienced individually or in a group; it can be focused on an empathetic response to a text or on information gathering and learning; it can be experienced via a personal connection to specific titles or through the process of escaping from day-to-day life into another world. Texts can be used to either confront or avoid difficult emotions; to provide comfort and familiarity; or to think about new perspectives and challenge existing thinking. Life circumstances as well as experiences of symptoms of mental health problems also affected people's choice of texts. Bibliotherapy was experienced on a very personal level, so that the outcome of an interaction between a person and a text was difficult to predict, given that people do not read texts *de novo*. Such interaction between reader and reading material is the key therapeutic component of bibliotherapy.

Understanding how people use reading to manage mental health problems contributes to a wider body of literature on the use of non-medical interventions for mental health, related to the use of self-help literature. It also contributes to debates about why people read, what motivates them to read, and the benefits of reading (Elkin, Train, and Denham 2003). People read because they enjoy reading, but also because it improves their mental health. Participants in this study used reading to access information and as a form of self-help-based psychotherapy, but they also found benefit relating to peer support in bibliotherapy groups, which contributed to the maintenance of mental health via shared reading.

A greater understanding of the ways that readers engage with and benefit from bibliotherapy could help people manage symptoms, understand experiences, and improve their well-being. Reading is an integral part of the participants' strategy for coping with mental health issues; it is used to manage difficult emotions and to experience catharsis, clarity, and empathy. It is not simply a leisure activity, as it can have wider benefits, including increasing self-understanding.

This study is an exploratory one aiming to investigate experiences, but it has highlighted that the meaning and aims of bibliotherapy are malleable, with those using bibliotherapy adapting it to meet their own needs. One finding of this research is that bibliotherapy produces a very personal connection between reader and book. While four outcome-based models of bibliotherapy were established, this was with a caveat that participants required and used different types of bibliotherapy throughout their lives.

A wide variety of texts can be used to elicit different therapeutic experiences, and participants located useful literature by various methods, including independent serendipitous discovery. Examining reading for health and well-being has helped identify the gaps in current understandings; an awareness of these gaps is essential to developing a better theoretical understanding of the processes of bibliotherapy. Previous literature has not explored the outcomes of undertaking bibliotherapy from a user perspective; this study has begun this process of exploration by showing that readers are finding diverse benefits in reading. Reading has the potential to provide solace and consolation in times of stress and to enable readers to find a supportive community that may help them to cope with mental health problems. The value of a well-stocked library and its impact on mental health cannot be underestimated.

Notes

1 Editors' note: See Steenberg in this volume for a report of studies of shared reading groups with clinical populations as practised within the Get into Reading program framework.
2 Editors' note: See Fuller and Rehberg Sedo in this volume.

References

Adler, Patricia A., and Peter Adler. 1994. "Observational Techniques." In *Handbook of Qualitative Research*, edited by Norman K. Denzin and Yvonna S. Lincoln, 377–91. London: Sage.
Atkinson, Paul, and Amanda Coffey. 1997. "Analysing Documentary Realities." In *Qualitative Research: Theory, Method, and Practice*, edited by David Silverman, 45–62. London: Sage.
Bentall, Richard P. 2009. *Doctoring the Mind: Is Our Current Treatment of Mental Illness Really Any Good?* London: Allen Lane.
Billington, Josie, Christopher Dowrick, Andrew Hamer, Jude Robinson, and Clare Williams. 2010. "An Investigation into the Therapeutic Benefits in Relation to Depression and Well-being." University of Liverpool and Liverpool Primary Care Trust. http://thereader.org.uk/get-into-reading/research
Brewster, Elizabeth. 2007. "'Medicine for the Soul': Bibliotherapy and the Public Library." MA thesis, Department of Information Studies, University of Sheffield. http://dagda.shef.ac.uk/dissertations/2006-07/External/Brewster_Elizabeth_MALib.pdf
———. 2011. "An Investigation of Experiences of Reading for Mental Health and Well-Being and Their Relation to Models of Bibliotherapy." PhD diss., University of Sheffield. http://etheses.whiterose.ac.uk/2006/
Brewster, Liz, Barbara Sen, and Andrew Cox. 2012. "Legitimising Bibliotherapy: Evidence Based Discourses in Healthcare." *Journal of Documentation* 68(2): 185–205.
Brewster, Liz, Barbara Sen, and Andrew Cox. 2013. "Mind the Gap: Do Librarians Understand Service User Perspectives on Bibliotherapy?" *Library Trends* 61(3): 569–86.
Broom, Alex. 2009. "Intuition, Subjectivity, and Le Bricoleur: Cancer Patients' Accounts of Negotiating a Plurality of Therapeutic Options." *Qualitative Health Research* 19(8): 1050–9.
Charmaz, Kathy C. 2006. *Constructing Grounded Theory: A Practical Guide through Qualitative Analysis*. London: Sage.
Clarke, Greg, Frances Lynch, Mark Spofford, and Lyn DeBar. 2006. "Trends Influencing Future Delivery of Mental Health Services in Large Healthcare Systems." *Clinical Psychology* 13(3): 287–92.
Cohen, Laura J. 1992. "Bibliotherapy: The Experience of Therapeutic Reading from the Perspective of the Adult Reader." PhD diss., University of New York.

Cuijpers, Pim. 1997. "Bibliotherapy in Unipolar Depression: A Meta-Analysis." *Journal of Behaviour Therapy and Expressive Psychiatry* 28(2): 139–47.
Davis, J., A. Macmillan, G. Mair, K McDonnell, and M. Weston. 2005. "Step into the World of Books: Final Report of the Get into Reading Project 2004–5." Liverpool: University of Liverpool. http://thereader.org.uk/get-into-reading/research
Dowrick, Christopher, Josie Billington, Jude Robinson, Andrew Hamer, and Clare Williams. 2012. "Get into Reading as an Intervention for Common Mental Health Problems: Exploring Catalysts for Change." *Medical Humanities* 38(1): 15–20.
Duffy, John, Jo Haslam, Lesley Holl, and Julie Walker. 2009. "Bibliotherapy Toolkit." Kirklees Council: Huddersfield. http://www.kirklees.gov.uk/community/libraries/bibliotherapy/bibliotherapy.shtml
Elkin, Judith, Briony Train, and Debbie Denham 2003. *Reading and Reader Development: The Pleasure of Reading*. London: Facet.
Erdelez, Sanda. 1999. "Information Encountering: It's More Than Just Bumping into Information." *Bulletin of the American Society for Information Science* 25(3). http://www.asis.org/Bulletin/Feb-99/erdelez.html
Fish, Stanley E. 1976. "Interpreting the Variorum." *Critical Inquiry* 2(3): 465–85.
Frude, Neil. 2005. "Prescription for a Good Read." *Healthcare Counselling and Pyschotherapy Journal* 5(1): 9–13.
Gold, Joseph. 1990. *Read for Your Life: Literature as a Life Support System*. Markham: Fitzhenry and Whiteside.
Hartley, Jenny. 2002. *The Reading Groups Book*. Oxford: Oxford University Press.
Hodge, S., J. Robinson, and P. Davis. 2007. "Reading between the Lines: The Experiences of Taking Part in a Community Reading Project." *Medical Humanities* 33(2): 100–4.
Iser, Wolfgang. 1995. "Interaction between Text and Reader." In *Readers and Reading*, edited by Andrew Bennett, 20–31. Harlow: Longman.
Jacobsohn, Rachel W. 1998. *The Reading Group Handbook: Everything You Need to Know to Start Your Own Book Club*. New York: Hyperion.
Kangas, Ilka. 2001. "Making Sense of Depression: Perceptions of Melancholia in Lay Narratives." *Health* 5(1): 76–92.
Leitch, Vincent B. 1995. "Reader-Response Criticism." In *Readers and Reading*, edited by Andrew Bennett, 32–65. Harlow: Longman.
Mains, Jennifer A., and Forrest R. Scogin. 2003. "The Effectiveness of Self-Administered Treatments: A Practice-Friendly Review of the Research." *Journal of Clinical Psychology* 59(2): 237–46.
Manguel, Alberto. 1996. *A History of Reading*. London: Flamingo.
Markless, Sharon, and David Streatfield. 2006. *Evaluating the Impact of Your Library*. London: Facet.
Miall, David S., and Don Kuiken. 2002. "A Feeling for Fiction: Becoming What We Behold." *Poetics* 30(4): 221–41.
Mol, Annemarie. 2002. "Cutting Surgeons, Walking Patients: Some Complexities Involved in Comparing." In *Complexities: Social Studies of Knowledge Practices*, edited by John Law and Annemarie Mol, 218–257. Durham: Duke University Press.
Nell, Victor. 1988. *Lost in a Book: The Psychology of Reading for Pleasure*. London: Yale University Press.

Oatley, Keith. 1995. "A Taxonomy of the Emotions of Literary Response and a Theory of Identification in Fictional Narrative." *Poetics* 23(1–2): 53–74.

———. 1999. "Meetings of Minds: Dialogue, Sympathy, and Identification, in Reading Fiction." *Poetics* 26 (5–6): 439–54.

Pilgrim, David. 2002. "The Biopsychosocial Model in Anglo-American Psychiatry: Past, Present, and Future?" *Journal of Mental Health* 11(6): 585–94.

Priest, R. G., C. Vize, A. Roberts, M. Roberts, and A. Tylee. 1996. "Lay People's Attitudes to Depression: Results of Opinion Poll for Defeat Depression Campaign Just before Its Launch." *British Medical Journal* 313(7061): 858–59.

Rosenblatt, Louise M. [1938]1970. *Literature as Exploration*. Reprint, London: Heinemann.

Ross, Catherine Sheldrick. 1995. "'If They Read Nancy Drew, So What?' Series Book Readers Talk Back." *Library and Information Science Research* 17(3): 201–36.

———. 1999. "Finding without Seeking: The Information Encounter in the Context of Reading for Pleasure." *Information Processing and Management* 35(6): 783–99.

———. 2009. "Reader on Top: Public Libraries, Pleasure Reading, and Models of Reading." *Library Trends* 57(4): 632–56.

Saldaña, Johnny. 2009. *The Coding Manual for Qualitative Researchers*. London: Sage.

Scheff, Thomas J. 1979. *Catharsis in Healing, Ritual, and Drama*. Berkeley: University of California Press.

Shaw, Ian, and Suw Taplin. 2007. "Happiness and Mental Health Policy: A Sociological Critique." *Journal of Mental Health* 16(3): 359–73.

Shrodes, Caroline. 1949. *Bibliotherapy: A Theoretical and Clinical-Experimental Study*. Berkeley: University of California Press.

Usherwood, Bob, and Jackie Toyne. 2002. "The Value and Impact of Reading Imaginative Literature." *Journal of Librarianship and Information Science* 34(1): 33–41.

Literary Reading as a Social Technology   12
An Exploratory Study on Shared Reading Groups

Mette Steenberg

This chapter presents an exploratory study on "shared reading" groups in clinical populations as practised within the *Get into Reading* program. Methodologically, the study is grounded in extensive fieldwork using participatory observation and involvement, as well as qualitative interviews. From this ethnographic approach I studied "shared reading" as a material practice that motivates and constrains social interactions. Through observations of reading sessions with psychotic and affective patients in both mental health and community settings, I describe how this practice comes to function as a *social technology*.

For the past ten years, the Reader Organization in the UK has practised a particular form of reading called "shared reading" within its Get into Reading (GiR) program. The program was developed not just to get more people reading, but also to get people reading more, so as to enhance their personal engagement in the reading experience. This is done through participation in weekly reading groups lasting for ninety minutes during which a literary text – often a short story or an extract from a novel, followed by a poem – is read aloud while a trained "shared reading" facilitator encourages participants to share responses and engage in open-ended reflections. Although GiR was not developed for therapeutic purposes, shared reading groups have demonstrated a solid "best practice" record of accomplishment.

Over the years, the program has accumulated an impressive number of positive evaluations within mental health settings. In 2007 the National Health Service (NHS) shortlisted GiR as the most innovative practice in mental health. Locally, the organization has a formal relationship with the Mersey Care NHS trust. Just the sheer number of groups served by this program testifies to the success of GiR as a successful intervention – there are more than 330 weekly reading groups in the Liverpool area alone. Approximately one-third of those are within mental health settings or aimed at people suffering from mental health problems in the community. The practice of shared reading seems to be particularly well-suited for people with mental health problems, as *in situ* reading allows for participation even in cases when reading and other demanding cognitive tasks have become inaccessible due to a reduced level of cognitive functioning whether as part of diagnosis or as an effect of medication (Robinson 2008). Preliminary research further suggests that shared reading represents a form of ecological remediation that strengthens the cognitive functioning level.

A recent study (Dowrick et al. 2012, 16) identified the following three factors as relevant to the therapeutic effects of shared reading: (1) the literary form and content, (2) facilitation, and (3) group processes along with the impact of the environment. A typical shared reading session is a ninety-minute session with "re-cap" period of ten minutes, followed by a "prose reading and discussion" for fifty to sixty minutes. In the course of reading, pauses are made. The first is usually eight to ten minutes into the reading session, to allow time for discussions "usually starting with issues, characters or situations contained in the material just read and often progressing to personal reflection and the sharing of opinions and experiences" (2012, 15). After the first pause, the facilitator encourages participants to read aloud. Prose reading is followed by "poetry reading and discussion" for twenty to thirty minutes (2012, 16).

Concerning literary form and content, Dowrick and his colleagues found that fiction "appeared to foster relaxation and calm," while "poetry encouraged focused concentration" (2012, 17). They explain the distinction between prose and poetry as a difference between a *fictional* mode afforded by a "continuous temporal sequence" that suspends the unfolding of real time where the "future takes care of itself," and a *poetic* mode that is "more exacting regarding levels of concentration and mental effort" (2012, 17). Thus they found that the latter "elicited more verbal expression of thinking, intensity of focus on individual words and meanings and, interestingly in light of increased difficulty, inclusiveness" (2012, 17). The article shows that though they work differently, "both literary forms allowed participants to discover new, and rediscover old or forgotten, modes of thought, feeling and experience" (2012, 17).

When it comes to facilitation, the research team observed how the facilitator, who was positioned as an experienced "expressive reader," was crucial both in making the literature come alive in the room and in modelling the range of potential adequate and appropriate literary responses (2012, 18).

The third factor for therapeutic success pointed out by Dowrick and his co-authors relates to group processes. Linguistic analysis of conversational patterns revealed that participants would engage in "reflective mirroring of one another's thoughts and speech habits" expressed through "verbatim or near-verbatim repetition of another participant's words" (2012, 18). The study documents that speakers also support one another through syntactic and prosodic mirroring. This is taken as a measurement of the social cooperation and confidence built within the group over time.

"Shared reading" presents an interesting case for researching the reading experience, for it cuts across traditional distinctions between pleasure and utility as well as between silent and expressive, and individual and social forms of reading. Such a case takes reading for pleasure seriously and lifts personal and non-expressed responses to the literary text into a collective setting of shared reflections. This occurs through *in situ* live reading, thereby expanding existing notions of what constitutes a reading experience and consequently challenging how to study it. I am as concerned here with the description of a new reading phenomenon as I am with methodological issues related to its study.

In Dowrick and colleagues' 2012 study, factors of relevance are isolated and analyzed as variables in relation to therapeutic change. Although it uses conventions from ethnographic and linguistic research methods, their design follows a traditional psychological intervention/effect model, with a focus on outcome measurements (i.e., on a depression scale). In contrast to this, I argue that an ethnographic approach to the study of "shared reading" allows for a stronger consideration of context, given that physical space and organizational structure are both important factors for the analysis of outcomes. More importantly, however, an exploratory qualitative study allows us to discern what I will here refer to as "unintended consequences," that is, outcomes that are non-stipulated by the design, in contrast to research agendas in which outcomes are identified by the design prior to the intervention. In the present case it was an objective to explore outcomes as they arose from the activity itself, although with the obvious aim of defining factors of relevance for future studies. To address those unintended consequences I established different kinds of groups to identify the importance of the following:

1. Setting and place: How does the actual physical place in which the reading group is conducted relate to outcomes? I had three different settings: a community setting, a clinical setting, and finally an acute care setting. In the latter case, I also explored the difference between open and secluded spaces.
2. Voluntary engagement: What is the role of voluntariness as it relates to outcome measures, in this case defined as engagement and pleasure of reading, and motivation to continue as an active reading group member?

Below, I report findings drawn from work with three groups set up within clinical mental health care settings. Then I turn to discuss results from work with groups set up in external contexts. This will enable me to directly address the importance of setting and voluntariness respectively.

Mental Health Hospital Settings

From autumn 2011 to spring 2013, I conducted and collected data from three different shared reading groups in mental health hospitals. The intention was to investigate whether shared reading would constitute a meaningful activity for patients at mental health hospitals. Two groups were conducted at Aarhus University Hospital in Risskov, Denmark, in 2011 and 2012. Group A was conducted in an acute care ward for patients with psychosis. Data were collected through participatory observation over a period of twenty weeks, with the reading sessions suspended only over the Christmas holidays. The ward had a capacity for sixteen patients; of these, between two to five patients would participate in the reading group. As the primary investigator, I participated as the reading group facilitator. Reading group members were informed that I was a literary scholar from the University of Aarhus with an interest in exploring social forms of reading in different settings. The hospital librarian also participated as part of her training to become a shared reading group facilitator and took over the role of facilitator halfway through; this allowed me to participate as an "ordinary" reading group member. The purpose of bringing in outsiders was to clearly mark and set the activity aside from ordinary treatment, although all activities are viewed within a framework of therapeutic treatment. It was further decided that two occupational therapists would join the group in turns in order for the intervention to become an integrated part of the activities at large, and to assist the reading group facilitator in potentially difficult situations. The occupational therapists also helped select and motivate those patients who would benefit most from participation in the reading groups. The reading group was announced at morning gatherings.

At the end of the intervention, qualitative interviews were conducted with the two assisting occupational therapists, the head nurse (who had commissioned the intervention), the librarian, and a single patient. I had considered using audio recordings so that I could transcribe the reading group sessions for the purpose of conducting a reader-response analysis of reading engagement, but with patients suffering with various forms of pyschosis, this proved impossible. Instead, I kept a detailed reading log.

Group B was conducted at a ward for patients with affective psychiatric disorders. It ran irregularly over a period of fifteen weeks in the spring of 2012. As with the other group, I participated as reading group facilitator, with one of the hospital librarians taking over halfway through. The group had between two to five participants. Of these, one was a regular member; the others participated between one and three times. Staff did not participate. At the end of the intervention, the librarian was interviewed.

Group C was conducted over a period of ten weeks by one of the hospital librarians at a day hospital in Silkeborg, Denmark, for patients with affective disorders. It was offered as a voluntary supplementary activity to the existing range of treatments on the ward. Four to six patients participated every week, with a core group of three members. On some occasions the occupational therapist would sit in on the reading. With this group I did not conduct participatory observation; instead, at the conclusion of the sessions I interviewed the occupational therapist as well as the head nurse who had commissioned the intervention.

When setting up these three groups, I was concerned with the differences between reading practices of people with psychotic and affective psychiatric disorders; in particular, I looked at the terms of engagement and the kinds of responses to texts. Two important aspects were pointed out by the involved research partners, patients and staff alike.

The first aspect concerns the reading group as a "free space," with particular emphasis on the importance of the activity being voluntary and on the presence of a skilled reading group facilitator who does not have a therapeutic relationship with the patients, thus keeping the aesthetic purpose of the activity in sight. In this regard, the importance of an "outsider" acting as a reader-in-residence, who came for the reading only and had no impact on or role in treatment, was stressed repeatedly by staff and by reading group members as well. In this context, the strategies of "shared reading" function as a technology for interacting with co-readers and building a shared world.

The second aspect identifies the active participation of staff members as engaged readers and their conceptualization of the reading group activity as integral to the relational work in their therapeutic activities at large. Within this understanding, the reading group became a way of creating – in the words of the staff – "human" and "sane" relations not just between patients but also between patients and staff. Although these two findings may seem contradictory, when it is taken into account that we were looking at "unintended consequences," it makes sense that an intervention conceived of as a purely aesthetic activity may carry unintentional effects.

Literary and Literal Responses: Grounding Meaning and Enabling Social Interactions

Shared reading proved to function as a social technology enabling psychotic patients to enter into an intersubjective domain with the text and with other reading group participants. Following Rosenblatt's (1978) ideas on literature as a "lived-through experience" – ideas that posit that the transaction between a reader and a text enables a literary response (and demands a non-psychotic response) – patients were able to leave their conditions behind and enter a realm of shared human experiences through the practice of shared reading. Previous to the intervention, it had been a concern that psychotic patients would be too disassociative to follow a story that lasted for more than half an hour. In practice, I observed that on the contrary, literary reading delimits the range of potential responses and motivates even strongly hallucinating patients to respond adequately to the text, even if such a response, in the case of psychotic patients, is often a literal response rather than a literary one.

A Lived-Through Experience: The Embodiment of Reading

At times, it was a shared embodied experience that allowed for social coordination. To illustrate this I describe here the reading of the Norwegian writer Lars Saabye Christensen's short story "Gensynet" (The Reunion). The story is about a young daughter being reunited with her father. Much of the text consists of a detailed description of an airplane flight in severe weather during which the flight personnel and main characters experience great anxiety and fear. As we read this story in the reading group session I observed how all participants, staff and patients alike, were sighing and jumping in their chairs, swaying to one side and the other as the light airplane was buffeted by the storm. When the plane finally landed and the main character could touch firm ground, we all looked around at one another, smiling in relief. At the beginning of the reading, there were many pauses during which participants discussed the characters and their motivations, but as the intensity of the flight unfolded, there was an explicitly stated eagerness to stay within the embodied experience of the reading and follow it to its conclusion. The subsequent discussion evolved around our own experiences of airplane flights, and our anxieties and fears of death in similar situations.

The sighs and the movements as well as the memories and experiences of fear that were brought to the table were all adequate literary responses to the style, voice, and content of the text. The active shared engagement in the embodied experience of the text placed all participants, both staff and patients, on an equal footing, and in the subsequent discussion there were no substantial differences between the kinds of experiences and responses that staff members and patients brought to bear on the reading. The text encouraged a common set of human responses based on fear of flying and fear of death, and participants responded in kind at the affective and conceptual levels.

Another example of shared reading involved the response to Karen Blixen's story "The Ship-Boy's Tale." Halfway through this session, one patient became clearly anxious in response to a situation suggestive of physical and mental abuse. This was an appropriate response as we all felt the suffocating fear of being held tight in the arms of the drunken sailor. Our responses led to reflections on the right to kill in self-defence and how to live with such a deed.

Very rarely did I observe psychotic participants responding in a disassociative or hallucinating manner. One female patient associated the concept of "milking" with her own breastfeeding, but even if the analogy was socially "out of place," the connection was still highly relevant. In fact it was much more often the case that participants would put pressure on a reading to become as literal as possible. When confronted with two possible readings, figurative and literal, psychotic participants in general opted for the literal. This was particularly evident with a female participant who when outside the reading group session experienced intense hallucinations, believing she was the creator of the universe. On one occasion she sat with a cup firmly placed on her head to prevent her brain from exploding; nevertheless, she insisted on the most concrete of all possible readings. In the post-reading session interviews, staff members explained that they know from experience that no matter how psychotic a patient is, a non-psychotic part of the person is always within reach. It is not always easy to access that part or to create space for its expression. Regarding the participant described above, reading was an activity that called for non-psychotic behaviour, and on the basis of this, a relation was built, on her own initiative. This included discussing literature and going to the hospital library, where she suddenly declared, "It's lovely being able to think like a normal person." The head nurse emphasized in the post-session interview the importance of the reading sessions in establishing a relationship with this particular patient in that they facilitated a conversation about "how to live a life with a strongly psychotic patient." Reading as an activity had been fundamental to the patient's conceptualization of her own recovery process. It represented a plan, something to go on with, perhaps in a more formal way an education, once she returned home.

The reading group thus seemed to encourage what staff members referred to as "sane" expressions. Therefore, despite the fact that a literal response is seldom an adequate literary response, and regardless that concrete thinking constitutes a symptom of cognitive inflexibility in schizophrenia, and as such represents an "unhealthy" response, in the reading group the concreteness functioned as an effort to ground meaning and to respond adequately.

For other psychotic patients the reading group was simply an occasion to sit down, to focus on something other than their condition. One participant who could not otherwise sit still for two minutes at a time sat through the whole session, saying nothing but listening and concentrating. The value of such an experience is articulated by an occupational therapist: "When you think about how miserable some of them were, how invalidated by hearing voices, just sitting quietly is quite an accomplishment."

Social Coordination outside of the Reading Experience

Previous to the intervention there had been concerns about the social aspect of shared reading. As a result of their mental illness, patients with psychosis often find social interactions difficult and therefore withdraw from the social milieu, which leads to isolation. Would such people be able to participate in a shared reading session? In general, there was a tendency for psychotic participants to interact primarily with the text and with the reading group facilitator. Responses were thus most often individual responses to the text, and less frequently responses to other participants. However, we did find that moving stories such as "Gensynet," where all participants shared the same embodied fear of flying, and "A Ship-Boy's Tale," enabled social interactions. When one patient became visibly frightened during the reading of "A Ship-Boy's Tale," a second adopted the role of protector with comments such as "don't be afraid, it's just a story" and exhibited an almost parental guidance throughout the reading of the text: "that's life, nothing we can do about it," "nothing to worry about," "it will be over soon, then everything will be all right." An occupational therapist expressed the effect of the shared experience in the following way: "It has often been intense, because you feel that the patients are engaged, we are all engaged, and that creates a pleasant experience and atmosphere in the reading group."

In post-intervention interviews it was mentioned that participation had many times led to social interactions outside the sessions. One staff member observed that patients who "could not stand one another," were able to sit side by side without provoking one another during reading. She also noted that patients who had participated in a shared reading session would suddenly contact one another to start a conversation in the sitting room area, or play a game together. Some would approach her wanting to discuss the story again, or talk over stories they had read before. She explained, "When it spreads like that, like rings in water, I find it truly fascinating, then it suddenly becomes completely different than just medication, medication, and we are the bad guys, then it becomes such a good and positive thing."

There was as described in the above section a real sharing of the literary experience and, perhaps most importantly, a shared non-psychotic experience that enabled participants to build relations and engage in social interactions. Also, the very act of participating in a social situation, sitting around a table with coffee, cake, and conversation, constituted an important aspect of the reading group. As such the shared reading group can also be seen, according to the head nurse, as an activity that supports the general training of social skills and thus fits well with the concept of cognitive milieu therapy, albeit in a more ecological form that explores already existing cultural practices.

Community and Clinical Settings

As mentioned above, in order to amplify the scope of my exploratory design addressing setting and motivation, two additional groups were formed. The first of these was recruited in the spring of 2012 through the local newspaper. The advertisement was targeted at older people, defined here as fifty-eight and older, who had a history of suffering from depression. It was stressed that the study was about "reading for pleasure." The group was commissioned by a joint project between the Danish Reading Society (*Læseforeningen*) and *Ensomme Gamles Værn*, an organization working to improve the lives of disadvantaged elderly people, with me acting in the dual roles of reading group facilitator and researcher. I informed participants that the primary aim was to conduct a number of shared reading groups for different target groups of elderly people in order to explore the benefits of participation. I also informed them that as a literary scholar I had a particular interest in exploring social reading in different settings.

The group met at a seniors centre. The hope was to recruit others who were using the centre for other recreational purposes. But contrary to expectations, the group was formed solely on the basis of responses to the advertisement. Typically, three to five participants attended; there were three core members and three others who were more loosely involved. All participants were women between the ages of fifty-seven and sixty-three. At the first meeting, the participants discussed the peculiarity of being recruited based on their mental illness diagnoses for a study on "reading for pleasure." The general opinion was that it felt safe to know that other members had an insight into the kinds of vulnerability associated with mental illness, but apart from that, the shared medical condition itself was not an issue that would arise during the readings; what *did* arise was its existential counterparts such as loneliness, isolation, and a longing to share.

While recruiting this community group, I worked with two psychologists to set up another shared reading group for explicit research purposes. The aim was to explore the extent to which shared reading could and would function as an ecological form of cognitive remediation in depressive patients in remission, for many depressive patients suffer from memory loss and poor concentration. Most participants were recruited through an ongoing research project on meta-cognition in depressive patients, and some through a webpage in which participants were informed about the aim of the study. Our hypothesis was that shared reading would increase the level of cognitive functioning. This hypothesis was shared with all potential participants on the webpage and in an information leaflet. All potential participants, excluding those with bipolar and psychotic diseases, underwent a diagnostic interview, were scored for levels of depression (i.e., Hamilton scale), and took a neurocognitive test consisting of a battery targeting working memory, attention span, and executive functions. After testing, twelve participants that met our inclusion criteria were selected for the shared reading group activity. I participated as reading group facilitator and investigator into social forms of reading. Each participant filled out a questionnaire to inform us about reading habits and forms of reading prior to the intervention. Also, a Likert scale was used to assert motivations and outcomes for each session. The sessions were audio- and video-recorded for subsequent analysis of reading responses and kinds of engagement.

It soon became apparent that recruitment and framing of the activity were important factors for social functioning and engagement in the reading groups. The community group recruited for "reading for pleasure" soon started to function as a group (after the third session), despite initial failures to integrate a vulnerable member, and continued as a group after the intervention period of ten weeks. In contrast, the clinical group recruited for research purposes outside of the reading experience itself (i.e., a study of concentration, attention, and memory) never managed to function as a group. Furthermore, in this group I experienced the greatest difficulties with motivation and engagement among participants. Some came irregularly, others tended to be absent-minded even when physically present. The general attitude was that of pupils in class trying to concentrate on what the teacher is saying, knowing that they ought to, but unable really to focus. Clearly this was an effect not of diagnosis (the community group shared the same clinical condition) but of setting. The fact that they were there because of a lack (of concentration or attention) and a perceived need and wish to regain former levels of cognitive functioning, and the fact that I was there to provide it, created an atmosphere of inequality, but also of demands, of unfulfilled hopes and expectations. Moreover, perhaps most importantly, those goals motivating their participation were at best derivative of the reading experience. A few participants – all of whom were already engaged readers (as stipulated in the questionnaire) – tried to pressure others for a different attitude, and although we had moments of real engagement, they were infrequent and I did not manage to mitigate my role as someone there to provide treatment.

In contrast, in the community group, which was conducted for the pleasure of the reading experience in itself, participants were highly motivated, and members would not miss a single session (in fact, they scheduled their vacations and other activities around it). Participants stayed attuned and attentive throughout the entire session, admitting that at times they had to go home and sleep afterwards because the experience was so intense. They never expressed frustration concerning the facilitation of the group or of the texts; rather, they were grateful that such an activity existed, free and for them.

Concerning neurocognitive outcomes, there is no way to compare the two groups, for my only source of data from the community group was my reading log based on observation, whereas data for the research group were collected and recorded both prior to and after the intervention. In the research group, there were statistically insignificant effects (due to the small sample size) on all neurocognitive measures. Those in the community group would spontaneously address their increased level of cognitive functioning through self-perception. They all admitted to having periods of difficulty reading due to depression; this is why the reading-aloud model suited them so well. However, during the period of the intervention, participants discovered that reading aloud encouraged sustained attention and concentration, and as a result, several members of the group took up this practice at home, either alone or with a partner.

Main outcomes in the community setting related to the social functioning of the group, high levels of commitment to and engagement with the reading activity, and (self-reported) renewed ability to read at home. In the research group, the main outcomes were in the neurocognitive domain, with hardly any related to social functioning and engagement in the experience. That neurocognitive effects are achieved even when social effects are lacking suggests that reading generally boosts cognitive functioning.

Sharing Minds and Embodied Experiences

Shared reading became a social tool for creating and entering a shared experiential world in the community setting. To illustrate this with data from my research, below I provide the text of "Bekjendelser" ("Confessions") by B.S. Ingemanns, followed by two excerpts from my research diary on my observations regarding the reading group members' responses to our reading of this poem.

B. S. Ingemanns "Bekjendelser" ("Confessions")
La bienséance est la moindre de toutes les loix & la plus suivie.
(Rochefoucauld)

I'm often glad, although I feel like weeping;
For no heart shares the joy in my sole keeping.
I'm often sorrowful, though laugh with glee,
So no one all my frightened tears may see.

I often love, although I feel like sighing;
For my heart needs be mute and hid from prying.
I'm often angry, though must wear a smile;
For those who anger are but fools that rile.

I often burn, yet in such heat I shiver;
The world's embrace is like an ice-cold river,
I'm often cold, yet sweat stands on my brow;
For many tasks lack love it seems somehow.

I often speak, though would refrain from prating,
Where mindless words for thought need not be waiting.
I'm often dumb, and would to ease my breast
Have thund'rous voice when it is most oppressed.

Oh! You alone who can my joy be sharing,
You at whose bosom I can weep uncaring,
Oh! dearest, if you knew me, loved me true,
I could be always as I am – with you.

I pause. Inga nods, she recognizes that feeling of being alone among other people. Susanne says: "Yes, that is how it is; in the reading group my inner life becomes shared reality, here I don't feel alone. I often walk around in the world feeling isolated, in my own dimension, because I don't work any longer and I'm not busy as other people. And the things I think about would like to talk about and don't discuss those with other people but here I do."

In the course of reading Susanne had taken her shoes off and lifted and folded her legs in the chair. While she was talking, I observed Inga suddenly taking off her shoes placing her bare feet on the edge of the chair. Without a word but with her body language mirroring Susanne's she was bodily expressing her agreement of the reading. Till that point this particular reader had been a very hesitant member of the group, voicing her doubts about whether she really belonged to it or not, now she embodied it.
(Excerpts from Researcher's Reading Log, community group)

The scene above highlights two important ways in which shared reading becomes a social technology through the synchronized embodied experiences of reading. The first concerns the way in which both Inga and Susanne by way of reading express lived experiences of their emotional life, in this case loneliness and belonging respectively. The second concerns the way in which sharing such newly rediscovered feelings becomes a technology for shaping emotional life itself. There seems to be a loop connecting embodied qualities and lived experience of the text, to the expression of those who are sharing, which in turn leads to a modulation of initial feelings. The feeling resonating with Inga was loneliness, as expressed in the first stanza of the poem, whereas the feeling resonating with Susanne was belonging, as expressed in the last stanza of the poem. Susanne expressed those feelings, and in that expression associated the reading group and its members with the potential other of the poem with whom the heart can be shared. Inga visibly embodied the feeling of belonging to the group, of being a member, thus modifying her initially expressed feeling of loneliness or isolation. Sharing itself became a technology in the group for modulating subjective feelings and sensations.

Although we hardly ever discussed the fact that all reading group members shared a diagnosis of depression, on a single occasion one reading group member facilitated a larger group discussion about depression when she responded to her reading of Danish author Hans Otto Jørgensen's "Jens Thorstensen," a story of an immaculate conception. The protagonist Jens Thorstensen is carrying a child and experiences overwhelming isolation and loneliness as he realizes that this is something that cannot be shared with anybody, not even his wife. One member of the reading group responded, "That is how it feels being depressed, no one can see it, you're all alone with this feeling inside of you, feeling ashamed and wanting to hide it." The others immediately jumped in with recognition and agreement. At the time, no further elaboration of this initial response was made, but there was a visible relief and relaxation, leading to an elevated atmosphere of joy during the remainder of the session. Then, when meeting the next time, group members engaged in a prolonged discussion prior to reading about their experiences of isolation and stigmatization as a result of depression.

Conclusion

The main outcomes I have identified are paradoxical, as the potential therapeutic effects related to social functioning and emotional well-being can only be achieved when the reading group intervention is not perceived as a therapeutic but rather as an aesthetic activity based on reading, and sharing responses. This implies that even when reading activities that take place at an acute care ward for mental health in hospitals form part of treatment, the reading groups can only support positive outcomes when they are carried out for aesthetic rather than clinical or therapeutic purposes. There is also evidence that positive neurocognitive effects on concentration, attention, and memory are also realized even when positive effects on social and emotional well-being are not apparent. Contrary to expectations, diagnosis did not have an effect on outcomes in terms of social functioning and emotional well-being. What *did* have an effect was the setting, including the formal organizational frame into which the activity was built, how well integrated it was into the general conception of relational work within a frame of milieu-therapy, and how well the distinct aesthetic purpose was kept in sight during the reading sessions. In the case of the acute in-ward section, this purpose was achieved by a professional reader-in-residence, and in the case of the community setting, by insisting on "reading for pleasure."

In this chapter my aim has been twofold: to conceptualize dimensions of the shared reading experience, and to describe specific affordances of particular kinds of material and cultural practices, in this case "shared reading." Through this approach, I have provided a methodology for studying the reading experience, one that includes both its qualitative dimensions and its reflective processes, as well as the cultural practice of reading. When researching the reading experience – in this particular case, its potential mental health benefits – it is essential to understand reading not as a uniform activity (e.g., decoding of meaning as in the formalist tradition) but rather as a practice that can be cultivated in various ways, each of which has certain affordances. I have argued that "shared reading" as a social technology facilitates co-construction of an intersubjective reality. For the potential application of research on reading, whether it be directed at mental health or other interventions, I have argued for the need not to just isolate factors but also to describe the processes and mechanisms involved as well as the qualitative dimensions of the reading experience.

References

Blixen, Karen. 1942. "Skibsdrengens fortælling [A Ship-Boy's Tale]. In *Vinter-Eventyr* [*Winter Tales*]." København: Forlaget Gyldendal.

Christensen, Lars Saabye. 2005. "Gensynet [The Reunion]." In *Oscar Wildes Elevator.* København: Athene.

Dowrick, Christopher, Josie Billington, Jude Robinson, Andrew Hamer, and Clare Williams. 2012. "Get into Reading as an Intervention for Common Mental Health Problems: Exploring Catalysts for Change." *Medical Humanities* 38(1): 15–20.

Ingemann, B.S. 2010. "Bekjendelser" [Confessions]. English translation by John Irons, "Another poem set to music by Carl Nielsen, by the Danish 19th century poet and hymn-writer B.S. Ingemann" (blog). http://johnirons.blogspot.dk/2010/04/another-poem-set-to-music-by-carl.html

Jørgensen, Hans Otto. 2010. "Jens Thorstensens andet liv" [The Other Life of Jens Thorstensens]. In *Kort fortalt: danske noveller 2000-2010* [*Shortly Told: Danish Short Stories*], edited by Nanna Mogensen and Klaus Rothstein. København: Tiderne skifter.

Robinson, Jude. 2008. *Reading and Talking: Exploring the Experience of Taking Part in Reading Groups in Walton Neuro-Rehabilitation Unit (NRU)*. Liverpool: University of Liverpool.

Rosenblatt, Louise M. 1978. *The Reader, the Text, the Poem: The Transactional Theory of the Literary Work*. Carbondale: Southern Illinois University Press.

Sikora, Shelley, Don Kuiken, and David S. Miall. 2011. "Expressive Reading: A Phenomenological Study of Readers' Experience of Coleridge's 'The Rime of the Ancient Mariner.'" *Psychology of Aesthetics, Creativity, and the Arts* 5(3): 258–68.

The Indescribable Described   13
Readers' Experiences When Reading about Tragic Loss

Eva Maria (Emy) Koopman

In recent years, the Netherlands – like many Western countries – has seen a surge of autobiographical and semi-autobiographical books about grave suffering, from depression to dealing with the death of one's child. Given the popularity of this type of literature, it is relevant to investigate why readers choose to read it and how they experience it. What feelings and thoughts does autobiographical literature about suffering evoke? The Dutch "requiem novel" *Tonio* (2011), in which author A.F.Th. Van der Heijden narrates the loss of his son, is a particularly successful example. People who had read *Tonio* were invited to share their ideas on the novel ($N = 67$). In addition, responses from other readers found online at the online bookstore bol.com and the social media site for readers goodreads.com were analyzed.[1]

The Catharsis Hypothesis

> I felt I must write about it ... If I was doomed to be sent to this island of punishment, of grief and bereavement, at least I wanted to map it in my way. I wanted to give my private names to everything that came to my being in this situation. I read books of other people who experienced something like that and they were good books and meaningful, and yet they did not give me my words. You know, a writer is someone who feels claustrophobia in the words of other people, and I had to find my own words, and to describe the indescribable. (David Grossman, on the Dutch television show *Boeken*, 16 September 2012)

This quotation expresses the strong need writers can feel to articulate painful experiences they have had to deal with – in Grossman's case, the loss of his child. Despite the struggle it often causes, it is far from surprising that many authors write about their suffering. What is more surprising is that there seems to be a large audience for these tragic stories. In the last decade, there has been a surge of novels and memoirs about intense suffering, from depression and disease to the death of a partner or child (e.g., Didion 2006;

Grossman 2012; Oates 2011; Vann 2008). While suffering in all its variety has always been an important subject for literature, the current market for memoirs and autobiographies that address excruciating life experiences seems unprecedented (Rak 2013). As we see book after book appearing in which acclaimed authors give expression to grief, pain, and despair, two questions arise: Why do people read the tragedies of others? And how do they experience them? This paper attempts to provide answers by looking at readers' engagement with the bestselling Dutch memoir *Tonio* (2011).

Deriving a certain satisfaction from consuming sad stories, in the form of a novel or a movie, can be termed the "drama paradox" (Oliver 1993; Zillmann 1998). Just as it seems commonsensical that stories are used in order to generate pleasant emotions (i.e., enjoyment), it seems illogical that they are also used to generate unpleasant emotions like fear and sadness (e.g., Oliver 1993; 2008; Vorderer 2003). An enduring explanation for why we voluntarily expose ourselves to unpleasant emotions through media and arts is the catharsis hypothesis. In Chapter 6 of his *Poetics*, Aristotle (n.d.) defined tragedy as "an imitation of an action that is serious, complete, and of a certain magnitude" that, by arousing "pity" (*eleos*) and "fear" (*phobos*), accomplishes the "purgation" (*katharsis*) of these emotions. The predominant translation of "catharsis" is "purgation," which leads to the assumption that simply experiencing certain emotions through a mimetic medium should bring about relief from those emotions. However, this "catharsis hypothesis" is widely debated. Empirical studies on media violence demonstrate that when exposed to a violent stimulus, people tend to become *more* agitated instead of less (e.g., Bushman, Baumeister, and Stack 1999). As Scheele has stated in a review on catharsis as purging, "the hypothesis of hedonistic purging (through pleasurable vicarious involvement) may be regarded as falsified for 'hostile aggression'" (2001, 212). Whether this also applies in the context of sadness or fear and literature is still unclear. Koopman (2011) has found retrospective self-reported cathartic effects (measured as feeling calmer and experiencing less negative emotions) in the context of finding comfort through literature in difficult times, but this experience of feeling calmer mainly had to do with being distracted from one's problems. In that sense, it was not "purgation" in the classic sense, which assumes that emotions have to be experienced in order to be diminished.

While it seems questionable that simply experiencing emotions through reading or watching a tragic narrative leads to their expulsion, we could redefine the catharsis hypothesis using the same passage from Aristotle (Khoo and Oliver 2013; Scheele 2001). Since Aristotle did not clearly explain what he meant by *katharsis*, the passage has given rise to extensive debate about how to interpret the term. Various scholars have argued that *katharsis* could also be translated as "clarification" (Golden 1968; Halliwell 1986; Keesey 1979; Nussbaum 1986). Translating *katharsis* as "clarification" would be consistent with Aristotle's idea, in Chapter 4 of *Poetics*, that we enjoy mimetic expression because we can recognize it and learn from it. Catharsis would result from sympathizing with and/or pitying characters as well as being horrified by their fate and from our subsequent reflection on these feelings, perhaps relating them to our own experiences. As Nussbaum (1986) has argued, this clarification is not purely intellectual: through experiencing certain emotions in response to a fictional drama, we intuitively understand these emotions, their triggers, and ourselves better. Through reading about another person's suffering we are confronted with our vulnerability and mortality. This may not be enjoyable, but it can be meaningful and valuable when we feel we have reached a deeper understanding of life.

Indeed, throughout her work on sad movies, Oliver (e.g., 1993; 2008; Oliver and Bartsch 2010; Kim and Oliver 2011) has stressed that theories assuming that media consumption is all about "enjoyment" or lifting one's mood simply do not cover the attraction of sad media. Empirical studies on mood management have shown that people who are sad often select sad rather than uplifting media. This has been shown both for music (e.g., Chen, Zhou, and Bryant 2007; Gibson, Aust, and Zillmann 2000; Knobloch and Zillmann 2003) and for television/film (e.g., Dillman Carpentier et al. 2008; Kim and Oliver 2011; Nabi et al. 2006). Clearly, media are used not only for entertainment and relaxation but also for "counter-hedonic" purposes, such as dealing with experiences one regrets (Nabi et al. 2006).

Literary scholars commonly share the idea that meaningful experience is at least as important as enjoyment when reading literature. This assumption is based on a general belief in the elevating properties of "art." Yet "meaningful experience" will likely be different for those who can directly relate the suffering of characters to their own experiences and for those who do not have any experience with the depicted events. If we conceptualize catharsis as clarification through having gained felt insight into human experience, we can assume that for readers who have direct experience with the type of suffering described, this does not occur, since these readers already know what the experience is like. The aspect of "fear" would be missing here, and it may not be so much "pity" that these readers feel for the characters, but identification and recognition. Indeed, the main functions of reading as identified by studies in bibliotherapy include recognition and support (e.g., Bernstein and Rudman 1989; Cohen 1992; Hynes 1980; Koopman 2011; Zeelenberg and Spiertz 1993).[2] Through recognition, certain readers may also derive new insights. Reading about another person's suffering may help them put their own experiences in context.

When exploring the experience of readers who willingly expose themselves to someone else's pain, Van der Heijden's *Tonio* (2011) provides a good example. This "requiem novel" is based largely on actual events – namely, the death of the author's twenty-one-year-old son in a traffic accident and the aftermath of this loss. The narration of this tragic event is intertwined with the meticulously preserved memories the author has of his son, and with his personal life events and reflections. While this is a non-fiction book, it is highly narrativized: Van der Heijden uses some conventions of the detective story. In the narrative, he tries to find out who the mysterious girl was that Tonio photographed not long before his untimely death. While Van der Heijden does not shy away from describing emotional events, his writing style remains rather cerebral, with a preference for long sentences with complex, sometimes archaic words and allusions to cultural knowledge. For example, he describes his memory of the last time he and his wife saw Tonio as follows:

> In all of my anxiety about his vulnerability I never once paused to reflect on the fact that the agile o's that smiled at me so lively through the name "Tonio" were typographically the same as those that stared at me through the rigid congruence of the word "death" [*dood*]. The last time Mirjam and I saw him, two drain plugs were sticking out of his forehead, a shorter one and a somewhat larger one, like horns ... With everything that went through me at that moment, there was apparently still a place within my brain for a scene out of the movie *Camille Claudel*, that I saw years before together with Mirjam.[3] (Van der Heijden 2011, 14–15)

Tonio has been highly successful. It won the prestigious Libris Literatuur Prijs as well as the popular vote of the NS Publieksprijs, and by June 2013 it had sold almost 200,000 copies, a huge number by Dutch book trade standards. The novel has been translated into English and various other languages. Given its commercial and critical success, *Tonio* offers a relevant case for studying why people read about suffering. In addition, the author himself has proposed a hypothesis about catharsis:

> Many people wrote to me that they recognized themselves in my book, because they had lost someone themselves ... But more people who read the book have not lost a child and still they read it. This is because of their own fears, these people read the book to allay their fears. Why did the old Greeks go to horrific plays? Because of catharsis. It did not happen to me, but it could happen to me. In some way this solves something. (Van der Heijden, on the television show *Nieuwsuur*, after receiving the Libris Literatuur Prijs)

Van der Heijden here is positing that people who have lost a child read his book for recognition, while parents who have not had to cope with such a loss experience read the book to reduce the intensity of their fears. Is he right in this analysis? How did readers experience *Tonio*?

Methods

To get responses from a varied group of people who had read *Tonio*, an online survey was distributed through three websites that were expected to be visited by different types of readers: 8weekly.nl (a website with reviews of literature, music, film, and visual arts), the Facebook page of the public library of Utrecht, and a forum for parents who had lost a child. The survey contained closed and open questions about motivations for reading *Tonio* as well as about thoughts and feelings during reading. It stayed online throughout July 2012. In addition, responses to two forums about *Tonio* were examined: bol.com (the Dutch Amazon) and goodreads.com. While the primary focus was the survey, responses to the forums were used to supplement the codes derived from responses to the survey.

Since the survey study used self-selecting respondents, the data may not be representative of all readers of *Tonio*. However, there was a satisfying variation in respondents' background characteristics. Sixty-seven readers responded – fifty-three women and fourteen men; the relatively low number of men corresponds with the generally lower tendency among men to read novels (Zill and Winglee 1988). Respondents' ages ranged between nineteen and sixty-nine years. Thirty-seven respondents had children, thirty did not (three of whom were childless after the death of their child). In total, seven respondents had lost a child.

On bol.com, twenty-eight readers had left remarks (of whom at least eighteen could be identified as female); on goodreads.com, ten readers (nine female) engaged in the discussion, only six of whom had read the novel. Most bol.com readers who provided age details fell within the age range of fifty and fifty-nine years ($n = 12$). The goodreads.com readers did not provide age details.

The answers to the survey questions were coded using a combination of quantitative and qualitative content analysis, with the aim of cross-case analysis (Schreier 2001, 2012). In response to the questions addressing feelings during reading, I expected to see both narrative feelings (designating affective responses directed towards characters and events) and aesthetic feelings (designating feelings directed towards stylistic elements, such as appreciating a beautiful sentence) (Kneepkens and Zwaan 1994; Tan 1996). Regarding narrative feelings, scholars have made useful distinctions between "empathy," "sympathy" and "identification." In several recent discussions on the subject, there seems to be some consensus that *identification* can be defined as imagining oneself in the position of the character and recognizing similarities, *empathy* as experiencing emotions perceived as similar to the character while acknowledging the difference between oneself and the character (i.e., feeling with), and *sympathy* as feeling for another without feeling what the other feels (e.g., Andringa 2004; Busselle and Bilandzic 2009; Coplan 2004; Keen 2006; Mar and Oatley 2008; Mar et al. 2011). While these distinctions were expected in readers' responses, in order to let the responses speak for themselves, no *a priori* categories were made.

In respondents' answers, the (theoretical) difference between empathy and sympathy turned out to be difficult to determine, as the Dutch word "*medeleven*" can mean either "empathy" or "sympathy," feeling with or feeling for. Where sympathetic and empathetic reactions were distinguished, they were frequently mentioned in quick succession, for example: "I felt a lot of compassion, and was sometimes very sad myself." The apparent alignment between these feelings for readers led us to combine empathetic and sympathetic reactions towards the characters and author in a single category called "Empathic emotions." Within this category, respondents could report multiple emotions, experiencing, for example, both "Pity" and "Sorrow/pain." Similarly, "Empathic emotions" is related to but distinct from "Recognition/identification," which includes all responses in which readers made an explicit connection between their own experiences and those of the character or author (e.g., fear of losing one's own child).

Motives for Reading *Tonio*

In response to a multiple choice question about the reasons for reading *Tonio*, the reasons most frequently given were: curiosity about Tonio's story ($n = 25$), curiosity about the stylistic quality of the book ($n = 18$), and being a fan of the work of Van der Heijden ($n = 16$). The latter could also be seen as a form of curiosity about the latest product of an admired author. Besides curiosity, seeking support was an important motive: ten readers indicated that they chose the book hoping to find support during their own grief process. Social factors – recommendations by friends and being part of a book club – were each ticked off by six respondents. Figure 13.1 shows the frequencies for the reasons to read *Tonio* based on the multiple choice question.

The answers to an open question about expectations showed similar motives for reading as responses to multiple choice questions: positive ideas about the author's reputation (Motives: Curiosity – Author), curiosity about the content (Motives: Curiosity – Story Tonio), interest in the style (Motives: Insight – Articulation grief), support during one's own grief process

Figure 13.1 Main Reasons for Reading *Tonio* (n=67)

(Motives: Insight –Support own grief process), and social factors. Particularly interesting were responses concerning curiosity about the style, since these did not simply repeat the multiple choice option. As the name of the qualitative code "Motives: Insight – Articulation grief" indicates, these responses to the open question appeared to be more about gaining a form of insight: these people wanted to know how grief can be articulated. A thirty-one-year-old male, for example, said: "The question rises to what extent the author can find a language to articulate such a sensitive subject." Another example of this is a forty-seven-year-old mother who stated that she wanted to know "how a father can cope with such an immense loss and the pain that comes with it ... how he could articulate that." As this latter quote shows, there appeared to be an overlap of an interest in the general subject (or theme, namely: loss) and the way this subject could be expressed. This need to learn more about grief was reported by those who did not appear to have experienced grave loss themselves. It could be characterized as seeking clarification of an experience beyond one's own comprehension.

While readers could be said to show a need for clarification, catharsis as purgation did not seem to be a main motive. In response to a question about the catharsis hypothesis (i.e., whether allaying one's fear was a motive to read the book), five of the sixty-seven respondents answered "yes." Five others partly agreed. To some extent, for these readers, gaining insight appeared to be a way to reduce their fears. One of the respondents who agreed with the catharsis hypothesis, a forty-five-year-old mother, also cited this motive of wanting to learn about grief: "I wanted to know how One copes with the loss of a child. I fear this is the worst thing that can happen to a parent." The capitalization of "One" emphasizes that this is a great concern for this woman, yet the emphasis on "knowing" suggests that the catharsis she was looking for comes closer to clarification. Of the ten readers reporting catharsis as purgation (partly or completely) as a motive, four later explicitly reported gaining existential insight.

Responses further showed that the motive for thirteen of the respondents had largely to do with general reading habits: to the question about expectations and/or the question about media attention, these respondents said they read practically anything ($n = 9$), or, in four cases, that they were looking for a good read for the holidays and that *Tonio* seemed to fit the profile.

Apart from the abovementioned motives, media attention appeared to play an important role; seventeen readers indicated in response to a closed question about media attention that they probably would not have read the book had it received less attention.

Narrative Feelings: An Emotional Experience

Most respondents ($n = 57$) said "yes" to a question whether *Tonio* evoked emotions, and twenty-three explicitly reported an intense emotional experience. While respondents made many remarks on their feelings both in response to characters/events (i.e., narrative feelings) and in response to the style (i.e., aesthetic feelings), remarks about narrative feelings clearly outnumbered those about aesthetic feelings. There was a high prevalence of remarks on empathy, sympathy, and pity. In addition, respondents reported admiration for the author, remarking on the "courage" he had summoned to write about this and the "vulnerable" position he had placed himself in. It needs to be stressed that the author as a character was often conflated with the author as a real-life entity. When respondents wrote that they felt compassion with "the author and his wife," it was not quite clear towards whom the emotional reaction was directed: the parents as presented in the book (as "characters"), the actually existing parents, or a self-constructed mixture of both. This conflation logically resulted from the autobiographical nature of the book.

As can be imagined, the intense emotional experience could be painful. Some respondents even indicated that they had trouble reading on. Of the five respondents who stopped reading, four did so because it was too painful for them. For two of the four, this had to do with their own grief. Even though the similarities observed by grieving readers were often painful, generally this recognition was highly appreciated. See for example this response by a fifty-three-year-old mother:

> I have experienced several miscarriages and a stillborn. Of course this played a large role while I read the novel and in my response to it. On the one hand

this was confrontational, difficult, raw, painful ... But also comforting and recognizable, you experience a certain support through the story.

The desire for recognition (explicitly reported by six people who sought support in their grief process) appeared to surpass the pain expected in reliving the loss experience. In line with findings from bibliotherapeutic research (e.g., Bernstein and Rudman 1989; Cohen 1992; Hynes 1980; Koopman 2011; Zeelenberg and Spiertz 1993), as well as with the hypothesis posed by Van der Heijden, grieving respondents felt known and acknowledged in their sorrow (i.e., "that's exactly how it is"), and they wrote about "comfort" and "support." This was confirmed by responses on bol.com.

Painful emotions were also experienced by those who had not lost a child themselves. To a certain extent, people reported having themselves felt the pain, sadness, and despair described in the book. For example, a sixty-one-year-old mother indicated that she felt "the despair of the parents, the pointlessness of everything after the death of a child," and a forty-five-year-old mother said that "at times I was intensely sad myself." Within responses of "identification," fear of losing one's own child had a special place. While the majority of respondents did not read to allay fears about losing a child, parents who read *Tonio* were clearly confronted with this fear. Of the thirty-seven respondents with children, half ($n = 18$) explicitly talked about the fear of losing a child when asked how having children themselves affected their response. In addition, seven respondents remarked that reading exacerbated this fear, for example, this fifty-three-year-old mother: "Allaying the fear, that doesn't work, it only gets bigger and more real. It's not a motive to start reading the book, it's something that happens during reading." Yet, as for most of those who re-experienced the pain of a loss, this was not a reason to stop reading or to not appreciate the novel. Indeed, experiencing fear went together with reporting more emotions in general. All of the respondents who talked about fear also reported empathic emotions, and they reported a higher frequency of emotions than those who did not speak about fear, while the frequency of reported thoughts did not differ.

Aesthetic Feelings: Appreciating the Unsentimental

While aesthetic feelings were less frequently reported than narrative feelings, most respondents ($n = 46$) did make positive remarks about *Tonio*'s style. The appreciation of the style, insofar as it was explained by respondents, mainly had to do with intricate and "beautiful" formulations and with "unsentimentality." Multiple readers emphasized that the book was "no tear-jerker," but relatively "distanced." On bol.com the rather cerebral style of the author was often lauded as realistic (e.g., "No false sentiments. Everything is so pure and real"). Many survey respondents also appreciated that the style was "not unnecessarily emotional."

As shown above, many respondents felt a strong and heavy emotional impact. However, eight readers indicated that the emotional impact of the novel was less fierce but still haunting. They explained that the emotional experience of the novel stuck with them, and they related this to the style, for example: "The choice of words made the theme very emotional, not in the sense of direct tears, but as a feeling that you as a reader take with you for the rest of the day." Or: "Serenely written. Not a book to really cry with, but one that makes you pause with what happened." These responses indicate that the book had a lingering presence for some and suggest this had to do with the intricacy of the style.

Distance and Ambivalence

While most readers appreciated the style, others were disappointed. As a nineteen-year-old man put it:

> I noticed that he remained very distanced. Often I thought: why don't you get to the core, to your feelings. That's probably because of Van der Heijden's grandiose, woolly vocabulary: this builds a sort of wall between the text and the reader.

Another reader, a fifty-five-year-old woman, even got angry for this reason: "His son died and yet he did not manage to move me??????" Similarly, while most parents ($n = 30$) indicated that having children influenced their reading experience, for some ($n = 7$) it did not. None of these seven parents felt strongly involved, and four even felt distanced. As a thirty-two-year-old mother indicated: "I had hoped the book would move me, but it did not, so there was no relation." The respondents to the survey who remained unmoved were a minority. On bol.com this type of reaction was not found, which could have had to do with the social pressure to be respectful to the grieving author in a pseudo-public space. In total, twelve readers did not feel involved in the story. Four of these readers indicated that the author was being "too personal" or "too egotistic."

Remarks about the author being too personal were also made by those who did feel narrative engagement, suggesting an ambivalent reading experience. Apparently, the deeply personal nature of memoirs is not readily accepted by all readers. For some, it still feels intrusive to read about the most intimate experiences of a well-known author. This was brought out clearly by four respondents who indicated that, although they felt emotionally engaged, they also struggled with the "voyeuristic" element. This reaction occurred on bol.com and goodreads.com as well. One thirty-year-old man in the survey noted that he constantly felt "like an intruder during an especially emotional and intimate phase in the life of two people," which made him feel "both shame and involvement."

Clarification and Other Insights

Relevant for the purposes of this study, thirteen respondents spoke of an experience that could be classified as "clarification." While they were not explicitly asked about it, these respondents wrote about gaining deep, meaningful insights (mostly in response to a question whether they would recommend the novel, but also in response to a question about thoughts). "I learned something about the despair and panic that can overtake a human being when confronted with a great loss," said a twenty-three-year-old female reader. And a thirty-one-year-old father: "This book [gives one] a deep inside view in what loss does to people, what grieving is."

These types of insights can be contrasted with more simple thoughts about the content, style, or author, such as, "What a shame Tonio's life ended so soon," and with self-implicating thoughts that did not show new existential insight: "It started me thinking about my relationship with my roommates." In this latter category also fell thoughts of the respondents who had lost someone themselves. They made comments about recognizing certain elements from their own lives. While these comments sometimes showed increased acceptance, they remained at a purely individual level instead of at the existential, for example: "I saw some differences, like that ... they had a sober funeral. We did that differently and I realized while reading that I am glad we did." Interestingly, there was no significant overlap between the motives of wanting to know more about grief (which could be seen as catharsis as clarification as a motive) and actually reporting existential insight. Of course, as existential insight was not explicitly asked about, the fact that readers did not report it does not necessarily mean they did not experience it.

While theoretically it was expected that clarification could be the outcome of confrontation with unpleasant emotions, responses about having gained existential insight did not show a particularly strong overlap with mentions of fear (only three of the thirteen respondents who gained existential insight also wrote about fear). Empathic emotions seemed more important – ten out of the thirteen respondents had reported these, and seven had specifically reported pity. However, statistical tests showed this was not that different from those who had not reported existential insight. Another interesting overlap was between finding meaning and appreciating the style: eleven out of the thirteen respondents who gained insight had made positive remarks about the style, none had made negative remarks. Again, however, this did not differ significantly from the other respondents, as people were generally positive about the style.

Yet, responses did suggest that style and meaning-making were closely connected. A response that appeared similar to having found meaning, albeit focused on style, was the expression of appreciation for the way Van der Heijden had articulated his experience. For example: "The writing process that occurred simultaneously with the grieving process is remarkable, and that the author has made art out of such a subject is something I greatly admire." Twenty-three people in total gave such a response, of whom seven combined terms such as "horrible subject" and "beautifully articulated" (e.g., "it's a nightmare, but incredibly well articulated"). Of these twenty-three people, ten had also reported fear of losing one's child. This relation also was statistically significant, suggesting a process of catharsis as clarification. All in all, this could indicate that a well-crafted stylistic formulation may help frame what frightens us.

Conclusion

The current case study into the "requiem novel" *Tonio* provided an exploration regarding readers' motives to read autobiographical books about suffering, in this case: tragic loss. As expected, for those who had suffered a grave loss themselves, finding comfort and support through recognition appeared a crucial motive for reading about someone else's grief, even if this meant re-experiencing painful emotions. In these cases, grief is endured because one can have the sense of sharing it. In the current study, reading for recognition and support did not seem to lead to existential insights, but it would indeed be rather too much to ask someone who is so personally involved in the narrative events to reflect upon general human issues. Instead, for those who are grieving, reading about grief can help put one's own experiences into perspective. This type of reading may, indirectly and in the longer term, elevate one's mood, yet within this case study that could not be determined. Of course, grief processes can differ substantially (Stroebe et al. 2001). It may be that when there is enough self-perceived distance, more general insights on human experience can arise.

For those who were not trying to work through their grief, the most prevalent reasons for reading *Tonio* were curiosity about the content and about the style. In addition, choosing to read this well-known "requiem novel" was determined by social factors (such as being part of a book club) and media attention.[4] *Tonio*'s autobiographical nature, in combination with the status of the author and the media attention the book received, are likely to have fuelled curiosity. Insofar as this curiosity is about the story of the death of a child and the grief of his parents, it could be labelled with the more negative term "voyeurism," about which some readers were troubled. Apparently, the "memoir boom" (Rak 2013) is not yet readily accepted by everyone; some readers felt uncomfortable reading a "real" account of someone's intimate and painful experiences. It can be argued, however, that being curious about such experiences is rather sensible and productive. If we do not look at the actual painful experiences of others, how are we to understand fundamental human emotions? We may benefit from authors like Grossman and Van der Heijden in that we gain insight vicariously.

Gaining insight did indeed appear as an important motive and experience. Curiosity about the content was not limited to sensationalism and seeking enjoyment. On the contrary, it largely appeared to have to do with insight-oriented motives: trying to find out more about how others deal with grief. Respondents' indications that they hoped Van der Heijden would find a way to articulate grief, "give shape" to it, showed a further need for clarification. Seeking and finding clarification was more prevalent than simply seeking and finding an expulsion or diminishment of negative emotions. The prevalence of the expressions about the way grief was articulated as well as the relation between appreciating the style generally and reporting existential insights seem to indicate that the structure and style of the literary expression of grief can provide a form of meaning. Describing the indescribable, as Grossman put it, can be invaluable for those who do not have the words and/or experiences themselves, possibly providing a frame for understanding human experience.

It is noteworthy, when describing the indescribable, that one does not need to stress the emotional to evoke feelings in readers. Despite Van der Heijden's tendency to intellectualize, reading *Tonio* still was an emotional experience for most readers. Empathic responses (empathy, sympathy, pity) were very pronounced. It seems that these had an attraction in themselves. People apparently like to feel moved, they like to feel empathy with (fictional) others as a way to realize their own emotional capacity (Zillmann 1998). However, not all emotional experiences were positive. Fear was one of the most salient emotions for parents who read the book, yet it appeared to be an emotion most parents would rather not have experienced. Yet the unpleasantness of the emotion did not stop most of them from reading or appreciating the novel. In contrast to what could have been expected following the catharsis hypothesis, readers did not appear to keep on reading to diminish their fear, at least not consciously. Also, reports of gaining existential insight were not clearly related to experiencing fear. However, the fact that respondents who experienced "clarification" did not mention fear does not preclude that they felt it, since the questions more openly asked about thoughts and feelings. As we do see that readers who talked about the beautiful articulation of grief also tended to experience fear, we can hesitantly conclude that there does seem to be a clarification process going on that includes unpleasant emotions. As noted above, clarification may be found in the way grief is articulated, in the style that frames the experience.

While this case study may have made it somewhat clearer why people choose to read a tragic memoir, it also raises further questions. To what extent do the different reader responses outlined above – gaining existential insight, experiencing fear, finding beauty in the articulation, the lack of reporting catharsis as purgation – call for a reformulation of the catharsis hypothesis? Scheele (2001) has suggested that the integration of cognition and emotion that characterizes catharsis as clarification can indirectly mediate the relaxation of tension. The question to what extent gaining existential insight is related to diminishing unpleasant emotions calls for further research, which could include physiological measures of fear and interviews to establish the type of insights gained. Does reading about suffering make one feel sadder but wiser, or calmer and wiser? And what is the role of style, narrative structure, and genre (fiction versus non-fiction) in this process?

For now, the current study shows that readers' experiences in reading about suffering go beyond the simple experience of enjoyment. The responses to *Tonio* suggest that empathy and stylistic appreciation can lead to the feeling of having learned something vital. *Tonio* is an example of how literature offers the opportunity to imagine extreme experiences that we hope we never have to encounter ourselves, and how that opportunity can expand our world view. Indeed, we can only encourage authors to keep describing the indescribable.

Notes

I would like to thank Els Andringa and Don Kuiken for their useful comments during the research process and on a previous version of this article.

1 Another article about the study this chapter discusses has been published in the journal *Scientific Study of Literature*, under the title "The Attraction of Tragic Narrative: Catharsis and Other Motives" (Koopman 2013). As the title indicates, that article focuses largely on motives for reading, while the current chapter focuses mainly on the reader's experience during and after reading. The current chapter also pays more attention to readers' qualitative responses, while the 2013 article is mainly quantitative. However, it needs to be noted that the two articles overlap.
2 Editors' note: See also the chapters by Brewster and Steenberg in this volume.
3 All translations in the following pages have been made by the author of this chapter.
4 Editors' note: See Fuller and Rehberg Sedo in this volume.

References

Andringa, Els. 2004. "The Interface Between Fiction and Life: Patterns of Identification in Reading Autobiographies." *Poetics Today* 25(2): 205–40.

Aristotle. (n.d.). *Poetics*. http://www.gutenberg.org/files/1974/1974-h/1974-h.htm#2H_4_0008

Bernstein, Joanne E., and Marsha Kabakow Rudman. 1989. *Books to Help Children Cope with Separation and Loss: An Annotated Bibliography*, vol. 3. New York: R.R. Bowker.

Bushman, Brad J., Roy F. Baumeister, and Angela D. Stack. 1999. "Catharsis, Aggression, and Persuasive Influence: Self-Fulfilling or Self-Defeating Prophecies?" *Journal of Personality and Social Psychology* 76(3): 367–76.

Busselle, Rick, and Helena Bilandzic. 2009. "Measuring Narrative Engagement." *Media Psychology* 12(4): 321–47.

Chen, Lei, Shuhua Zhou, and Jenning Bryant. 2007. "Temporal Changes in Mood Repair Through Music Consumption: Effects of Mood, Mood Salience, and Individual Differences." *Media Psychology* 9(3): 695–713.

Cohen, Laura J. 1992. "Bibliotherapy: The Therapeutic Use of Books for Women." Journal of Nurse-Midwifery 37(2): 91–95.

Coplan, Amy. 2004. "Empathic Engagement with Narrative Fictions." *Journal of Aesthetics and Art Criticism* 62(2): 141–52.

Didion, Joan. 2006. *The Year of Magical Thinking*. New York: Random House.

Dillman Carpentier, Francesca R., Jane D. Brown, Michele Bertocci, Jennifer S. Silk, Erika E. Forbes, and Ronald E. Dahl. 2008. "Sad Kids, Sad Media? Applying Mood Management Theory to Depressed Adolescents' Use of Media." *Media Psychology* 11(1): 143–66.

Gibson, Rhonda, Charles F. Aust, and Dolf Zillmann. 2000. "Loneliness of Adolescents and Their Choice and Enjoyment of Love-Celebrating versus Love-Lamenting Popular Music." *Empirical Studies of the Arts* 18(1): 43–48.

Golden, Leon. 1962. "Catharsis." *TAPA* 93: 51–60.

Grossman, David. 2012. *Uit de tijd vallen. Een verhaal in stemmen. [Falling Out of Time: A Story in Voices]*. Amsterdam: Cossee.

Halliwell, Stephen. 1986. *Aristotle's Poetics*. London: Gerald Duckworth.

Hynes, Arleen M. 1980. "The Goals of Bibliotherapy." *The Arts in Psychotherapy* 7(1): 35–41.

Keen, Suzanne. 2006. "A Theory of Narrative Empathy." *Narrative* 14(3): 207–37.

Keesey, Donald. 1979. "On Some Recent Interpretations of Catharsis." *The Classical World* 72(4): 193–205.

Khoo, Guan Soo, and Mary Beth Oliver. 2013. "The Therapeutic Effects of Narrative Cinema through Clarification: Reexamining Catharsis." *Scientific Study of Literature* 3(2): 266–93.

Kim, Jinhee, and Mary Beth Oliver. 2011. "What Combination of Message Characteristics Determines Hedonic and Counter-Hedonic Preferences? An Examination of the Interplay Between Valence and Semantic Affinity." *Media Psychology* 14(2): 121–43.

Kneepkens, E.W.E.M., and Rolf A. Zwaan. 1994. "Emotions and Text Comprehension." Poetics 23: 125–38.

Knobloch, Siliva, and Dolf Zillmann. 2003. "Appeal of Love Themes in Popular Music." *Psychological Reports* 93: 653–58.

Koopman, Emy M. 2011. "Predictors of Insight and Catharsis among Readers Who Use Literature as a Coping Strategy." *Scientific Study of Literature* 1(2): 241–59.

———. 2013. "The Attraction of Tragic Narrative: Catharsis and Other Motives." *Scientific Study of Literature* 3(2): 178–208.

Mar, Raymond A., and Keith Oatley. 2008. "The Function of Fiction Is the Abstraction and Simulation of Social Experience." *Perspectives on Psychological Science* 3(3): 173–92.

Mar, Raymond A., Keith Oatley, Maja Djikic, and Justin Mullin. 2011. "Emotion and Narrative Fiction: Interactive Influences Before, During, and After Reading." *Cognition & Emotion* 25(5): 818–33.

Nabi, Robin L., Keli Finnerty, Tricia Domschke, and Shawnika Hull. 2006. "Does Misery Love Company? Exploring the Therapeutic Effects of TV Viewing on Regretted Experiences." *Journal of Communication* 56(4): 689–706.

Nussbaum, Martha C. 1986. *The Fragility of Goodness: Luck and Ethics in Greek Tragedy and Philosophy*. Cambridge: Cambridge University Press.

Oates, Joyce Carol. 2011. *A Widow's Story: A Memoir*. New York: HarperCollins.

Oliver, Mary Beth. 1993. "Exploring the Paradox of the Enjoyment of Sad Films." *Human Communication Research* 19(3): 315–42.

———. 2008. "Tender Affective States as Predictors of Entertainment Preference." *Journal of Communication* 58(1): 40–61.

Oliver, Mary Beth, and Anne Bartsch. 2010. "Appreciation as Audience Response: Exploring Entertainment Gratifications beyond Hedonism." *Human Communication Research* 36(1): 53–81.

Rak, Julie. 2013. *Boom! Manufacturing Memoir for the Popular Market*. Waterloo: Wilfrid Laurier University Press.

Scheele, Brigitte. 2001. "Back from the Grave: Reinstating the Catharsis Concept in the Psychology of Reception." In *The Psychology and Sociology of Literature: In Honor of Elrud Ibsch*, edited by Dick H. Schram and Gerard J. Steen, 201–24. Amsterdam/ Philadelphia: John Benjamins.

Schreier, Margrit. 2001. "Qualitative Methods in Studying Text Reception." In *The Psychology and Sociology of Literature: In Honor of Elrud Ibsch*, edited by Dick H. Schram and Gerard J. Steen, 35–56. Amsterdam/Philadelphia: John Benjamins.

———. 2012. *Qualitative Content Analysis in Practice*. London: Sage.

Stroebe, Margaret S., Robert O. Hansson, Wolfgang Stroebe, and Henk Schut. 2001. *Handbook of Bereavement Research: Consequences, Coping, and Care*. Washington, DC: American Psychological Association.

Tan, Ed S. 1996. *Emotion and the Structure of Narrative Film: Film as an Emotion Machine*. Mahwah: Lawrence Erlbaum Associates.

Van der Heijden, A.F.Th. 2011. *Tonio: Een requiemroman*. [*Tonio: A Requiem Novel*]. Amsterdam: De Bezige Bij.

Vann, David. 2008. *Legend of a Suicide*. New York: HarperCollins.

Vorderer, Peter. 2003. "Entertainment Theory." In *Communication and Emotion: Essays in Honor of Dolf Zillmann*, edited by Jennings Bryant, David R. Roskos-Ewoldsen, and Joanne Cantor, 131–53. Mahwah: Lawrence Erlbaum Associates.

Zeelenberg, Leo W., and Vivian Spiertz. 1993. "Depressie en Bibliotherapie: Over het gebruik van boeken bij depressie." [Depression and Bibliography: The Use of Books for Depression]. PhD diss., Utrecht University.

Zill, Nicholas, and Marianne Winglee. 1988. *Who Reads Literature? Survey Data on the Reading of Fiction, Poetry, and Drama by U.S. Adults during the 1980s*. Washington, DC: National Endowment for the Arts.

Zillmann, Dolf. 1998. "Does Tragic Drama Have Redeeming Value?" "SPIEL – *Siegener Periodikum zur Internationale Literaturwissenschaft* 16(1): 1–11.

When Comics Set the Pace   14
The Experience of Time and the Reading of Comics

Lucia Cedeira Serantes

> I remember with *Blankets*, I sat, it was a Saturday and I remember sitting at the Denver Public Library and just reading it, in one afternoon, not really looking up. (Alison)

Reading, like other everyday practices, has temporal and spatial dimensions. Rosenblatt defines reading as a transaction that involves "a reader and a text at a particular time under particular circumstances" (1982, 268). These circumstances are described by readers in different ways. In Alison's quote above, she talks about reading the graphic novel *Blankets* in terms that are recognizable for many readers when she describes a particular reading experience, in a particular place, with a particular pace and duration. In my research into the experience of young adult readers of comics, time emerged as a critical factor that affected their reading experiences. The relevance of time resides in its potential to explain the importance and resurgence of comics as reading material. Parents, educators, and librarians have often explained youth's interest in comics based on their visual component. On the one hand this component is undeniably relevant in the process of understanding and enjoying comics; on the other hand it is worrisome that this element is so often connected to ideas of "light reading" or "easy reading." My research (2009; 2014) along with studies by Botzakis (2008; 2011) and Sabeti (2011; 2013) seeks to open up new lines of debate about this issue. Here I examine the connection between reading, comics in particular, and the experience of time in order to show a growing complexity in this relationship. I argue that this complexity partly arises from the dual processes of adaptation and resistance to the temporal requirements that readers live under in the digital era. As an example of these processes I put forward the following thought shared by another of my participants, Shalmanaser:

> I think the thing that gets me about comics ... is that they can do something that neither books nor movies can ... It's almost like *you have time to go over it without taking too much time*, you have all the visuals of a movie except

that there's much more detail, *you have all the time to look at them*, taking the details, and you have all the plot of a book but without all the descriptions. (Cedeira Serantes's italics)

Shalmanaser succinctly summarizes the temporal duality in the experience of reading comics. The first sentence in italics introduces an idea of efficiency, how the characteristics of the medium provide a quick but also satisfying reading experience. The second sentence in italics describes a different condition, one that I relate to processes of slowing down, of deceleration, even resistance to the way time is currently experienced in society.

To be able to successfully explain this dual role that comics play it is important to understand the temporal experiences and requirements that surround readers. I will first set out recent scholarly discussions about acceleration and deceleration in contemporary society. This review is not meant to be comprehensive; rather, it is limited to understandings, studies, and concepts that can inform the contextualization and interpretation of my participants' experiences. I will introduce previous studies that examine the relationship between time and reading. These scholarly works mostly come from a time-use perspective, but there are also some unique examples from a phenomenological approach that guide my work to a particular attitude towards the reading experience. Finally, after establishing this context, I will bring to the discussion my participants' thoughts and experiences to address the overall question of comics' potential contribution (supportive and/or antagonistic) to the experience of time in contemporary society.

Time in Society: Acceleration, Deceleration, and the Pace of Life

The concepts of "time–space compression" (Harvey 1990), "timeless time" (Castells 2000), and "dromology" (Virilio 2006) are examples of time's prominent role in the explanation of structural, social, and economical changes, especially in connection to late capitalism and emergent digital technologies. Time has also become a critical topic in the study of everyday practices. Early arguments that connected time and everyday life can be seen in pioneers like Durkheim ([1912]1976), who declared that the rhythm of social life is the basis for time, or more recently Lefebvre ([1992]2004), who defended the study of quotidian rhythms to explore the connections between individuals and the social.

The concept of acceleration is directly connected to time. In the digital age "time is characterized by acceleration, speed and instantaneity" (Reading 2012, 144). Rosa and Scheuerman note the importance of acceleration in current analyses, but they also observe an apparent inconsistency in that while "*acceleration* figures as a striking feature of prominent diagnoses of contemporary social development" (2009, 2), this phenomenon lacks a strong sociological analysis and "too often the simplistic claim is made that in modern societies more or less everything is speeding up" (2009, 2).

Rosa identifies three analytical and empirical categories to analyze the relationship between social phenomena and social acceleration (2009, 81): technological acceleration, acceleration of social change, and acceleration of the pace of life. In the explanation for the third dimension, the acceleration of the pace of life, Rosa brings up the concept of "scarcity of time" (2009, 85–87). Intuitively, technological acceleration should bring an increase of free time since it should decrease the time we need to carry out daily activities and processes, leaving more time for leisure. Rosa says that "if less time is needed, time should become more abundant," but if the result is that time has become scarcer, "this is a paradoxical effect that calls for a sociological explanation" (2009, 85). Inspired by Rosa, Leccardi focuses on this paradox and also observes that the saved time that technological acceleration generates has been "swallowed up" by social acceleration (2007, 27), consequently feeding the current feelings of time scarcity and burnout. Leccardi converts the paradox into a pertinent question: how can one keep a social time that is increasingly rapid and fragmented together with the richness and the specific tempo of inner time? (2003, 39). As I will present, reading comics offers a partial but sensible answer to this question.

Rosa calls for the need to measure the pace of life, immediately introducing subjective and objective approaches. The subjective approach focuses primarily on individuals' experience of time with a focus on the increase of feelings of time scarcity, hurry, and time pressure, thus "making plausible the argument that the 'digital revolution' and the processes of globalization amount to yet another wave of social acceleration" (2009, 86). Time-use studies are the typical result of scholarly works using an objective approach. These studies identify how we distribute our time in relation to the activities we perform. Their main goal is to detect processes whereby activities are compressed into less time or result in practices such as multitasking.

In this process of studying and theorizing acceleration and the pace of life, Rosa detects the overuse of the idea of the acceleration cycle to help explain the dynamics related to speed and growth present in Western societies. In contrast to the acceleration cycle, he proposes the exploration of three factors that influence the aforementioned three dimensions: an economic motor, a cultural motor, and a structural motor. A closer look at the cultural motor is pertinent in this section since Rosa links it to his explanation of the phenomenon of the scarcity of time.

First, Rosa reminds us of a notable change in modern Western society. The ideas of happiness and life fulfillment are no longer connected to a "higher life"; citizens seek self-realization by trying to live through "as many options as possible from the vast possibilities the world has to offer" (2009, 91). The problem is that the options offered by the world always outgrow those realizable in a lifetime and thus the acceleration of the pace of life becomes a potential way of addressing this divergence. Basically, the acceleration of the pace of life is our attempt to adapt to the increase of possibility accentuated by the cultural motor. Rosa concludes that "acceleration serves as a strategy to erase the difference between the time of the world and the time of our life" (2009, 91).

Rosa considers the process of speeding up to be asynchronous and demands an effort to "understand the status, function, and structure of those phenomena that escape dynamization or even represent forms of slowdown and deceleration" (2009, 93). In his own study he distinguishes five different forms of deceleration and inertia (92–97). Among the intentional forms of slowing down there is one that shows how citizens are trying to adapt and cope with current temporal requirements. Rosa explains them as "limited and temporary forms of deceleration that aim at preserving the capacity to function and further accelerate within acceleratory systems" (95). As examples he mentions yoga and taking time out in monasteries. Reading has already been linked to practices that help this process of slowing down (Miedema 2009); the uniqueness of comics reading is that it can potentially support both acceleration and deceleration.

Time in Reading

In research about reading habits, studies of time management and distribution are not uncommon. Addressed are such topics as the influence of reading time on academic achievements and on the improvement of literacy skills, and the distribution of time among competing media practices (e.g., Gallik 1999; Johnsson-Smaragdi and Jönsson 2006; Hughes-Hassell and Rodge 2007; Mokhtari, Reichard, and Gardner 2009). In contrast, the subjective approach is less prevalent and is mainly represented by phenomenological studies of reading (Heap 1977; Hunsberger 1985, 1992).[1] Gallik (1999) and Hughes-Hassell and Rodge (2007) are two examples of time-use studies where reading, time, and academic achievement are interconnected. Gallik found that time spent reading for pleasure outside of school was a useful predictor for reading comprehension, vocabulary, and speed. During breaks and vacations, magazines were the most popular reading material while comic books were the least popular, with 88 percent of students reporting that they rarely or never read comic books (Gallik 1999, 485). Eight years later, Hughes-Hassell and Rodge (2007) reported that comics were the second favourite, along with magazines. Their study focused on the leisure reading habits of 584 urban-minority middle-school students; in their case, the connection between school achievement and time spent in leisure reading was already established and served as a factor to justify the need for a closer examination of the leisure reading practices of urban youth. Gilbert and Fister (2011) examined the idea of reading as being at risk among the college student population. Their participants declared that they did not have much time to engage in reading for pleasure during the school year, although they did have positive feelings about reading. The researchers did not include graphic novels as an option in their survey, but they indicated that this material often appeared in the write-in choices of the students.

Although time is central to these projects, the analysis is centred on quantitative issues – how much time is being dedicated – and on the consequences of this time allocation. For example, the choice of comics and magazines is often linked to the following: issues of low literacy levels; the instrumental role of the visual element to support an easier reading experience; and the participants' interest in the content. Alternatively I propose that some characteristics of comics support a reading experience that better adapts to the ways young adults organize their lives.

A phenomenological approach has had a presence in the study of reading, particularly since the emergence of reader response theory. The works of Wolfgang Iser (1972; 1978) and Georges Poulet (1969) are two early examples. Yet there are very few examples that employ a subjective approach to the study of reading and time. The works of Heap (1977) and Hunsberger (1985; 1992) are two highly relevant examples. As part of his theoretical examination of one reading act, Heap explored the temporal structure of reading, always understood as a situated and embodied activity. Heap located reading as occurring "within a certain intersection of world time and inner time" (1977, 109). According to Heap, reading has an intrinsic temporal structure that he compares to a clock. The reader controls one hand of this clock and can step it up, slow it down, or even halt time (1977, 112). However, texts still have an "ideal" reading time that, although modifiable by the reader, is partly responsible for the text's "unity of sense." Therefore, the reader needs to know and orient her reading act to how the text is supposed to be read (1977, 112). For Heap, it is crucial to understand the relationship between reading and time in order to understand reading as sense-making. Hunsberger (1992) also understands reading as an embodied and individual lived experience, but in contrast to Heap, she explored this experience empirically through interviews with a group of readers. Like Heap, Hunsberger identifies a difference between an "objective, or clock" perception of time and an "experienced, or inner" perception that is part of the many "complexities of thinking about – and living in – time." Based on these complexities, she asked, "What then happens to time during reading? How is it experienced?" (1992, 65). Among the several issues that she briefly discusses, one is especially relevant for my analysis – her treatment of "not-time," a feeling of standing outside time. Based on her participants' comments, Hunsberger explores two qualities: "stillness and freedom from daily concerns" (1992, 90). These two qualities describe how readers escape or feel as if the world rests while they are reading. Finally, she argues that "reading gives an opportunity to experience time in various ways, to start difficult but significant thinking, to glimpse not-time, and to stretch out imaginative limits" (1992, 91).

These two studies touch on aspects of the temporal experience in reading and help ground my project in a scholarly tradition that understands reading as situated and embodied and that acknowledges the relevance of temporal experiences and questions. In my study I privilege the social-temporal requirements and experiences that surround my participants. This context is important for a more active and reflective re-engagement with time and temporality, especially in relation to mediated experiences and, in this particular case, to reading (Keightley 2013, 59).

Comics Readers, the Experience of Time, and the Possibilities of Comics

> I am a reader, but not, I don't know ... It's not something I choose to do all the time, it's something that I'd do as I'm going to bed or if I'm on the train or I don't know, if I'm waiting for something ... But I, it's something I choose to fill my free time with. This is why I like comics 'cause it's such a lighter read. I feel like I can get through a comic, it's less dense than reading a novel. I find comics much more enjoyable. (Preacher)

Up to this point I have talked mainly about time but not much about comics reading. When one thinks about comics reading, the concepts of "light" reading and reluctant readers often arise (Krashen 2004). However, Preacher's words above reveal a complex experience, especially so when the analysis uses a temporal approach to raise some alternative understandings of this idea of "light" reading.

First we need to question several assumptions. In the context of Preacher's words, where do we find this quality of being "light"? Is it connected to the form, the content, the experiential context, or a combination of these? Does it mean easy, simple, entertaining, or maybe adaptable? For instance, the immediate association of "light" with the content of comics shows a lack of critical engagement with the diversity in comics publishing and an oversimplification of this reader's taste. Preacher's reading preference is defined by works such as *Maus*, *Watchmen*, *Batman: The Killing Joke*, and *Y: The Last Man*. None of these titles can be described as simple or easy to read.

Properly addressing these assumptions is beyond the scope of this paper, but they show an assumed simplicity in relation to the study of the comics reading experience. The introduction of a temporal perspective helps reveal this understudied complexity. Preacher's description is not exceptional; rather, it reflects the perspective of an average citizen in a Western urban centre. He chooses to read mostly to fill time; he reads during the fractions of time that become free in his daily life. Furthermore, the influence of time availability on his reading experience justifies the inclusion of a temporal lens in the analysis. One might ponder then whether there are certain characteristics that make comics simply highly adaptable to readers' time availability. In the case of Preacher, it represents the significant relationship between social time and an individual's pace of life, illustrating comics' adaptability to these different temporal experiences.

This brief analysis richly illustrates the considerable potential that including a temporal perspective brings to the analysis of the reading experience. Below I explore how the experience of reading comics can potentially adapt to and resist the social-temporal requirements of the digital era.

Efficiency and Time Scarcity: How Comics Adapt to Temporal Demands

> It's not necessarily easier than reading text, but it's easier than reading a textbook text or a History text or stuff that I have to. It's definitely a welcomed break. (HunterS)

Participants constantly mentioned the idea of time scarcity. Except for two participants, they were students or had just finished their university degree, and time scarcity was explained primarily in connection to the constant work of time management to balance academic and leisure activities with related feelings of stress and pressure. Daniel describes his days as extremely busy: he is an undergraduate in university, works at a comics bookstore, and has several leisure activities that occupy his free time. Economic pressures play a pivotal role in the way he organizes his time. University is very expensive, hence a priority for his time allocation. But he also states that he tries to "steal time for myself whenever I can." These two attitudes reveal a tension that manifests itself even more clearly during his commuting time. When he rides the bus he tends to read comics, but this simple act precipitates a "crisis of conscience" since he should be using his time for school work. Marian raises a similar tension when she describes the opportunity to go to the public library as a "luxury." The library is her main access point for reading material, especially comics, and this lack of time affects her reading practices. The language used by these two participants denotes feelings of stress and pressure that connect their experiences with the aforementioned ideas about the subjective experience of social acceleration (Rosa 2009, 86).

Participants implement some practices to alleviate these feelings. For example, for HunterS, Templesmith, and Devi, comics reading becomes their preferred activity for breaks from academic work. Devi, an English student, qualifies comics as a "treat" in comparison with the many readings she has to do for class. Preacher describes comics as "sort of therapeutic"; when he is stressed or worried, comics help him "immerse myself and make that the only thing on my mind." For these participants, comics reading is a leisure activity that easily fits among academic responsibilities, provides some time for oneself, and can easily insert itself into daily work routines.

This struggle for time is not unique to work/study activities. The lives of these young adults are overloaded with activities, so time management often expands into leisure time. This struggle connects with Rosa's discussion about the acceleration of the pace of life. The constant competition for time can be understood as a manifestation of the conflict between the modern process of self-realization and the impossibility of experiencing everything that is available to us. Daniel has already given some thought to this struggle for time. He sees photography as his main calling, but as it is a demanding activity, it is sometimes difficult for him to keep up with it. He explains that without this interest and some other activities, his time for reading would certainly increase. However, the lack of these other activities would make him "feel like something would be missing in my life because I wouldn't be being creative." In the middle of this race for leisure time, comics have one little advantage in that "they are a creative piece of art, they're art, they're stories," so for Daniel they manage to reconcile many of his interests. In this case the visual element of comics is not something that makes them easier or lighter, but something inspiring that can inform some of Daniel's other leisure activities.

Shade justifies the importance of comics based on their publishing format. As he explains:

> Sometimes when I get home [in the evening] I want to read stuff right away ... I have a relatively short attention span so I can't really sit and do one thing for a long time so usually I'll watch a tv show and then I'll go and read a couple of comic books and then I'll go do work or something and then I'll go and read a couple more comic books, these [pointing at the comic books he has brought] are good for that, where you can just get a couple even before I go to work or something, if I want to read them I can.

Monthly comic books can develop long and complex story arcs, and the quality of some titles satisfies Shade's expressed preference for reading material that "brings something new, that can make me think about something." These comic books are also a convenient option: their requirements for time and attention adapt to Shade's evening routine, one clearly populated by many different activities.

The visual element of comics emerges as an important factor in explaining these participants' preferences. For them, that element supports a quick immersion in the narrative, thus making effective and efficient use of the available time for reading. Shalmanaser articulates this concisely when he says that "[comics are] something that you can just pick up and drop whenever you want to and you can get back into the story very easily." When the participants feel that time is scarce, the capacity to immediately immerse oneself in the story is invaluable. This characteristic also enables the reader to stop the reading experience without dreading the moment of starting again. As Shalmanaser explained, achieving the reading "momentum" is easier and faster with comics. This idea of reading "momentum" can be better explored with the help of the concept of "flow."

The psychologist Csikszentmihalyi uses the concept of "flow" to explain why some activities are enjoyable and absorbing. This state is defined through four principles: control, challenge, feedback, and focus. He explains these as follows:

> At the core of the flow experience is enjoyment. For an activity to be truly enjoyable, it must have clear goals, permit immediate feedback, require effortless involvement, and have a clear chance of completion. A truly enjoyable experience leads to an altered sense of time duration, a sense of control over one's own action, and the emergence of a stronger sense of self. (1990, 50)

Csikszentmihalyi identified reading for pleasure as one of the most frequently reported flow activities. Although the role of time is mentioned explicitly only in connection to the manipulation of inner time, it is implicit in relation to the other characteristics: How fast can you achieve the goals of the activity or reach completion? How immediate is "immediate feedback"? In the case of comics reading, one essential factor is that less time is needed to achieve a potentially satisfactory reading experience. The availability and distribution of time are complex and fragmented, and comics seem to adapt well to these external conditions because readers can get into a story faster. The combination of achieving a satisfactory reading experience in a relatively short period of time and the ability to smoothly enter and exit the narrative connects comics with the experience of "flow."

Ziolkowska and Howard (2010) explored the comics reading experience using the concept of "flow." They interviewed nine adult participants who were avid comic readers to address the question of why adult readers choose to read comics. They determined that the relatively short length of comics supports a quick completion that in turn provides readers with immediate satisfaction and positive tangible feedback. It is tempting to equate quick with easy, but this fast experience was also demanding because it required textual and visual literacy skills as well as knowledge about the medium itself (2010, 164). In the case of my participants, Baa powerfully reinforces these conclusions with one sentence: "[Comics] can tell you so much and you can finish them in a day." This sentence makes more evident the importance of the balance between providing a satisfactory experience and having that experience in a short period of time. Nevertheless, it is also crucial to keep in mind the diversity in comics publishing and how different formats and art styles can affect the reading experience. For example, Marian explains the difference between reading a mainstream manga and an American trade paperback:

> It's the fact that a manga volume would take an hour to read and then it's like, ok, I have to find another soon or otherwise I'll forget what was happening or I'll just waste an hour ... [Pointing at *Unwritten*] This one has more text in it. A trade is kind of ... worthy ... not worthy but I just find that there's just more satisfaction, it takes more than one sitting to read.

We can gather from this quote that undemanding comics or reading experiences that are too short can be problematic. Comics are not the perfect reading material for the twenty-first century reader, but certain qualities make them more gratifying. Comics respond to the time requirements prevalent in the digital era: they are easily inserted into busy daily work routines, and they are successfully adjusted to the high volume of other daily activities. Comics also seem to provide a high level of satisfaction without requiring a substantial time investment.

In the following section I narrow the focus to one concrete aspect of the reading experience in order to examine how readers slow down the reading experience and potentially resist the fast-paced rhythm of their daily lives.

Resistance: Slowing Down the Reading Experience with Comics

> You can read a comic quickly but you've not necessarily read it at all. With comics I try not to go too quickly because you're not taking everything in, there's a lot of visual information there, it's almost like reading between the lines of a novel. (Daniel)

Reading has often been linked to processes of slowing down, creating time, or taking time for oneself. For example, in her research about female romance readers Radway determined that these women used reading as a way to carve out their own space and time in the midst of demanding caring roles in domestic life (1991). Comics reading seems to play a similar role for some of my participants. As I have previously mentioned, Preacher sees comics reading as relaxing and explains his reading routine as a reaction to the chaos of dormitory life. He likes to read when it is quiet, when "everyone is asleep or everyone is chill[ed] out a little bit or while they're studying." He also looks for privacy, "away from everybody else." So he reads at night, in bed or on a couch, making himself physically and emotionally comfortable. Reading helps him find or create a moment for himself. However, as I have said, this characteristic is not unique to reading comics, but supported by many reading experiences. So, what is actually unique about comics?

Certain characteristics of comics fit rather well into fast-paced social time. However, the possibility exists that comics also support the conditions for an antagonistic temporal experience, allowing the reader to take time, to stop, and to contemplate. In Daniel's quote (above) he talks about not reading "too quickly" in order to be able to take everything in. Devi describes a similar deceleration process when she characterizes comics as treats because she "can take time" with them, especially in contrast to her required academic reading. When she tries to describe the uniqueness of comics, she describes an act of contemplation, how she can "spend a lot of time on a page." The dual nature of comics makes this act of contemplation possible. As an experienced reader of comics, Devi knows that text and images need to be read together, but she likes to appreciate the images on their own and also sometimes to revisit the text. Atkinson (2012) introduces a temporal explanation in relation to this duality in his study of reading and contemplation in comics. He uses Peeters's "double temporalité" to explore the difference between the viewing experiences of reading comics and visiting a gallery (2012, 69). When a reader is looking at a panel, two reading possibilities are open to her. One is that of looking at the panel as a "tableau" (i.e., as a picture or a painting where the reader remains looking at a single image), and the second is as a "récit" (i.e., as a narrative, where sequentiality and storytelling inevitably push the reader forward). Inspired by Eisner, Atkinson also explains how creators design the stories with a certain rhythm; readers then reconstitute that temporal continuity for the comics to have a meaning (2012, 70). However Atkinson finds that the structure of comics and the practice of comics reading inevitably push readers away from the act of contemplating:

> The ease with which we read comic books is largely dependent on the transparency of the narrative or the legibility of the process of reading but this involves turning away from the "trace picturale" or the plasticity of the line and not persisting in the contemplation of the visual properties of any one image. (2012, 72)

Conversely, Schneider (2010) considers a series of comics that challenge Atkinson's premise. Based on comics that focus on everyday life stories, Schneider identifies different strategies proper to the language of comics capable of arousing everyday moods in the reading experience. She is particularly interested in those cases where a sense of slowness is introduced, thus manipulating the temporal dimension. For example, Schneider finds that contemplation is connected to "engagement, curiosity and attention" and that the act of contemplating is often explored in comics through repetition, the manipulation of the direction of the gaze in the panel, or the inclusion of "small and telling differences" (2010, 59). According to her, these comics produce this slowdown process. But does this process need to be sought purposefully by the creator? Or can it be achieved independently by the reader?

Schneider and Atkinson focus on text analysis; my interest lies on the reader experience. As described by my participants, this process of temporal re-creation and meaning creation is not closed to possibilities of reader's agency. For instance, Promethea explains how she intentionally looks at the pages and panels as "tableaux" because she wants to appreciate the art: "I look at the pages first 'cause I know that if I get to the story I won't even ... I'll forget about the page, I'll forget to appreciate the page so I'll always stare at the art work first for a while before finishing the story." Kalo expands this idea when she says that she was "purposefully waiting and stopping and looking [at] every little thing." If comics, as Atkinson explains, primarily impose a high speed to be able to re-create the narrative – the "récit" – then perhaps we should wonder if the act of slowing down is an act of rebelling against this imposed rhythm. Schneider brings up Michel de Certeau's comparison between walking and reading in her discussion of Jirô Taniguchi's *The Walking Man* (2010, 62). Following de Certeau, Schneider explains that reading can be understood as a way of wandering through an imposed system. Expanding on this, I propose that in this imposed system there is also an imposed speed. This imposed speed can be internal, as part of the text created by the author, and/or external, as the high speed that surrounds the reading experience. The uniqueness of comics is that they create the possibility for a double speed during the same reading experience. This duality gives readers the agency to choose. Although the experience of reading comics is often linked to high-speed reading and brevity, this should not be essentialized; rather, it should be opened to multiplicity and, in some cases, even resistance. Evidently, as Schneider studied, there are works that are created with this slowness embedded in them. However, the always present possibility of enjoying a panel as a "tableau" allows readers to individually slow down the experience.

Hunsberger concludes her phenomenological study of time and reading by saying that "reading is an area of life that provides excellent ground for the imagination to challenge time or any other practical constraints" (1992, 90). The experience of reading comics gives readers a clear possibility not just to challenge time but to make it malleable, which potentially contributes to the development of "lines of resistance" (Keightley 2012, 206) to a single fast-paced time experience.

Conclusion

> There was a period of time when I wasn't reading at all, because I thought I was so busy and didn't have any time but then I decided that reading is important to me, that it makes me happy so I need to make time every day to do it. (Selina)

For Selina, reading is a powerful force in her life. She sometimes thought without time for reading, she would "go off the deep end." In a time when it is rather difficult to develop structured and solid routines, Selina established a simple but effective strategy: always travelling and moving with reading material. It does not matter how brief the time periods, she always uses them for reading. Therefore Selina needs reading material that can both fulfill her need for reading and adapt to her pace of life. Lately that reading material has been comics.

This scenario reveals the importance of reading. Although not all participants shared Selina's intensity, they did identify themselves as comics readers and shared the substantial role that comics reading plays in their lives. For example, if reading is conceptualized as a "focal practice" (Sumara 1996, 9) that rearranges readers' lives, one might wonder how the current temporal structures can potentially affect my participants' identity as readers. Rosa points to the relevance of this question when he says that "changes in the temporal structures of modern societies transform the very essence of our culture, social structure, and personal identity" (2003, 17–18). Daniel's words about "stealing time for [him]self" and Kalo's description of her lack of time for pleasure reading as "heartbreaking" already indicate the reality of time scarcity and point to issues of lack of and need for control. Having or not having time at their disposal is affecting their present status as readers. For

Shalmanser, lack of time may even be affecting his future identification with reading:

> If I don't have time to read I tend to read less and less and mainly even when I do have time again I might not think of reading because I just got out of practice, but if I do have time to read typically I will, I will use all of it, I have a limit to how long I can read for one stretch of time but otherwise I try to use [it] to its fullest extent. If I don't have very much time I might stop reading as much in the future.

If the lack of time is affecting the practices of readers and can potentially affect their identities as such, time is a variable that clearly should be included more often in discussions about the reading experience. As I have discussed, this is especially crucial for comics reading since it helps defy stereotypes about comics reading. It speaks to Leccardi's inquiry about how we grapple with a rapid social time and a specific inner time (2003, 39). In this study, I have shown how my participants construct comics as complex narratives that smoothly adapt to the temporal requirements connected to a current state of time scarcity. Moreover, in this age where time seems to be defined by acceleration, speed, and instantaneity, readers also appreciate the quality of comics to allow for moments of contemplation.

Note

1 Editors' note: See chapters by McKenzie and Davies and by Cliff Hodges, respectively, in this volume, for more on aspects of temporality in reading and on time–space elements in the reading experience.

References

Atkinson, Paul. 2012. "Why Pause?: The Fine Line between Reading and Contemplation." *Studies in Comics* 3(1): 63–82.

Botzakis, Stergios. 2008. "'I've Gotten a Lot Out of Reading Comics': Poaching and Lifelong Literacy." In *57th Yearbook of the National Reading Conference*, edited by Y. Kim, V.J. Risko, D.L. Compton, D.K. Dickinson, M.K. Hundley, R.T. Jimenes, K.M. Leander, and D.W. Rowe, 119–29. Oak Creek: National Reading Conference.

———. 2011. "'To Be a Part of the Dialogue': American Adults Reading Comic Books." *Journal of Graphic Novels & Comics* 2(2): 37–41.

Castells, Manuel. 2000. *End of Millennium*, 2nd ed. Oxford: Blackwell.

Cedeira Serantes, Lucia. 2009. "'I'm a Marvel Girl': Exploration of the Selection Practices of Comic Book Readers." Paper presented at the Canadian Association for Information Science Conference: Mapping the 21st Century Information Landscape: Borders, Bridges, and Byways, Ottawa.

———. 2014. "Young Adults Reflect on the Experience of Reading Comics in Contemporary Society: Overcoming the Commonplace and Recognizing Complexity." PhD diss., University of Western Ontario, London.

Csikszentmihalyi, Mihaly. 1990. *Flow: The Psychology of Optimal Experience*. New York: HarperCollins.

Durkheim, Emile. [1912]1976. *The Elementary Forms of Religious Life*. 2nd ed. London: Allen and Unwin.

Gallik, Jude D. 1999. "Do They Read for Pleasure? Recreational Reading Habits of College Students." *Journal of Adolescent & Adult Literacy* 42(6): 480–88.

Gilbert, Julie, and Barbara Fister. 2011. "Reading, Risk, and Reality: College Students and Reading for Pleasure." *College & Research Libraries* 72(5): 474–95.

Harvey, David. 1990. *The Condition of Postmodernity: An Enquiry into the Origins of Cultural Change*. Cambridge, MA: Blackwell.

Heap, James L. 1977. "Toward a Phenomenology of Reading." *Journal of Phenomenological Psychology* 8(1): 103–13.

Hughes-Hassell, Sandra, and Pradnya Rodge. 2007. "The Leisure Reading Habits of Urban Adolescents." *Journal of Adolescent & Adult Literacy* 51(1): 22–33.

Hunsberger, Margaret. 1985. "The Experience of Re-Reading." *Phenomenology + Pedagogy* 3(3): 161–66.

———. 1992. "The Time of Texts." In *Understanding Curriculum as Phenomenological and Deconstructed Text*, edited by William F. Pina and William M. Reynolds, 64–91. New York: Teachers College Press.

Iser, Wolfgang. 1972. "The Reading Process: A Phenomenological Approach." *New Literary History* 3(2): 279–99.

———. 1978. *The Act of Reading: A Theory of Aesthetic Response*. Baltimore: Johns Hopkins University Press.

Johnsson-Smaragdi, Ulla, and Annelis Jönsson. 2006. "Book Reading in Leisure Time: Long Term Changes in Young Peoples' Book Reading Habits." *Scandinavian Journal of Educational Research* 50(5): 519–40.

Keightley, Emily. 2012. "Conclusion: Making Time – The Social Temporalities of Mediated Experience." In *Time, Media, and Modernity*, 201–10. London: Palgrave Macmillan.

———. 2013. "From Immediacy to Intermediacy: The Mediation of Lived Time." *Time & Society* 22(1) (25 March): 55–75.

Krashen, Stephen D. 2004. *The Power of Reading: Insights from the Research*. 2nd ed. Westport: Libraries Unlimited.

Leccardi, Carmen. 2003. "Resisting 'Acceleration Society.'" *Constellations* 10(1): 34–41.

———. 2007. "New Temporal Perspective in the 'High-Speed Society.'" In *24/7: Time and Temporality in the Network Society*, edited by Robert Hassan and Ronald E. Purser, 25–36. Stanford: Stanford University Press.

Lefebvre, Henri. [1992]2004. *Rhythmanalysis: Space, Time, and Everyday Life*. New York: Continuum.

Miedema, John. 2009. *Slow Reading*. Duluth: Litwin Books.

Mokhtari, Kouider, Carla A. Reichard, and Anne Gardner. 2009. "The Impact of Internet and Television Use on the Reading Habits and Practices of College Students." *Journal of Adolescent & Adult Literacy* 52(7): 609–19.

Poulet, Georges. 1969. "Phenomenology of Reading." *New Literary History* 1(1): 53–68.

Radway, Janice. 1991. *Reading the Romance: Women, Patriarchy, and Popular Literature*. Chapel Hill: University of North Carolina Press.
Reading, Anna. 2012. "Globital Time: Time in the Digital Globalised Age." In *Time, Media, and Modernity*, edited by Emily Keightley, 143–62. London: Palgrave Macmillan.
Rosa, Hartmut. 2003. "Social Acceleration: Ethical and Political Consequences of a Desynchronized High-Speed Society." *Constellations* 10(1): 3–33.
———. 2009. "Social Acceleration: Ethical and Political Consequences of a Desynchronized High Speed Society." In *High-Speed Society: Social Acceleration, Power, and Modernity*, edited by Hartmut Rosa and William E. Scheuerman, 77–111. University Park: Pennsylvania State University Press.
Rosa, Hartmut, and William E. Scheuerman. 2009. "Introduction." In *High-Speed Society: Social Acceleration, Power, and Modernity*, edited by Hartmut Rosa and William E. Scheuerman, 1–29. University Park: Pennsylvania State University Press.
Rosenblatt, Louise M. 1982. "The Literary Transaction and Evocation Response." *Theory and Society* 21(4): 268–77.
Sabeti, Shari. 2011. "The Irony of 'Cool Club': The Place of Comic Book Reading in Schools." *Journal of Graphic Novels and Comics* 2(2): 37–41.
———. 2013. "'A Different Kind of Reading': The Emergent Literacy Practices of a School-Based Graphic Novel Club." *British Educational Research Journal* 39(5): 835–52.
Schneider, Greice. 2010. "Comics and Everyday Life: From *Ennui* to Contemplation." *European Comic Art* 3(1): 37–64.
Sumara, Dennis J. 1996. *Private Readings in Public: Schooling the Literary Imagination*. New York: Peter Lang.
Virilio, Paul. 2006. *Speed and Politics*. Los Angeles: Semiotext(e).
Ziolkowska, Sarah, and Vivian Howard. 2010. "'Forty-One-Year-Old Female Academics Aren't Supposed to Like Comics!' The Value of Comic Books to Adult Readers." In *Graphic Novels and Comics in Libraries and Archives: Essays on Readers, Research, History, and Cataloging*, edited by Robert G. Weiner, 154–66. Jefferson: McFarland.

Comics

Carey, Mike (w) and Peter Gross (a). 2009. *The Unwritten*. 9 vols. New York: Vertigo.
Moore, Alan (w), Dave Gibbons (a), and John Higgins (c). 2013. *Watchmen*. New York: DC.
Moore, Alan (w) and Brian Bolland (a). 2008. *Batman: The Killing Joke*. New York: DC.
Spiegelman, Art. 2003. *The Complete Maus*. London: Penguin.
Thompson, Craig. 2009. *Blankets: An Illustrated Novel*. Marietta: Top Shelf.
Taniguchi, Jiro. 2004. *The Walking Man*. London, Rasquera: Fanfare, Ponent Mon.
Vaughan, Brian K. (w), Pia Guerra (a), Goran Sudžuka (a), and Paul Chadwick (a). 2002–8. *Y: The Last Man*. 10 vols. New York: Vertigo.

Reading Groups in Swedish Public Libraries 15

Kerstin Rydbeck

This chapter presents results from a study investigating the reading group activities connected to Swedish public libraries.[1] Reading groups are common in Sweden and have been so for a very long time. As in most Western European countries, the rise of reading communities in Sweden was closely connected to the development of the modern book market and the press and to what Habermas calls the public sphere of bourgeois society. Circulating libraries and literary societies developed in Sweden during the late eighteenth century and the first part of the nineteenth. Some literary salons also existed – the most famous was Malla Silfverstolpe's salon in Uppsala, which began in 1820 and continued for several decades (Sørensen 1998). The first use of the Swedish word *läsecirkel* (i.e., reading circle) is found in a text published in 1824 (*Svenska akademiens ordbok* 2015). From that time onward, the word "circle" in the Swedish language became closely connected to the free educational work of small groups comprising people with similar interests. During the nineteenth century, however, it was part of a secular reading culture and used largely in connection to groups belonging to the upper classes (Rydbeck 2013c).

Sweden also had a strong religious reading culture. By the mid-eighteenth century, about 90 percent of Swedes – both men and women – were literate. This was a consequence of the Church Law of 1686, which required local pastors to organize yearly assessments of literacy and of knowledge of Luther's catechism, for all members of their parishes. The results were written down in church examination registers (*husförhörslängder*) (Appel and Fink-Mortensen 2011; Lindmark 2011). The Swedish religious culture was also strongly affected by pietism; in the nineteenth century the pietists – as an outgrowth of their intensive study of the Bible, introduced a new, reflective reading, which is why they were called "readers" (Ambjörnsson 1998). This new way of reading and studying the Bible was generally conducted in small local groups of laypeople, referred to as conventicles. However, as in England and Scotland, Sweden had a Conventicle Act that forbade such religious assemblies in private homes without the presence of a clergyman from the Church of Sweden. When this act finally was abolished in the 1860s, the Free Church Movement developed quickly as the first of several important popular and social movements in the country.

According to Ambjörnsson (1998), the temperance and labour movements, which also developed during the late nineteenth century, adopted this style of reflective reading. Together, the three popular movements came to play an important political role in the development of modern, democratic Sweden, and at an early stage they privileged educational work. With ideological influences primarily from the Chautauqua movement in United States and from British Bible circles, a pedagogical concept for self-education in small local study groups developed within the Swedish temperance movement at the turn of the twentieth century. These groups, called *studiecirklar* (i.e., study circles), followed a few basic principles. At the beginning of the year, the circle purchased as many books as it had members; the books were then circulated in the group, and meetings were organized on a regular basis, for discussion and reflection on this literature. The study circle did not have a teacher in the traditional sense, but one member served as leader. The circle amounted to a forum where an active search for knowledge was conducted through democratic interactions among all participants, leading to empowerment (Rydbeck 1995).

Study circles soon became the dominant approach to free educational work in general. This was an important reason why so-called *folkbildning* (i.e., popular education) quickly developed into a mass activity in Sweden. The choice of the word "circle" for local study groups indicated that the new social movements had absorbed the circle concept. Still, circles could be described as small groups with similar interests, engaged in educational activities. The members of these groups were often from the working class or lower middle class, and as a consequence, the close connection between the word circle and the upper classes soon disappeared. In twentieth-century Sweden, circles involved people from all strata of society (Rydbeck 2013c).

As early as 1911, the study circles had begun receiving subsidies from the government provided that they were to be organized *studieförbunden* (study association). Consequently, during the first half of the twentieth century, study associations evolved under the auspices of various popular movements and non-governmental organizations. Until the end of the 1940s, these subsidies were given as books valued at a certain sum of money (i.e., not in cash). At the end of the year, when the circle's work came to an end, these books were brought together, and in this way circle libraries gradually took form. A large number of circle libraries emerged, largely in connection with the temperance or labour movements; some such libraries assembled quite comprehensive collections. However, these organizations lacked the financial resources to continue supporting the study circle libraries, so instead, they handed their libraries over to the new public libraries, run by municipalities, that were being founded in Sweden in the first half of the twentieth century (Rydbeck 2013c). Indeed, in many parts of Sweden in the early years, books from study circle libraries constituted an important part of the collections in public libraries. In some old books – borrowed from, for example, the public library in Uppsala – it is still possible to find an inscription stating that the book belongs to the circle library of some local temperance lodge in the county of Uppsala.

It is important to grasp this historical process in order to understand how reading group activities developed the way they did during the twentieth century. It became the duty of public libraries to supply study circles with literature, but generally the libraries themselves did not organize any circle activities. That was the responsibility of the study associations, which became the main organizers of reading group activities in Sweden throughout the twentieth century. Those associations are still very important today

Especially in the early years, before the 1920s, the study circles were characterized by a rather free and process-oriented educational ideal, and the reading material was often fiction. Study circles functioned in much the same way as today's reading groups or book clubs. But gradually the activities changed. The circles became more oriented towards specific subjects, with curricula, textbooks, and traditional teachers. The circles dedicated to reading fiction became known as *litteraturcirklar* (e.g., literature circles), and their proportion gradually decreased. They became – and still are – regarded as a subcategory within the main study circle concept (Rydbeck 2013c).

The massive early public support for popular education in Sweden is probably the reason why, in the twentieth century, reading groups organized by bookshops never became important. The bookshops could of course supply the study associations with books, which were partly paid for with government funds. But to receive state subsidies, the educational work had to be explicitly non-commercial. Even today, reading groups are rare in Swedish bookshops. Although the national book market is now paying more attention to social reading and reading groups, it is nothing compared to how Fuller, Rehberg Sedo, and Squires (2011) describe the situation in North America and Great Britain. But this is slowly changing, and some (mostly independent) bookshops now organize reading groups. In 2011, for the first time, Kulturrådet (the Swedish Arts Council) funded local reading promotion projects organized by bookshops – for example, reading group activities (Kulturrådet 2012).

Every adult Swede knows what a study circle is. According to one survey, about 60 percent of us have participated in study associations (Orbe and

Theorell 2013). Since we all are familiar with the study circle concept, study circles have arisen in various contexts outside popular education. Independent, freestanding reading groups existed throughout the twentieth century, but it is difficult to estimate to what extent. It is likely that the first of these groups were old-fashioned upper-class-oriented reading circles. And since men controlled the new study associations, much of the educational work connected to the women's movement – also an important social and popular movement launched in the late nineteenth century – took root outside these study associations (and consequently without public support) throughout the twentieth century. The most important women's organization in Sweden during the second wave of the women's movement, in the 1970s, was called Group 8. This organization started precisely as a local study circle (with eight women) that discussed political literature focusing on women's issues, and grew concurrently with new study circles around the country (Rydbeck 2013b).

"Study circle" has been the common term over the past hundred years in Sweden for all reading or study groups. Their focus has always been on literature that is *not* fiction, regardless of any formal links to institutionalized popular education. "Reading circle," "book circle," and "literature circle" have became synonyms for reading communities that focus specifically on fiction. It is possible that the word *bokcirkel* (i.e., book circle) – the most common term today – in the beginning referred to freestanding groups, but this is no longer the case. Henceforth I will use the term "book circle" for Swedish reading communities.

However, some international influences in the Swedish terminology can be noticed. The term "club" is gaining ground at the expense of "circle." For example, public libraries often use "reading club" for groups focusing on children – perhaps because children are expected to like "clubs" of different kinds. I have also seen several freestanding groups that call themselves "book clubs." This could reflect a North American influence, since a book club in Sweden more often means a commercial organization that supplies its members with books by mail.

Book Circles in Study Associations and Public Libraries during the Last Decade

It is often claimed in the Swedish press that the number of book circles has increased dramatically in recent years – so much so that one can, in fact, talk of a new social movement (e.g., Kellman Larsson 2012; Stensman 2011)! Stereotypical assumptions are sometimes expressed about the participants – for example, that book circles are dominated by middle-aged, well-educated urban women who combine book discussions with wine drinking (e.g., Kadefors 2009). However, few studies have been undertaken about Swedish book circles.

Statistics are available about the study associations' circle activities since the beginning of the twentieth century. To gather data about the circles focusing on fiction, I examined the statistics from 2002–11 collected by Folkbildningsrådet (the National Council of Adult Education) and Statistics Sweden (SCB) indicating the number of circles for each study association in each municipality (in Sweden there are 290 in total) and the number of male and female participants, placed into four age cohorts. It is important to point out here that circle activities for children under thirteen years of age do not receive any state subsidies, which means there are no book circles for children in the study associations.

The national statistics concerning public libraries were quite rudimentary during the twentieth century, but since 2007, those libraries have had to report every year to the Royal Library and SCB the different types of activities organized – including, for example, for reading promotion. Closed book circle meetings form one category. I have examined the figures for 2007 to 2011, which tell us the number of circle meetings in all municipalities. Unfortunately, the figures give no information at all about the participants, except for the proportion of children among them.

In 2011 the Swedish study associations – in total there are ten today – organized more than 280,000 study circles with almost 1.8 million participants (note that the entire population of Sweden is about 9.5 million).[2] By far the largest categories were connected to the practising of music of various kinds. Only 1.7 percent (almost 4,600) related to book circles, and the number – quite contrary to assumptions – decreased considerably between 2002 and 2011 (by 27 percent). In the book circles, women predominated (85 percent in 2011) (Rydbeck 2013a). This is hardly surprising: it has long been a well-known fact that women read more than men (Hartley and Turvey 2002; Long 2003; Poole 2000). But it should also be noted that the proportion of participants in the oldest age category – 65 years or more – increased significantly and in 2011 comprised 81 percent (17 percent were 25–64 years of age, 2 percent in 13–24 range). Most book circle participants today are retired women, and when they disappear, the study associations seem to have great difficulty recruiting new, younger participants (Rydbeck 2013a). For young adults who want to start book circles, the study associations are not attractive partners any more. Perhaps less generous state subsidies and the expanding administrative apparatus surrounding the circle activities could be an explanation, in combination with declining book prices. Nowadays, contrary to the situation fifteen to twenty years ago, books are cheap in Sweden. Normally a paperback novel does not cost more than a magazine or two daily papers. One reason for this is the low value-added tax on books – to promote reading it was changed from 25 to just 6 percent in 2002. Why bother with the study associations and their regulations when one can buy some paperbacks, find some friends and get started?

The figures for the public libraries, however, show a totally different development. Library-based circles were rare during the twentieth century, but the number of book circle meetings in libraries increased dramatically between 2007 and 2011 (up 187 percent). So did the proportion of municipalities with library circles (about two-thirds in 2011). Undoubtedly, public libraries have recently put a lot of effort into supporting social reading and organizing reading communities, especially for adults, although about one-third of the library circles have been directed to children (Rydbeck 2013a). A more user-oriented perspective in reading promotion work during the last decade could explain this. Also influential have been the British Council's Reader Development program and the library project Opening the Book; both include reading groups (Van Riel, Fowler, and Downes 2008).[3]

This interest from the libraries for social reading also includes reading communities based on digital communication. In 2010 the Swedish county libraries jointly took over the responsibility for the most important Swedish virtual reading community, *Bokcirklar.se* (Bookcircles.se), from the librarian Nina Frid (2012), who had started it as a private initiative four years earlier.

It is difficult to compare the statistics for book circles in libraries with those of book circles in study associations, because the former show the number of meetings per year, and the latter only the number of circles. My estimate, however, would be that about 900 library circles existed in 2011 in Sweden (Rydbeck 2013a), while the overall number was about 5,500. Thus, the number of circles connected to the study associations still formed a far larger group. But it must be emphasized that the freestanding, independent circles are not included here. Though not supported by any official statistics, my assumption is that today they form the largest and probably fastest-growing type.

The statistics tell us that although the number of book circles in study associations and public libraries was high in densely populated urban areas around the big cities of Stockholm, Göteborg, and Malmö, a significantly greater proportion of the residents were engaged in book circle activities in small municipalities, in rural areas in sparsely populated parts of the country (Rydbeck 2013a). Probably, this is explained at least partly by the fact that big cities always have a lot of other cultural activities going on, competing with book circles for people's spare time. This is not always likely in small places.

The municipality with the largest proportion of citizens involved in book circle activities connected to study associations was Pajala, in the far north of Sweden, close to the Torne River and the Finnish border. Älvdalen, an isolated region in the centre of Sweden, close to the Norwegian border, was the municipality with the largest proportion of citizens in library-based circle activities. An interesting fact is that quite a lot of men were active in the Pajala circles, which were all organized by the temperance-movement-based study association NBV, although the labour-movement-based ABF is by far the largest organizer of book circles on a national level (with 51 percent of all circles) (Rydbeck 2013a). This can probably be explained by the fact that this part of the country is still strongly influenced by the Laestadianism, a conservative pietistic movement, for whose members temperance is important. It is also a region where the Finno-Ugric Meänkieli, one of Sweden's official minority languages, is spoken. Related to this, Älvdalen also has its own language, an ancient dialect of the old Norse spoken in Scandinavia, Iceland, and the Faeroes about 1,000 years ago. An interesting question is whether the book circles in Älvdalen and Pajala were used actively as tools for preserving and developing regional minority culture. Hopefully, further studies will answer this.

Book Circles in Public Libraries – Organization and Participants

As previously mentioned, the library statistics do not give any information about the readers taking part in book circle activities. Furthermore, they do not tell us how the circles are organized, or anything about the ideas behind this involvement in social reading activities from the libraries' or the participants' perspectives. My contacts among public librarians have shown that book circle activities can be very different, not only between different municipalities but also between different library units connected to the same library organization. This was why I decided to conduct a study that delved deeper into the public libraries' book circle activities. I organized a Web-based survey in March 2013, directed to the public libraries in all 290 Swedish municipalities. The questionnaire had three parts. The first had questions for all library units, whether or not they were involved in circle activities The second part had some general questions for libraries with ongoing circles, and the third part focused on the activities of one specific circle. The questionnaire offered the possibility of describing activities in five different circles. More than 1,000 library units were contacted by email. I received 486 answers from units in 259 of the 290 municipalities. The answers represent libraries both with and without book circles. This comprehensive material clearly illustrates that circle activities can be organized in many different ways. The purpose here is to point out some results. The information in the remaining part of this chapter is based on this library survey.

Library Circles ... or Not?

One would think that book circles organized by public libraries would be an easily defined group, since the activities each year have to be reported for national library statistics. However, it seems that the libraries have different views regarding what a library circle is, as opposed to an independent circle. Some libraries stated that they do not organize book circles, but that they support some independent circles, primarily by offering space in the library for meetings. Sometimes the library also recommends books and provides copies for the circle to use. Those libraries do not consider themselves circle organizers, unless librarians take part in the meetings as leaders. Other libraries stated that they *do* organize book circles but that some of the circles work totally independently – the only support they get is a room for their meetings. Some respondents even stated that they provide circle leaders with keys to the library so that the meetings can take place outside opening hours.

From these answers one must conclude that there are a great number of circles in which librarians serve as leaders, using some of their working hours for circle activities; but at the same time, a fairly large number of circles are connected to public libraries while using almost no personnel resources. It is also interesting that clearly, circles are keen on having their meetings in libraries, although they do not use the library resources in any other way. This also means there are considerably more book circle activities going on in Swedish public libraries than what is actually seen in the official statistics.

Another important finding is that book circle activities are rapidly affected when the library is hit by financial cuts. Several respondents reported that their libraries used to organize book circles but can no longer afford to do so. One example is the previously mentioned Älvdalen. Of all municipalities in the country, it had the highest proportion of citizens engaged in library book circle activities in 2011. But in 2013, this library did not organize any such activities at all, because of budget reductions.

Circle Participants: Middle-Aged, Educated Female Professionals

The library survey showed that many participants in library circles are elderly retirees over 64 years of age (42 percent), although this group is not as predominant as in the circles of the study associations. The share of adults of working age (from 25 to 64 years) is higher in the libraries (36 percent). The circles for children and teenagers up to 17 years also constitute a fairly large group (22 percent). Obviously, a major challenge for the libraries today (as it is with the study associations) is reaching young adults, from 18 to 24 years. Not one single answer in the survey referred to a circle with participants of that age. Also, the libraries have great difficulties attracting male readers. As in the study associations, there was a heavy predominance of women. Only 2 percent of the libraries' book circles had only male participants or a majority of men, and only 6 percent had a balance between men and women. Ninety-two percent of circles had a majority of women, or only women.

When accounting for their most important reason for organizing book circles in the library, 60 percent answered they considered it part of the library's reading promotion work. However, a great majority of the respondents also noted that most participants would be reading a lot, borrowing a lot from the library, and visiting the library regularly regardless of the circle. If reading promotion for the libraries means strengthening the reading habits of those who seldom or never read books, the question is whether book circles make any difference. At the same time, this activity could lead to a broadening of the participants' reading habits, for we know that participants may, through reading group engagement, come to read literature they otherwise would not get in touch with (Devlin-Glass 2001).

In the survey I tried to map the reading group participants' education and professional background. The librarian respondents had to answer in their own words. Some wrote that they had never reflected on this matter. They did not consider it relevant, given that the mission of public libraries is to offer services to *all* citizens, whatever their social background. In one way, I sympathize with this argument. However, if it is part of the libraries' mission to organize activities and promote reading, it is important for them to have some knowledge about the impact of the activities from a social perspective.

What the survey clearly reveals is that the majority of participants in Swedish library circles are well-educated people, often with a university education. Consequently, the educational level of the Swedish participants looks quite similar to that of the British reading groups studied by Jenny Hartley (Hartley and Turvey 2002) and to the North American book club members studied by DeNel Rehberg Sedo (2004). Professions connected with the health care sector and the educational system are especially often mentioned by respondents. This is hardly surprising, considering that most of the participants are women and that the public sector – and especially professions related to health care and education – is where the great majority of Swedish women work. Based on the answers, the most typical Swedish library circle participant is a middle-aged or retired nurse or schoolteacher.

Library Circles' Reading Preferences: Literary Fiction, Biographies, and Memoirs

The last aspect I touch on here is the books actually read. Which types of books do the library circles read and discuss? The simple answer is that they read novels, published in Sweden and from other parts of the world. The majority of respondents (55 percent) only read fiction; 44 percent occasionally read non-fiction as well, with biographies or memoirs as the most common categories. Hardly any circles read non-fiction exclusively. Non-fiction circles probably regard the study associations as their natural partners, not the libraries.

Some circles focus on one particular genre – for example, science fiction or fantasy. But by and large, the librarians emphasize that the circles mix a lot and that diversity in reading selections is highly valued. That said, fixed themes or genres are common in the circles, such as classics, historical novels, women writers, or travel literature. Award-winning books seem to be a popular theme – for example, Nobel Prize winners. Some read the same literature as the book circle of the Swedish public broadcasting company, a popular radio program that has been running for several years, mostly with different well-known Swedish writers reading and discussing classics (*Bokcirkeln*). But there are more odd themes, such as library books that have never been borrowed, books written the year the participants were born, and books with ugly covers. Some respondents report that their circles sometimes read crime novels, which is hardly surprising, for Sweden has many bestselling contemporary crime writers, several of them internationally recognized. However, more respondents claim that they avoid this type of literature. There is a great demand for novels focusing on subjects such as, for example, "life stories," "relations," "sorrow," and "reconciliation." In other words, the participants seem to prefer literature dealing with universal issues connected to human lives and social relations, issues that affect all of us, regardless of time and space. And perhaps this is what many participants find attractive about book circles. They offer the possibility of discussing important and sometimes difficult matters related to life, but without getting too personal. You can connect to your own life and experiences but at the same time keep a certain distance from the personal and private, for the discussion focuses mainly on the book. This is an important finding in past research (Hartley and Turvey 2002; Long 2003; Nybacka 2011).

Some information from this survey remains to be analyzed, concerning for example how the circle work is organized and how reading selections are made. Another important issue is how the libraries interact with independent book circles in the neighbourhood. For example, some libraries quite recently started to lend what they call "book circle bags" containing five to seven copies of the same novel, sometimes even including a handbook for book circles or a manual with preformulated questions for launching discussion of this particular book.

Statistics show that book circles have become a common activity in Swedish public libraries over the past decade. The results from my 2013 survey indicate that there is a great dominance in the library circles of quite well-educated middle-aged or elderly women, reading novels – both classics and contemporary literature, written both by Swedish writers and by writers from many other parts of the world, often focusing on issues related to human lives and social relations. So, while this library survey begins to provide a picture of the collective reading experiences of book circles in public libraries, work remains to be done that will give voice to reading circle participants.[4]

Notes

1. This study forms a part of a larger research project on reading communities in contemporary Sweden: "Readers' Circles: A Sociological Study about Social Reading and Reading Communities in Contemporary Sweden," Uppsala University, http://www.abm.uu.se/research/Ongoing+Research+Projects/Readers'+circles/
2. Some general information in English about the study associations' activities today are given in *Facts on Folkbildning in Sweden* (2011) The ten study associations are *ABF* (multiple organizations and political parties connected to the labour movement), *Bilda* (Free Church movement and other Christian churches except the Church of Sweden), *Folkuniversitetet* (University Extension Organization, universities and students' unions), *Ibn Rushd* (Muslim based), *Medborgarskolan* (Moderate Party and other conservative organizations), *NBV* (Temperance Movement), *Sensus* (Church of Sweden, YMCA–YWCA, scouts, etc.), *Studiefrämjandet* (multiple nature and environmental organizations), *Studieförbundet Vuxenskolan* (Liberal Party, Centre Party, Federation of Swedish Farmers), and *Kulturens bildningsverksamhet* (multiple cultural organizations focusing on music and choirs).
3. The British Opening the Book project was mentioned in a book promoting book circle activities in Swedish public libraries as early as in 2004 (Lundin 2004).
4. The aim of another survey in this research project, carried out in 2013–14, was to estimate the volume of book circle activities in the county of Uppsala (in total eight different municipalities) by getting in touch with as many of the active circles as possible, and to collect information from the participants themselves about them and their circle work. This study resulted in questionnaires from 231 different reading communities. Their answers still wait to be analyzed.

References

Ambjörnsson, Ronny. 1998. *Den skötsamme arbetaren: idéer och ideal i ett norrländskt sågverkssamhälle 1880–1930* [The conscientious worker: Ideas and ideals in a sawmill village in the north of Sweden 1880–1930]. Stockholm: Carlsson.

Appel, Charlotte, and Morten Fink-Jensen. 2011. "Books, Literacy, and Religious Reading in the Lutheran North." In *Religious Reading in the Lutheran North*, edited by Charlotte Appel and Morten Fink Jensen, 1–14. Newcastle upon Tyne: Cambridge Scholars Publishing.

Bokcirkeln [The Book Circle]. Sveriges Radio. http://sverigesradio.se/sida/default .aspx?programid=3349

Devlin-Glass, Frances. 2001. "More Than a Reader and Less Than a Critic: Literary Authority and Women's Book-Discussion Groups." *Women's Studies International Forum* 24(50): 571–85.

Facts on Folkbildning in Sweden: A Brief Overwiew. 2011. Stockholm: Folkbildningsrådet. http://www.folkbildningsradet.se/globalassets/fakta-om-folkbildning/facts-on-folkbildning_2011_web.pdf

Frid, Nina. 2012. *Slutet på boken är bara början – om bokcirklar och bibliotek* [The end of the book is just the beginning: About book circles and libraries]. Lund: BTJ Förlag.

Fuller, Danielle, DeNel Rehberg Sedo, and Clare Squires. 2011. "Marionettes and Puppeteers? The Relationship between Book Club Readers and Publishers." In *Reading Communities from Salons to Cyberspace*, edited by DeNel Rehberg Sedo, 181–99. Houndmills: Palgrave Macmillan.

Hartley, Jenny, and Sarah Turvey. 2002. *The Reading Groups Book: With a Survey*. Oxford: Oxford University Press.

Kadefors, Sara. 2009. "Oviljan känns i hela kroppen – Sara Kadefors om bokcirklar" [I can feel the repugnance in my whole body – Sara Kadefors about book circles]. December, *Piratförlaget*. http://www.piratforlaget.se/serie/tema-bokcirklar-2

Kellman Larsson, Johan. 2012. "Därför älskar vi att läsa i grupp [The reason why we love reading in groups]. *Metro*, 27 September.

Kulturrådet. 2012. "Litterära evenemang i Sverige för bokhandlar" [Literary events in Sweden for book shops]. 12 May. http://www.kulturradet.se/sv/bidrag/beviljade _bidrag/ 2012/Litterara-evenemang-i-Sverige-for-bokhandlar

Lindmark, Daniel. 2011. "Popular Education and Religious Reading in Early Nineteenth-Century Sweden." In *Religious Reading in the Lutheran North*, edited by Charlotte Appel and Morten Fink Jensen, 191–215. Newcastle upon Tyne: Cambridge Scholars Publishing.

Long, Elizabeth. 2003. *Book Clubs: Women and the Uses of Reading in Everyday Life*. Chicago: University of Chicago Press.

Lundin, Immi. 2004. *Cirkelbevis: Läsecirklar på bibliotek* [Circle evidence: Reading circles in libraries]. Lund: Bibliotekstjänst.

Nybacka, Pamela Schultz. 2011. *Bookonomy: The Consumption Practice and Value of Book Reading*. PhD diss., Stockholm University. http://su.diva-portal.org/smash/get/diva2:409635/FULLTEXT01.pdf

Orbe, Johan, and Caroline Theorell. 2013. *Allmänhetens attityder till studieförbunden 2013* [Public attitudes towards the study associations, 2013]. Survey conducted by Swedish Institute of Public Opinion Research (SIFO). Stockholm: Folkbildningsförbundet.

Poole, Marilyn. 2000. "Between the Covers: Women's Reading Groups." TASA 2000 Conference: Sociological Siyes/Sights. Adelaide: Flinders University.

Rehberg Sedo, DeNel. 2004. "Badges of Wisdom, Spaces for Being: A Study of Contemporary Women's Book Clubs." PhD diss., Simon Fraser University. http://summit.sfu.ca/system/files/iritems1/8708/b3524580a.pdf

Rydbeck, Kerstin. 1995. *Nykter läsning: den svenska godtemplarrörelsen och litteraturen 1896–1925* [Sober reading: The Swedish Good Templar Movement and literature 1896–1925]. PhD diss., Uppsala University. English summary: http://uu.diva-portal.org/smash/get/diva2:398502/SUMMARY01.pdf

———. 2013a. "Läsargemenskapernas komplexa landskap: om bokcirkelbegreppet och utvecklingen av svensk bokcirkelverksamhet, med speciellt fokus på folkbibliotekens och studieförbundens cirklar" [The complex landscape of reading communities: The book circle concept and the development of Swedish book circle activities, with special focus on circles in study associations and libraries]. In *Libraries, Black Metal, and Corporate Finance: Current Research in Nordic Library and Information Science*, edited by Kersti Skans Nilsson and Anders Frenander, 112–35. Borås: Borås University.

———. 2013b. "Popular Education and the Empowerment of Women: A Historical Perspective." In *Popular Education, Power, and Democracy: Swedish Experiences and Contributions*, edited by Ann-Marie Laginder, Henrik Nordwall, and Jim Crowther, 50–71. Leicester: National Institute of Adult Continuing Education (NIACE).

———. 2013c. "Det sociala läsandet förr och nu" [Social reading then and now]. In *Lärandets mångfald: om vuxenpedagogik och folkbildning*, edited by Andreas Fejes, 37–54. Lund: Studentlitteratur.

Stensman, Ann. 2011. "Samling kring boken" [Gathering around the book]. *Helsingborgs Dagblad*, 26 November.

Svenska Akademiens Ordbok. 2014. s.v. "cirkel I.10.b." http://g3.spraakdata.gu.se/saob

Sørensen, Anne Scott, ed. 1998. *Nordisk salongskultur: en studie i nordiske skønånder og salonmiljøer 1780–1850*. [Nordic salon culture 1780–1850]. Odense: Odense universitetsforlag.

Van Riel, Rachel, Olive Fowler, and Ann Downes. 2008. *The Reader-Friendly Library Service*. Newcastle upon Tyne: Society of Chief Librarians.

part 3
politics

"I readed it!" (Marissa, four years)
The Experience of Reading from the Perspective of Children Themselves: A Cautionary Tale

Lynne (E.F.) McKechnie

Marissa was within three months of her fourth birthday when the following incident was observed during a visit to her local public library with her mother. She was sitting on a small stool in the picture book area. She had a copy of Denise Fleming's *Lunch* (1992) in her hands. This is the story of a little mouse that, page after page, eats his way through a series of foods. Though not explicitly, the text and illustrations of this patterned tale invite children to identify fruits and vegetables and their colours as they move through the book. Visual clues are included to suggest what the mouse might find and eat on the next page, making this a story of prediction as well. But for Marissa, a child who had yet to "read" in the traditional sense of being able to decode text, the book presented an opportunity to really *read*. Marissa insisted that her mother, then eight and a half months pregnant, settle in on the floor in front of her to "sit, look, and listen" while she conducted a small storytime. She started by showing the cover and saying the title, *Lunch*. She moved on to the title page and repeated the title while pointing to the little mouse, whom she described as being very hungry. And then she *read*. Very few of her words matched those in the text, but she told a most compelling story. In some ways I found her narrative to be better than that of the author. For example, Marissa added a wonderful refrain to her telling. Every time the mouse moved on to find a new food, she emphatically said "Lunch. I want lunch!" This refrain captured the heart of the story and added a feature, a repeated refrain, often found in patterned books. Now and then Marissa's mother helped with the reading. For example, when Marissa hesitated when she encountered blueberries, her mother reminded her that they had eaten this fruit for lunch a few days ago, scaffolding Marissa's *reading* by grounding it in her daughter's own life experiences. When Marissa completed the story, she closed the book, held it up once more to show the cover to her audience, and proclaimed in a very self-satisfied tone, "*I readed it!*"

Marissa was one of thirty girls who participated in my doctoral research project where I observed the children and recorded their naturally occurring language during a trip to their public library. While not one of the girls could actually "read" (in terms of being able to decode written text), all but one identified themselves as readers, often with Marissa's almost iconic phrase "*I readed it.*" I wasn't about to argue with Marissa. This vignette is a fine example of an emergent reading in which many of the early literacy skills are evident (e.g., understanding how narratives work, the ability to predict, and the role of more competent readers in supporting the reading). But the most intriguing thing I learned from Marissa and the other children was how important the construction of self as reader was in the long and complex process of becoming a reader. Marissa was a *reader*. She never doubted that she could and would *read*. This self-confidence has likely served her very well.

Children's Experiences of Reading

New Zealand scholar Marie Clay (1972, 1975) coined the term "emergent literacy" in 1967 when her research made it apparent that reading did not start with a child's ability to decode text correctly but rather was grounded in emergent literacy practices that immersed a child in language experiences. Clay expanded the notion of literacy to include listening, speaking, writing, and reading language, with all four processes developing simultaneously. This shift in understanding spurred a frenzy of research. Representative landmark work was conducted by scholars such as Dorothy Butler (1979, 1980) from New Zealand, William Teal and Elizabeth Sulzby (1986) from the United States, and Gordon Wells (1986) from the UK. Becoming a reader was and is still recognized as a process that begins at or even before birth and that continues throughout one's lifetime.

My own research has looked at the intersection of children, reading, and public libraries. I sought and continue to investigate how libraries can best support children on their journey to becoming readers. An important element in this work was an emphasis on capturing data that reflected children's own perspectives on this topic. Examples from three studies serve to illustrate this: the baby storytime study (four sites, about fifteen families per site, children from birth to two years old); the library visit study (thirty girls, four years old); and the book ownership study (107 children, four to twelve years old).

The first study was an exploration of early literacy in the context of Baby Storytime (McKechnie 2006), a program commonly offered by public libraries for children and their caregivers. As the children, aged from birth to two years, were too young to interview or survey, this was primarily an observation study. My field notes include the following observation of Louise, eight months old at the time, who was attending baby storytime with her mother:

Context: Librarian is reading a story where a double-spread illustration of an animal is followed by a double spread showing the animal making its characteristic sound.

Observation note: Louise is leaning forward and smiling in anticipation of the page turning. Librarian turns the page. Librarian and the Moms roar like a lion. Louise excitedly waves her arms up and down all the while smiling.

Immediately after this, Louise became quite quiet. She leaned forward staring intently at the librarian and the book in anticipation of the next page turning. While baby storytimes can often appear quite chaotic, with children crawling and toddling around the room, interacting with others, and playing with toys and other books, as with Louise, many if not all of the children involved in the study also participated in and demonstrated early reading behaviours.

Elissa, another child in my doctoral library visit study (McKechnie 2001), was browsing through the picture book section of the children's area looking for materials to borrow when she pulled Eric Carle's *The Very Hungry Caterpillar* (1987) from the shelf. This is what she said to her mother:

Elissa: You know what?
Mother: What?
Elissa: This is it. This is the caterpillar one.
Mother: What happens to him?
Elisa: Gets big.
Mother: And then what?
Elissa: Then ... He gets more bigger.
Mother: Uh, huh?
Elissa: And then he gets fat.
Mother: Right! And then when he finishes eating and getting big and fat, what happens at the end?
Elissa: Butterfly! [Elissa and her mother both laugh joyfully]

Even this early in her development as a reader, Elissa shows herself to be very competent. She demonstrates an emerging knowledge of children's literature and her own history as a reader when she recognizes *The Very Hungry Caterpillar*. Her familiarity with narrative structure is reflected in her retelling of the story. Elissa's mother supports her daughter's reading by providing prompts and clues when needed. It is important to note that Elissa takes the lead in this conversation with her mother, who enables rather than controls Elissa's retelling of the story.

After my visits to the library with the girls, I asked the mothers to keep a diary for one week to record any incidents involving the library. Sarah's mother noted this in her diary on the day after their visit to the library with me:

> Diary Entry: In the afternoon I had to drop off one book [at the library], and Sarah remembered the study being done yesterday. Wondered if Lynne was there again with the red jacket and the baby tapes, etc. She then remembered mention of being in a book for the study [the thesis]. She wants to know if she's going to be a heroine, good/bad character, maybe the mother of the family in the book!

The drive for story is strong in young children. Sarah managed to "story" both the research process and my thesis. The library visit study validated the role that public libraries play in the development of children as readers. None of the girls had started formal education. None had received instruction in reading. Not one could print her first name. Yet all, like Melissa, Elissa, and Sarah, were *readers*.

The book ownership study (McKechnie 2004) involved interviews with older children centred on their own personal collections of reading and information materials. Zach, nine years old at the time of the study, showed me his copy of *The Pokeman Handbook* (Barbo 1999). His enthusiasm is evident in this excerpt from his interview:

> Zach: I've read that [*Pokeman Handbook*] like 16 times. And I've tooken it everywhere.
> Researcher: Where would you take it?
> Zach: I took it to school. I took it up north. Um, I take it to read in the car.

While research has shown that boys often read less than girls (McKechnie 2007), some boys are enthusiastic about reading, especially if, like Zach, they are able to choose their own reading materials.

Factors that foster reading in children are evident in my research and that of others. These factors, especially those that arise from children's own behaviours and perspectives, are summarized in *Reading Matters: What the Research Reveals about Reading* (Ross, McKechnie, and Rothbauer 2006):

- hearing stories read aloud by a parent or other caring adult
- having opportunities to do emergent story readings
- having ready access to reading materials

- having free choice of reading materials so that stories are enjoyed and the experience is pleasurable
- having the space and time for shared and individual reading
- being part of a "readerly" family
- having opportunities to talk about reading
- having a sense that reading is a valuable activity
- having access to an enabling adult

Interventions in Children's Reading

Kelly Gallagher, author of *Readicide: How Schools Are Killing Reading and What You Can Do about It* (2009), dedicates his book to "those educators who resist the political in favor of the authentic" (iii). He provides the following definition:

> Read-i-cide *n*: The systematic killing of the love of reading, often exacerbated by the inane, mind-numbing practices found in schools. (2009, 2)

Three prominent practices serve to illustrate how readicide is evident in the early literacy endeavours of today's libraries and schools: the overemphasis on particular skills, the promotion of dialogic reading, and the implementation of levelled reading.

Overemphasis on Particular Skills

In "Becoming a Nation of Readers: The Report of the Commission of Reading," an early US government–sponsored document on the importance of reading, it is noted that "the single most important activity for building the knowledge required for eventual success in reading is reading aloud to children" (National Academy of Education [US] 1985, 2). A companion piece for parents (Binkley 1988) identified five simple practices parents could follow to support this – talking, singing, reading, writing, and playing. These basic early strategies were grounded in research, including the studies mentioned earlier (Clay 1972, 1975; Sulzby and Teal 1986; Wells 1986). They were confirmed in later works such as Krashen's (2004) meta-analysis of the literature on reading and reiterated recently in "Leisure Reading: A Joint Statement of the International Reading Association, the Canadian Children's Book Centre, and the National Council of Teachers of Education" (International Reading Association 2014).

While these basic strategies continue to be promoted, others that focus on very particular aspects of early reading experiences have emerged. The National Early Literacy Panel was convened in 2002 by the US Congress "to identify interventions, parenting activities, and instructional practices that promote the development of children's early literacy skills" (2008, vi). The result was a report (2008) that identified six crucial early literacy skills: print motivation, phonological awareness, vocabulary, narrative skills, print awareness, and letter knowledge. Other variables were uncovered, but it was the emphasis on these six skills that was adopted by organizations working with young children (birth to five years). "Every Child Ready to Read @ your library" was and continues to be an important initiative by the Public Library Association (PLA) and the Association for Library Service to Children (ALSC), divisions of the American Library Association, devoted to "teaching parents and other caregivers how to support the early literacy development of their children" (Meyers and Henderson 2014). The first edition of this manual for public libraries (Every Child Ready to Read @ your library 2004) provided curriculum and materials to use for parent education. These centred on the six emergent literacy skills. The ALSC and PLA were diligent in promoting this initiative with libraries and librarians. They also undertook studies to evaluate the effectiveness of the program and continued to follow current research in the area. In the wake of this, they made modifications to the program and published a new and expanded edition of "Every Child Ready to Read @ your library" (2011). While additional factors influencing early literacy were addressed by this revision, the core six early literacy skills remained. And very specific activities were recommended to cultivate these skills. A quick perusal of public library websites provides evidence that Every Child Ready to Read @ your library has been adopted by many if not most public libraries in the United States and Canada. While admirable, especially in intent and in the rigour brought to the important issue of helping children become readers, the problem with programs such as Every Child Ready to Read @ your library is that their focus on particular skills can cause us to ignore other aspects of emergent reading that are arguably just as important. The complexity of the reading process can and is being overlooked.

Dialogic Reading

With all the research that sought to identify particular skills related to emergent reading came an understanding that the *how* of reading was almost as important as the simple *doing* of reading in fostering the development of strong readers. A number of techniques emerged, with dialogic reading being a prominent example. Dialogic reading was developed by Grover J. Whitehurst through his Stony Brook Reading and Language Project (2001). Whitehurst notes:

When most adults share a book with a preschooler, they read and the child listens. In dialogic reading, the adult helps the child become the teller of the story. The adult becomes the listener, the questioner, the audience for the child. No one can learn to play the piano just by listening to someone else play. Likewise, no one can learn to read by listening to someone else read. Children learn most from books when they are actively involved. (1992, para. 7)

Dialogic reading involves the PEER sequence, an interaction between the adult and the child in which the adult:

- prompts the child to say something about the book
- evaluates the child's response
- expands the child's response by rephrasing and adding information to it
- repeats the prompt to make sure the child has learned from the expansion (Whitehurst 1992, para. 8)

While the long-term direct effects of dialogic reading on conventional reading success have not yet been substantiated (Salinger 2001), some research supports its effectiveness especially for children from low-income families (e.g., Lonigan and Whitehurst 1998). Many public libraries have implemented workshops to teach first staff and then parents the techniques of dialogic reading so that they can implement these in library programs and bedtime reading for young children.

But does all dialogic reading go well? A search for "dialogic reading" on YouTube, a popular site for sharing videos, yields some interesting examples. Raising a Reader Massachusetts is a not-for-profit organization dedicated to fostering early literacy. It has posted a number of short videos to YouTube. One of these, "Dialogic reading in action!" (2012), is described as follows:

> Pheap and her son Kayden show us that Raising A Reader MA is about more than just reading a book, it's an engaging activity that promotes interaction between adults and children. Before Raising a Reader MA, Kayden's teacher said, "He has hardly said a word at school the entire year! He murmurs under his breath and often covers his mouth when speaking. He also tends to restrain himself from smiling or laughing." The addition of a simple reading activity can help open up children to the world of words and paves the way to academic success throughout a child's life.

In the scene presented in this video clip, Pheap and Kayden are sharing a picture book by Rosemary Wells, one of her award-winning titles about two little rabbits named Max and Ruby. While lively talk occurs between mother and child, what happens here appears more like an oral worksheet emphasizing traditional preschool academic skills as Kayden's mother asks him to point to and count objects in the illustrations and identify colours. There is little or no sense of story and narrative. There is no linking of the story to Kayden's own life. And Pheap is definitely the one controlling this "reading" – not once does Kayden ask a question or offer a comment of his own.

A major problem with dialogic reading, then, is that it can be implemented as reading controlled by the adult rather than by the child. While interest may be high at first, it may quickly be experienced by the child as work. The success of dialogic reading depends very much on the skills of the adult involved. While the techniques can be taught, unless the adult is a reader her/himself, it will be very difficult to implement them appropriately.

Levelled Reading

A phenomenon that has become increasingly evident in the last twenty years is the implementation of levelled reading in both children's formal reading education and their pleasure reading. Brabham and Villaume note that "in general, levelled text refers to reading materials that represent a progression from more simple to more complex and challenging texts. Texts that have been levelled include books created for commercial purposes, selections for basal reading anthologies, and children's literature" (2002, 438). Many schemes are used, including Fountas and Pinnell's text-level gradient and Lexile scores. Some of these measures have associated commercial programs for structuring, guiding, and measuring children's reading achievements, including the Lexile Framework for Reading and the Accelerated Reader program. More and more children's literature is being levelled. For example, HarperCollins's iconic *I Can Read* series of beginning-to-read books for early elementary school-age children, which includes many classics of children's literature such as Caldecott medal-winning *Frog and Toad Are Friends* (Lobel 1970), now includes not just a "level" on the front cover but also a description of the scheme and the characteristics of each of the three levels on the back of each book in the series. *NoveList K–8 Plus*, the popular readers' advisory database, lists Lexile scores for all children's materials. Teachers, parents, and some librarians welcomed this labelling as it helped them identify texts at a child's reading level. But problems quickly emerged. The pedagogical approaches and the algorithms for assigning levels to texts each use different criteria so that the same book might be labelled as appropriate for very different levels. Also, as Brabham and Villaume point out, "some schools are caught up in 'leveling mania' ... [They] become so enamored with leveled text that they lose sight of other important aspects of effective reading instruction" (2002, 438). Rather than allowing children to select texts that interest them, some teachers and parents restrict them to texts that are at their designated level. Any book that has not been levelled with the scheme in use in a particular school will not be allowed and probably will not be in the school library collection. "Traditional unrestricted browsing behaviors are profoundly changed when [Accelerated Reader] selections are mandated by teachers ... When the book level numbers on the library book spine is an obvious number, students not only focus on that number as they browse, they often shun other books that do not fit their [Reading Level] criteria" (Cregar 2011, 42). The American Association of School Librarians, a division of the American Library Association, has adopted the following statement on reading labels:

> One of the realities some school librarians face in their jobs is pressure by administrators and classroom teachers to label and arrange library collections according to reading levels. Student browsing behaviors can be profoundly altered with the addition of external reading level labels. With reading level labels often closely tied to reward points, student browsing becomes mainly a search for books that must be read and tests completed for individual or classroom point goals and/or grades. (2011)

Unfortunately, the mania continues.

Do Children Know about Readicide?

Excerpts from the data from my book ownership study (McKechnie 2004, 2007) show that children clearly do know about readicide. When asked if he liked to read, Rick (twelve years) responded: "It depends. If somebody goes and picks a book for me and tells me to read it and I don't like it, that's when I don't like reading. But if I pick a book that I think I'll like, that's when I like it. I'd rather read when I know I like it." Quiet Rebel (eleven years) had a large set of children's literature classics like *Treasure Island* and *Robinson Crusoe* on his bookshelf. When asked if he had read all the titles, he responded, "Not one." When asked whether he planned to read them one day, his response was pointed and terse: "Maybe in 10 or 26 years." Jonathon (twelve years) only held eight titles, the smallest collection of any of the children in the study. His books were manuals for computer and tabletop strategy games. When asked to describe his reading, he said: "Well, I don't really read novels or anything like that ... I just read little passages." He had already learned that some types of reading, the sort of reading he liked to do, didn't count. This was affirmed by John (eight years). Pointing to a non-fiction book in his collection, he confirmed that it was the "favourite of the ones that give me all the information" while also noting that "it doesn't look like it's a *real* book." John had already learned that *real* books, those privileged by the teachers, librarians, and other adults in his life, were fiction books and not very much like the books he particularly enjoyed reading. This is consistent with the results of Smith and Willhelm's *Reading Don't Fix No Chevys* (2002), a study of the literacy in the lives of young adult men, which found that schooled reading, the reading valued by teachers and imposed on students, was seen as involving work rather than pleasure and overlooked the rich and varied reading practices of these boys.

Healing

We know a lot about reading. And we know a lot about what brings people, including children, to become readers. While the development of particular technical skills is important, becoming a reader is a far more complex process. Focusing our energy on very specific aspects of the reading process and associated techniques such as dialogic and levelled reading to improve reading skills overlooks factors that seem to be more foundational, more salient.

Stephen Krashen in *The Power of Reading*, a meta-analysis of the research on reading, now in its second edition, identifies a powerful but extraordinarily simple potential solution:

> The cure for this kind of literacy crisis lies, in my opinion, in doing one activity, an activity that is all too often rare in the lives of many people: reading. Specifically, I am recommending a certain type of reading – **free voluntary reading** (henceforth FVR). FVR means reading because you want to. For school-age children, FVR means no book reports, no questions at the end of the chapter, and no looking up every vocabulary word. FVR means putting down a book you don't like and choosing another one instead. It is the kind of reading highly literary people do all the time. (2004, x)

Small and Arnone describe another sort of reading that they think of as an antidote to readicide: "Reading is often thought of as a skill, something to be learned and practiced. But reading can also be considered a creative art, capturing the imagination of the reader in ways that result in creative thought and expression. Think of this as **creative reading**" (2011, 13). They go on to note: "Critical to the avoidance of readicide is encouraging the notion that the pleasure of reading in and of itself is its own reward – not stickers, incentives, unrelated incentives or forced reading" (15).

The notions of free voluntary reading, creative reading, and reading for pleasure appear to be simple, but I argue that they are foundational to the development of readers. Children appear to know this well, until they learn something different, as John and Jonathon did. I close this paper with the words of Genevieve (four years), a participant in my library visit study. Genevieve's mother had left her in the picture book area of the library with instructions to choose some books she wanted to borrow. When she returned she found Genevieve seated on the floor with a large pile of books on either side.

    Mother: Genevieve! How many books do you have?

    Genevieve: [Looking at the piles of books] One more.

    Mother: Just one more! Remember how many books I said?

    Genevieve: Yup.

    Mother: How many?

    Genevieve: [Holding up three fingers] Four.

    Mother: I said five. And I think you've got more than five.

    Genevieve: I do ... I do have more.

    Mother: Ya. We're going to have to put some back.

    Genevieve: [Picking up and looking at the books one at a time] I want this one. Where's that one? That one. That one.

    Mother: OK. I leave you for three minutes and look, you've cleaned out the library.

    Genevieve: That one. I need a book like that one and that one.

Genevieve, the reading addict, and her mother left the library a few minutes later with six books. At four she was already a fervent free voluntary and creative reader with ready access to a large and rich collection of reading materials and well on her path to becoming a *reader*. I can only hope that the well-intentioned literacy strategies and interventions of some of the adults surrounding Marissa, Genevieve, and children everywhere do not disrupt this important journey.

Note

This chapter was developed from a keynote address given at "Researching the Reading Experience," a conference held at Oslo and Akershus University College of Applied Sciences, Oslo, Norway, 11–12 June 2013.

References

American Association of School Librarians (AASL). 2011. "Position Statement on Labeling Books with Reading Levels." *AASL, American Library Association*. http://www.ala.org/aasl/advocacy/resources/position-statements/labeling

Association for Library Services for Children (ALSC), and the Public Library Association (PLA). 2004. *Every Child Ready to Read @ your library*. Chicago: ALSC and PLA, American Library Association.

Association for Library Services for Children (ALSC), and the Public Library Association (PLA). 2011. *Every Child Ready to Read @ Your library*, 2nd ed. Chicago: ALSC and PLA, American Library Association.

Barbo, Maria S. 1999. *The Official Pokeman Handbook*. New York: Scholastic.
Binkley, Marilyn R. 1988. "Becoming a Nation of Readers: What Parents Can Do." Washington: Office of Educational Research and Improvement, US Department of Education.
Brabham, Edna Greene, and Susan Kidd Villaume. 2002. "Leveled Text: The Good News and the Bad News." *The Treading Teacher* 55(5): 438–41.
Butler, Dorothy. 1979. *Reading Begins at Home: Preparing Children for Reading before They Go to School*. London: Heinemann.
Butler, Dorothy. 1980. *Babies Need Books*. London: Bodley Head.
Carle, Eric. 1987. *The Very Hungry Caterpillar*. New York: Philomel.
Clay, Marie M. 1972. *Reading: The Patterning of Complex Behaviour*. Auckland: Heinemann.
Clay, Marie M. 1975. *What Did I Write?* Portsmouth: Heinemann.
Cregar, Elyse. 2011. "Browsing by Numbers and Reading for Points." *Knowledge Quest* 39(4): 40–45.
"Dialogic Reading in Action." 2012. *Raising a Reader Massachusetts*. 11 December. http://www.youtube.com/watch?v=62wDFYeGORk
"Every Child Ready to Read @ Your library." 2014. *Association for Library Service to Children*. http://www.everychildreadytoread.org
Fleming, Denise. 1992. *Lunch*. New York: Henry Holt.
Gallagher, Kelly. 2009. *Readicide: How Schools Are Killing Reading and What You Can Do about It*. Portland: Stenhouse.
International Reading Association. 2014. "Leisure Reading: A Joint Statement of the International Reading Association, The Canadian Children's Book Centre, and the National Council of Teachers of English." *International Reading Association*. http://www.reading.org
Krashen, Stephen D. 2004. *The Power of Reading: Insights from the Research*, 2nd ed. Westport: Libraries Unlimited.
Lobel, Arnold. 1970. *Frog and Toad Are Friends*. New York: HarperCollins.
Lonigan, Christopher J., and Grover J. Whitehurst. 1998. "Relative Efficacy of Parent and Teacher Involvement in a Shared-Reading Intervention for Preschool Children from Low-Income Backgrounds." *Early Childhood Research Quarterly* 17: 265–92.
McKechnie, Lynne (E.F.). 2001. "Ethnographic Observation of Preschool Children." *LISR* 22(1): 61–76.
———. 2004. "'I'll Keep Them for My Children' (Kevin, 9 years): Children's Personal Collections of Books and Other Materials." *Canadian Journal of Library and Information Science* 28(4): 73–88.
———. 2006. "Observations of Toddlers in Library Settings." *Library Trends* 55(1): 190–201.
———. 2007. "'Spiderman Is Not for Babies' (Peter, 4 years): The Boys and Reading Problems from the Perspective of the Boys Themselves." *Canadian Journal of Library and Information Science* 32(1–2): 57–67.
Meyers, Elaine, and Harriet Henderson. 2014. "Overview of Every Child Ready to Read @ Your library." *Association for Library Service to Children*. http://www.everychildreadytoread.org/project-history%09/overview-every-child-ready-read-your-library%C2%AE-1st-edition

National Academy of Education (US). 1985. *Commission on Reading: Becoming a Nation of Readers: The Report of the Commission on Reading*. Washington: National Academy of Education.

National Early Literacy Panel. 2008. "Developing Early Literacy: A Scientific Synthesis of Early Literacy Development and Implications for Intervention." *National Center for Family Literacy*. https//www.nichd.nih.gov

Ross, Catherine S., Lynne (E.F.) McKechnie, and Paulette M. Rothbauer. 2006. *Reading Matters: What the Research Reveals about Reading, Libraries, and Community*. Westport: Libraries Unlimited.

Salinger, Terry. 2001. "Assessing the Literacy of Young Children: The Case for Multiple Forms of Evidence." In *Handbook of Early Literacy Research*, vol. 3, edited by S.B. Neuman and D.K. Dickinson, 390–420. New York: Guilford Press.

Small, Ruth, and Marilyn P. Arnone. 2011. "Creative Reading: The Antidote to Readicide." *Knowledge Quest* 39(4): 12–15.

Smith, Michael W., and Jeffrey D. Willhelm. 2002. *Reading Don't Fix No Chevys: Literacy in the Lives of Young Men*. Portsmouth: Heinemann.

Teale, William H., and Elizabeth Sulzby, eds. 1986. *Emergent Literacy: Writing and Reading*. Norwood: Ablex.

Wells, Gordon. 1986. *The Meaning Makers: Learning to Talk and Talking to Learn*. Portsmouth: Heinemann.

Whitehurst, Grover J. 1992. "Dialogic Reading: An Effective Way to Read to Preschoolers." *Reading Rockets*. http://www.readingrockets.org/article/400

———. 2001. "Emergent Literacy: Development from Prereaders to Readers." In *Handbook of Early Literacy Research*, vol. 2, edited by S.B. Neuman and D.K. Dickinson, 11–29. New York: Guilford Press.

Reading the Readers
Tracking Visible Online Reading Audiences

Marianne Martens

17

Robert McChesney (2013) has described how the political economy of communication is transforming the media industries. This chapter will address how one such media industry, publishing, is increasingly using digital technologies to engage readers in constructing bestsellers. According to John B. Thompson (2010), in the transnational conglomerate model, to remain competitive, publishers must focus their resources on books that could become bestselling cultural commodities. The combination of digital technologies and the political economy of the publishing industry has shifted reader response theory by providing visible examples of young people's reading experiences.

Researching reading has long been an elusive process. Reader response theory helps uncover some of the perceived relationships between readers and texts in the print environment. New digital technologies enable online book-related environments in which readers provide concrete evidence of their tastes, while building visible virtual communities of reading audiences. Three such communities will be explored in this chapter: (1) peer-to-peer reviewers on Random House's proprietary Random Buzzers website (Randombuzzers.com 2013); (2) an online community of brand readers centred on the Twilight Saga (Hachette Book Group 2013), a bestselling transmedia phenomenon; and (3) publisher-created digital extensions of book characters from Alyxandra Harvey's (2010) series *The Drake Chronicles* that seek to engage readers via the social media platforms they occupy.

In exploring these sites, this chapter attempts to demonstrate how we have moved from communities of "implied readers" (Iser 1974) to online communities of participating reading audiences that cross geographic boundaries, unite readers around common reading interests, and display concrete evidence of how readers (and authors and publishers) engage with texts.

Reader response theorists who have tackled reading in print formats include Wolfgang Iser, whose "implied reader" (1974) is the reader an author expects to encounter: a reader who is pure, unbiased, and uninfluenced, unlike the *actual* (and mostly invisible) reader who encounters a text. Louise Rosenblatt (1978) considered reading to be a transaction between the reader and the text and saw reading as a continuum residing between aesthetic texts (those written for pleasure or beauty) and efferent texts (those written as informational texts). Digital formats have shifted these definitions: today, aesthetic texts have blurred with efferent texts, as hyperlinks allow the reader of a novel to seek information (e.g., Alyxandra Harvey includes pronunciation guides to character names in electronic versions of *The Drake Chronicles*). Stanley Fish (1980) who studied professional, academic readers, described how a reader's own background, beliefs, and experiences cohere with his or her own understanding and interpretation of texts. Interpretive communities (which are not necessarily physical communities) are directly related to what a reader brings to a text.

Janice Radway's *Reading the Romance* (1984) provides an interesting analog counterpart to studies of online reading communities. Using questionnaires and interviews, Radway conducted an in-depth study of sixteen women customers of a particular bookstore owned by "Dot," in "Smithtown." In an attempt to understand their preferences for lowbrow romance novels, Radway interviewed the women about their reading histories – from their favourite childhood books, to their knowledge of romance novels, to their leisure patterns. Arguably, Dot's newsletters served as an *ur*-blog for her readers, informing them about the latest developments in the genre. Publishers (of romance novels) would send her galleys to review, and her recommendations would lead to purchases by customers who trusted her opinions. For publishers, this model was labour intensive: they had to seek out key booksellers like Dot, send them advance review copies (ARCs) of books ahead of publication, and hope for favourable reviews that would translate into book sales. Today, publishers use online services such as NetGalley (*NetGalley.com* 2013) to distribute texts electronically to professional readers ahead of publication, and materials are reviewed on peer-to-peer sites, as discussed below.

In Radway's study, while the subjects all bought books at Dot's bookstore, and presumably used her newsletter for recommendations, the women did not actually know one another ahead of the study. As a bookseller making selections and recommendations for her customers, Dot served as a mediator, in much the same way that adult gatekeepers – including librarians, teachers, parents, and booksellers – traditionally served as mediators for young adult literature prior to the age of digital reading technologies. The Internet, however, has allowed for the removal of a layer of gatekeeping.

Disintermediated Reading Spaces

Tiziana Terranova argues that the Internet is a site of "disintermediation" (2007, 34) that eliminates the middleman, who in the case of books is the librarian or bookseller. Publisher-based websites for teens serve as such sites of disintermediation, for they are removing a layer of gatekeepers (librarians, teachers, parents, booksellers) that has long stood guard between books and the teens who read them. This has disrupted the traditional means of disseminating books to young people that has been in place since the early twentieth century.

In the case of publishers' websites, teens' affective labour amounts to an excellent source of surplus labour that provides free consumer research, peer-to-peer reviewing, marketing, and even content creation. Maurizio Lazzarato describes such labour as work that "involves a series of activities that are not normally recognized as 'work' – in other words, the kinds of activities involved in defining and fixing cultural and artistic standards, fashions, tastes, consumer norms, and, more strategically, public opinion" (2013, 132). Coté and Pybus describe affective labour as that which manipulates "a feeling of ease, well-being, satisfaction, excitement or passion," and write that "historically this labour has been unpaid and has been commonly regarded as 'women's work'" (2007, 90). This might explain why a 2007 Pew Institute study found girls to be more active in creating content than boys, and why girls (and women) are the dominant participants in online content creation. Perhaps it also connects to essentialist views on women: Coté and Pybus write about immaterial labour on Myspace and other social networks as a form of identity-building, and they write about affective immaterial labour in the context of caring for *Neopets*, equating this type of labour involving "caring and well-being" (para. 7) to the traditional realm of women's work as caregivers. Terranova calls those participating in free labour in the social factory "NetSlaves" (2007, 33). If we accept that such labour is being done in the context of making books, then teens participating on publisher-based sites are performing the same type of affective, immaterial labour (meaning labour that is done on an unpaid and voluntary basis out of a feeling of goodwill), carried out in this case on the Internet and feeding into products published through other media channels.

While this type of participation is relatively new in the realm of books and literature, other media channels have long solicited consumer participation. Mark Andrejevic (2008) describes the *Television Without Pity* (TWoP) website, through which viewer/participants exercise self-empowerment, first by having a creative voice in the direction of the programs, and second by impressing fellow members of the TWoP community with their snarky or pithy criticism of particular shows; all the while, the producers benefited from free market research. The difference here is that solicitation of consumer participation is now occurring in what has always been considered what Bourdieu (1984) refers to as an inalienable field of cultural production: literature.

Research on audiences argues that the interactivity of "new media" serves to "disaggregate audiences" (Butsch 2011, 162), but in the case of online sites centred around books, the reverse is true. An active audience is aggregated via its visible evidence of participation, as members leave comments, contribute content, and leave other tangible evidence of their presence. An audience is constructed in part via the layers of comments and user-generated content left behind by the participants. One such disintermediated website is Random House's *Random Buzzers*.

Random Buzzers: Disintermediated Reviews

By around 2007, most of the Big Seven transnational conglomerates had created teen-specific participatory sites (Martens 2012). This enabled a convergence of readers and critics to supplement or even replace the role of reviewers like Radway's Dot.[1] The *Random Buzzers* (2013) website was especially sophisticated: members called "Random Buzzers" could earn "Buzz Bucks" by posting pictures, answering surveys, taking quizzes, writing essays, voting, posting comments to a message board, clicking on links and sending them to friends, emailing and sending instant messages directly from the site, and "recruiting" friends. A social networking component allowed participants to "friend" other reviewers in order to follow their recommendations (Martens 2012, 178).

By spring 2009, a direct discourse between publishers, authors, and teen consumers had been established on the *Random Buzzers* and *Twilight Saga* websites (*Twilight Saga* will be discussed next). Publishers were able to communicate directly with their readers by building websites that attracted teens by providing them with access to their favourite books and authors; the same websites provided participants with agency by soliciting their feedback, advice, and user-generated content related to books released by those publishers.

On the *Random Buzzers* site, in exchange for their labour, participants could earn Buzz Bucks, a form of virtual currency. This money had no value anywhere beyond the site's walls; but within the site, it could be exchanged for other Random House products, including posters, ARCs, and published books, all at a low cost to the publisher.

As a result of the convergence of technology, labour, and the new disintermediated relationships between publishers and young readers, teens' book-related labour in online environments has become a rich source of information for publishers. For the past few years, publishers have been carefully monitoring the Web for users' opinions, feedback, and content related to the books they publish. By creating proprietary online sites that emulate and link to what the teens are doing independently on blogs and fan sites, publishers can create and exploit a venue for affective peer-to-peer marketing, all within a proprietary digital enclosure (Andrejevic 2007) governed by the site's rules for participation. The community of peer-to-peer reviewing that exists on the *Random Buzzers* site has extended the types of book recommendations found in Dot's newsletter (Radway 1984) across geographically distributed communities. Reviews are no longer limited to literary experts, but are in the hands of the readers, as they build connections with other readers and create a venue for a visible reading audience in which members interact with their favourite authors, as well as with one another via peer-to-peer recommendations and other activities. Within the overarching genre of young adult literature, reading participants display elite levels of cultural capital by posting badges next to their names, and by the number of reviews they submit (those who post more receive higher-ranked badges). This has redefined our notion of what constitutes a "reading expert." No longer is it just traditional gatekeepers – parents, trained librarians, or expert booksellers (like Janice Radway's "Dot") – who recommend reading material; instead, recommendations are made by peers who have been certified and validated by the number and rank of badges earned. Theoretically, publishers can channel readers' contributions and feedback on their websites to create and sell books tailored to readers' displayed expressions of taste.

With the print model, romance readers, depended on their geographic proximity, could perhaps attend a favourite author's book tour; by contrast, in an online community, readers have access to their favourite authors via interactions such as online question-and-answer sessions. This allows them to build a personal connection with their favourite authors; it also enables what Pattee (2006) describes as the literary mode of production – by bringing the readers closer to the production of the books. These online interactions between readers and authors provide publishers with clear snapshots of readers' tastes. On the *Random Buzzers* site, readers were able to get close to their favourite authors by participating in activities such as "Question of the week." Participants submitted questions to a selected author, and if featured, that question was highlighted on the site's home page. Most likely, *Random Buzzers* had far more members than Dot's newsletter had readers/subscribers; certainly, the website's geographic reach was far wider. As of 5 April 2012, there were 67,524 *Random Buzzers* subscribers (Martens 2012).[2]

One example of such participant–author interaction was between participant fan "Pabkins" and author Page Morgan, as follows:

> Pabkins: "When mapping out your male love interest, how did you decide what you wanted to do with him?" (Pabkins 2013).
>
> Page Morgan, author of The Beautiful and the Cursed (TB&TC), answered: "I liked having a few different male love interests to map out in TB&TC. I could do different things with each of them. Nolan is sarcastic and dangerous with a sword. Luc is quiet and strong and Vander is intelligent and a bit more gentle." (Morgan 2013)

Upon receiving the author's response, Pabkins posted the following enthusiastic response:

> "OH My Goodness! I didn't even realize my question got picked! Woohoo!" (Pabkins 2013)

In addition, Pabkins earned twenty-five Buzz Bucks for posting this question. The virtual space provides a type of proximity to a favourite author, allowing readers to form affective relationships with the author, the site, and the publisher who enables this contact. Similar goals are evident in the next site I discuss: the Twilight Saga site.

The Twilight Saga Site

User input has been invaluable to publishers as they shape the literature they produce for young adults. Websites and blogs are effective vehicles for getting feedback from these consumers, and publishers are co-opting these models on their own proprietary sites, where teens are actively involved with the books they love. These sites foster an affective relationship between publishers, who appreciate the free consumer research, and their reading consumers, who become participating fans of particular books and authors. Publishers can use the input from their sites to attract and market to other teenagers, thus exploiting affect and co-opting teens' online activities for marketing purposes. According to the end-user licensing agreements governing use of the sites, such content can be used as the site owners wish, including to create new content.

Online interaction arose broadly around the bestselling *Twilight* series. It was the readers themselves who established a bottom-up, organically constructed, textual community of fan sites, blogs, and other content, all of which took root around what was initially a single book. But that first book quickly became a bestselling series and generated an online community of brand reader fans; this eventually spawned an entire genre of "teen paranormal romance." This community was initially comprised of readers of print editions of the books, and also of participants in social interactions that extended from the books onto the Web, where readers shared opinions, news, gossip, fan fiction, and more. With *Twilight*, the publisher expanded on this natural development, using the associated textual communities for financial gain. Emulating material already on the Web, the *Twilight Saga* website was launched in 2007 and gained a strong following by billing itself as the *official* site for news and information related to books and films in *The Twilight Saga*. In doing so, it channelled individuals' fan sites onto its proprietary site.

In 2013, after the publication of all four books and the release of all five movies in the *Twilight* series, there were still seventy groups on Hachette's *Twilight Saga* site (Hachette Book Group 2013). When Janice Radway conducted her research for *Reading the Romance*, Dot, the bookstore owner, was at the centre of a community of more or less anonymous readers who were united around a taste for romance novels, a bookstore, and Dot's newsletter. Overall, feedback from readers was limited to conversations Dot had with her customers, which may or may not have influenced her reviews for publishers. In contrast, today, feedback can now be received almost effortlessly from globally distributed fans who are united around a common fandom and a common language (English), as they contribute their opinions and content across online participatory sites. As on the *Random Buzzers* site, participants served as peer-to-peer reviewers (albeit without free ARCs), peer-to-peer marketers, providers of free consumer research, and even content providers as they voluntarily uploaded materials ranging from fan fiction to songs based on the series. Of course, any content that was uploaded by users onto Hachette's proprietary site was governed by the site's end-user licensing agreement, which in turn meant that site owners maintained certain rights over user-generated content posted on the site.

The four books in the *Twilight* series (Amazon.com 2013a) appeared between 2005 and 2009, and the five movies between 2008 and 2012 (IMDB.com 2013). The *Twilight* series maintained its blockbuster status for several years. In 2011, Diane Roback wrote in the trade journal *Publishers Weekly* that "sales of *Twilight* books, while still significant, cooled somewhat last year – just over 8.5 million books sold in 2010 vs. 26.5 million in 2009 and 27.5 million in 2008" (Roback 2011).[3] The height of activity on the site occurred in 2009, with several question-and-answer (Q&A) sessions that allowed readers to post questions, which the author, Stephenie Meyer, selected from to answer.[4] Even after sales of the books, movies, and related merchandise shrunk, site membership continued to grow. As evidence of the series' continued popularity, on 15 May 2013 there were 500,276 members on *TwilightSaga.com* (Hachette 2013), representing a slight increase from May 2012, when there were 499,355 members (Martens 2012).

When the *TwilightSaga.com* site was created, the groups within it were modelled after existing fan sites on the Web, and the OlderWomanGroup emulated the online website *TwilightMOMS.com* (Hansen 2013), which later became a commercial site with sponsored advertising. The OlderWoman-Group (*TwilightSaga.com, OlderWomanGroup* 2013) remained active (posts appeared daily in May 2013), and its 2,339 members had close parallels to Janice Radway's romance readers. The group described itself as follows: "It's more than an obsession ... It's a sisterhood." About readers of romance novels, Radway wrote:

> The romance community then, is not an actual group functioning at the local level. Rather, it is a huge, ill-defined network composed of readers on the one hand and authors on the other. Although it performs some of the same functions carried out by older neighborhood groups, this female community is mediated by the distances of modern mass publishing. Despite the distance, the Smithton women feel personally connected to their favorite authors because they are convinced that these *writers know how to make them happy*. (1987, 97; author's emphasis)

The "sisterhood" of OlderWomanGroup may have felt an affective, personal relationship with author Stephenie Meyer, in part because of her presence (direct and indirect) on the site, but the real sisterhood was among the group's members, who were united as brand readers of *Twilight*. "Goodwill towards brands ... has arguably become even more important in contemporary times" (Jarrett 2003, 344). Exploiting the affective labour of the consumer is quickly becoming a new strategy for producers. A study of the conversations on the group reveals themes of friendship, *Twilight* fandom, and shared confessions, as seen in Table 17.1.

Participants clearly enjoyed identifying with a community of similar tastes and sharing in the guilty pleasure of reading (and viewing) *Twilight*. As seen in Table 17.1, women demonstrated a sense of community and friendship, with comments like "were [sic] all nuts but I'm proud of it," and "So nice to know I'm not the only crazy older woman around." The comments in the table were from 2009. By 2013, aside from occasional posted pictures of the main characters "Edward," "Bella," and "Jacob," the conversations on the site had very little to do with *Twilight* and were much more representative of a community of friends catching up with one another. For example, among a barrage of Mother's Day greetings to one another, WhyCantEdwardBeReal? (2013) posted a description of her return home from a vacation to Barcelona:

> Hello everyone, doing a quick drive by. Will come back to cmment later. Barcelona was great w great weather – we are so exhausted tho. Still on whacked out time. The flight coming home was cancelled so we came home a day late. Trying to catch up.[5]

Table 17.1 Twilight Fandom (from *twilightsaga.com*, OlderWomanGroup 2009)

"Name" of poster	Friendship	Fandom	Confessions
Dark Star	"Look forward to joining in with discussions about the wonderful Twilight with my new friends in the OlderWomanGroup :o)	"wonderful Twilight"	"I've never been a part of a forum or anything like this before so I'm a bit nervous"
Bridget	"Hope to get to know lots of you ladies and share in the love that we have for the Twilight Saga!!!"	"… what do you now, within the first chapter I was hooked."	"I am 27 and a mother of 3 great kids that keep me busy but I still find time to get my Edward and Bella fix, lol!!"
Joanne		"I bought a copy of Teen magazine last night at the grocery story … Edward and Bella were on the cover"	"So nice to know I'm not the only crazy older woman around"
Tina	"I'm excited to be among others who find themselves obsessed.. and just plain nuts over this whole series."	"I just couldn't get enough then and still can't."	"I ignored my family and stayed up till all hours of the night … I think [my husband] sees me eyeing the 22 year old hot young guys. Oh my god what did I admit to……I am certifiable."
tracey engdahl	"I am so happy to have these outlets to discuss the phenom that is Twilight."	"Saw the movie [for the fifth time] last night at the cheap seat theater … I have read the saga four times."	"My husband rolls his eyes when he walks by the computer and sees my wallpaper."
Saga-momma	"I am glad to read that I am not alone!"	I have read the Twilight Saga (all 4 books) more than 20 times … I feel that I know the characters personally, and they are a part of my life."	"I feel really silly with the amount of energy I put towards Twilight. Everytime my husband sees me on the computer or reading a Twilight book (which is all the time) he just smiles and rolls his eyes … I feel like a teenager again."
Joi	"Isn't this fun!"	"I've seen the movie 14 times and I'm reading the books for the 2nd time … I spend all my spare time … searching the internet for updates about anything Twilight."	"OK, were all nuts but I'm proud of it."

Spelling and grammar rendered faithfully as on site. All comments are from 13 February 2009.

Clearly, this kind of affective support experienced by a community of brand readers is not only possible but also visible in online communities like the Twilight Saga site. Aside from the allusion to the lead character Edward in the poster's username, her (assuming poster is female) post has absolutely nothing to do with the series. The virtual friendships that started around the *Twilight* fan community had grown into real friendships. While Radway's romance readers were not part of an actual, tangible community of readers (physical or digital), she writes

> that through romance reading the Smithton women are providing themselves with another kind of female community capable of rendering the so desperately needed affective support. This community seems not to operate on an immediate local level although there are signs, both in Smithton and nationally, that romance readers are learning the pleasures of regular discussions of books with other women. (1984, 96)

The affective and immaterial labour by visible readers, which so far has been explored in this chapter around *Random Buzzers* and *The Twilight Saga* in terms of peer-to-peer reviews, marketing, focus-group research, and user-generated content, is expanded upon by authors and publishers as well. Publishers and authors must also engage in new forms of labour, and one such example will be explored in the next section. *The Drake Chronicles* by Alyxandra Harvey is supported via the author's own social media and Web presence, but also via the publisher's social media efforts.

Digital Character Extensions via *The Drake Chronicles*

Before the Internet, authors of books for young people helped promote their own books by going on book tours and school visits and attending author signings, and this continues to be an important way of marketing books, especially those by top-selling authors. But in the new political economy of the publishing industry, technological innovations mean that marketing has moved beyond being directed mainly by the publishing company; it is now considered a collaborative effort involving marketers, authors, and readers. In terms of authors, social media enable a larger than ever focus on do-it-yourself (DIY) marketing. Alyxandra Harvey, author of the *Drake Chronicles* series, is one such engaged author; she maintains an extensive Web presence via her website, *AlyxandraHarvey.com*. Readers are able to post questions to her in different places on the site, and she answers many of them.[6] Questions on the frequently asked questions (FAQ) portion of that site often have formulaic answers that defer to her publisher; see Table 17.2. Other

Table 17.2 Alyxandra Harvey's Q&A (Harvey 2009)

Questions	Answers
Q: Will you come to my town/school?	A: I can only go where I am invited and where my awesome publishers can send me … but let them know where you are, it never hurts to ask!
Q: Will there be a Haunting Violet sequel?	A: Haunting Violet is currently a standalone novel. That said, I wrote a sequel for my own enjoyment, so the possibility is there. It depends on publishers and reader demand, I suppose. So if you want it, let Bloomsbury/Walker & Co know! and make sure to let your local bookshops know you want to read more.

questions, such as those posted under the "Appearances" tab (Harvey 2012), had a more personal tone, featuring informal language and grinning emoticons.

In addition to Harvey's own efforts at connecting with fans via her website, in 2011, her publisher's marketing department (Martens 2012) collaborated with the author to develop digital extensions of characters via the social media sites inhabited by readers, such as Facebook and Twitter, and by having the characters interact with one another via status updates and Twitter feeds. Staying in the right voice was a challenge for her publisher's marketing team; they accomplished it by keeping books on their desks and double-checking how characters' voices might sound. Recently, a group of graduate students read the series. When they analyzed the corresponding social media content, they found that often the voices did not remain consistent. One such example that was criticized was the character of Solange, who was born into an old vampire family. While her speech is formal and Old Worldly in the series, the students noticed that on social media, Solange suddenly spoke like a contemporary American teenager (Martens 2012).

As evidenced by her enthusiasm in describing the company's digital campaigns, Harvey's marketer enjoyed the creativity of coming up with this supportive storyline, and enjoyed assuming the identities of the fictional characters from *The Drake Chronicles* and continuing their storylines via Twitter feeds. She especially enjoyed watching the teens' reactions. In these cases, social media are redefining the workday for marketers, for this work has no clearly defined schedule or boundary. Twitter feeds and Facebook statuses have to be updated, and often censored for plot "spoilers" or bad language almost around the clock. While social media sites such as YouTube rely on Amazon Mechanical Turk (Amazon.com 2013b) to monitor content, publishers do not appear to be using the same, which means that the monitoring remains a combination of algorithms that can eliminate coarse language, and constant policing by publishers' staff.

In creating such online character extensions, the publisher blends fiction with reality as people become book characters and book characters come to (virtual) life. The collaborative community marketing effort, involving publishers' marketing staff, authors, and the participating young readers, points to how the field has been reconfigured.

Technology also provides evidence of consumers' tastes. Teens have long been an ephemeral and unpredictable market; today, however, Web analytics allow book marketers to find out what young readers like most, including which parts of a given website most engage them (Martens 2012). Surveillance gathered from users via sophisticated Web analysis tools then informs the content of the books, as well as what sorts of activities will be developed to promote the books online. By revealing what they are most interested in (based on information gathered from Web analytics), teens become co-creators of the cultural products made for them.

Publishers have made significant financial investments in digital formats,[7] and there is an assumption on the part of publishers that young people enjoy and even expect these multiplatform/transmedia formats.[8] The publishers' and authors' views represent the development of new ideas related to young people's reading through technological innovations, as opposed to the construct of the largely invisible and "implied reader" (Iser 1974) that existed before.

Conclusion

This chapter has described visible reading audiences within online communities of readers, from the *Random Buzzers* site to *TwilightSaga.com* and the *Drake Chronicles*. Technology has allowed a progression from Iser's (1974) "implied readers," blurred the relationship between aesthetic and efferent texts described by Rosenblatt (1978), and redefined Fish's (1980) "interpretive communities." Clearly, reading audiences demonstrate their tastes and form communities around shared interests in books: from labouring as peer-to-peer reviewers, to brand reading (in the case of adults sharing embarrassment over reading books created, ostensibly, for teens). And while such communities of affect benefit readers by providing them with agency and a personal relationship with the authors, publishers may be benefiting most of all, for the large amounts of focus-group-style data, supplied by readers completely free of charge, theoretically allows them to create products that teens want to read (and, of course, buy).

The sites considered here enable much scrutiny of readers. Beyond the websites and social media platforms described in this chapter, the amount of data about readers that is available via e-reading platforms provides even more visibility on consumers' reading habits, and is an important area for future research on reading. In *Digital Book World*, Brandhorst (2013) writes: "We'll be able to tell what a reader of an e-book is reading at any given instant; how many pages she's read; where she dropped off; where, geographically, she's reading; and what factors influenced her purchase in the first place. And on and on." Clearly, e-readers present even more visibility on reading, allowing for a staggering amount of data to be collected about readers, and pointing to a loss of privacy that would have been unacceptable in the era of print.

Notes

1 In 2013, Penguin and Random House merged, so that there was now the Big Six (Bosman 2013), which included HarperCollins, Hachette, Macmillan, Penguin Random House, Scholastic Corporation, and Simon & Schuster.
2 As of 2013, *Random Buzzers* membership has been extended across social media sites like Facebook and Pinterest, and a new analysis should be undertaken to see if participation via social media has exceeded or replaced participation on the original website.
3 For more about the TwilightSaga site, see Martens 2012 and Martens 2010.
4 No new Q&A sessions have appeared since 2009.
5 Spelling and punctuation as on website.
6 Of course it is an assumption that the author is answering questions on her website.
7 According to the Pew Internet and the American Life Project, as of May 2011, 12 percent of adults (over eighteen) in the United States own e-book reader, which is double the number (6 percent) who owned one six months earlier, in November 2010. Holiday 2010 was the tipping point for e-books and digital readers (Purcell 2011).
8 The fact that adults are buying e-book versions of young adult novels is another reason for publishers to commit to this format.

References

Amazon.com. 2013a. "Twilight." http://www.amazon.com/s/ref=nb_sb_noss_2?url=search-alias%3Dstripbooks&field-keywords=twilight+.
———. 2013b. "Amazon's Mechanical Turk." https://www.mturk.com/mturk/welcome
Andrejevic, Mark. 2007. *iSpy: Surveillance and Power in the Interactive Era*. Lawrence: University Press of Kansas.
———. 2008. "Watching Television without Pity: The Productivity of Online Fans." *Television & New Media* 9(1): 24–46.
Bosman, Julie. 2013. "Penguin and Random House Merge, Saying Change Will Come Slowly." *New York Times*, 2 July. http://www.nytimes.com/2013/07/02/business/media/merger-of-penguin-and-random-house-is-completed.html.

Bourdieu, Pierre. 1984. *Distinction: A Social Critique of the Judgement of Taste*. Cambridge, MA: Harvard University Press.
Brandhorst, Tim. 2010. "Closing the Gap between Publishers and Readers." *Digital Book World*, 23 April. http://www.digitalbookworld.com/2010/closing-the-gap-between-publishers-and-readers
Butsch, Richard. 2011. "Audiences and Publics, Media and Public Spaces." In *The Handbook of Media Audiences*, edited by Virginia Nightingale, 149–68. Oxford: Blackwell.
Coté, Mark, and Jennifer Pybus. 2007. "Learning to Immaterial Labor 2.0: Myspace and Social Networks." *Ephemera* 7(1): 88–106. http://www.ephemerajournal.org/sites/default/files/7-1cote-pybus.pdf
Fish, Stanley. 1980. *Is There a Text in This Class?: The Authority of Interpretive Communities*. Cambridge, MA: Harvard University Press.
Hachette Book Group. 2013. *TheTwilightSaga.com*. http://thetwilightsaga.com
Hansen, Lisa. 2013. *TwilightMOMS.com*. http://www.TwilightMOMS.com
Harvey, Alyxandra. 2009. "Alyxandra Harvey's Frequently Asked Questions." *AlyxandraHarvey.com*. http://alyxandraharvey.com/faq
———. 2010. *Hearts at Stake* (Book #1 in the *Drake Chronicles* Series). New York: Walker Books.
———. 2012. "Alyxandra Harvey Appearances." *AlyxandraHarvey.com*. http://alyxandraharvey.com/on-tour/comment-page-13/#comments
IMDB.Com. 2013. "Twilight." http://www.imdb.com/find?q=twilight&s=all
Iser, Wolfgang. 1974. *The Implied Reader*. Baltimore: Johns Hopkins University Press.
Jarrett, Kyle. 2003. "Labour of Love: An Archaeology of Affect as Power in e-Commerce." *Journal of Sociology* 39(4): 335–51.
Lazzarato, Maurizio. 2013. "Immaterial Labor." http://www.generation-online.org/c/fcimmateriallabour3.htm
Martens, Marianne. 2010. "Consumed by Twilight: The Commodification of Young Adult Literature." In *Bitten by Twilight: Youth Culture, Media, and the Vampire Franchise*, edited by M. Click, J. Stevens Aubrey, and L. Behm-Morawitz, 243–60. New York: Peter Lang.
———. 2012. "A Historical and Comparative Analysis of Multiplatform Books for Young Readers: Technologies of Production, User-Generated Content, and Economics of Immaterial and Affective Labor." PhD diss., Rutgers, State University of New Jersey.
McChesney, Robert W. 2013. *Digital Disconnect: How Capitalism Is Turning the Internet Against Democracy*. New York: New Press.
Meyer, Stephenie. 2005. *Twilight*. New York: Little, Brown.
———. 2006. *New Moon*. New York: Little, Brown.
———. 2007. *Eclipse*. New York: Little, Brown.
———. 2008. *Breaking Dawn*. New York: Little, Brown.
NetGalley.com. 2013. "Welcome to NetGalley." https://www.netgalley.com
Pabkins. 2013. "OH My Goodness!" *Randombuzzers.com*. http://www.randombuzzers.com/things-to-do/question-of-the-week/view/writing/when-mapping-out-your-male-love-interest-how-did-you-decide-what-you-wanted-to-do-with-him/#42957 (page no longer accessible).
Pattee, Amy. 2006. "Commodities in Literature, Literature as Commodity: A Close Look at the Gossip Girl Series." *Children's Literature Association Quarterly* 31(2); 154–75.

Purcell, Kristin. 2011. "E-reader ownership doubles in six months." PEW Internet and the American Life Project. June 27. http://pewinternet.org/Reports/2011/E-readers-and-tablets/Report.aspx

Radway, Janice. 1984. *Reading the Romance: Women, Patriarchy, and Popular Literature*. Chapel Hill: University of North Carolina Press.

Random Buzzers. 2013. http://www.randombuzzers.com

Roback, Diane. 2011. "Franchises Flying High: Children's Books: Facts & Figures 2010 Series Dominate with Huge Numbers; e-Book Needle Jumps." *Publishers Weekly*, 21 March. http://www.publishersweekly.com/pw/by-topic/childrens/childrens-book-news/article/46543-franchises-flying-high-children-s-books-facts-figures-2010.html

Rosenblatt, Louise. 1978. *The Reader, the Text, the Poem: The Transactional Theory of the Literary Work*. Carbondale: Southern Illinois University Press.

Terranova, Tiziana. 2007. "Futurepublic: On Information Warfare, Bio-Racism, and Hegemony as Noopolitics." *Theory, Culture, & Society* 24(3): 125–45.

Thompson, John B. 2010. *Merchants of Culture: The Publishing Business in the Twenty-First Century*. Cambridge and Malden: Polity Press.

TwilightSaga.com, OlderWomanGroup. http://thetwilightsaga.com/main/search/search?q=older+woman+group

WhyCantEdwardBeReal. 2013. "Barcelona." *TwilightSaga.com, Older Woman Group*. 15 May. http://thetwilightsaga.com/group/olderwomangroup?groupUrl=olderwomangroup&xgi=&test-locale=&exposeKeys=&xg_pw=&xgsi=&groupId=&id=2570916%3AGroup%3A214552&xg_disable_customizations=&xn_debug=&test_embed=&test_baz_7722=&test_baz_6713=&categoryId=&page=5#comments.

Literature in Common

18

Reading for Pleasure in School Reading Groups

Teresa Cremin and Joan Swann

This chapter considers the reading experiences of voluntary reading groups in schools, their collaborative interpretation of children's/young adult literature, and their construction of reader identities. We focus on a study of secondary school reading groups in different parts of the UK as they took part in a scheme to "shadow" the judging of two prestigious children's book awards: the Carnegie Medal and the Kate Greenaway Medal. The groups spent part of the summer term reading and discussing books that had been shortlisted for one or both of these awards. They were then able to compare their views with those of the judges. Our study of this process was carried out in collaboration with the Chartered Institute of Library and Information Professionals (CILIP), which runs the awards and the shadowing scheme and wished to evaluate the success of shadowing. The work was funded by the Carnegie UK Trust.

A strong theme that emerged in the study was that, despite their institutional settings and, to some extent, their alignment with curricular priorities (e.g., many were reported as contributing to their school's literacy strategy), the groups presented themselves as determinedly extracurricular. While reading for pleasure is part of the curricula for English in the UK, group leaders and members saw English as dominated by objectives-led approaches to reading and by assessment. By contrast, reading group experiences were characterized as being about "fun," "enjoyment," and "choice." Groups were partly defined by their contrast with curricular reading, and considerable work went into creating and sustaining this distinctiveness. But also, in a context in which reading is often regarded as "geeky," an activity for "boffins," groups sought to create reading communities in which the pleasure of reading could be shared.

In this chapter we consider, in turn, evidence from interviews and conversations with reading group members, and observations and audio-recordings of reading group meetings. In combination, these demonstrate how "non-school" reading practices, relationships, and identities are worked at and maintained: both accounted for in talk about reading and enacted within reading group practices.

Theoretical and Policy Contexts for the Study of School Reading Groups

Our study of school reading groups, here shadowing the Carnegie and Kate Greenaway book awards, has two starting points. The first of these is the recent emergence of a discourse analytic approach to literary reading (e.g., Allington and Swann 2009; Peplow et al. 2016; Swann and Allington 2009). This has much in common with other approaches to the study of reading experiences that see reading and readers as historically and socially positioned, such as aspects of the history of reading (e.g., Crone and Towheed 2011; Halsey 2009); qualitative media reception studies (see review in Staiger 2005); and ethnographic studies of contemporary reading practices and reading events, including reading groups/book clubs (e.g., Cherland 1994; Long 2003; Radway [1984]1991; papers in Rehberg Sedo 2011; and Lang 2012). Hall (2006) characterizes such approaches as "literature as social practice," an echo of Street's (1984) somewhat larger conceptualization of literacy as social practice. For Hall, applying this to literature provides a much-needed emphasis on "people's reading and writing activities in the broader context of their lives and interactions ... what people do with texts and how they find value in literature within the constraints of their own social contexts" (2006, 451).

As its name suggests, a discourse analytic approach adds to this an interest in the discourse through which people construct reading experiences: both the accounts readers provide of their reading (e.g., in interview data) and, of more recent interest, the discursive interpretation of literary texts evident in joint reading activities. Examples include Allington and Swann (2011) on historical and contemporary evidence of reading; Benwell (2009) on the reception of diasporic fiction; Ericksson Barajas and Aronsson (2004; 2009) on school "booktalk"; Peplow (2014) on the discursive construction of reader identities; Swann (2012) on creative interpretive activity in reading groups; and Whiteley (2011) on "professional" and "non-professional" readings of poetry. Discourse analysis may be used to identify recurrent themes in discourse. It may also focus on the communicative strategies employed by participants – in literary discussion, for instance: how interpretations are collaboratively co-constructed between readers; how they are developed sequentially within interactions; how they are embedded in particular sets of social and interpersonal relations; and how they are, in other respects, socially/culturally and historically contingent.

For those adopting such a contextualized approach to reading, school reading groups provide an interesting instance of literary reading in a particular institutional setting, where the informal practices associated with reading groups rub up against, and may be in tension with, certain institutional preoccupations, roles, and relationships. We were concerned to document the kinds of reading experiences, and literary discourse, that would be constructed in such settings. A second motivation for the study had to do with educational issues: the increased attention afforded in recent years to the significance of reading for pleasure. Successive international surveys have documented a decline in young people's participation in and enjoyment of reading in England relative to other countries (OECD 2002, 2010; Twist et al. 2003, 2007, 2012). UK studies have affirmed these findings, highlighting in particular that young people's interest in reading declines with age, as does the pleasure they find in it (Clark, Osborne, and Akerman 2008; Maynard et al. 2007); the two most recent UK surveys revealed highly significant differences between 8-to-11-year-olds, 11-to-14-year-olds, and 14-to-16-year-olds in terms of their reading enjoyment (Clark 2012, 2013). In the autumn 2012 survey, which drew on the views of 34,910 young people from 8 to 17 years, over half of the 11-to-14-year-olds (the most common age range in the current study) reported enjoying reading only "a bit" or "not at all." In this age group, daily reading and the time spent reading showed continual decline, with three-quarters noting that they read for less than thirty minutes at a time and nearly one-third reporting reading one or no books in the last month (Clark 2013).

Such findings are of considerable concern within education. Reading for pleasure is seen as a worthwhile activity in its own terms, but it has also been associated, directly and indirectly, with reading attainment (Clark 2012; OECD 2010; Sullivan and Brown 2013; Twist et al. 2012). It is suggested that being a frequent reader affords more of an advantage than having well-educated parents (OECD 2002), and an examination of twenty-seven nations' family practices argues that children growing up in homes with a wealth of books receive the advantages of approximately three years more schooling, as measured by their national tests, than children from "bookless homes" – a finding that is independent of parents' education, occupation, and class (Evans et al. 2010).

Alongside such research studies, reports from the Office for Standards in Education, Children's Services, and Skills (Ofsted) in England have expressed concern about the lack of a coherent policy for reading in many schools. In a review of evidence from their last three English surveys, they comment: "In recent years the view has developed, especially in secondary schools, that there is not enough curriculum time to focus on wider reading or reading for pleasure" (Ofsted 2012, 29).

The development of wider reading/reading for pleasure forms part of the national curricula for English/literacy in England and Wales, Scotland, and Northern Ireland. It enjoys increased prominence in the new national curriculum for English in England, which includes a persistently repeated statutory requirement that pupils "should be taught to develop pleasure in and motivation to read" (DfE 2013, 26). The accountability and assessment regimes associated with English as a subject have not altered, however, and it is argued that the new curriculum fails to recognize the diversification of young people's contemporary reading preferences and practices (Maynard et al. 2007; Clark 2012). The curriculum also makes the assumption that teachers have sufficient knowledge of children's literature to foster reader development and children's motivated engagement in fiction, although the evidence suggests that, at least at the primary level, this is not the case, and that teachers depend too heavily on a narrow range of well-known authors (Cremin et al. 2008a, 2008b).

Given such concerns about young people's reading for pleasure, the potential of extracurricular reading groups to increase participation in reading becomes of interest within education, as does the potential of specific initiatives such as shadowing children's book awards to broaden reading opportunities for children and young people. Our study was carried out in light of this. The evidence we provide also contrasts with the documentation of general trends in large-scale surveys, whether national or international. While we did examine UK-wide data on shadowing, our study, in common with contextualized and discourse analytic approaches to the reading experience discussed above, included a major qualitative component, exploring the ways in which readers interact with others around texts, as well as their discursive practices and identities as readers. In this chapter, we focus on these latter aspects of the reading experience.

The Shadowing Study

The shadowing study took place over two years (2011 and 2012). As mentioned above, it included a quantitative component, focusing largely on the demographic characteristics of groups, the motivations of group leaders registering for the scheme, and the reading activities reported for their groups. In addition, a qualitative component allowed us to explore "shadowing in practice" in a small number of groups: we carried out semi-structured interviews with the leaders of thirty-one shadowing groups in different parts of the UK; we also visited and observed a sub-set of these groups, four in 2011 and six in 2012. Of these ten groups, seven were secondary-school extracurricular reading groups that undertook shadowing in the summer term. In this paper we focus on data from these seven reading groups.[1]

The groups were selected to ensure as diverse a range as possible along several dimensions: geographical location; a social and cultural mix; the inclusion of boys as well as girls; and a range of abilities across the sample (see Appendix). Most groups were visited two or three times across the shadowing period during the summer term. In two groups, as well as observing shadowing, we were able to observe an English lesson participated in by some group members. Complementary data from a variety of methods[2] enabled us to construct "rich descriptions" (Geertz 1973) of reading experiences by examining the social construction of readers and reading, the particular reader identity positions of both young people and adults, the nature of reading activities, and the development of group interpretations of literary texts. We addressed several research questions, of which two are particularly relevant here:[3] How do group members and group leaders account for their experiences in reading groups; how do they position themselves as readers within these groups? And what is the nature of the groups' reading practices and how are these collaboratively constructed and maintained?

Accounting for Reading Experiences: Interviews and Conversations

In interviews and informal conversations, group leaders and members represented reading groups, and particularly shadowing, as a high-culture activity concerned with "good quality literature," "the best of children's reading," "something worthwhile." Shadowing was widely seen as extending young people's reading repertoires beyond popular fiction – for example,

> Group leader: [It] pushes them up from Roald Dahl etc.
> Group member: It opens your eyes and makes you read different things.

This allowed young people to try on new identities as readers. In a striking example, Katie, identified by herself and by her group as a keen reader of vampire books, recounted a dramatic shift: on reading *My Sister Lives on the Mantelpiece*, she put aside her vampire books to complete the whole Carnegie shortlist:

> With My Sister Lives on the Mantelpiece it's like really good, 'cos like you would like read it and it would just make you want to read more and I was actually starting to read it and I think "Hang on I could actually put my Twilight – my Vampire books to aside for a bit and actually read these ones."

Katie's "conversion" to Carnegie became a recurrent theme in this and other discussions, referred to, often jocularly, by herself and other participants.

While reading in English is also about high-quality literature, group leaders and members distinguished their activity from English and indeed tended to define their groups in contrast to English, an observation also noted by Hippisley (2009). A major focus was on different reading practices. Reading in English was described as more prescriptive and less volitional, as in the following comments from group members:

> We had to, we were told which book to read and then we had to read them and it was sort of like, our teacher suggested that we did reading over the holidays and he gave a list of books that he suggested for us to read, but it was like books that he had read and books that he thought were good in a literary way, whereas we wanted books that had a good plot and story and things that aren't in English.

> When you read in class ... it is reading for the sake of reading, sort of thing, it is reading so that the teachers know you can read and everything. But when you are here, it is like, you read because you enjoy reading and you want to like broaden your horizons of books that you like to read.

Reading groups granted readers greater choice and autonomy in terms of how they read:

> There is no set book, so you can see what appeals to you and think "I'll try that."

> You just sort of pick up a book and read it if you like it and you can stop half way through if you really think you can't go on with it.

Interestingly, while books such as those shortlisted for awards were seen as good-quality literature, distinguished from popular fiction, some group leaders also represented them as differing from "English" texts:

> I want to make them realize that reading isn't all about Shakespeare and Dickens and what they have to read in English, as much as those authors are exciting and are enjoyable. I don't want them to feel that that is what it is all about. Reading is a choice and there is a lot of choice out there, and for them to explore. So, you know, it is reading for pleasure.

> I know ... they do Great Expectations and Lord of the Flies and things, whereas these [Carnegie shortlist] are more modern and [have] been written recently, so they are about events that will, or could occur presently or have done, so [young people] kind of understand them more.

Reading groups were therefore seen as extending young people's reading in two directions: both beyond popular fiction and also into worthwhile contemporary literature outside the traditional literary canon.

In contrast to the perceived task-focused nature of English, which was dominated by assessment, reading groups and shadowing were about pleasure and enjoyment. A group leader commented:

> We are doing it for fun, we are doing it to enjoy the books, to share a group activity that they all like doing ... Nobody is going to be marking what they are doing ... I mean you do try and make group activities in English fun and [include] group discussion, but you always want an end product in a class situation, you want something you can assess, tick a box.

Both group leaders and members repeatedly referred to pleasure and enjoyment in reading – the single most commonly used word was "fun."

In emphasizing reading as a pleasurable activity, some group leaders contrasted this with prevailing perceptions of reading as something for "geeks" or "boffins" – for instance:

> I would say there is quite a lot of negativity towards reading, and if you are a reader that you are a bit of a boffin – that term "boffin" comes up quite a lot.

Group members also commented on negative reactions to their interest in reading, a point developed in the following dialogue:

> A: I think it is quite hard to find a place to go and read because it gets quite noisy in the library.
>
> B: And if you go and sit on the field people take it as, see it as –
>
> C: "Boffin."
>
> B: Yeah, "boffin."
>
> B: You are being a geek if you sit and read because you are not doing what everyone else is doing, because they promote, round here they like, they like big up all the sports, if you don't do that then you sit and read, even if you sit and do your homework on the field they will call you a "boffin" because you are doing it in school.
>
> I: How do you handle that, because you are readers?
>
> A: I just ignore it.
>
> Sev: Yeah.
>
> A: I had umm, we were allowed to revise for our exam in English yesterday and umm and I instead sat on the field and read outside, and it was like they try to distract you because they think it is funny that you are reading, because they don't, because you are –
>
> B: Like different.
>
> A: Yeah, like a minority.
>
> (I = interviewer; A, B, and C = reading group members)

Such perceptions are consistent with evidence from larger surveys. For instance, one-third of the upper primary/lower secondary students questioned by Clark and colleagues viewed readers as "geeks" or "nerds," while one-quarter perceived them as "boring" (2008, 17).

In the context of such negative perceptions of reading, our interviews highlighted the perceived value of reading groups in providing space for communities of readers. A group leader noted:

> Sometimes I think even if you're in a top set that culture in the classroom might not exist where you can sit and rave on about your favourite books 'cos there'll always be one or two people in the class who are like – oh that's a bit geeky em whereas here they're quite secure and feel quite safe about you know being passionate about something that they're reading.

This was also a frequent theme in interviews with group members:

> It's like being with other people that love books as much as me. So yeah, I kinda like fit in.

> It gave a great sense of community because if you read books you often read on your own, and the Carnegie Medal – it gave a sense of community in a group and we could come along and share ideas and discuss the books.

In one group, members humorously reclaimed the perceived difference/minority status of being an avid reader. A young reader commented positively on the "weirdness" of some of the group in reading "two, three, four different books at a time" and also recounted a story of when she was caught reading a Carnegie book under the desk in a biology lesson:

> I usually get them [books] taken off us 'cos I'm trying to read during lessons [laughter]
> I do it's like [xxx] with A Monster Calls I was into an interesting bit so I was leaning back on my chair in biology with the book under the desk [laughter]
> And it was like Miss was like:
> – Amy.
> – Yes.
> – Can you answer this question.
> – No. [other participants join in to chorus this response] [laughter]
> – And why not.
> – I was kind of distracted.
> With the book under the desk.
> [laughter]

This is a well-known and much enjoyed story within the group. Other participants in the interview respond with laughter to the representation of the teacher and the student, Amy, in the dialogue and chorus Amy's long-drawn-out "No." The story humorously fuses "high-culture" reading with an activity more usually thought of as counter-cultural.

As communities of readers, reading groups are characterized as informal and, importantly, non-hierarchical. Young readers talked about being "free" to express opinions and "say what we actually think." Group leaders and other adults referred to being "on a level" with young people during meetings, and English teachers often contrasted this with their experiences and positions in class. For example:

> I come in part because in this group I can be a reader – you know one of the group, whereas in class I have to be the leader and the teacher. Here it's different, I can be me.
>
> It's vastly different and I enjoy this so much more because with Carnegie they tell me about the book, rather than me asking questions, and sometimes I've not read it and even if I have, it's different and we're more equal.

Some of the young people commented that the English teachers who attended their shadowing groups were different, and less teacher-like in this context:

> G: Miss K is different when she is here because normally she is like a Drama teacher and an English teacher ...
>
> M: ... more relaxed.
>
> G: And she like, she treats you as one of the pupils like everyone else, but when we come here she treats us like ...
>
> M: Friends.
>
> F: Friends – like, someone that we can talk to, we can talk about the books and have our own opinion whereas like in drama if say, we say something like, we didn't like what we are doing, we would be made to do it anyway.
>
> G: And she is more relaxed here

The transition for English teachers was not, however, always straightforward. One teacher pointed out that she became "a little bit more task-oriented" in her library reading group, which she felt might take the enjoyment out of reading. The extent to which it may be possible for teachers to step out of their teacher frame, characterized by one as an "objectives/assessment focused literary mindset," was pondered upon by several group leaders, including in the following reflection from a school librarian, who contrasted her own role with that of a teacher:

> As an English teacher I don't know whether you'd be able to switch off that English teacher bit of your brain that says you know kind of right now we

need to talk about the plot, what did you think about the character what did you think about the – and I don't tend to do it like that particularly. I'll try and draw it out of them sometimes but often – I mean they've all done it today – just spoken naturally about those sorts of things as it's occurred to them, rather than making it a focus point and getting in the way of their enjoyment of the text maybe.

Such tensions, reflected by English teachers themselves, by librarian group leaders, and by young group members, connect to Wenger's argument that the multiple identities of any individual – including here the contrasting identities of English teacher and reading group member – create a nexus of multi-membership that is the living experience of boundaries (1998, 78). As Wenger observes, it requires work to reconcile these different forms of membership, which may well be in tension. Despite this, however, it appeared that for some English teachers the reading group offered an opportunity to engage personally and to adopt a more dialogic and discursive stance towards reading. In so doing, positioned as fellow-readers, they arguably altered the lived experience of reading both for themselves and for other group members.

Reading in Practice: Observations and Recordings of Discussion

The interviews discussed above provide accounts, by reading group members and group leaders, of their reading experiences and associated sets of values. Observation provides a different kind of evidence, allowing the researcher to catch reading/interpretive activity on the hoof, as it occurs in particular settings. Audio recordings of discussion enable a more detailed analysis of the co-construction of reading: how readers jointly produce interpretations of literary texts. This is, necessarily, embedded in interpersonal activity: literary interpretation involves the co-construction of particular sets of social relations between readers. In our data, both observations and the analysis of discussion provide evidence of the enactment of relatively informal and non-hierarchical relations between readers, broadly consistent with the accounts provided by group members in interviews. We illustrate this aspect of reading group activity below.

Evidence of informal/non-hierarchical reader relations was immediately apparent in the layout of reading spaces. In the schools in which we were also able to observe English lessons, the contrast was striking. Figures 18.1 and 18.2 provide an illustration from a school in which we followed children directly from an English lesson into their library reading group. In the classroom, children sat in regularly arranged desks facing the front of the room. In the library, they sat around larger tables rather more haphazardly arranged.

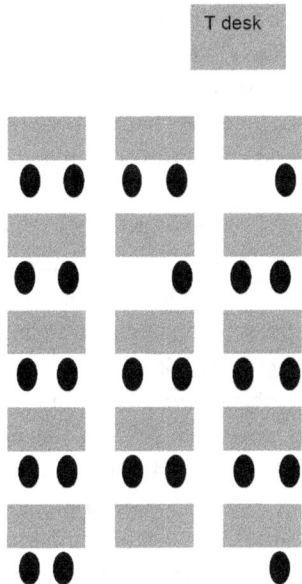

Figure 18.1 Seating arrangements, English classroom

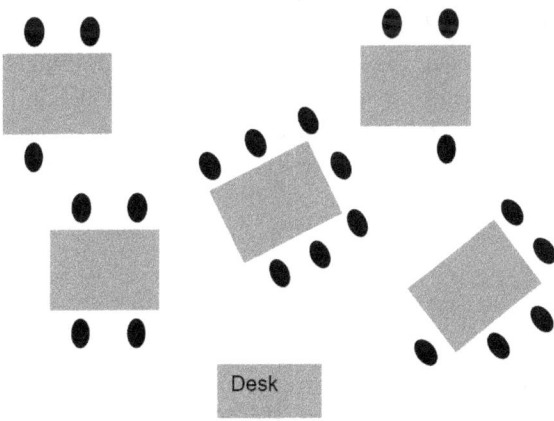

Figure 18.2 Seating arrangements, library reading group

Although there was a library desk, there was no obvious "front" to which members oriented. Adults sat among children around the tables. In other groups, members sat around tables like this, or, in smaller groups, around a single large table, adults and children usually together.[4] In one classroom setting, desks were moved together to make a large table. In another setting, the group moved from a classroom to a conference room in which they could sit more comfortably. Group members sometimes sat on the tables. They lounged back in their chairs. In one group a teacher lay on her side on the library issue desk, whilst another in a very relaxed mode sat with her feet on the desk eating her lunch. This adult behaviour was not a focus of attention by younger group members, who were also sitting informally. Adults and young people did not always remain in the same place – sometimes they moved around from one table to another to join different groups.

In all the settings we observed, reading was accompanied by the consumption of food and drink: children brought lunches or snacks. Group leaders often provided biscuits. In one group, members took it in turn to bring cakes they had baked themselves. Group members often made jocular references to food ("I know the biscuits are important to you ..."). Figure 18.3 comes from a group website announcing the start of their shadowing activity in 2012. The reference to eating biscuits or crisps, "which is strictly forbidden..ahem," accompanied by a smiley emoticon, seems to position the activity, humorously, as mildly counter-cultural.

The creation of such physical spaces for reading, how group members occupy those spaces (body orientation, movement, etc.), and the consumption of food and drink as an accompaniment to reading are indicators of, and arguably help construct, the informal and relatively non-hierarchical relationships that obtain in reading groups and that are highlighted in interviews. Where we have comparative evidence, this differs from practices in English lessons. While the reading activity the groups engage in is clearly

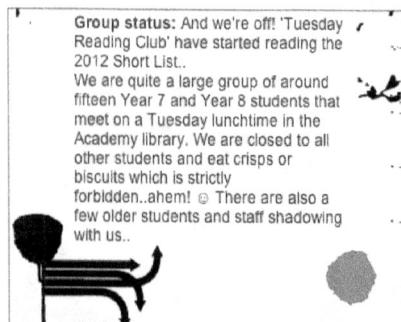

Figure 18.3 Eating in the Library: Group Website Extract

high-culture, some practices may have elements of the counter-cultural (the consumption of food and drink where this is not meant to happen, highly relaxed body positions including lying prone on the issue desk), something we also referred to earlier in relation to the story of reading Carnegie books under the desk.

Relatively non-hierarchical relationships were evident in frequent humorous episodes in the groups, produced in interaction between group members and group leaders and other adults. We mentioned jocularity and food above, but there were many other sources of humour. Humour is consistent with interview accounts of reading group experiences being about "fun." The following examples come from field notes from a group meeting in which, following earlier discussion, group members give brief presentations on a favourite book:

> A boy down to present later leaves the room briefly, commenting "I'll be back in two seconds," then in a sing-song voice "dum dum dum!" The librarian calls out "You'd better be back!" and everyone laughs. A teacher offers humorously: "I'll take over – I'll just dance!"

> There is a sports match taking place outside the library and the shouting can be heard clearly through the window. The librarian comments: "I love the way that Lily gives a really nice speech and outside we're all hearing ... [in a rough voice, she imitates the loud exclamations from the sports field]." Group members laugh at this.

> As he walks to the front, a boy comments ironically on the presentation he is about to give: "I may have achieved a new level of choosing ... clichés but we'll just have to see!" The audience laughs.

The construction of reading relationships is also accomplished discursively in group members' discussion of literary texts. In facilitating the discussion of texts, group leaders often position themselves as co-readers, albeit more experienced than young people in the group. Our observations and recordings show that group leaders both elicited contributions from group members and gave their own interpretations alongside those of group members; group members raised questions and issues about the texts, which were responded to by others, and some took extended speaking turns without adult intervention. Sometimes they disagreed with group leaders, as in the extract below from a mixed-aged group discussing *The Bride's Farewell* by Meg Rosoff. Here two group members, Emily and Rosie, have negative views of the central character of *The Bride's Farewell* – they say there is not much to like about her and she is "not a moral character." The interaction continues between the librarian group leader (L) and group members Emily (E) and Sarah (S):

1 L: I don't think that's necessary and I don't know why you don't like her because I think she is an amazingly strong character, why doesn't she work for you?

2 E: She just doesn't really do a lot [pause] if you think about what she does.

3 L: She moves away and therefore is going to get married to Mr O'Reilly!

4 E: But she didn't consider that and that ended up with her [unclear]. I think if you're going to be –

5 S: I agree with Emily.

6 L: Do you?

7 S: Absolutely 100% because the very narrative moves from one haphazard event to another and I think she's very gullible, a victim of her own naïveté.

Group members continue to voice their dissatisfaction with the central character, though the librarian views her more sympathetically ("It sort of feels like my life you know …"). The librarian concedes that people tend to have strong opinions about Meg Rosoff's writing! While Sarah aligns her interpretation of the central character with that of Emily (Turn 5), interpretations from the librarian and group members are constructed in opposition to one another. The librarian maintains her positive reading of the novel, but also explicitly recognizes and shows interest in the young people's views, despite their divergence from her own. Below is a longer extract from a discussion of *My Sister Lives on the Mantelpiece* by Annabel Pitcher, that is more clearly "led" by the librarian group leader – the librarian takes virtually every second turn in the interaction. The transcript adopts discourse analytic conventions that include details of the pattern of turn-taking between participants (see note below transcript). We also include a brief commentary on the discursive strategies adopted by the librarian.

1	L:	Cos this is so completely different to anything you normally read Katie	L shows awareness of K's reading preferences; engages K in talking about her favourite book.
2	K:	It is	
3	L:	I can't believe that this is your favourite	
4	K:	It – I know but I actually read it and I actually enjoyed that one out of all the ones that I'm busy – even this one I enjoyed that one the most	

5	L: Right so why do you think that is	She encourages K to say more, and to give reasons for her views.
6	K: It's like cos like the story is really exciting the way it's like been set out it's made the story intense and it makes want to read on (.) I think I got like to chapter four uhm like I put it down cos I was so tired (.) I actually didn't want to put the book down it like it leaves you like on a bit of a cliffhanger	
7	L: Is it the way the story is set out and the way the story develops or is it the characters do you think that [pull you	L encourages a focus on narrative structure: plot and characterization.
8	K: [it's	K overlaps L's speaking turn.
9	L: along and [makes you determined	
10	K: [it's the way the	
11	L: [to finish it	
12	K: [it's both – it's the way the story and the characters are developed that makes you want to read on it has got that (xxx) tension that makes you want to sit on the edge of your seat	
		L starts to address another reader but notices E and brings her into the discussion.
13	L: (xx[x) right come on Ella	
14	E: [I	
15	L: [you are bursting to say something	
16	E: [I used to have a very bad reputation of putting a book down after a few chapters and you are like "I will read you" (.) (xxx) I forget it exists this one I was like "Mam I'm not going to bed yet [no" (laughter)	L and E overlap here and below.
17	L: [Because this is not the thing – the kind of thing you read either [Ella is it	L shows her awareness of E's reading preferences.
18	E: [No I usually never finish one in a day and I finished it in an entire day I was like "Ahh you amazing book"	
19	?: What –	Others comment on E's experience
20	?: You're like me	
21	L: So can you explain [what it is that	L encourages E to say more.

22	E:	[I just loved it there was like mini plots in it er as well as the main one that you just had to know what is happening "Oh my god that's happened wait how does that affect that"	
23	?:	Yeah	
24	E:	"Why does he hate that	
25	K:	so much"	K completes E's turn.
26	E:	Yeah like why	
27	L:	So you were trying to keep one step ahead of the story all the time ...	Librarian acknowledges/reformulates E's reading.

(L = librarian; K = Katie; E = Ella. Square brackets indicate the beginning of overlapping speech; (.) = a brief pause; double curved brackets = nonverbal features, here ((laughter)); quotation marks indicate reported speech or thought; (xxx) = unclear words that could not be accurately transcribed.)

While the librarian tends to direct the discussion (usually selecting speakers; at Turn 7, encouraging a focus on plot and characterization), this can be seen largely as a facilitator role (eliciting interpretations from Katie and Ella, encouraging them to expand on these). Across the interaction as a whole, this ensures that all speakers are able to say something about the book(s) they have read. The librarian demonstrates her awareness of Katie's and Ella's reading preferences, a feature commented on by group members, and contrasted with practice in English lessons, where the focus is on texts selected by the teacher and students' own interests are not acknowledged. Group members themselves comment on others' interpretations of the books, and their reading practices (though here only minimally, Turn 20). The interaction is characterized by overlapping speech and by speakers completing one another's turns (here Katie completes Ella's turn – Turns 24/5). Overlaps and joint speaking turns are characteristic of relatively informal dialogue. It is noticeable that the librarian is frequently overlapped by other speakers; on one occasion (Turn 13), she abandons what she was about to say to support Ella, who had overlapped her. In their discussion of books, then, the librarian and group members are also discursively constructing particular reader relations. Although the librarian leads the discussion, this still has features of informal and relatively non-hierarchical dialogue, and the librarian's turns are facilitative, supporting other speakers. Such broad characteristics are shared by other groups in our sample, although specific interactional strategies may differ (compare the interaction on *The Bride's Farewell*).

Some of these characteristics are evident in adult reading groups meeting outside institutional settings (e.g., Peplow 2014; Swann 2012). These latter are equally diverse (they may or may not have a facilitator; occasionally one member takes on this role informally, or temporarily), but they share a general orientation towards supportive and non-hierarchical dialogue. Informality and lack of hierarchy are evident in the physical space. And, famously, literary discussion is accompanied by food and drink (one of us was recently given a fridge magnet with the words: "My reading group only reads wine labels"). The idea of a reading group brings with it certain expectations about reading experiences and reading practices that, in schools, come to characterize this type of extracurricular event and differentiate it from more formal schooled reading.

Conclusion

School reading groups seem to occupy a liminal space on the fringes of education, concerned with a high-culture literary activity consistent with the aims of reading for pleasure in English curricula yet identified as apart from, and in contrast to, curricular reading. Reading groups in general represent a kind of reading experience that is positioned outside and sometimes against "the academy," and we have suggested that they bring with them certain expectations (informality, reading for fun and enjoyment) that persist in their importation into schools.

We have discussed how this identification is accomplished in the accounts group leaders and group members give of their reading practices and themselves as readers; and in the conduct of reading itself – from the layout of rooms and the presence of food and drink through to the interactional detail of literary discussion. The work we have discussed reflects a broadly qualitative, contextualized approach to literary reading, one that focuses on the way a particular reading experience is embedded in certain reader identities, and sets of relations between readers.

The research raises educational issues in a context in which there is a desire to increase young people's participation in reading for pleasure and enjoyment, and few schools are seen to attend to this challenge (Ofsted 2012). The effective promotion of reading for pleasure/enjoyment seems unlikely to be achieved in current approaches to literary reading in secondary school classes, a distinct reading practice that takes place in a hierarchical setting in which young people are obliged to attend to and make sense of a text generally chosen by someone else (a teacher, head of department, examination board), and where they will be assessed on their response to the text. It is interesting to consider what benefits might accrue if the discussion of literature in English classes were approached more like a reading group, with young people exercising greater choice, and a greater focus on both individual and social experiences of reading. Are the reading experiences evident in school reading groups, defined as extracurricular, more effective if their distinctiveness is maintained? Or do such experiences have something to offer educationists as ways are sought to alter the decline in adolescents' attitudes to and pleasure in reading?

Appendix: Case Study Groups

Groups visited in 2011:

A reading group in a girls' secondary school in the West Midlands, with a high number of ethnic minority students. The group shadows the CILIP Carnegie Medal. It is run by an English teacher, with an active membership of up to 15 students in Year 8 (aged 12–13 years).

A reading group in a mixed independent school in southwest England shadowing the CILIP Carnegie Medal from the long list through to the final decision. The group is run by a librarian and has an active membership of up to 20 members from Years 7–10 (ages 11–15), who met in two subgroups.

Groups visited in 2012:

A mixed-gender reading group (more boys than girls) in a comprehensive school in Scotland. The school has students from a mix of cultural backgrounds. The shadowing group is made up of 24 S1–S3 students (ages 11–14). It is led by the school librarian, and three English teachers also attend meetings. The group shadows the CILIP Carnegie Medal.

A mixed-gender (though only one boy) and mixed-ability reading group in a comprehensive school in North East England. Students are mainly white British. This is a group of 15 older students – Year 10–13 (aged 14–18). The group is led by the school librarian, and shadows the CILIP Carnegie medal.

A mixed-gender and mixed-ability group in a comprehensive school in the East Midlands. The school includes students from different cultural backgrounds and has a relatively high number of students eligible for free school meals. The group has 14 members in Years 7–8 (ages 11–13). It is shadowing both the CILIP Carnegie and Kate Greenaway Awards and is led by the school librarian.

A mixed-gender group of Years 7–8 students (ages 11–13) in a comprehensive school in southeast England. The school includes 13 students from a range of cultural backgrounds. The school librarian, who runs the shadowing group, describes the group members as "very able" in terms of reading ability. They are shadowing the CILIP Carnegie Medal.

A mixed-gender group (though with only one boy) in a comprehensive school in a rural area of southwest England. Most students come from a white British background. The group is mixed-age, with 25 members drawn from Years 7–10 (ages 11–15). It is run by the school librarian and is shadowing the CILIP Carnegie Medal. Three members of the English department and two volunteer helpers also attend meetings.

Notes

We would like to thank the reading group members who kindly allowed us to observe and record their meetings, and so made our research possible. We are also grateful for the continuing support of the Chartered Institute of Library and Information Professionals (CILIP), and to the Carnegie UK Trust for generously funding the research.

1 While shadowing most frequently involves school reading groups, particularly at secondary level, it may also take different forms – for example, a one-off initiative; integration into the literacy curriculum. Given our focus on voluntary, extracurricular reading, we do not discuss such initiatives here.
2 Our data for the groups included the following: semi-structured interviews with group leaders (mainly librarians; one English teacher) and with other adults involved in the groups (e.g., teachers, a voluntary helper); in most cases, semi-structured group interviews with young people in the groups; in two cases, timetabling made this difficult and group members completed adapted interview schedules individually and in writing; "as and when" informal conversations with group leaders/members; observations of meetings, recorded as field notes; audio recordings of activities, allowing a closer focus on group interaction; in two schools, observations of an English lesson; mapping of physical spaces: diagrams plus photographs; collection of any documents or other evidence (e.g., posters, book reviews written by some group members).
3 Ethically the work was guided by the British Educational Research Association Ethical Guidelines (2011). All data are anonymized, and pseudonyms are used throughout.
4 An exception was a group of younger secondary school children who enjoyed games and competitions. The librarian often stood up to manage these.

References

Allington, Daniel, and Joan Swann. 2009. "Researching Literary Reading as Social Practice." *Language and Literature* 18(3): 219–30.
———. 2011. "The Mediation of Response: A Critical Approach to Individual and Group Reading Practices." In *The History of Reading*, vol. 3: *Methods, Strategies, Tactics*, edited by Rosalind Crone and Shafquat Towheed, 80–96. Basingstoke: Palgrave Macmillan.
Benwell, Bethan. 2009. "'A Pathetic and Racist and Awful Character': Ethnomethodological Approaches to the Reception of Diasporic Fiction." *Language and Literature* 18(3): 300–315.
British Educational Research Association (BERA). 2011. *Revised Ethical Guidelines for Educational Research*. Nottingham: BERA.

Cherland, Meredith Rogers. 1994. *Private Practices: Girls Reading Fiction and Constructing Identity*. London: Taylor and Francis.

Clark, Christina. 2012. *Children's and Young People's Reading Today: Findings from the 2011 National Literacy Trust's Annual Survey*. London: National Literacy Trust.

———. 2013. *Children's and Young People's Reading in 2012: Findings from the 2012 National Literacy Trust's Annual Survey*. London: National Literacy Trust.

Clark, Christina, Sarah Osborne, and Rodie Akerman. 2008. *Young People's Self-perceptions as Readers: An Investigation Including Family, Peer, and School Influence*. London: National Literacy Trust.

Cremin, Teresa, Marilyn Mottram, Eve Bearne, and Prue Goodwin. 2008a. "Exploring Teachers' Knowledge of Children's Literature." *Cambridge Journal of Education* 38(4): 449–64.

———. 2008b. "Primary Teachers as Readers." *English in Education* 42(1): 1–16.

Crone, Rosalind, and Shafquat Towheed, eds. 2011. *The History of Reading*, vol. 3: *Methods, Strategies, Tactics*. Basingstoke: Palgrave Macmillan.

DfE (Department for Education). 2013. *English: Programme of Study for KS1–4: Draft for Consultation*. February 2013. London: Department for Education. http://www.education.gov.uk/nationalcurriculum

Eriksson Barajas, Katarina, and Karin Aronsson. 2004. "Building Life World Connections during School Booktalk." *Scandinavian Journal of Educational Research* 48(5): 511–28.

———. 2009. "Avid versus Struggling Readers: Co-construed Pupil Identities in School Booktalk." *Language and Literature* 18(3): 281–300.

Evans, M.D.R, Jonathan Kelley, Joanna Sikora, and Donald Treiman. 2010. "Family Scholarly Culture and Educational Success: Books and Schooling in 27 Nations." *Research in Social Stratification and Mobility* 28(2): 171–97.

Geertz, Clifford. 1973. *The Interpretation of Cultures: Selected Essays*. New York: Basic Books.

Hall, Geoff. 2006. "Literature as a Social Practice." In *The Art of English: Literary Creativity*, edited by Sharon Goodman and Kieran O'Halloran, 451–59. Basingstoke: Palgrave Macmillan.

Halsey, Katie. 2009. "'Folkstylistics' and the History of Reading: A Discussion of Method." *Language and Literature* 18(3): 231–46.

Hippisley, Sulaxana. 2009. "Girl Talk: Adolescent Girls Constructing Meaning in Book Groups and the Classroom." *Changing English* 16(2): 221–30.

Lang, Anouk, ed. 2012. *From Codex to Hypertext: Reading at the Turn of the Twenty-First Century*. Amherst: University of Massachusetts Press.

Long, Elizabeth. 2003. *Book Clubs: Women and the Uses of Reading in Everyday Life*. Chicago: University of Chicago Press.

Maynard, Sally, Sophie MacKay, Kimberley Reynolds, and Fiona Smyth. 2007. *Young People's Reading in 2005: The Second Study of Young People's Reading Habits*. London: NCRCL, Roehampton University, and Loughborough: LISU, Loughborough University.

OECD. 2002. *Reading for Change: Performance and Engagement across Countries. Results from PISA 2002*. New York.

———. 2010. *PISA 2009 Results: Learning to Learn: Student Engagement, Strategies, and Practices*, vol. 3. http://dx.doi.org/10.1787/9789264083943-en

Ofsted. 2012. *Moving English Forward: Action to Raise Standards*. Office for Standards in Education, Children's Services and Skills. http://www.ofsted.gov.uk/resources/110118

Peplow, David. 2014. "'I've Never Enjoyed Hating a Book So Much in My Life.' The Co-construction of Reader Identity in the Reading Group." In *Pragmatics and Literary Stylistics*, edited by Siobhan Chapman and Billy Clark, 152–71. London: Palgrave.

Peplow, David, Joan Swann, Paula Trimarco, and Sara Whiteley. 2016. *The Discourse of Reading Groups: Integrating Cognitive and Sociocultural Perspectives*. New York/Abingdon: Routledge.

Radway, Janice. [1984]1991. *Reading the Romance: Women, Patriarchy, and Popular Literature*. Reprint, London: Verso Press, 1991.

Rehberg Sedo, DeNel, ed. 2011. *Reading Communities: From Salons to Cyberspace*. Basingstoke: Palgrave Macmillan.

Staiger, Janet. 2005. *Media Reception Studies*. New York: NYU Press.

Street, Brian. 1984. *Literacy in Theory and Practice*. Cambridge: Cambridge University Press.

Sullivan, Alice, and Matt Brown. 2013. *Social Inequalities in Cognitive Scores at Age 16: The Role of Reading*. CLS Working Paper 2013/10. London: Centre for Longitudinal Studies.

Swann, Joan. 2012. "Creative Interpretations: Discourse Analysis and Literary Reading." In *Discourse and Creativity*, edited by Rodney Jones, 53–71. London: Pearson Education.

Swann, Joan, and Daniel Allington. 2009. "Reading Groups and the Language of Literary Texts: A Case Study in Social Reading." *Language and Literature* 18(3): 247–64.

Twist, Liz, Marian Sainsbury, Adrian Woodthorpe, and Chris Whetton. 2003. *Reading All Over the World* (PIRLS: Progress in International Reading Literacy Study). Slough: NFER.

Twist, Liz, Ian Schagen, and Claire Hodgson. 2007. *Readers and Reading: The National Report for England* (PIRLS: Progress in International Reading Literacy Study). Slough: NFER.

Twist, Liz, Juliet Sizmur, Shelley Bartlett, and Laura Lynn. 2012. *PIRLS 2011: Reading Achievement in England*. Research Brief.

Wenger, Etienne. 1998. *Communities of Practice: Learning, Meaning, and Identity*. Cambridge: Cambridge University Press.

Whiteley, Sara. 2011. "Talking about 'An Accommodation': The Implications of Discussion Group Data for Community Engagement and Pedagogy." *Language and Literature* 20(3): 236–56.

Desire and Becoming – Multilingual Pupils' Reading Experiences

19

Joron Pihl and Kristin Skinstad van der Kooij

Today the understanding of the reading experience within educational institutions is dominated by accountability discourses about acquisition of basic reading skills, reading strategies, and reading proficiency.[1] Reading assessment is based on standardized tests that assume a linear relationship between test scores and the ability to read. Assessment ranks good, fair, and poor readers and identifies readers as "at risk," with a critically low reading competence (Kjærnsli and Roe 2010). Thus, the reading experience in schools is intimately linked to discourses about reading deficiencies and compensatory education (Pihl 2009a). Teachers are pressured to teach to the tests (Davies and Bansel 2007), even though the documented negative effects on student motivation and learning are significant (Amrein and Berliner 2002; 2003). In schools the emphasis on reading skills is closely related to the interpretation of texts (Holland [1968]1989; Iser 1978). Consequently, perhaps the most important questions get little attention: What makes children become passionate readers? And what does the reading experience do with and to the reader?

The rationale for such research questions is the assumption that independent and passionate reading develops from actual reading experiences. From an educational and democratic perspective, development of independent reading guided by the reader's desire is a precondition. A key question in education, then, is how schools can contribute to the development of passionate readers, regardless of the pupils' socio-economic and socio-cultural backgrounds. In the following we analyze the reading experiences of multilingual pupils from the perspective of multiple literacies theory (MLT) (Masny and Cole 2009). These pupils participated in the project "Multiplicity, Empowerment, Citizenship Inclusion Through Use of the Library as Learning Arena," conducted in Norway from 2007 to 2011.[2]

Multiple Literacies Theory

Multiple literacies theory (Masny and Cole 2009) is a theoretical framework inspired by the philosophical works of Gilles Deleuze and Félix Guattari (Deleuze 2004; Deleuze and Guattari 1988; 2004) that provides tools for analyzing complex phenomena and relations that may lead to new foci, research questions, and understanding. Within MLT, the theoretical focus is on what the reading experience *does* with the reader: Masny and Cole (2009) describe the reading experience as "reading the world and self." MLT is founded on an ontology in which being is conceptualized in terms of *becoming* rather than what a person "is" at a given time. This ontological foundation has implications for conceptions of time and agency: acquisition of basic skills cannot be measured against specific requirements at specific levels of age. The time frame for assessment of reading is short-term and is limited by external requirements to reading proficiency. The act of reading fiction is a slow process. Intrinsic to the reading experience is reflection. Readers acquire linguistic and cultural competence while reading (Elley 1991, 1992; Roe 2011).

The philosophy of Deleuze and Guattari conceptualizes multiplicity as "difference in itself" (Deleuze 2004). Thus, multiplicity (difference) is not defined as "the Other," as deviance from a norm or from "the same," but rather as a fundamental condition of all being. "Ideas are multiplicities: every idea is a multiplicity ... Everything is a multiplicity in so far as it incarnates an Idea. Even the many is a multiplicity; even the one is a multiplicity (2004, 230)." As multiplicity is plural, it cannot be identical to itself but is always in a process of becoming. These two concepts – multiplicity and becoming – are strongly interrelated (Deleuze 2004) and have important methodological implications (Masny and Cole 2009). Roughly speaking, one might say that multiplicity is looking for difference, not sameness or unity of identities.

According to Deleuze and Guattari, processes of becoming develop somewhat like a rhizome, connecting multiplicities horizontally in any direction and in multiple ways. They contrast this to relations, which are structured vertically, and illustrate their point by referring to a tree with roots, a trunk, and a canopy. "A rhizome as a subterranean stem is absolutely different from roots and radicles ... Any point of a rhizome can be connected to anything other, and must be. This is very different from the tree or root, which plots a point, fixes an order" (Deleuze and Guattari 1988, 7). Thus, desire is understood as a primary active force generated by multiplicities generating processes of becoming that strongly differ from an understanding of desire as a reactive response to unfulfilled needs.

In this chapter we analyze interviews with children using rhizo-analysis – a method of examining texts by rhizomatic mapmaking (Alvermann 2000).

The structure of the mapmaking is horizontal. We plot the children's statements about their reading experiences and their expressions about what the reading does to them, and analyze the processes of becoming that emanate from their reading. We do not analyze hierarchies or linear relations, but rather linkages and discontinuities. Initially we used NVIVO software for qualitative analysis and Free Nodes in order to map the data thematically in a horizontal manner, creating a map of each child's statements about her/his reading experience.

The data consist of interviews with fourteen multilingual learners – eight girls and six boys – who had varying levels of competence with the Norwegian language. The pupils volunteered for the interviews from three different classes at one of the project schools. According to the teachers, some were good readers, some were average, and some were poor. The interviewers were not informed about the teachers' evaluations of the children's reading proficiency.

The Multiplicity Project

The Multiplicity project was a research and development project and an intervention study conducted at two elementary schools in Norway from 2007 to 2011 (Pihl 2011; 2012b). The project's aim was to develop reading engagement through literature-based literacy education (Elley 1991), extensive use of library resources, and collaboration between teachers and librarians. At the time of the interviews our informants had been engaged in the Multiplicity project for two years.

The children we interviewed attended an urban school in the most underprivileged part of the city in terms of the socio-economic status, levels of education, unemployment, and involvement in social services. The housing consists primarily of large apartment buildings with single houses in between. The only facilities for children and young people in the area are the school, a public library branch, and a football field. Seventy-five percent of the pupils at the project school are multilingual. At this school, the children's scores on national reading tests are on average in the lower range, just above or below the "critical limit." This is a great concern for the principal and teachers at the school, whom educational authorities hold accountable for these weak test results.

The literacy project involved partnership and collaboration between two schools, two teacher education institutions, and a public library. Teacher educators, teachers, and librarians collaborated systematically during the project. The work consisted of educational planning and literature dissemination in a variety of forms. In particular, the teachers provided the children with fiction and non-fiction instead of textbooks. The project prioritized voluntary reading among children in and out of school. The major focus was on reading fiction, but non-fiction was included. The children were exposed to a broad range of literature in different genres and of different levels of complexity. They had regular access to the literature in classroom libraries, at the school library, and in public libraries. At school, a "culture for reading" was developed. Teachers and children shared their reading experiences and read and recommended literature to each other; the children dramatized stories they had read, produced art, and wrote stories related to their reading. The project generated extensive reading engagement among the pupils and wide use of the libraries in an inclusive reading environment (Pihl 2009b; 2012a; Tonne and Pihl 2012; van der Kooij and Pihl 2009). Regardless of their proficiency in the language of instruction, the children formed one group in literacy education and school subjects within the Multiplicity project. They were not placed in tracked reading groups according to their level of reading competence.

Reading the World and Self

In the interviews, we asked the children about their reading experiences as well as about their use of the school and public libraries. We invited them to talk about books they were reading at the time of the interview. Geetha was reading a book about an animal, which ended up in a hospital. She expresses her reading experience in the following way: "I love to read. I think it is really fun … It is fun to know about things. I like to read, it's just fun." This is a strong affirmation of positive sensations and emotions related to reading. To Geetha the act of reading is a highly affective mode of being. "I enjoy reading because I experience new things … They have many strange things at the hospital. A place where the dead people are." For Geetha, it is a new experience that they have dead people at the hospital. She probably associates the hospital with treatment of sick people. That they have a room where they keep dead people transcends her own life experiences. The fact that she expresses joy of reading, and relates this to her encounter with death and a room for the dead, is intriguing. Geetha appreciates this transcendental experience. It extends her knowledge of the world to the extent that she feels sheer joy. Surprising connections to things and experiences – known, conceptualized, and imagined – generate sensations of joy and desire, corresponding to how Deleuze conceives of desire as both a force and a focus (Knight 2009).

In our analysis, we focused on what the reading experience does with and to the child. Geetha's expression of the joy of reading is typical. Ameena expresses her feelings about reading in the following way: "I noticed that when we started to read more, I got an urge [*lyst*] to read more. When we didn't read that much, I didn't have an urge [*lyst*] to read at all." Ameena uses the Norwegian concept of *lyst*, which people commonly use for something they like to do. However, it also has erotic connotations: it is used to express desire, similar to the German concept *Lust*. Ameena explicitly says that her desire to read was generated from the reading itself; this links her desire to the collective dimension of the reading experience. "When *we* started to read more, I got an urge to read more." "We" refers to her class and classmates at school, who started voluntary reading of fiction within the literacy project in 2008. The fact that "we" started to read more, and that she reads more than before, has generated in Ameena a desire to read more. Affect is central to her reading experience.

The Deleuzian concept of affect implies emotions and feelings but is not limited to individual sensations. "Deleuzian affects are essentially collective and cannot be isolated in the subject or bracketed solely with emotions and feelings" (Cole 2009, 73). In other words, affect is intrinsic to collective desire (Deleuze and Guattari 2004). This has implications for how we conceptualize the reading experience. In contrast to discourses about acquisition of basic reading skills and strategies, which focus extensively on individual acquisition and performance, we draw attention to the reading experience as an event in which the collective dimension is important: the sharing of the literacy events with others. MLT also allows us to privilege children's literacy experiences in school as a desire for aesthetic experiences and knowledge. Although desire is a fundamental force in the lives of children as well as adults, reading in school traditionally devotes little attention to this when providing children with opportunities to read.

Geetha also draws attention to the social dimension of the reading experience:

Interviewer: What do you think about choosing yourself what to read?
Geetha: Good ... but I like best that someone recommends to me.
I: Who recommends to you?
Geetha: Mmm ... lots of times my sisters, sometimes friends and sometimes my teacher.

Geetha's description of having recommendations made for her reading connects to the Deleuzian notions of affects, percepts (units of perception), and concepts as elaborated by Cole below:

> According to the Deleuzian conception of affects, these essential parts of the thinking subject are not just feelings or emotions, but are forces that influence

the body's mode of existence or its power ... The power to be affected, together with the corresponding power to affect constitutes an organizational structure that Deleuze insists is entirely filled with passive and active affections. These affections also determine Deleuzian becoming ... Deleuzian affective literacy may therefore be imbued with becoming in that it is about change in agency – or subjects deepening their power through the breaking and reconsideration of habit through alignment with others. (2009, 67)

In terms of Cole's analysis of affect, the interviews show that the children reflect on how the reading experience affects and changes them. They talk about what they read, their choices of literature, and their understanding of self in relation to others. They reflect on what is "normal" or not and on how one might live. The question of how one might live is also central to the philosophy of Deleuze and Guattari (May 2005), and something that the children reflect on time and again in the interviews. For example, they relate their visions for their own future to their reading experiences. Ameena experiences the development of her imagination while reading: "When I started reading more books, I developed more imagination, and when I didn't read books, I didn't have imagination at all." Ameena has a meta-perspective on her own imagination. She discovers that her ability to imagine and think has changed in relation to her reading. She is in a process of becoming, a change she explicitly links to her actual reading experience.

The children were also invited to talk about what they like to read.[3] One student's response illustrates another experience of the process of becoming, through reading engagement. The interviewer asks Anzor:

I: What do you think about reading?

Anzor: I think it's fun, and I think it is very interesting to read different stories. Sometimes science books where you investigate things ... I have read a lot about *Titanic*. I borrowed the book at the library.

I: Which books do you like the most?

Anzor: *Wolfbrother*. The very best book I have read.

I: What's it about?

Anzor: It's about a boy, and his mother is dead. He has no sisters or brother. He lives with his father. He sees a bear and every time the bear comes, it kills people and it gets bigger. Then it kills his father, and the father says before he dies: "You must find a mountain with clouds, you must have such eyes, and you must do very much to save this town and don't let the bear take over everything ... You shall find the pathfinder, and that is the wolf" ... It was so exciting and every time I read a chapter, I could not put the book away ... My favourite animal is the wolf.

The drama apparently affects Anzor deeply. In his narrative, he draws particular attention to the moral imperative in the story and the fact that the wolf finds a way to kill the bear, which had killed the father and the people in the village. When we analyze this within the conceptual framework of multilingual literacies theory we see that Anzor is in a process of becoming while engaging with the literature – in a process of "becoming wolf." Anzor was four years old when he came to Norway, and he describes his understanding of the context of his life at that time:

> Anzor: That was when there was war in Chechnya, which is why we came here ... It isn't really total war, but very dangerous to live there. My cousin was killed last year because he drove a car, and then the car was bombed by a Russian plane. Twenty boys died ... And when some boys go hiking in the woods and shoot, they were killed because someone thought they were bandits. My father knew the boys that were killed ... If you do something silly, the police or military just kill you without asking anything. There is a lot of crime there.

These experiences constitute his point of departure while reading *Wolfbrother*. Anzor's older sister and grandmother and most of his family still live in Chechnya. He came to the Norwegian school when the Multiplicity project started. He spent a lot of time in the library in fourth grade, and today he uses the public and school libraries regularly, often every day. He uses the main branch of the public library every Sunday with his older sister. Anzor was eleven years old at the time of the interview.

> Anzor: I read every day – in different places – if I don't read books, I read on the Internet, I read newspapers or listen to books on a CD. [He reads Russian and Norwegian.] Now I have found a very interesting book. It is about a boy named Stefan, in the old days. It was in Jerusalem when there was fighting between Christians and Muslims. Stefan is a very clever knight. His mother and sister were captured as slaves, and his father was captured to become a warrior. He must fight, even though he doesn't want to. Stefan was also captured, but in a different place. Then came the French, and the Christians thought they would be saved, but a Christian man was hit in the head by an axe. But then comes Stefan on a horse, and everyone mounts their horses and rides away. But then he is hit by an arrow in the shoulder and faints. When he wakes up, the people there say that he saved them. And then he travels on to save his family. I have read two of these books, and now I will read the third. We have five in this series in the classroom library.

Anzor and his family have experienced violent social and political oppression in Chechnya. His narratives show that he reads books about violent social conflicts. He chooses to read books in which the main characters are brave and fight against violent oppression. The narratives transcend the oppression to which the characters are subjected. What does the reading do for Anzor? We suggest that he engages with the world and his family's traumatic experiences while reading: "And when I am bored when I read, it's much more interesting to sit at the library. So, I am not bored in my spare time. I think books *help* [Anzor's emphasis]. I plan to have a library in my home when I am grown up." Anzor sees himself in the future as an adult reader – a reader for whom reading is so important that he will have a library in his own home. His narrative manifests processes of becoming – in his case becoming "a reader" and perhaps a pathfinder – a wolf.

Many of the children emphasize that when they read, it may help them become what they want in the future. Waqas says:

> If I read, I know more things, and then I have a better chance of becoming what I want [a doctor]. You have to be smart, you get good grades at school. And other things that are important. That is very important to me, because if I become a doctor, I can help other people ... If I were not able to read, I wouldn't get my exam.

Waqas is aware that reading is a source of knowledge in the school sense of this concept. Reading has an instrumental function – it helps him do well on exams. But at a more profound level he has a desire to become a doctor. He expresses agency while envisioning himself as a future doctor. Moreover, beyond these pragmatic aims, Waqas is aware that there is more to reading than its function of providing him with a good education and access to the profession he wants. He says that reading gives him insight into "other things that are important" – in other words, things other than those measured by exams in school and getting the job he prefers. He apparently has learned other things through reading besides what he perceives as the school concept of knowledge – "Other things that are important to me." This aspect of the reading experience drives Waqas to read, whether it has benefits for school or not. Thus, the reading experience generates a desire to read that is partly independent of the school context. Again, we see that reading generates agency and processes of becoming, and this shows promise for future reading and his future intellectual and emotional development. Several of the children are convinced that reading can help them realize their ambitions in life. Hacer wants to become a police officer, and when asked how she will achieve this, she replies: "Read a lot, work hard."

Some of the children are explicit about their intellectual curiosity and which books they want to read:

> Mario: I usually read about animals and books about the Earth planet. What happens with lava and things like that. I read about it *because I like it*. [Mario's emphasis]
>
> I: Do you have books at home?
>
> Mario: ... eh we have a book about wild animals. I like that one. We have no books about lava or such books about the Earth, but I would like to buy ... or borrow such books to read.

Mario's answer indicates that his access to books at home is limited. We have reason to believe that his opportunity to buy books is also rather limited. He does not expand on this, but goes on to point out that he can borrow books that interest him at the library. He will choose books about animals and the Earth *because he likes it*.

The children attach great importance to their individual choice of books. It is in the classroom library, the school library, and the public library that they have access to books. Anzor tells us: "I don't like fantasy that much, because I think they exaggerate. I like facts the most. Then I get to know a lot. So, I have read a lot about *Titanic* and such things. I borrowed the book at the library."

We asked the children to compare their own life experiences with the main characters in the books they are reading. Hacer says she has had a similar experience to Stine (the main character), who did not want to go into the swimming pool in the story she was reading. "I don't either, because I cannot swim. And Stine cannot either. I think it is normal. I thought it is only me ... that this only happens to me. But when I read such books, I believe it happens to everybody." Hacer feels abnormal for not being able to swim, but through her reading, she understands that she is not the only one who cannot swim. She is "normal."

In a dialogue with Geetha, the interviewer asks her about differences between herself and Judy Moody, a character in a book she is reading. Geetha explains that Judy Moody lives in a house: "She has a garden and lots of things. I want to live like that, too. I don't want to live in an apartment building." Geetha explains that if children play inside her apartment, they disturb the neighbour on the second floor. When the family has visitors in the living room, the children must sit still and be quiet. Lack of space and poor housing conditions limit Geetha's opportunities to play at home with her siblings. Through the reading experience, Geetha learns that Judy Moody and other children, who live in houses, do not have such problems. This is why she wants to live in a house and not an apartment building. Geetha learns about living in a house through her reading, and she sees herself living in a house in the future. Her conception of self is in a process of becoming. For Deleuze and Guattari, the very idea of thinking differently about one's life and interactions with others and the world is essential. This is very different from theories of social and cultural reproduction, which ascribe cultural deprivation to pupils with poor and working-class backgrounds. These theories are very influential in schools and shape the socialization of children and the teachers' conceptualization of them (Coleman 1979).

The interviewer asks Geetha whether she likes her school. Geetha responds by commenting on other people's negative opinions of her community and school:

> Geetha: Many people say that my school is not a very good place, but I think that even if other children go to other schools, the books are the same.
>
> I: What do you mean by that?
>
> Geetha: Many say that we have these and these books. But we also have those books.
>
> I: And what do you think then?
>
> Geetha: That both schools are good.

She is aware that her community has low social prestige and reputation in the city where she lives, and she addresses the social inequalities and the devaluation of her community in her response. Geetha's answer is interesting because she does not acknowledge the low status of her community and school. Her decisive argument and rebuttal against those who devalue her community is that her school has "the same books." This is a quality criterion, according to her. Equal access to the same books as children in wealthy communities is, according to Geetha, an equalizer. The stigma attached to her part of the city does not influence her evaluation of her school. This indicates that the reading experience has a major impact on her perception of the world and self. Her reading experiences influence her to the extent that she has an independent view of the quality of her community and school. The fact that she has access to "the same books" is liberating. It transforms her conceptualization of the world and her position in it. Access to the same books is a manifestation of quality: quality of education at her school, and quality of the people and relations within her school.

Discontinuities and "Lines of Flight"

In multicultural and multilingual societies, the language of instruction in public schools is the official, dominant language. In Norway, multilingual children are taught to read mainly in their second language. In these circumstances, how can schools contribute to the development of passionate readers? In this case study, the children communicate about their reading experiences in their second language – Norwegian. Given the rather limited vocabulary and halting syntax in several of the narratives, our first impression was that the children's reading experiences were limited. However, when addressing how the children read the world and self, we explored what reading does with and to the children. We focused on the content of the children's narratives and on the impact of their reading on their understanding of self and the world. This is in contrast to assessment of basic reading skills, which is the usual focus of educational researchers. Based on a close reading of the interviews and our theoretical and methodological approach, we found that there was a lot more to the children's reading than we first thought.

What did reading do to the children? It gave them access to the world and to the lives of others in ways that influenced their perceptions of self and others. It filled them with strong sensations – excitement, joy, and a desire to read. The interviews indicate that their reading experiences had profound intellectual and emotional impacts. Many of the children's narratives show that they felt empowered by reading, for it opened up new horizons to them, giving them ideas and hopes for what they might do and become. Reading helped them understand problematic experiences in their lives. The children saw themselves in relation to others from new perspectives – no longer were they limited by the underprivileged community in which they lived, or by their past. They could look beyond their community and articulate desires to engage with the world and others in new ways. We read this as manifestations of agency and processes of becoming.

If we had judged the children's reading in terms of their linguistic proficiency, we might have concluded that the outcome of their reading was rather limited. In this regard, we argue that contrary to what assessments of literacy proficiency assume and predict, the reading experiences of the children were in fact unpredictable. Unpredictable events are what Deleuze and Guattari call "lines of flight" (Deleuze and Guattari 1988). Had the school provided the children with books based solely on their linguistic proficiency in the Norwegian language, it is questionable whether they would have had the reading experiences they had. In the literature-based literacy project, the pupil's individual choice of books was crucial. This was facilitated by abundant access to books and by the sharing of literary events among the children, teachers, and librarians, as well as by the children's extensive use of library books and resources. We found that this was critical to the development of reading engagement among the children (Tonne and Pihl 2012).

Our major finding relates to the discontinuity between the children's linguistic proficiency in a second language and the impact of reading experiences on the children – that is, on their desire to read and their processes of becoming. The children express that their reading experiences are transcendental in several respects and therefore more profound than we perhaps might expect if we were to judge solely by their linguistic competence in the second language. The interviews indicate that when children are given the opportunity to voluntarily read fiction and other books in a reading-friendly environment together with other readers, they read books first and foremost because they enjoy it. They read books that are *at* but also *above* their supposed proficiency level. They do so because they are interested in the story or the topic. Positive reading experiences generate a desire to read.

Yet traditional pedagogical work with reading in schools rests on the assumption that children should read books *at* their competence level. Reading programs are based on assessments of reading proficiency. Books are produced for specific competence levels, thus providing children with "tracked reading" or "levelled reading." A consequence of this is that "poor readers" are provided with books that are simple in both linguistic and literary terms. We suggest that in fact, access to a broad variety of books in different genres and of varying complexity is fundamental to the development of passionate readers at all levels of reading proficiency. This is an important argument against "tracked or levelled reading" for "clever," "middle range," and "poor readers" (Tonne and Pihl 2013; van der Kooij and Pihl 2009; McKechnie in this volume).

Desire and Assemblage

Through rhizo-analysis focusing on the desire to read, processes of becoming and discontinuities, we were able to identify a striking discontinuity between the children's linguistic competence and their reading experience in the second language. Thus, the traditional assumption in schools that linguistic proficiency predicts and determines the reading experience seems too simple. The reading experience is complex, and the desire to read generates processes of becoming and of agency that transcend linear conceptions of relations between reading proficiency and the reading experience. The children's narratives about their reading indicate that there is no linear relationship or parallel between reading proficiency and reading experience. The children discover themselves through assemblage, by making connections to literature and the world through their reading. The importance of this can hardly be overestimated, especially in the present context, in which individualism and competition forcefully shape socialization and learning in schools and society (Barstad 2013; Biesta 2012; Davies and Bansel 2007).

In middle-class homes with educated parents, the children often have access to books and to a culture of reading; in poor areas, many children grow up with neither. These differences contribute substantially to the reproduction of social inequality (Kjærnsli and Roe 2010) and will continue to do so (Hvistendahl and Roe 2004) as long as dominant discourses about basic skills, standardized testing, and accountability prevail. If proficiency level in reading is *the* precondition for the provision of books, and if schools continue to assign pupils to "tracked reading," poor readers will stay poor readers.

Alternative conceptual frameworks are needed in order for pedagogy and literacy education to provide children with reading experiences that excite and challenge them in interaction with others. The reading of textbooks generally does not provide such challenges or develop passionate readers (Limberg 2003). The advantage of MLT is that it provides concepts that facilitate literacy education in ways which emphasize desire and processes of becoming, in contrast to understandings of literacy and learning firmly based on assessment of what a child "is."

Deleuze and Guattari argue that desire produces something new, a desire that exists in rhizomatic assemblages (Deleuze and Guattari 1988; Jordan 1995). The design of the Multiplicity project is such that it connects assemblages – schools and libraries, teachers and librarians, children and books – thereby producing desire in particular instances, that is, assembled desire. This desire has nothing to do with natural or spontaneous desire, or determination. Again, this highlights the collective quality of multiplicities, which generate becoming, transformation, and transcendence when put to work so as to interact in horizontal networks. Rhizomatic assemblages or networks are horizontal and unpredictable, mutable and peculiar to each incidence. This facilitates the production of desire and creativity (Knight 2009). These uses, functions, and productions are vital in an analysis. The research reported here affirms the potential of rhizomatic assemblages, as opposed to assessment of learning, accountability, and predication of performance. This latter concept of learning is not conducive to learning, because it is founded on what worked in the past (Biesta 2012).

We have argued that literacy education and reading should be conceptualized from a long-term perspective. Of course this does not mean that we are not concerned about improving reading competence. Rather, the underlying ontology, the concepts and methodologies of MLT, open ways of working with reading and literacy that embrace the unpredictable and non-linear aspects of reading events, reading experiences, and developments. This is particularly important in relation to multilingual pupils and poor pupils. Schools too often underestimate these children if they fail to reach the competence levels prescribed at a given age and stage (Pihl 2009a). Based on standardized assessments, teachers tend to interpret low scores as individual deficiencies and subsequently misunderstand children's potential to become passionate readers.

Conclusion

If we assume that reading is a creative process, we also need to take into account that the act of reading is a slow process and not solely an exercise in use of reading skills. The act of reading develops in interaction with literature that challenges the reader in multiple ways, based on the artistic, linguistic, and other qualities that engage the reader. The act of reading also entails collective dimensions in that it involves sharing literary experiences with others. This ought to inform literacy education in schools. But in order for this to happen, new theories and pedagogical practices are required. MLT provides affirmative concepts within literacy education – multiplicity, desire, becoming, and assemblage – that facilitate reading the world and self beyond assessment regimes and accountability paradigms, both of which limit reading experiences and the desire to read among children in schools.

Engagement with interesting literature in classroom libraries, school libraries, and public libraries, voluntary reading, and the sharing of reading experiences transform readers beyond the limits that schools place on readers who have been assessed as poor readers. This appears to be the case whether the readers are multilingual and poor, or monolingual and wealthy. These very same readers can, through reading experiences, become agents who read the world and self and act upon it in unforeseeable ways, long after they have finished school. This has the potential to be one of the most important lessons learned in school. Multiplicity, desire, and becoming are productive in informing literacy and education, for they link extensive engagement with literature – both inside and outside school, in assemblage, and in classrooms, school libraries, and public libraries – with the potential to generate passionate readers and desiring social agents.

Notes

1 See for example, international reading assessments: PISA, http://www.oecd.org/pisa/pisaproducts/46619703.pdf; and PIRLS, http://timssandpirls.bc.edu/pirls2011/downloads/P11_IR_Executive%20Summary.pdf.
2 In previous publications we have analyzed the data from this project from the perspectives of new literacy studies and socio-historical activity theory (Pihl 2011; Tonne and Pihl 2012; van der Kooij and Pihl 2009).
3 We present coherent accounts of their narratives in order to make the content understandable in spite of grammatical imperfection.

References

Alvermann, Donna E. 2000. "Researching Libraries, Literacies, and Lives: A Rhizoanalysis." In *Working the Ruins: Feminist Poststructural Theory and Methods in Education*, edited by Elizabeth St. Pierre and Wanda S. Pillow, 114–19. London: Routledge.
Amrein, Audrey L., and David C. Berliner. 2002. "High-Stakes Testing Uncertainty and Student Learning." *Educational Policy Archives* 10(18). doi:http://dx.doi.org/10.14507/epaa.v10n18.2002
———. 2003. "The Effects of High-Stakes Testing on Student Motivation and Learning." *Educational Leadership* 60(5): 32–38.
Barstad, Kristin. 2013. "Qualification Frameworks and the Concept of Knowledge: From Aristotle to Bologna, Brussels, and Norway." In *Teacher Education Research between National Identity and Global Trends: NAFOL Year Book 2012*, edited by Anna-Lena Østern, Kari Smith, Torill Ryghaug, Thorolf Krüger, and May Britt Postholm, 185–215. Trondheim: Akademika.
Biesta, Gert. 2012. "Becoming Educationally Wise: Towards a Virtue-Based Conception of Teaching and Teacher Education." In *Teacher Education Research between National Identity and Global Trends: NAFOL Year Book 2012*, edited by Anna-Lena Østern, Kari Smith, Torill Ryghaug, Thorolf Krüger and May Britt Postholm, 29–53. Trondheim: Akademika.
Cole, David R. 2009. "Deleuzian Affective Literacy for Teaching Literature: A Literary Approach for Multiple Literacies." In *Multiple Literacies Theory: A Deleuzian Perspective*, edited by Diana Masny and David R. Cole, 63–78. Rotterdam: Sense Publishers.
Coleman, James Samuel. 1979. *Equality of Educational Opportunity*. New York: Arno.
Davies, Bronwyn, and Peter Bansel. 2007. "Neoliberalism and Education." *International Journal of Qualitative Studies in Education* 20(3): 247–59.
Deleuze, Gilles. 2004. *Difference and Repetition*. London: Continuum.
Deleuze, Gilles, and Felix Guattari. 1988. *A Thousand Plateus: Capitalism and Schizophrenia*. London: Althone Press.
———. 2004. *Anti-Oepidus Capitalism and Schizophrenia*. London: Continuum.
Elley, Warwick B. 1991. "Acquiring Literacy in a Second Language: The Effect of Book-Based Programs." *Language and Learning* 41(3): 375–411.
———. 1992. "How in the World Do Students Read?" Hamburg: International Association for the Evaluation of Educational Achievement.
Holland, Norman N. [1968]1989. *The Dynamics of Literary Response*. Reprint, New York: Columbia University Press.

Hvistendahl, Rita, and Astrid Roe. 2004. "The Literacy Achievement of Norwegian Minority Students." *Scandinavian Journal of Educational Research* 48(3): 307–24.

Iser, Wolfgang. 1978. *The Act of Reading: A Theory of Aesthetic Response*. Baltimore: Johns Hopkins University Press.

Jordan, Tim. 1995. "Collective Bodies: Raving and the Politics of Gilles Deleuze and Felix Guattari." *Body & Society* 1(1): 125–44. doi:10.1177/1357034x95001001008

Kjærnsli, Marit and Astrid. 2010. *På rett spor Norske elevers kompetanse i lesing, matematikk og naturfag i PISA 2009* [*On the Right Track. Norwegian Pupils' Skills in Reading, Mathematics, and Natural Sciences in PISA 2009*]. Oslo: Universitetsforlaget.

Knight, Kinda. 2009. "Desire and Rhizome: Affective Literacies in Early Childhood." In *Multiple Literacies Theory: A Deleuzian Perspective*, edited by Diana Masny and David R. Cole, 51–61. Rotterdam: Sense Publishers.

Limberg, Louise. 2003. *Skolbibliotekts pedagogiska roll: En kunnskapsöversikt* [*The Educational Role of the School Library: A Literature Review*]. Stockholm: Skolverket.

Masny, Diana, and David R. Cole, eds. 2009. *Multiple Literacies Theory: A Deleuzian Perspective*. Rotterdam: Sense Publishers.

May, Todd. 2005. *Gilles Deleuze: An Introduction*. Cambridge: Cambridge University Press.

Pihl, Joron. 2009a. "Ethno-Nationalism and Education." In *Paradoxes of Cultural Recognition: Perspectives from Northern Europe*, edited by Sharam Alghasi, Thomas Hylland Eriksen, and Halleh Ghorashi, 111–33. Farnham: Ashgate.

———. 2009b. "Interprofessional Cooperation between Teachers and Librarians: Analysing Theoretical and Professional Arguments for Cooperation in an Era of Globalization." In *Nordic Voices: Teaching and Researching Comparative and International Education in the Nordic Countries*, edited by Halla B. Holmarsdottir and Mina O'Dowd, 41–59. Rotterdam: Sense Publishers.

———. 2011. "Literacy Education and Interprofessional Collaboration." *Professions and Professionalism* 1(1): 52–66. http://urn.nb.no/URN:NBN:no-29831

———. 2012a. "Can Library Use Enhance Intercultural Education?" *Issues in Educational Research* 22(1): 79–90. http://www.iier.org.au/iier22/pihl.pdf

———. 2012b. *Multiplisitet, Myndiggjøring, Medborgerskap: Inkludering gjennom bruk av biblioteket som læringsarena* [*Multiplicity, Empowerment, Citizenship: Inclusion through the Use of Libraries as Learning Arena*], HiOA report vol. 6. Oslo: Høgskolen i Oslo og Akershus.

Roe, Astrid. 2011. *Lesedikdaktikk – etter den første leseopplæringen*. [*Reading Didactics: After the First Reading Education*]. Oslo: Universitetsforlaget.

Tonne, Ingebjørg, and Joron Pihl. 2012. "Literacy Education, Reading Engagement, and Library Use in Multilingual Classes." *Intercultural Education* 23(3): 183–94.

———. 2013. "Andrespråkseleven, leseprøver og litteraturbasert leseopplæring." [The Second Language Pupil, Reading Tests, and Literaure-Based Reading Education] *NORAND* 8(1): 91–114.

van der Kooij, Kristin Skinstad, and Joron Pihl. 2009. "Voices from the Field Negotiating Literacy Education in a Multicultural Setting." In *Nordic Voices: Teaching and Researching Comparative and International Education in the Nordic Countries*, edited by Halla B. Holmarsdottir and Mina O'Dowd, 167–79. Rotterdam: Sense Publishers.

Experiencing the Social Melodrama in the Twenty-First Century
Approaches of Amateur and Professional Criticism

Cecilie Naper

Over the past ten years a new kind of bestseller has reached the top of the popularity lists, one aimed at a female audience, written by internationally acclaimed writers like Jamie Ford, Kathryn Stockett, Victoria Hislop, Chris Cleave, Tatjana de Rosnay, and Sue Monk Kidd. Two special features characterize these novels. First, the plots turn around a group of protagonists who fight intensely against violence and oppression and who are willing to sacrifice personal safety in the struggle for fundamental human rights – freedom, equality, and justice. Second, the stories are attached to momentous turning points in history that have sunk into oblivion in the collective memory of the West. In this chapter I have limited my analysis to readers' experiences of three of the better-known novels of this genre: Victoria Hislop's *The Island* (2005), Kathryn Stockett's *The Help* (2009), and Jamie Ford's *The Hotel on the Corner of Bitter and Sweet* (2009).[1]

Each novel features a unique historical setting. In *The Island*, the plot concerns the internment of lepers on Spinalonga, off the coast of Crete. The plot in *The Hotel* relates to the internment in the United States of American citizens of Japanese origin after the attack on Pearl Harbor during the Second World War. *The Help* explores the living conditions of black maids in the American Deep South in the early 1960s.

I have labelled this genre *social melodrama*: "social" because it follows the tradition of *critical realism* by addressing themes relating to social problems, and "melodrama" since all the novels of this genre insist on "poetic justice" (i.e., virtue is rewarded and vice is punished). The Russian formalist Sergej Balukhaty (Gerould 1978) has formulated a precise description of the melodrama. As early as in 1927 he pointed out that its most characteristic feature is to provoke strong and unambiguous emotions among audiences and readers. According to Balukhaty, at the centre of the melodramatic plot we find a young and defenceless heroine. To facilitate the readers' vicarious identification with the heroine, the plot then has a kind of roller-coaster design that aims to facilitate the readers' vicarious identification with the heroine. Peter Brooks (1995) expanded the concept to include both canonical literature and popular fiction. According to Brooks, the melodrama is fundamentally characterized by the fact that meaning, continuity, and cohesion emerge from the apparent chaos and meaninglessness in life. This underlying melodramatic tone strengthens the potential "fascination factor" of novels because it conveys the legitimacy of the protagonists' quests.

Researching Reviewers' Reading Experiences: Booklovers and Professionals

The new social melodramas enjoy popularity throughout the Western world, and such novels receive fulsome praise on sites like *Goodreads* and the Norwegian website *Bokelskere.no*, where avid readers offer insights into their reading preferences and evaluation criteria. On *Bokelskere*, social melodramas are highly valued. However, critics in the Norwegian papers with the highest literary and cultural profiles – *Morgenbladet* and *Klassekampen* – do not share this enthusiasm. The literary editors of these newspapers have declared that they consider the novels' standardized literary formulas to be redundant and unworthy of individual review in their columns (Farsethås 2013; Haugen 2013). The wider media do review these novels, and of the three novels selected, I have found seven reviews: three in the most widely distributed Norwegian newspaper, *Aftenposten*, two by the Norwegian Broadcasting Corporation (NRK), and two in the most culturally oriented of the tabloids, *Dagbladet*. For this paper I have further analyzed all amateur reviews of the three books found on *Bokelskere.no* over a period of three months – in total, about 1,500 reviews.

The Reading Experience and Genre Features of the Social Melodrama

An analysis of the reviews of ordinary (amateur) critics indicates that many regard literature and literary experience as one of many phenomena in their daily lives, rather than as a specific aesthetic event. In order to understand what it is about these novels that fascinates readers, it is necessary to analyze both the literature and its audience. Hans Robert Jauss's (1982) reception study of a number of novels published over a hundred years or so provides a framework for understanding the different ways readers relate to and identify with protagonists and their projects. In a successful encounter between readers and literature, the expectations of the reader merge with the textual attributes of genre, rhetoric, and composition. Furthermore, a successful literary experience relies on readers being situated both historically and culturally to be capable of and open to the different perspectives inherent in literature. Jauss's concept of the reader's "horizon of expectations" refers to a number of aesthetic norms: a given text will be met by readers who possess the requisite "cultural capital" (Bourdieu 1984). However, Jauss does not consider that within one culture there exist several types of readers with different horizons of comprehension, different literary competence and preferences, and different expectations of genre. To understand the variations among the reviews discussed here, it is crucial to expand Jauss's theory to include factors related to differences in literary understanding, genre expectations, and cultural capital.

Following Jauss, when a genre becomes institutionalized, it functions as a kind of blueprint for authors and readers. The stories of the social melodrama grow out of a Manichean moral universe where the distinctions between good and evil are very clear, and the protagonists are portrayed in ways that permit easy identification. The plots are set in a different historical setting than that of the author and reader, and the protagonists live in societies without any kind of social security. The fact that the characters are left to fight so desperately for themselves underscores their inner independence and strength. The stories are simple to understand and follow the well-established patterns of the historical novel. A general principle is a retrospective plot consisting of two stories: a framing story of the present, and another story set in the past, where the main part of the story unfolds. The story begins in the present from the point of view of a storyteller who unravels a story of the past, which turns out to be a basis for understanding the storyteller's own life. This reinforces the underlying melodramatic perspective: human existence may seem fragmented and incomprehensible, but it still possesses profound meaning.

The most significant characteristic of the social melodrama novel, however, is that it can be read as a contemporary version of the *Bildungsroman*. Just as in the traditional *Bildungsroman*, the story follows the pattern: at home – abroad – at home. In the traditional version, however, the protagonist starts an odyssey as a young and rebellious character, looking for his own footing in the world. By the end of the story he has returned home wiser, but also somewhat more resigned to the vagaries of life. In the social melodrama, the young female protagonist leaves a hierarchical society steeped in old traditions to set out and search for her own identity and her own place in the world. By the end of the story, the values for which she has fought have given her a new understanding of the world and a "new home." For example, Skeeter in *The Help* leaves her home in Jacksonville, where racial policies judge its citizens by skin colour. She creates a "room of her own" in a publishing house in New York.

There are many common features in these novels, but there are also significant differences. Though the more standardized ones are predictable in terms of characterization, plot, language, and style, other novels of this genre may run counter to readers' expectations. In *The Island*, the melodrama is fully developed; the story is filled with love and jealousy, murder, deception, and yearning. Its denouement is a happy ending portraying how the hero, Dr. Kyritsis, has miraculously succeeded in portraying the lepra germ. An omniscient storyteller leaves nothing to the imagination. In keeping with the structure of the melodrama, the main interest is the private and personal sphere of each individual; the grander designs of society function as a backdrop.

The Hotel should be regarded as a text in between the traditional melodrama and the realistic and more problem-oriented novel. This is a story of two adolescent lovers, Chinese American Henry and Japanese American Keiko, who towards the end of the novel reunite after having been separated for forty years. Coincidentally, they have become widow and widower more or less at the same time. Alongside this story the readers witness how American authorities after Pearl Harbor displaced Japanese American communities into internment camps.

In *The Help*, as with the other two novels, poetic justice must prevail. One good example of this is the fate of the novel's "witch," twenty-three-year-old Hilly Holbrook, who as a reflection of the lawful segregation of the times, constructs a separate lavatory to be used only by the family's black nanny. Sweet revenge occurs when arrogant Hilly one morning finds her own lawn covered by the waste of many lavatories. Apparently to soften Hilly's anger, nanny Minnie offers to bake Hilly's favourite chocolate cake. When Minnie later reveals that the cake contains a special ingredient – Minnie's own poop – the alarm of becoming the community laughingstock turns out to be stronger than her thirst for revenge.

The storyteller's voice in *The Help* is more subdued than in the other two novels. In perhaps the most emotional scene in this novel, we hear the voice of one of the central characters, the black maid Abileen. She has lost her own son and developed strong relationships with the white children for whom she cares in spite of her awareness that they will most likely perpetuate the oppression of herself, her family, and her friends. When asked why she never works in the same household for more than twelve years, she responds simply that she quits while the children are still "colourblind."

Typical of the genre is how the wheels of history in *The Help* function as more than just a backdrop for the story about the individuals and their relationships. In the telling of the stories of Skeeter, the young white heroine, and the black maids Abileen and Minnie, different life experiences are contrasted. By fighting injustice and tyranny, Skeeter risks both friendships and love. The maids, by contrast, risk their work and homes, and even their lives, in a narrow society in which the activities of the Ku Klux Klan are rampant.

Through the close reading of texts, I examined the seven reviews published in national Norwegian papers and broadcasting, with particular attention given to identifying the differing sets of criteria used in assessing the novels. This method, however, could not be applied to the 1,500 or so amateur reviews on *Bokelskere*. To document the quality and complexity of this enormous corpus I present a condensed quantitative analysis, illustrated with some typical examples taken from the reviews.

Tracing the Experiences of the Amateur Critics

Readers use the website *Bokelskere* in different ways. Some write rather comprehensive reviews, but most of the contributions are relatively short, as are their contributions in discussion groups. Table 20.1 shows to what extent the readers were interested in the different novels, lists how many discussions were going on for each novel by the end of the data collection period, and gives a range for the number of reviews on each thread.

In the reviews of Kathryn Stockett's *The Help* there were two recurring arguments. First, the readers claim that it was difficult for them to put the novel down because they become so involved with the protagonists and their projects. Second, they expressed that the picture they had of the living conditions of black people in the Deep South of the 1960s had become more balanced and that they had learned something they did not know. About her relationship to the characters in *The Help*, Lena[2] for instance writes:

Table 20.1 Reader Interest in the Three Novels

Novels	Followers	Dice throwers	Dice values	Discussions/reviews
The Island	3,268	1,002	4	41 discussions with 14 to 18 reviews published on each thread
The Help	1,394	448	5	11 discussions with 9 to 57 reviews published on each thread
The Hotel	1,398	395	4	11 discussions with 6 to 65 reviews published on each thread

"Dice value" refers to average values among reviewers, out of possible score of 6. The now common practice – and not just in the tabloid papers – of evaluating books, concerts, dance performances, and so on, by dice numbers has been adopted by the amateur critics of *Bokelskere*.

"A fantastic book that made me think about the characters for a long time afterwards. Sat there feeling empty when I had read the last page."

A great many readers stated that they tried to savour the novel. For example, Tone wrote that she tried to take breaks in her reading to draw the experience out as long as possible: "However, this approach did not really work out for me," she states, "it was so terribly simple to become hooked and be literally devoured by this novel. It is so incredibly satisfying when a novel has such a pull in its prose! J."

Vivi pointed out a parallel between the conditions of African American maids who worked in the United States in the 1960s and the conditions of maids working in Brazil today:

> The situation of the housemaids [in the United States of the 1960s] is not very different from what we see in Brazil today. These housemaids are poor and often of African or Indian descent. They have little education, can hardly read or write, many are regarded as downright stupid. They sleep in a small babysitter, often they eat in their own private kitchen, have a separate toilet, and social contact between white masters and black servants is not accepted.

The most frequent contributor among the "booklovers" was Rosemarie. This reader was interesting because her views typically represented those of many readers. She pointed out that she had had no idea how strongly the white community regulated itself: "To cross the line between black and white was something you simply did not do. The fear of jeopardizing your own social status was simply too great. I thought I had read quite a lot about the racial policy, but this was very well and intensely portrayed, and it gave me many new and valuable insights."

The contributions related to Jamie Ford's *The Hotel* are different. Here the readers were split in two completely different groups, and their judgments were so disparate that it was hard to believe they were commenting on the same novel. What made the most profound impression on the readers of the first group was the treatment of American citizens of Japanese origin during the Second World War. A great many of these reviewers stated that they had not realized how this particular ethnic group had been treated. Rosemarie observed:

> When Japan attacked the US Pacific Navy, the result was a paranoid attitude against all Japanese that lived in the US (the same as we have seen with communists during the Cold War and against Muslims after 9.11). This novel tells the story of what happened to them. They were exposed to what we today may call illegal infringement. Not only were they the victims of constant persecution, but they were deported from their homes to end up in concentration camps under miserable conditions. The reason this is not well known today, is that history is always presented by the victorious.

This group also frequently commented on the novel's composition and style. For instance, Cathrine said: "The language of this novel is simple and elegant. The fact that the novel is acted out in two different periods of time, is something the author has executed with a steady hand." These readers, however, found the denouement irritating. Mari, for instance, wrote: "The ending, however, he could have left out. This is too much glam à la Hollywood."

The second group of readers did not comment on language and style. They immensely enjoyed the happy ending, where Henry and Keiko, each recently widowed, meet up after being separated for forty years. The readers Solveig, Anne-Christin, and Elin characterized the novel as "sweet, charming, and moving." These readers also quite frequently used phrases like "I got a lump in the throat" or "tears in the eyes."

There were three main views of Victoria Hislop's *The Island*. A great many readers had a rather low opinion of the novel. Riveroflaroo posted the most scathing attack: "I managed to read half of it before I almost collapsed by boredom. Too much sentimentality. The descriptions are bombastic and there is too much focus on details." Some readers were moderately enthusiastic. Ragnhild said: "This is a heartbreaking story from a period when leprosy provoked lots of prejudice in people. The author relates in a very moving way about love and deceit, about the life on Spinalonga in all its facets." Like the readers of *The Hotel*, many readers of *The Island* admitted to crying. For instance, Astrid Marte wrote: "My greatest sob came when I was near the end. A super book!"

The most striking theme in the reception of *The Island* was how some readers were fascinated by the little-known story of the leprosy camp on Spinalonga but at the same time were annoyed by the stereotypical characters or the highly detailed storytelling. Mari said:

> By all means, fascinating reading about the life in a colony for lepers, but I like the characters to possess some interesting dimensions. So far, Fontini and the doctor seem to be the only ones who are painted in shades of gray, whereas the rest of the characters are portrayed in black and white, good and bad. I ought to give up on this, but I am probably too stubborn.

Randi put it like this: "An important theme, but wrapped up in a trivial setting and banal language." To this Toril commented: "I became so fascinated by the story I had to finish the book, in spite of unimaginative language and uninspired storytelling."

The Professional Readers

The Help was reviewed by Marta Norheim (2010) on Norwegian National Broadcasting (NRK) and by Hans H. Skei (2010) in the nationally distributed paper *Aftenposten*. Norheim emphasized that the novel, in addition to its thematic qualities, possessed some of the qualities that characterize a successful action thriller. She pointed out that the characters and setting had been conveyed in a complex and comprehensive way and with a depth exceeding what is found in novels of mere entertainment. Likewise, Skei (2010) praised the novel's composition. "*The Help* is in many ways a good, old-fashioned novel. At the same time it is modern in describing the process that leads up to the writing of the story, thus undermining this approach by recounting how the story was really put to paper." Both Norheim and Skei underscored how the novel portrayed a unique context and thus conveyed important historical knowledge. Skei wrote:

> We are in Jackson, Mississippi, early in the 1960s in the middle of decisive historical events that shake up segregation all over the South. What we experience at close hand is a very slow transformation of the relationship between black and white people, a transformation that has been forced upon state authorities against their own will.

The Hotel was reviewed by Mie Hidle (2009) on NRK and by Maja Troberg Djuve (2010) in another nationally distributed paper, *Dagbladet*. Both these critics were preoccupied with the cognitive dimension of the novel – what the reader could learn, and what the critic presumably had learned from it. Djuve pointed out that Japanese Americans had been treated as spies and infiltrators in the United States after Pearl Harbor. Both admired Ford's storytelling, his language, and the structure of the novel. Hidle stated, for example, that "the novel shows impressive craftsmanship and is unique in its composition." But neither critic was pleased with the denouement. Djuve stated that the novel became "softer and more predictable towards the end," and Hidle delivered a gruesome verdict on how Ford had chosen to end his story (see below, the subsection "Sense and Sensibility").

The Island was the most widely reviewed novel in my material. In *Aftenposten*, Knut Ødegård (2007) emphasized that the story about the leper community on Spinalonga was a moving and involving read. He went on to say that the novel's strength lay in its description of the disease and that the relationship between the healthy and the sick was convincingly rendered. When it came to the artistic dimension, however, Ødegård drew attention to the language, which he characterized as "full of clichés"; he also commented on the omniscient storyteller, who "spells out everything in such a way that nothing is left for the imagination." In reviews of one of Victoria Hislop's later novels, *The Return,* Catherine Krøger (2009) and Anne Merethe K. Prinos (2009) also referred to *The Island.* Krøger wrote: "With *The Island,* Victoria Hislop found her own recipe, like it often is with a surprising bestseller." Prinos, on the other hand, stated scathingly: "I know I am at risk of being regarded as a 'besserwisser' [know-it-all] and an elitist ... Both *The Island* and *The Return* are outstanding examples of what is not good entertainment."

Sense and Sensibility versus Affective Reading Responses

In general terms, the professional and amateur critics were all well-educated, although specific details of the professional critics are more readily available. One of the professionals, Skei, is a professor of literature who holds a doctoral degree, as does Hidle; the remaining professionals possess master's degrees. Two of the professional reviewers have received the Critic of the Year Award – Norheim in 2002 and Prinos in 2007. A comparative study of *Bokelskere.no* and the Hungarian site *Moli.hu* (Toth and Audunson 2012) portrays the typical contributor as a young, well-educated woman with an urban background. This study found that as many as 62 percent of the Norwegian participants had high levels of education.

Again, in general terms, there were marked differences between amateurs and professionals with regard to style of writing and descriptions of the reading experience. The amateurs wrote informally and used slang for effect liberally, whereas the professionals conformed to the conventions of literary criticism. Also, the amateurs' reviews were much shorter; yet there was a dynamic complexity in their assessments, which we can read in the context of an ongoing discussion that allowed for continual refinement of their own views.

The analysis revealed two categories of reviewers: all of the professionals and around half the amateurs were in the first group; the rest of the amateurs were in the second. The groups diverged in genre expectations as well as in literary preferences and tastes. The first group used criteria that were widely accepted by the leading members of the literary establishment; the second applied criteria that were of little or no value to literary experts. The first group evaluated the novels by standards belonging to a tradition of realistic and problem-oriented fiction; the second applied standards from the classic melodrama tradition.

The first group of critics could be categorized under the term "sense and sensibility." In their language and style, the amateurs compared favourably with the professionals, even if they sometimes broke free from the conventional tracks of literary criticism. Members in this group tended to be concerned with the ethical, cognitive (i.e., sense-making), and aesthetic dimensions of the novels. "Booklover Mari" expressed her view thus: "[*The Help*] insists that you ask yourself what you are willing to do for your fellow man when you know this may have consequences for your own life." Similarly, Djuve wrote about *The Hotel*: "It was done for the sake of their own [Japanese American] safety, it was said, but as a group they were treated as potential spies and collaborators."

These critics were fundamentally concerned with how the novels conveyed knowledge of the unknown as well as with composition, language, and style. Nevertheless, if these dimensions pulled in different directions, the majority gave priority to the cognitive or learning dimension. It is particularly striking that this tendency was as strong among the professionals as among the amateurs. For example, professional critic Mie Hidle was not very impressed by the denouement of *The Hotel*: "Towards the end, Ford throws away all his inhibitions … one death after the other, together with the confessions and words of truth; everything in order to gather all loose ends and to move the characters in the direction of a happy ending." However, having torn the denouement to pieces, she stated:

> This novel possesses something quite unique, i.e. an historic backdrop that will represent something new to many readers … Anyway, for this reader it was new to what extent the skepticism of Americans developed into a paranoia only comparable to the later fear of communism. People of Japanese origin were exposed to indiscriminate arrests and restrictions. Along the West Coast, like in Seattle, they suffered curfew, and were later deported to concentration camps deeper into the country.

The same tendency was apparent in Skei's review of *The Help*. For him, the novel was "an engulfing read over the first couple of hundred pages. Then it is basically more of the same until the story is being wound up relatively pointlessly." Notwithstanding these artistic deficiencies, Skei continued in a laudatory vein: "If this were not a work of fiction, the chapters told by Abileen and Minnie could have been part of an in-depth anthropological examination of the condition that the blacks lived under in the deep South during the sixties."

Affective Reading Responses

Compared to the critics in the first group, the second group of reviewers wrote shorter contributions, their vocabulary was more limited, and their reviews were more packed with emotionally laden terms like "beautiful," "touching," and "heartwarming." They also reported visceral reactions when reading these novels. Astrid Marte, for example, wrote that she "got the creeps" when Elena in *The Island* had to leave her husband and children upon being infected by the leprosy bacterium to settle at the island of the lepers, Spinalonga.

The cognitive dimension, however, received little attention from these readers. A number of them focused on the happy denouement, with quite a few stating that the happy ending was vital to making *The Hotel* a good read. Also important to these critics was the moral dimension. In line with the melodramatic storytelling tradition, this dimension was linked to the relationships between the characters rather than to the societies that had perpetrated a social injustice.

This group did not comment on language or composition, though many reviewers expressed a preference for "easy reads." Qualities like predictability and clarity in characterization and plot contribute to easy reading. So it is not surprising that for this group, *The Island* and *The Hotel* were their favourites, given that these two novels were the most closely based on literary formulas. This goes in particular for *The Island*, in which the omniscient storyteller regularly assists the reader by breaking into the narrative to summarize the events.

Aesthetic Experience, Enjoyment, and Fascination – Revisited

In the social melodrama novel, two different storytelling traditions are juxtaposed: on the one hand, the classic melodrama with its inclination to utilize strong effects and convenient coincidents; and on the other, a more realistic and problem-oriented storytelling that aims to create an "illusion of reality." Nevertheless, these novels belong to the same genre. According to Jauss (1982), a genre is created when a sufficient number of people have perceived that a number of texts share a significant number of characteristics and therefore belong together. The reviews demonstrated this interpretation by referring to the novels as "such books," "this type of book," and so on. In the online discussions, many statements were structured in terms of "If you liked 'book x,' you'll like 'book y' as well." When Elin and Solveig on *Booklovers.no* agreed that the love story of *The Hotel* was very moving, Elin recommended *The Island* to Solveig. And when Rosemarie and Tone agreed on how impressively *The Hotel* had related the predicament of Japanese Americans after Pearl Harbor, Rosemarie recommended *The Help* to Tone.

Readers who possessed more cultural capital seemed to prefer *The Help*, whereas those at the other end of the scale seemed to prefer *The Island*. *The Hotel* was situated in between and was praised by almost everybody. There was, however, much that readers agreed on. This is hardly surprising: they live their lives within the same historical epoch and the same general culture, and they have been socialized into a contemporary view of what female identity implies. It is through this triangulation of historical epoch, culture, and gender that I have explored the appeal and fascination that the social melodrama has on contemporary female readers. Jauss (1982) is particularly interested in how aesthetic enjoyment or fascination evolves when a group of readers identify with or at least involve themselves actively in one or more of the protagonists and their projects.

> In particular, I fell for Minnie, who doesn't let anyone interfere in her own affairs. She is also quite willing to take the consequences of her own decisions, and not once does she sit down to sulk or to take on a sacrificial role ... She is simply a strong and straightforward woman. (Rosemarie on *Bokelskere.no*)

This is a fine example of how newer feminist representations of women have contributed to and shaped social melodrama and readers' fascination with and experiences of the genre, whichever of the two distinct groups they belong to. Whether through the positive evaluation of the social melodrama's ability to convey knowledge of historical settings or by approving and having a great experience in reading books centred around strong and self-aware women, both groups adhere to and favour the new assertive heroine, who by the mid-1980s had entered bestselling literature.

From around 1850 to the early 1980s, popular novels featured heroines characterized by traditional female virtues such as patience, self-sacrifice, and compliance. After that, readers began to reject novels with passive female protagonists (Naper 2007). As the First Wave feminist movement focused its activities on family roles and intimacy, a new type of "anti-patriarchal" love story evolved. In this literature, loving couples support each other so that both partners can live their lives as free human beings unencumbered by traditional gender roles. The bottom line is that true love is only possible in a relationship characterized by mutual respect and equality (Naper 2007).[3]

During Second Wave feminism, the emphasis shifted to the social position of women rather than their familial role.[4] Bestselling novels during this phase focused more on strong female protagonists who fought relentlessly for equality and justice rather than on love stories. These bestsellers had active and assertive female protagonists but could also be classified as *Bildungsroman* (with a smattering of melodrama). This type of historical novel drew on well-known historical facts to convey some sort of ideology or moral lesson relevant to the present. Together with the basic rhythm of the melodrama, this new dimension has helped underscore the legitimate and meaningful quest of the protagonists, and it is the concept of the *Bildungsroman* more than anything else that binds these novels together. Now that the focus is on the female protagonist's fight for freedom, equality, and justice, the question of female identity and women's place in society is an overriding theme in the new millennium.

Notes

1. Hereafter, *The Hotel*.
2. All quotes in this chapter are from the website https://bokelskere.no. To simplify matters I have chosen to refer to the reviewers only by name. In the references, the readers can be retrieved by name under the heading Bokelskere.no.
3. My findings are from the Norwegian literary scene. In *Global Infatuation*, Eva Hemmung Wirtén (1988) has documented the same pattern in the love stories of the leading distributor of serial novels in the Western World, the Canadian-based novel factory Harlequin.
4. Still, there is left to see how gender and gender roles will be depicted in tomorrow's bestsellers. The female protagonists of the largest commercial successes over the past few years, Stephanie Meyer's Bella (The *Twilight* series) and E.L. James's Anastasia Rose (*Fifty Shades of Grey)* have just as many common features with the traditional heroine as with the postfeminist one.

References

Bourdieu, Pierre. 1984. *Distinction*. London: Routledge and Kegan.
Brooks, Peter. 1995. *The Melodramatic Imagination*. New Haven: Yale University Press.
Djuve, Maja Troberg. 2010. "Lesverdig bestselger" [Commendable Bestseller.] *Dagbladet*, 6 November.
Farsethås, Anne. 2013. Email interview with author. 9 February.
Ford, Jamie. 2009. *The Hotel on the Corner of Bitter and Sweet*. New York: Ballantine Books.
Gerould, Daniel. 1978. "Russian Formalist Theories of Melodrama." *Journal of American Culture* 1(1): 153–68.
Haugen, Karin. 2013. Email interview with author. 9 February.
Hidle, Mie. 2009. "Hotellet på hjørnet av bitter og søt" [The Hotel on the Corner of Bitter and Sweet]. *NRK* [National Norwegian Broadcasting]. 9 December.
Hislop, Victoria. 2005. *The Island*. London: Headline.
Jauss, Hans Robert. 1982. *Aesthetic Experience and Literary Hermeneutics*. Minneapolis: University of Minnesota Press.
Krøger, Cathrine. 2009. "Lidenskapsløst om lidenskapen" [Unpassionate on Passion]. *Dagbladet*, 14 April.
Naper, Cecilie. 2007. *Kvinner, lesning og fascinasjon* [*Women, Reading, and Fascination*]. Oslo: Pax.
Norheim, Marta. 2010. "Sterk sørstatsroman" [Strong southern state novel.] *NRK*, 30 April.
Ødegård, Knut. 2007. "De rene og urene av hjertet." *Aftenposten*, 5 August.
Prinos, Anne Merethe K. 2010. "Nitrist underholdning" [Dreary entertainment]. *Aftenposten*, 19 April.

Skarpenes, Ove. 2007. "Den legitime kulturens moralske forankring" [The Moral Anchoring of the Legitimate Culture]. *Tidsskrift for samfunnsforskning* 48(4): 531–63.
Skei, Hans. 2010. "Nesten oppbyggelig" [Close to Uplifting]. *Aftenposten,* 16 May.
Stockett, Kathryn. 2008. *The Help.* London: Penguin.
Toth, Mate, and Ragnar Andreas Audunson. 2012. "Websites for Booklovers as Meeting Places." *Library Hi Tech* 30(4): 655–72.
Wirtén, Eva Hemmungs. 1998. *Global Infatuation: Explorations in Transnational Publishing and Texts: The Case of Harlequin Enterprises and Sweden.* Publications from the Section for Sociology of Literature at the Department of Literature 38, Uppsala University.

Bokelskere.no commentary:

Anne-Christin. 2013. Bokelskere.no.http://bokelskere.no/diskusjoner/finn/?finn=hotellet+på+hjørnet
Astrid Marthe. 2012. Bokelskere.no. http://bokelkerenodiskusjonerfinn/?side=5&finn=%C3%B8ya
Cathrine. 2013. Bokelskere.no. http://bokelskere.no/diskusjoner/finn/?finn=Hotellet på hjørnet av bitter og søt
Elin. 2013. Bokelskere.no.http://bokelskere.no/diskusjonerfinn/?finn=hotellet+på+hjørnet
Elisabeth. 2013. Bokelskere.no. http://bokelskere.no/diskusjoner/finn/?finn=hjemkomsten
Hilde. 2013. Bokelskere.no. http://bokelskere.no/diskusjoner/finn/?finn=little+bee
Lena. 2013. Bokelskere.no. http://bokelskere.no/tekst/31744
Mari. 2013. Bokelskere.no.http://bokelskere.no/diskusjoner/finn/?finn=fontini
Mia Maria. 2013. Bokelskere.no. http://bokelskere.no/tekst/31744
Ragnhild. 2013. Bokelskere.no. http://bokelskere.no/diskusjoner/finn/?side=5&finn=%C3%B8ya
Randi. 2013. Bokelskere.no. http://bokelskere.no/diskusjoner/finn/?side=5&finn=%C3%B8ya
Riveroflaroo. 2013. Bokelskere.no. http://bokelskere.no/tekst/30863
Rosemarie. 2013. "Comment on *The Help.*" Bokelskere.no. http://bokelskere.no/tekst/37351
Rosemarie. 2013. "Comment on 'The Hotel on the corner of bitter and sweet.'" Bokelskere.no. http://bokelskere.no/bok/hotellet-paa-hjoernet-av-bitter-og-soet/192742
Solveig. Bokelskere.no. http://bokelskere.no/diskusjonerfinn/?finn=hotellet+på+hjørnet
Tone. 2013. Bokelskere.no. http://bokelskere.no/tekst/37351
Toril. 2013. Bokelskere.no. http://bokelskere.no/tekst/2218
Vivi. 2013. Bokelskere.no. http://bokelskere.no/diskusjoner/finn/?finn=Barnepiken

The Republic of Readers   21
Book Clubs in the United Kingdom of The Netherlands, 1815-1830

Arnold Lubbers

It has been assumed that when the Netherlands was merged with Belgium and Luxembourg to form the United Kingdom of the Netherlands, patriotic feelings were shared by the majority of the Dutch population. Indeed, after the country was liberated from the rule of Napoleon Bonaparte, there was an increase in the production of texts with patriotic themes, which makes that assumption plausible. Since literature, and reading material in general, was the principal means of spreading ideas or information in the early nineteenth century, it is hypothesized that Dutch readers likely showed interest in those texts. It is even thought that the spread of that specific reading material contributed to the spread of patriotic feelings, or early nationalism, in the Netherlands. This in turn could have contributed to the development of a Dutch national identity.

In 1842, on the fiftieth anniversary of the book club *Idle Hours Usefully Spent* (*Ledige Uren Nuttig Besteed*), chairman Anske Koopmans addressed an audience from the village of Oude Bildtzijl. In his speech, he looked back on previous decades and stressed the initial main goal of the book club: to assuage the yearning for knowledge and to spread enlightened thought. He said that reading served those purposes, but that the very structure and dynamics of the book club could help achieve that goal as well (Norder 1991, 10). In Koopmans's opinion, the structured way in which the members of the book club treated one another served as an example for society in general: "A good administration and good rules and regulations are inseparable from each other. This counts as much for a book club as for society as a whole" (1991, 18–19). According to him, "a book club is a republic in [microcosm] as it were" (1991, 22).

Koopmans's remarks suggest that book clubs did contribute to the formation of a national civil society. Most of them were founded by people "below" the upper and the upper-middle classes of society. These readers' institutions provided more than access to topical reading material; they also offered a social setting where people could practise democratic norms and values, before a democratic constitution was implemented in the Netherlands in 1848. The mere existence of book clubs may well have contributed to the development of a national identity. The fact that book clubs in effect blocked women from membership – along with lower- and lower-middle-class people – because they could not afford the mandatory subscription fees provides insight into the differential access that various social groups had to civil society and the public sphere.

In this chapter, I examine the minutes, rules, regulations, and book-purchasing habits of sixty book clubs in the northern Netherlands (today's Netherlands) from 1815 to 1830.[1] I begin by describing the cultural and societal climate and situating it among existing theories of nationalism and civil society. Then I place the information from the minutes of the book clubs against the description of the contemporary cultural and societal climate and recent studies on literary production from that period to answer this question: To what extent did Dutch book clubs contribute to the formation of national unity?

The Cultural Climate

The process of nation-building in the Netherlands in the early nineteenth century has been described as follows:

> National feeling and national sensitivities [are] socialized under a much larger group, in which – put disrespectfully – "semi-intellectuals" like teachers, journalists, writers and poets play an important role: the stereotypical men that shaped the Dutch nationalism and national culture during the long nineteenth century in terms of the myth of the Golden Age. (Van Sas 2005b, 46–47)

The cultural transfer carried out by these semi-intellectuals in books and magazines around the years 1815 to 1830 was strongly related to European developments in the first half of the nineteenth century as described by Leerssen: the history of a country no longer hinged on the leaders of that country, but much more on the nation as a whole. "The people" were seen as the new foundation of society, and this led to a vision in which ethnicity became entangled with the politically demarcated society. Such ideas were expressed, for example, in the historical novels that were increasingly being launched on the book market, such as those of Walter Scott. These books enabled readers to identify with their nationally shared cultural past – in essence, with their "own" past (Leerssen 2003, 76–79). According to Bank, these national notions in texts strongly appealed to and influenced readers: their recollections of such a past fed their patriotism (1990, 33–34).

As awareness of a shared national past gained ground, so did the notion that themes, values, and achievements from the past were part of a collective national heritage (Weichlein 2006, 77). This led contemporaries to link "tradition" to "national identity." Such historical awareness took root in Europe in the uncertain times after the Napoleonic Wars as technological and political developments rapidly changed society. However, the nation as an idea remained a cultural concept and was not yet used to denote a political order (2006, 77).

Leerssen (2003, 80–83) associates this societal need for harmony with the romantic view of the past in which contemporaries saw traditional community life as worth upholding. The values and standards bestowed on this period of the United Kingdom of the Netherlands have been summarized as the "Jan-Salie-spirit" (referencing a character from an influential nineteenth-century novel). According to Johannes, these values and standards could be divided into those that were worth pursuing and that could expect criticism. On the one hand, the Dutch harboured virtues such as generosity, domesticity, piousness, tolerance, simplicity, patriotism, and Orangeism. On the other, the Dutch were also narrow-minded, petit bourgeois, and closed to art, beauty, and passion (1997, 7).

Several scholars have shown there was a widely shared yearning for unity and peace in the United Kingdom of the Netherlands that was addressed by emphasizing national values and standards (Lok and Scholz 2012, 36; Van Zanten 2004, 44–45). The desire for unity and the development of a national identity went hand in hand in the period after 1815. That is why, according to Aerts, in voluntary organizations there was little room for politics: controversy was to be avoided. The national values of domesticity, Christian love, and harmony dominated the public spirit. Society was seen as one big family with the king as its father (Aerts 2010, 224). A socially shared national identity and a harmonious community were viewed as expressions of cultural nationalism and patriotism. These things were also seen as part of a societal dynamic that would lead to a civil democratic society. An examination of voluntary organizations like book clubs can shed light on these developments.

The Role of Literature

Despite various attempts by both the government and intellectuals, the inhabitants of the northern and southern parts of the United Kingdom of the Netherlands would not meld together culturally. Thus, some have characterized this period as a failed experiment (Aerts 1999, 61). The problems encountered by the merger make it clear that the desired nation, to use

Anderson's term, was an "imagined community," but only in the sense that it was the *authorities* who felt an affinity with the notion of the nation as a whole. According to Anderson (2006), the production of a national literature had a unifying effect on such a society. Previous research has shown that national sentiments and characteristics were often, through literature, conveyed to inhabitants of the kingdom, who by reading were educated to be true patriots. "'National' literature meant: original literature, texts written in impeccable Dutch, not translated and preferably with a story set on home ground, with patriotic characters and a description of domestic morals and customs" (Petiet 2009, 188). According to Mathijsen, between 1815 and 1830, publishers, poets, teachers, and vicars jostled one another in marketing a torrent of patriotic reading material (2010, 51–52). These peak periods of patriotic publishing were closely related to two epochs in the early nineteenth century during which national theatre enjoyed popularity (Jensen 2008, 144–48); according to Jensen, such novels, poetry, and plays reached a large audience (2008, 21). In short, patriotism and the production of books seem to have gone hand in hand in the period of the United Kingdom of the Netherlands.

A study of book clubs can inform us about the reading preferences of *groups* of people. The assumption is that individual preferences played a minor role in these clubs, whose choice of reading material would probably have reflected the middle-class ideals of self-development and pursuit of knowledge. It is likely that these clubs purchased pious, literary, historical, and political works of a useful or moralizing character. Kloek and Mijnhardt's research (1988, 63) on a Middelburg bookseller has shown that book clubs mainly purchased novels, travelogues, newspapers, and magazines.

Civil Society and Nationalism

Kloek and Mijnhardt characterized book clubs as organizations for the well-to-do middle class. The lower classes of the Netherlands were served mainly by libraries. Middle-class voluntary organizations were related to the development of civil society. Around 1800 the conviction gained ground that citizens could lay the foundations for knowledge, virtue, and happiness only through voluntary associations such as clubs, societies, and circles of friends (Mijnhardt 1988, 94). Such was civil society: the (self-)organization of a large group of people who were, as an outgrowth of various objective relations – economical, geographical, religious, linguistic, and so on – linked to one another and capable of reflecting on that. Three of these relations are essential:

(1) a "memory" of some common past, treated as a "destiny" of the group – or at least of its core constituents; (2) a density of linguistic or cultural ties enabling a higher degree of social communication within the group than beyond it; (3) a conception of the equality of all members of the group organized as a civil society. (Hroch 1996, 79)

The development of Dutch civil society was related to the unifying policies of King William I with regard to the first and second points: he tried to promote the idea of a shared past, and he encouraged the growth of linguistic and cultural associations. Within the confines of the book clubs, such notions of equality were practised. The trend towards voluntary self-organization had taken root in the eighteenth century, but it seems to have flowered especially in the civil nineteenth century (Van Sas 2005a, 21–22).

The term "civil society" has no precise definition.[2] It refers not only to the values and ideals of the middle classes but also to social reality itself. It is closely related to the public sphere: to debate, and to the public contemplation or expression of opinions – for instance, on politics or literature (see Habermas 1989). In the theoretical framework of the public sphere, societies and magazines are important because they facilitate and shape the debate. Conceptually, though, the public sphere is only that part of civil society in which public opinion is shaped (Janse 2008, 107).

From the perspective of civil society it is possible to link identity to the development of national unity: "Early nineteenth-century organizations function primarily as a unifying element in society; they contribute to an open civil society with a public sphere, in which enlightened ideals, democratic values and standards and the development of a national identity are spread" (De Vries 2006, 104).

Dutch history shows that civil society contributed to the achievement of democracy (Aerts 2010, 234). The civil society perspective therefore lends itself well to research on the period of the United Kingdom of the Netherlands because it exposes the practical consequences of the national pursuit of unity. Between 1815 and 1830, civil society was related to values and standards, originating in patriotism, that blended together with the aforementioned need for harmony and peace. The nation as a community bound together by language and culture was "unmistakably related to the liberal interpretation of state and society, but ... focused on togetherness" (Bank 1990, 41). This vision, which can be placed under the rubric of cultural nationalism, was an effort to express and reinforce a new sentiment of unity and emerging national consciousness. According to Bank (1990, 41), this cultural nationalism was middle class in character and was perpetuated by civil initiatives. Leerssen contends that such civil initiatives, including book clubs, have played a role in the spread of cultural nationalism (2006, 170).

According to this vision, book clubs were a social, civil framework in which books and magazines circulated. We can assume that reading material of and about the national culture was purchased and distributed among club members. Given that book clubs were a potential catalyst for cultural nationalism in the early nineteenth century, the question remains: To what extent have book clubs contributed to the cultivation of a national culture?

The Members of Dutch Book Clubs

What kind of people joined book clubs in the nineteenth century? It was not easy to become a member. Most book clubs voted by ballot, which guaranteed that membership remained restricted to a relatively small social circle. In the first half of the nineteenth century, book clubs were much more exclusive than their eighteenth-century predecessors. In the 1820s and 1830s, women were gradually excluded and the lower middle classes lost their welcome (De Vries 2007, 52). Especially in urban areas, reading society members were often intellectuals or had an artistic profession: local nobility, men in the liberal professions, well-to-do artists, ministers, teachers, and booksellers. Merchants and manufacturers seemed less interested (De Vries 2007, 54). There were also book clubs whose members were drawn mainly from one extended family (Dongelmans 1990, 201). The members of a book club in the village of Leens included a day labourer and a peddler. The presence of these show that book clubs – at least outside the urban areas – offered a setting in which relations could cross social boundaries (Lubbers 2010, 288).

The book club "Idle Hours Usefully Spent" in Oude Bildtzijl attracted members from a wide range of professions. They included a bartender, a farmer, a former sailor, a principal, a public servant, a butcher, a painter, a baker, a mason, a former lawyer, a cobbler, and a blacksmith (Tresoar Frisian Historical and Literary Centre n.d., 342-13, 20). In the village of IJzendijke, about one-third of the members were agricultural workers, and the rest were public servants, craftsmen, ministers, and medics (Franken 1995, 116).

Research on multiple subscription lists and archival records has shown that the number and composition of members of book clubs in the Netherlands between 1781 and 1850 was extremely diverse (Jansen 1988). We can cautiously conclude that preferences in reading material, gender, age, religion, and residence were potentially decisive factors in becoming a member or founder of a book club (Jansen 1990, 182).

The Scope of the Phenomenon

To understand the quantitative development of book clubs, Jansen studied subscription lists for books encompassing more than 100,000 individuals and organizations. He estimated that there were at least 924 and as many as 1,629 book clubs in the Netherlands between 1781 and 1849. This number seems to have grown until the 1830s. Between one half and three quarters of the book clubs were in the western provinces of Holland and Zeeland. One quarter to one fifth were in the middle, eastern, and northern provinces of Utrecht, Gelderland, Overijssel, Drenthe, Groningen, and Friesland. Less than 5 percent of book clubs were found in the southern provinces of Limburg and Noord-Brabant. In the southern province of Limburg, only two book clubs were discovered (Jansen 1990, 185).

But according to Jansen, the estimates based on his research were probably too low. The number of book clubs he found, based on an inquiry into the cultural life of the province of Groningen under teachers, was six times higher than what could be found through the study of subscription lists. It is possible that this multiplication holds true for the entire country (Jansen 1990, 186). This would mean that instead of an annual average of 271 book clubs (my estimate based on Jansen's numbers), there were 1,626 book clubs in existence at any given moment in the United Kingdom of the Netherlands in this period.

From 1815 to 1830, the northern part of the United Kingdom of the Netherlands had between 2.1 and 2.3 million inhabitants. That would mean there was one book club for every 8,487 Dutch. Sometimes people belonged to more than one organization (Brouwer 1995). What follows is a thought experiment: Multiply by six times (as mentioned above) and we arrive at one book club for every 1,414 Dutch. Based on the still extant minutes of the book clubs, we can determine that the average number of members was between twenty and thirty. This means that at any given moment, 5,420 to 8,130 Dutch belonged to a book club, which corresponds to between 0.2 and 0.4 percent of the total population; when multiplied by six, we arrive at 32,530 to 48,780 members – 1.2 and 2.4 percent of the entire population. Furthermore, memberships in book clubs were continuously changing. Each year, members left and new ones arrived. In the village of Leens, for example, between 1815 and 1830 a total of 101 individuals were members of the book club at some point. If this practice was common – and the minutes of some book clubs indicate it was, but this is by no means an absolute truth for all – then instead of a minimum of 5,420, there were 27,371 Dutch temporary members of book clubs, corresponding to 1.2 percent of the total population. Multiplied by six, that would account for a minimum of 164,226, meaning at least 7.2 percent of the total population belonged to a book club at some point. That would be the most positive estimate.

As mentioned before, book club members were largely from the middle classes, and probably specifically from the lower middle classes – especially if they lived in villages or towns. The lower middle classes constituted roughly 23 percent of the Dutch population – at that time, around 529,000 people. The upper middle classes, which in urban areas also provided book club members, were 3 percent of the population – around 69,000 people. This suggests that the total number of potential members was 598,000. Applying the lowest estimate above, that would mean that at least 0.9 percent were actually members. The highest estimate, however, would mean that 27.6% of the potential members at some point belonged to a book club.

Rules and Regulations

Most book clubs followed more or less the same rules and regulations. Perhaps the members, when drawing up their own, were inspired by the rules and regulations of other book clubs, which sometimes printed theirs. The high degree of similarity indicates that the organizations were comparable, which is why we can draw general conclusions when studying the book clubs collectively.

The main objective of the book clubs was to circulate reading material among their members, who read individually – reflection after reading was not part of their mandate. The ways in which the book clubs were managed, and the relations between the administration and the regular members, can be interpreted as an exercise in self-discipline. The administrative functions circulated among all members, and the choices of reading material were made democratically. Officially, there was no guidance by experienced readers, but it is not hard to imagine that this happened in reality. Still, based on the democratic approach to choosing reading material, we can surmise that the literary socialization of the middle classes had advanced much further than previously thought.

The clubs' regulations ensured that members conducted themselves appropriately during annual meetings; they also called for careful treatment of the reading material. Voluntary adherence to the strict rules and regulations makes it plausible to conclude that members actually read the reading materials that circulated. Members were allowed to keep the reading materials in their possession for on average fourteen days. Because the number of members was restricted, as was the geographical area from which they could be recruited, this reading period did not have to be shortened.

Strong self-discipline was demanded of the book club members. This can be related to civil ideals of order, tranquility, and self-restraint. Because controversial topics were ruled out when it came to choosing reading material, clashing viewpoints between different social groups were suppressed; possibly, this furthered social cohesion (De Vries 1989, 17). One might then ask whether book clubs contributed to the formation of national unity in the Netherlands. Even though that ideal was not explicated in the rules and regulations of the book clubs, mere participation in a book club made possible a sense of shared purpose.

The question remains: Did the choice of reading material express this democratizing process? As previously mentioned, several researchers have noted that the early nineteenth century saw a boom in patriotic texts. Did the members of book clubs show any interest in these? The rules and regulations of book clubs seem to have been rooted in a widely shared yearning for social peace, harmony, and unity. The reading materialthat circulated therefore offers an entry point for reflecting on the interests of a significant segment of the Dutch middle class.

Choices in Reading Material: National Heroes?

In a recent study, Jensen (2008, 219–20, 222, 224) identified sixty plays, poems, and novels published between 1815 and 1830 that focused on national heroes. Based on the titles of books mentioned in the minutes of book clubs, it is possible to make a reasonable estimate as to whether these books interested contemporary readers. When we correlate Jensen's titles with the minutes, it is clear there was no obvious interest in national heroes – less than 2 percent of the clubs purchased one of the titles identified by Jensen.

It seems then that in the period of the United Kingdom of the Netherlands, book clubs could hardly be called distribution channels for explicit nationalism or patriotism. Even when we apply a broad definition of nationalistic or patriotic reading material – texts that in some way or another include national themes such as Dutch history, geography, literature, or fiction – only about 10 percent could be classified (albeit not explicitly) as nationalistic.

When we consider this limited number of purchases with national themes and are reminded of the peak periods during which patriotic texts were published – the years just after the liberation from Bonaparte and around the secession of Belgium – it seems that patriotic reading material was primarily embraced in periods when the nation was or had been violated. This supports the idea, outlined by Mathijsen (2010, 51) that there was growing appreciation for national literature in the years 1810–14 and around 1830.

Does it then come as a surprise that only a small part of the reading material in Dutch book clubs between 1815 and 1830 was about historic, patriotic heroes? Not when it comes to novels: the patriotic historical novel blossomed in a later period, with a peak between 1835 to 1842 (Jensen 2008, 209). Furthermore, the Dutch production of novels was low in absolute numbers: publishing houses released only twenty to thirty-five novels annually, and most of these were translations (Streng 2011, 70). It could well have been that original Dutch novels were more expensive than translated ones.

Other reasons could account for the low number of Dutch novels in book clubs. The members may have viewed reading material with explicit patriotic themes as too controversial. Inspired by a yearning for peace and harmony, perhaps they decided that these themes were not suitable for their small social circle. Perhaps material about national heroes would have reminded the members too strongly of conflicts in the national past that continued to simmer. So perhaps reading material with less obvious patriotic themes was read.

Choices in Reading Material: A National Literary Heritage?

In another recent study, Petiet (2011) identified eighteen national literary histories and anthologies published between 1815 and 1830. After correlating these with the minutes of the book clubs, it is clear that only a small number of book clubs purchased them. Does this mean there was no interest in national literary heritage among the Dutch book clubs? We cannot be completely certain: anthologies are instructive and are also intended for purposes of education. It is conceivable that the book club members felt they did not need to be further educated. They could simply purchase the new editions of seventeenth-century texts without having to be told of their existence. The lack of literary histories and anthologies could actually support the idea that in general, the Dutch middle classes were more literary than has been previously thought.

Another reason for the seemingly low interest in literary heritage can be found in the attitude of book clubs: as mentioned before, they wanted to preserve peace and avoid controversy. Nationalism might be on the rise, but there was no consensus on the national past. Disputes from the past, between Catholics and Protestants or patriots and Orangeists, were unresolved themes in older literary works. Book clubs were not the ideal setting to circulate national or patriotic reading material that might have led to an unofficial ban on Dutch literary heritage.

Perhaps anthologies as a category of reading matter did not suit the objectives of book clubs; this sort of material could be used as study material or for reference, whereas in book clubs the reading material circulated continuously. So it is plausible that literary histories and anthologies were better suited for purchase by individuals. The study of private spending habits at the bookseller Van Benthem in the city of Middelburg around 1800 supports this assumption: reference books make up 14.4 percent of total private spending, but only 1.7 percent of the purchases of book clubs (Kloek and Mijnhardt 1988, 62). The absence of anthologies supports the idea that from 1815 to 1830, book club members were hardly interested in patriotic or national themes. The reference books that *were* present in book clubs highlight this point – these were books about general history, famous people from home and abroad, and criminal affairs.

Rock (2010) studied Dutch texts from the Middle Ages as well as from the seventeenth century; of these, he identified sixteen new publications between 1815 and 1830. After comparing the minutes of book clubs with these publications, it is clear that new editions of old texts were completely absent from the lists of purchased reading material in Dutch book clubs. Perhaps this was because these editions were few in number: in the Netherlands in that period, around 16,500 titles were published in total, but only sixteen new editions of old texts (Rock 2010).

Even editions by Willem Bilderdijk, one of the best-known Dutch writers of that period, were not bought by book clubs. This supports Leerssen's observation that even though there was an increased interest in the Middle Ages (2006, 53), the literature from that period received a half-hearted reception (2006, 100–101).

Choices in Reading Material: Domesticity?

Krol (1997) identified books in which domesticity – considered a prominent national value – was an important topic. She compared her information with the minutes of book clubs and found that when clubs purchased such books, they were principally translated works of German writers like August Lafontaine and Heinrich Clauren.[4] These purchasing habits suggest that domesticity was a typical Dutch trait, part of the national character. The reading material in book clubs suggests that at least part of the Dutch national character or identity was linked to contemporary European developments, in this case demonstrated by translated German reading material.

This habit of purchasing translated works is not surprising: in Dutch book clubs, either most or all of the novels purchased were in translation. In the Leens' book club, novels constituted 27 percent of all the reading material purchased. In book clubs in the village of Cadzand and in two in the city of Dordrecht, the percentages were respectively 27, 22, and 30. These numbers are comparable to the results from the aforementioned study of the Middelburg bookseller (Kloek and Mijnhardt 1988, 63).[5] It seems that members of the book club "De Eendragt" (The Concord) from the city of The Hague purchased fewer novels – 15 percent – but half their total spending was on French reading material, which could well have included novels. A confessional book club in Dordrecht had other objectives: it focused on religious or pious reading material, so it is no surprise only 4 percent of its books were novels. As a rule, book clubs purchased nearly twice as many novels as books, plays, and poetry that can be loosely characterized as patriotic or national. For each patriotic book there were two "international" books. Did this reflect a conscious international orientation? The question is valid, given that Dutch book clubs were heavily criticized in the early nineteenth century for buying only the most recently published materials (Brouwer 1995, 147). The critics claimed the book club members were not really interested in the actual content of the reading material, just as long as they could read. To a large extent they seemed to satisfy that particular need by buying translations, which, as mentioned before, hardly comes as a surprise, given that Dutch production of novels was low.

Here we see several developments converging. In tandem with the rise of nationalism and patriotism, the book trade professionalized itself during this period and the reading public was emancipated. As literary production became more international and commercial, translations were feared as competitors to original Dutch productions (Johannes 1997, 63). In countries like France and England, translations were unnecessary to meet the increasing demand for reading material as "these two countries *produce* a lot of novels (and good novels, too), so they don't need to buy them abroad" (Moretti 1999, 151).

Choices in Reading Material: Origins?

Contemporaries who criticized the reading of translated material related this to an apparent lack of patriotism. People spoke of a translating frenzy. Contemporaries also criticized Dutch writers for not writing enough original work, and Dutch readers, lacking affinity with a national culture, showed no preference for good, patriotic reading material (Johannes 1997, 64). A preference for translations was, according to the critics, nothing but cultural submissiveness and a marker of low self-respect (Heilbron 1995, 217). Especially after 1800, the criticism of translations took on a nationalistic slant (Korpel 1993, 8). At the same time, between 1815 and 1830 a sort of cosmopolitanism came into vogue. Were these two developments related to each other? Some, like the famous writer Jan Fredrik Helmers, viewed cosmopolitanism as integral to patriotism (Jensen 2011).

More implicitly than travelogues, which were often read in that period, translated novels wafted their readers to foreign settings and situations, opening a portal to thoughts and ideas from other cultures. Could a preference for the ideal of cosmopolitanism explain the extensive purchase of these novels? Such novels – Scott's, for example – offered a colourful opportunity to identify with a national or foreign past (Leerssen 2003, 79). The question then is whether a sizable corpus of translated novels signified the choice of reading matter of a true cosmopolitan?

For book clubs whose members read primarily for pleasure (as the critics suggested), the dependence on foreign book production was strong. An analysis of registers from a subscription library in the city of Haarlem in the second half of the nineteenth century confirms an increase in demand for recreational reading material during that time. The library mostly lent novels, and most of those were in original Dutch (De Vries 2007, 59). It is conceivable that the demand for recreational reading material was already present between 1815 and 1830 but that it could not be met by the level of the national book production. Publishing houses were aware of the tastes and demands of the reading public and responded to those, which could explain the high production of translated novels.

Buijnsters has ascertained that in eighteenth-century book clubs, the members strove to become better world citizens by reading collectively (1984, 188). If we define cosmopolitanism broadly as an open, interested attitude towards other countries and cultures, extensive spending of translated reading matter suggests that members of Dutch book clubs at least did not shy away from international ideas or foreign themes.

Reading Matter and the Cultural Climate

At first glance, in Dutch book clubs in the United Kingdom of the Netherlands, there seems to have been little interest in the home country. As mentioned before, that period saw a widely shared yearning for social harmony and peace. It seems that certain reading material was chosen because of this yearning. In that particular societal climate, writers like Hendrik Tollens and Cornelis Loots contributed to a discourse of reconciliation, taking an impartial attitude towards conflicts between various groups from the national past, which furthered national unity (Maas 2007, 2).

People read a multitude of travelogues and many foreign books in translation. In positive contemporary critiques, it was pointed out that translations could contribute to the development of Dutch language and culture. Translated reading material introduced useful foreign knowledge, values, and customs; it also cultivated literary judgment and taste by acquainting Dutch readers with foreign texts (Korpel 1993, 9–10). This could indicate a wish to take note of other cultures, a development that had already started in the eighteenth century. Intellectuals developed "an interest in knowing about other peoples, their manners and culture, and their 'national' character" (Dann 2006, 121). This follows the statement by Mathijsen that patriotism in literature was stimulated by making comparisons with literature from abroad (2010, 49). Still, it is more likely that books in translation were read because of there were so few original Dutch novels.

Of course, it is impossible to look into the minds of the members, but based on the purchasing habits of Dutch book clubs, their choices were rooted more in the wish to read for pleasure than in a consciously cultivated vision of cosmopolitanism or a wish to become better national citizens by learning about foreign values or customs. In short, people chose not to read patriotic reading matter for pleasure, or such materials were simply too expensive.

Conclusion

Dutch book clubs did not need reading matter with patriotic themes to contribute to national unity. The clubs were organized in a way that furthered social cohesion and, by extension, sentiments of social and national unity among the Dutch. The contribution of book clubs to the national cause can primarily be found in the democratic behaviour within these voluntary organizations. A statement by a member of the book club of Oude Bildtzijl illustrates this point well: "the general meeting was the main point, the reading was of secondary importance" (Norder 1991, 45). Early democratic ideals contributed to social consensus. Collective choices for reading material were devoid of blatantly patriotic themes; care was taken to avoid conflicts and debates. All of this reflected the ideals of the book clubs in the United Kingdom of the Netherlands.

So it is not surprising that purchasing habits did not exhibit a clear preference for explicit ideologies or any convincing interest in national or patriotic themes. Although certain aspects of what was believed to be the typical, ideal patriot can surely be detected in the reading matter, it is unwarranted to characterize this as a choice originating from a conscious decision born from national or patriotic sentiments. By steering clear of explicit themes in their choice of reading matter, the members of Dutch book clubs demonstrated the widely shared discourse of reconciliation, from a collective desire for harmony and peace. Paradoxically, the choice to avoid national themes turned out to be a unifying one.

Notes

1 This is all the archival material remaining of book clubs in that period.
2 The concept is explained in further detail by Hoffmann (2003; 2006).
3 The inquiry was studied in P.Th.F.M. Boekholt and J. van der Kooi, eds., *Spiegel van Groningen: Over de schoolmeesterrapporten van 1828* (Assen: Van Gorcum, 1996).
4 Similar conclusions were drawn by Van Zonneveld (1983).
5 It has not been possible, however, to identify whether such a topic ran through more reading matter in a more or less concealed way.

References

Aerts, Remieg. 1999. "Een staat in verbouwing: Van republiek naar constitutioneel koninkrijk, 1780–1848" [A Nation in Development: From Republic to Constitutional Monarchy]. In *Land van kleine gebaren: Een politieke geschiedenis van Nederland 1780–1990, [Country of Little Gestures: A Political History of Netherlands 1780–1990]*, edited by Remieg Aerts and Henk te Velde, 11–95. Nijmegen: SUN.
———. 2010. "Civil Society or Democracy? A Dutch Paradox." *BMGN: The Low Countries Historical Review* 125(2–3): 209–36.
Anderson, Benedict. [1983]2006. *Imagined Communities: Reflections on the Origins and Spread of Nationalism*. London: Verso.
Bank, Jan, Th.M. 1990. *Het roemrijk vaderland: Cultureel nationalisme in Nederland in de negentiende eeuw. [The Glorious Fatherland: Cultural Nationalism in the Netherlands in the Nineteenth Century]*. 's-Gravenhage: SDU.
Brouwer, Han. 1995. "Lezen en schrijven in de provincie. De boeken van Zwolse boekverkopers 1777–1849" [Reading and Writing in the Province: The Books of Zwolle Booksellers 1777–1849]. PhD diss., Utrecht University.
Buijnsters, P.J. 1984. *Nederlandse literatuur van de achttiende eeuw: Veertien verkenningen. [Dutch Literature of the Eighteenth Century: Fourteen Explorations]*. Utrecht: HES and De Graaf.
Dann, Otto. 2006. "The Invention of National Languages." In *Unity and Diversity in European Culture c. 1800*, edited by Tim Blanning and Hagen Schulze, 121–33. Oxford: Oxford University Press.
Dongelmans, B.P.M. 1990. "Over intekenaren, kopers en lezers: Een zoektocht naar het Leesgezelschap te Nieuwenhuis" [About Subscribers, Buyers and Readers: A Search for the Book Club of Nieuwenhuis]. *De Negentiende Eeuw* 14(2–3): 189–204.
Franken, A.F. 1995. "'Liefde voor waarheid en deugd'. Een leesgezelschap te IJzendijke, 1807–1864" [Love of Truth and Virtue: A Book Club in IJzendijke, 1807–1864]. In *Bijdragen tot de geschiedenis van West-Zeeuws-Vlaanderen [Contributions to the History of West-Zeeuws-Vlaanderen]* 23: 113–32.
Habermas, Jürgen. 1989. *The Structural Transformation of the Public Sphere: An Inquiry into a Category of Bourgeois Society*. Cambridge: MIT Press.
Heilbron, Johan. 1995. "Nederlandse vertalingen wereldwijd. Kleine landen en culturele mondialisering" [Dutch Translations Worldwide: Small Countries and Cultural Globalization]. In *Waarin een klein land. Nederlandse cultuur in*

internationaal verband [*In Which a Small Country: Dutch Culture in International Contexts*], edited by Johan Heilbron, Wouter de Nooy, and Wilma Tichelaar, 206–52. Amsterdam: Prometheus.

Hoffmann, Stefan-Ludwig. 2003. *Geselligkeit und Demokratie: Vereine und zivile Gesellschaft im transnationalen Vergleich 1750–1914* [*Conviviality and Democracy: Civil Society Organizations and the Transnational Comparison 1750–1914*]. Göttingen: Vanderhoeck and Ruprecht.

———. 2006. *Civil Society, 1750–1914*. Basingstoke: Palgrave Macmillan.

Hroch, Miroslav. 1996. "From National Movement to the Fully-Formed Nation: The Nation-Building Process in Europe." In *Mapping the Nation*, edited by Gopal Balakrishnan, 78–97. London and New York: Verso.

Janse, Maartje. 2008. "Towards a History of Civil Society." *De Negentiende Eeuw* 32(2): 104–29.

Jansen, D.W.K. 1988. "Niet velen, maar veel: Onderzoek naar het aantal leesgezelschappen in Nederland, 1781–1850" [Not Many, but Much: Survey of the Number of Book Clubs in the Netherlands, 1781–1850]. PhD diss., Utrecht University.

Jansen, Dick. 1990. "Uitgerekend op intekening: De kwantitatieve ontwikkeling van het leesgezelschap in Nederland, 1781–1850." [Exclusively on Subscription: Quantitative Development of the Book Clubs in Netherlands, 1781–1850]. *De Negentiende Eeuw* 14: 181–88.

Jensen, Lotte. 2008. *De verheerlijking van het verleden: Helden, literatuur en natievorming in de negentiende eeuw* [*The Glorification of the Past: Heroes, Literature, and the Development of the Nation in the Nineteenth Century*]. Nijmegen: Vantilt.

———. 2011. "Wereldburgerschap als verzetsdaad: Kosmopolitisme en patriottisme bij Jan Frederik Helmers" [Global Citizenship as an Act of Resistance: Cosmopolitanism and Patriotism with Jan Frederik Helmers]. *De Negentiende Eeuw* 35(1–2): 59–72.

Johannes, G.J. 1997. *De lof der aalbessen: Over (Noord-)Nederlandse literatuurtheorie, literatuur en de consequenties van kleinschaligheid 1770–1830* [*In Praise of Red Currants: About (Northern) Dutch Literary Theory, Literature and the Consequences of Small Scale 1770–1830*]. Den Haag: Sdu Uitgevers.

Kloek, J.J., and W.W. Mijnhardt. 1988. *Leescultuur in Middelburg aan het begin van de negentiende eeuw* [*Reading Culture in Middelburg at the Beginning of the Nineteenth Century*]. Middelburg: Zeeuwse Bibliotheek.

Korpel, Luc. 1993. *In Nederduitsch gewaad. Nederlandse beschouwingen over vertalen 1760–1820* [*In Nederdutch Robes: Dutch Reflections on Translation 1760–1820*]. Den Haag: Stichting Bibliographia Neerlandica.

Krol, Ellen. 1997. "De smaak der natie. Opvattingen over huiselijkheid in de Noord-Nederlandse poëzie van 1800 tot 1840" [*The Taste of the Nation: Conceptions of Domesticity in the Northern Dutch Poetry from 1800 to 1840*]. PhD diss., University of Amsterdam.

Leerssen, Joep. 2003. *Nationaal denken in Europe. Een cultuurhistorische schets* [*National Thought in Europe: A Cultural-Historical Sketch*]. Amsterdam: Amsterdam University Press.

———. 2006. *De bronnen van het vaderland. Taal, literatuur en de afbakening van Nederland 1806–1890.* [*The Sources of the Homeland: Language, Literature, and the Demarcation of the Netherlands 1806–1890*]. Nijmegen: Vantilt.

Lok, Matthijs and Natalie Scholz. 2012. "The Return of the Loving Father: Masculinity, Legitimacy, and the French and Dutch Restoration Monarchies (1813–1815)." *BMGN: Low Countries Historical Review* 127(1): 19–44.

Lubbers, Arnold. 2010. "Lezen in Leens tussen 1815 en 1830: Over boeken en hun lezers tussen verlichting en vaderlandsliefde" [Reading in Leens between 1815 and 1830: About Books and Their Readers between Enlightenment and Patriotism]. *De Boekenwereld* 26 (5): 284–98.

Maas, Beyke. 2007. "'Gedeeltelijke flaauwheid & gedeeltelijke scheuring': Literatuur als arena van concurrende idealen: het geval Jacob van Lennep" [Partially Embarassment and Partially Rupture: Literature as an Arena of Competing Ideals: The Case of Jacob van Lennep]." *Neerlandistiek.nl* 7(10d). http://www.meertens.knaw.nl/neerlandistiek

Mathijsen, Marita. 2010. "De paradox van het internationale nationalisme in Nederland 1830–1840 [The Paradox of International Nationalism in the Netherlands 1830–1840]." In *Naties in een spanningsveld. Tegenstrijdige bewegingen in de identiteitsvorming in negentiende-eeuws Vlaanderen en Nederland* [*Nations in Tension: Conflicting Movements on Identity Formation in Nineteenth-Century Flanders and the Netherlands*], edited by Nele Bemong, Mary Kemperink, Marita Mathijsen, and Tom Sintobin, 49–64. Hilversum: Uitgeverij Verloren.

Mijnhardt, W.W. 1988. *Tot Heil van 't Menschdom. Culturele genootschappen in Nederland, 1750–1815* [*For the Good of Humanity: Cultural Societies in the Netherlands 1750–1815*]. Amsterdam: Rodopi.

Moretti, Franco. 1999. *Atlas of the European Novel 1800–1900*. London and New York: Verso.

Norder, Maart. 1991. *Het leesgezelschap "Ledige uren nuttig besteed" 1792–1992.* [*The Book Club "Idle Hours Well Spent" 1792–1992*]. Oude Bildtzijl: [unknown publisher].

Petiet, Francien. 2009. "'Ieder mensch toch is verplicht om zijn vaderland lief te hebben.' Het streven naar nationaal geluk in de eerste decennia van de negentiende eeuw" ["'Every Man Is Still Obliged to Love His Country': The Pursuit of National Happiness in the First Decades of the Nineteenth Century]." In *Geluk in de negentiende eeuw* [*Happiness in the Nineteenth Century*]. Amsterdam: Bakker.

———. 2011. "'Een voldingend bewijs van ware vaderlandsliefde.' De creatie van literair erfgoed in Nederland, 1797–1845 ["A Conclusive Proof of True Patriotism": The Creation of a Literary Heritage in the Netherlands, 1797–1845]." PhD diss., University of Amsterdam.

Rock, Jan. 2010. "Papieren monumenten. Over diepe breuken en lange lijnen in de geschiedenis van tekstedities in de Nederlanden 1591–1863" [Paper Monuments: Over Deep Fractures and Long Lines in the History of Text Editions in the Netherlands 1591–1863]." PhD diss., University of Amsterdam.

van Sas, N.C.F. 2005a. "De metamorfose van Nederland" [The Metamorphosis of the Netherlands]. In *De metamorfose van Nederland. Van oude orde naar moderniteit 1750–1900* [*The Metamorphosis of the Netherlands: From Old Order to Modernity 1750–1900*]. Amsterdam: Amsterdam University Press.

———. 2005b. "Nederland. Een historisch fenomeen" [The Netherlands: A Historical Phenomenon]. In *De metamorfose van Nederland. Van oude orde naar moderniteit 1750–1900* [*The Metamorphosis of the Netherlands: From Old Order to Modernity 1750–1900*], 41–65. Amsterdam: Amsterdam University Press.

Streng, Toos. 2011. "Een kwestie van vraag en aanbod. Lezers en kopers van romans in Nederland, 1790–1899" [A Question of Supply and Demand: Readers and Buyers of Novels in the Netherlands, 1790–1899]." *Jaarboek voor Nederlandse Boekgeschiedenis* [*Yearbook for Dutch Book History*] 18: 69–96.

Tresoar Frisian Historical and Literary Centre. [Copies of testaments, genealogical notes, notes concerning and member list of the book club *Idle Hours Usefully Spent* in Oude Bildtzijl]. Collection H. Sannes (342–13, 20).

de Vries, Boudien. 1989. "Een eeuw vol gezelligheid: Verenigingsleven in Nederland, 1800–1900" [A Century Full of Fun: Social Organizations in the Netherlands, 1800-1900]. *Documentatieblad voor de Nederlandse kerkgeschiedenis na 1800* [*Bulletin of Documentation for the Dutch Church History after 1800*] 28(63): 16–29.

———. 2006. "Voluntary Societies in the Netherlands, 1750–1900." In *Civil Society, Associations, and Urban Places: Class, Nation, and Culture in Nineteenth-Century Europe*, edited by Boudien de Vries, Graeme Morton, and R.J. Morris, 179–83. Aldershot: Ashgate.

———. 2007. "Lezende burgers. Cultuuridealen en leespraktijk in burgerlijke kringen in de negentiende eeuw" [Reading Citizens: Cultural Ideals and Reading Practices in Bourgeois Circles in the Nineteenth Century]." *Groniek* 40: 39–64.

Weichlein, Siegfried. 2006. "Cosmopolitanism, Patriotism, Nationalism." In *Unity and Diversity in European Culture c. 1800*, edited by Tim Blanning and Hagen Schulze, 77–99. Oxford: Oxford University Press.

van Zanten, Joeren. 2004. *Schielijk, Winzucht, Zwaarhoofd en Bedaard: Politieke discussie en oppositievorming 1813–1840* [*Political Debate and Opposition Formation 1813–1840*]. Amsterdam: Wereldbibliotheek.

van Zonneveld, Peter. 1983. "Het leesgezelschap Miscens Utile Dulci" [The Book Club Miscens Utile Dulci]. In *Boeken verzamelen. Opstellen aangeboden aan Mr J.R. de Groot bij zijn afscheid als bibliothecaris der Rijksuniversiteit te Leiden* [*Collecting Books: Drafts Offered to Mr J.R. de Groot at His Retirement as Librarian of the University of Leiden*], edited by J.A.A.M. Biemans et al., 345–56. Leiden: Bibliotheek der Rijksuniversiteit Leiden.

"Crazy Thirst for Knowledge"
Chinese Readers and the 1980s "Book Series Fever"

Shih-Wen Sue Chen

22

In 2009, the Chinese Communist Party (CCP) organized a series of events to celebrate sixty years of the People's Republic of China. Amidst the numerous commemorative activities, surveys were conducted to compile a list of the six hundred most influential books over the past sixty years. The three hundred most influential books in the thirty years since "reform and opening up" had been announced the previous year *(Zhongguo tushu shangbao* 2009). Reading has always been an important part of Chinese culture, but during the rule of Mao Zedong, especially during the Cultural Revolution (1966–76), most intellectual and cultural activities had been suppressed and the majority of Chinese people had had little access to reading material other than Mao's *Little Red Book*.

Then in 1979, the influential monthly journal *Dushu* (*Reading*) published a seminal article titled "No Forbidden Zones in Reading," which marked a turning point for reading in China. The author, Li Honglin, who was working at the time for the Central Propaganda Department of the CCP, advocated that readers should have freedom to choose what they want to read and urged that previously censored books be made available. The publishing sector witnessed considerable growth after 1980, when CCP General Secretary Hu Yaobang urged publishers to "make more books, and make good books" (*duo chu shu, chu hao shu*). Interested in new thoughts, new perspectives, new disciplines, and new knowledge, Chinese readers turned to texts other than the works of Mao, Marx, Engels, Stalin, and Lenin.[1] It was no exaggeration to use the term "crazy reading" to describe the reading phenomenon of the 1980s, noted Peking University's Wang Zizhou (in Zhao and Xiao 1986, 3). In this chapter, I examine one particular cultural phenomenon during that decade: the "book series fever" (*congshu re*) of the mid-1980s, during which more than 1,500 book series were published within the short space of three years (Fang, Teng, and Chen 1988).

At the end of the 1980s, Chen Sha claimed that the book series fever had been a direct result of the breakdown of cultural monopoly and conservatism after the end of the Cultural Revolution. He urged the writing of a "developmental history of the 1980s book series craze" (Fang, Chen and Yu 1988). That history has so far failed to materialize, though a few English-language studies have touched on the book series fever. But those studies have focused on the impact of the transformation of publishing on intellectual audiences (see for example, Lee 2009; Chen and Jin 1997, 125). *Consuming Literature*, Shuyu Kong's notable work on recent Chinese publishing history, concerns bestsellers of the 1990s (Kong 2005) and mentions the book series fever only in passing. This chapter fills the gap in the research by asking the following questions: What was the appeal of these book series? Under what circumstances were they being read? What did readers feel they learned from the books? Before addressing these questions, I provide some background information on the publishing industry in China and attitudes towards reading in the 1980s. I then focus on the emergence of book series in the mid-1980s. Using sources such as blog entries, personal interviews, memoirs, correspondence columns, and newspaper opinion pieces, I examine the experiences of book series readers, with a focus on readers of the popular Fifty Cent Series (*wujiao congshu*) published by the Shanghai Culture Publishing House. Finally, I ask why many readers have fond memories of the book series of the 1980s. I argue that Chinese readers over a certain age, disillusioned with today's Chinese consumer culture, have constructed idealized narratives of their reading experiences in the 1980s. Their wistful longing for a more innocent past serves as a critique of the present.

Publishing and Reading in the 1980s

In May 1978 the China National Publishing Administration (CNPA, *Guojia chubanju*) reprinted thirty-five literary classics (both Chinese and foreign), with an initial print run of 15 million. But even with this, the demand for books far surpassed the supply, resulting in a book shortage in the early 1980s known as *shuhuang* or "book drought" (*Guoren* 2010). Many sources on reading during this time describe readers trying to satisfy a hunger or thirst after an era of intellectual drought or famine. For example, according to *Southern Weekend*, this was a decade when Chinese readers "eagerly drank Western milk" (He 2000). They were willing to read any book they could obtain because they had been deprived for so long. Netizen Senlin shuiche (Forest Waterwheel) describes his reading during the 1980s as "*hulun tunzao*" (eating the date whole). Faced with a torrent of new books, he swallowed the information in them very quickly without digesting and analyzing it (in "*Wo jioushi*" 2011). Another writer paints an image of the 1980s reader as a "greedy glutton" who felt exhausted from too much eating (Xiao, n.d.). As

Zhang Yiwu puts it, "at that time, we were enthusiastic about reading and our discussions could replace our meals" (in Hou 2011). They were so engrossed in their discussions of reading that they forgot to eat. Hunger for knowledge took priority over physical hunger. These are just a few examples among the various descriptions of 1980s reading as "consuming."

According to the poet Bei Dao, the mid-1980s "was a very special epoch in China, commercialism had not yet started, people were enthusiastic about knowledge" (in Lee 2009, 194). Voracious readers were willing to queue for hours in front of bookstores to obtain reading material and readily sacrificed money allocated to meals in order to buy books. Newly opened bookstores such as the Shanghai BookMart were welcoming an average of 15,000 customers a day. Long queues were common along Fuzhou Road and other streets in the Shanghai book district. According to literary scholar Chen Pingyuan, he lined up with many others in front of a bookstore at midnight to purchase a Chinese translation of *Anna Karenina* ("*Guoren*" 2010). Scholar Chen Dezhong remembers that during his sophomore year at university, he spent the 100 yuan he had received from donating blood on books rather than on extra food to supplement his diet (Zhuang 2010). For readers like Wang Luxiang, physical nourishment was not as important as "spiritual nutrients" that fed the soul and enhanced one's spiritual life (*Tiantian New News* 2009). At the 1986 Beijing Book Fair, Dong Xiuyu, former chief editor of SDX Publishing (Beijing), was deeply touched when two girls used their lunch money to buy books at the SDX stall that was located at the end of the room. As she later proclaimed, this was *fengkuang de zhishi xuqiu de shinian*, "the decade of crazy thirst for knowledge" ("*Renwen*" 2008).

Those who could not afford books relied on libraries. Chen Dezhong recalls happily spending most of his university days in the new Beijing Library (in Zhuang 2010). Many library borrowers charged those who were unable to apply for a library card for the privilege of reading books they had checked out. These library books were passed from hand to hand so often that they became known as "flying books" (*feishu*) because they were rarely returned. The library's patron did not worry about late returns, for his or her sub-borrowers paid more than enough fees to cover the fines (Link 2000, 240).

The Emergence of Book Series

For most of the 1980s, the CNPA monitored and regulated publications. It was also responsible for the Xinhua bookstore distribution network and the Publishers Association of China. After late 1983, state control over publishing began to loosen and publishing houses had more freedom to produce books on a wider range of topics. Regulations regarding book distribution became less stringent, and the state-owned Xinhua bookstores faced increasing competition from private booksellers. By 1988, nearly two-thirds of the book market was controlled by private and collective stores; compare this to 1979, when 95 percent of the market was dominated by Xinhua bookstores.[2]

Facing increased competition and financial strain after the CNPA withdrew subsidies and increased taxes, publishing houses started paying more attention to the tastes and preferences of the reading public (Chen 1992). They began producing book series (usually selected according to genre, theme, or target audience) in an effort to generate more profits by attracting loyal readers. Book series had been popular even during the Republican era (1912–49) because they could be produced more quickly. From the publishers' point of view, it was easier to issue books than magazines because it was more difficult to obtain permission to establish a new periodical at a time when censorship was still an important factor. Books in series could be released more quickly, and readers were more likely to buy new titles because they had read previous ones in the collection. Doing so provided them with a sense of continuity and completeness (Shiao 2010, 220).

Because profits could be quite high for a successful book series (Keyser 2003, 124), editors often copied from other texts and sent publishers works that were not carefully scrutinized or polished, as Dingxin Zhao discovered during interviews with some editors who were active in the 1980s:

> The so-called book series selects a set of related topics. The topics should be attractive and should look new: such as the arts of love, the secret of life, or how to reduce suffering. Then you find a publisher. When they agree to publish the series, you start to organize people to write it ... [The writing] is actually copying the content from other books. It is getting a number of books from the library and lifting the content. Some people do not even bother to hand copy. They just make Xerox copies, cut them down, and connect them. It goes to the publisher after that. (in Zhao 2001, 65)

However, not all editors were so focused on making money that they sacrificed quality for quantity. An editor from the Shanghai-based Academia Press (*Xuelin*) remarked, "we expect to lose money and are prepared for failure, but as long as half of the books in the Young Scholars book series [*Qingnian xuezhe congshu*] can be circulated, it means that we greatly succeeded. The future of academia lies in young scholars, so the publishing industry is responsible for helping them" (Dong 1986, 44).[3]

Academic Book Series

The restoration of the college entrance examination system in 1977 and the social demand for an educated workforce meant that in the early 1980s, youth were mostly reading to achieve academic success so that they would be deemed employable (Zhou 1987). They were imbued with the idea that China's future rested on patriotic citizens who were able to acquire knowledge of the world and learn how to help their country become a "fully developed civilization" among the nations. Books had a vital role to play in this process of education and modernization. Therefore, people did not read merely for pleasure; there was often a more serious motivation for reading.

Eager to pursue knowledge previously inaccessible to the general public, readers bought books in academic book series and attempted to devour them as quickly as possible without pondering whether they fully comprehended the content (Wang 2003). They read with urgency because they felt they had missed so much due to the "Ten Years of Chaos" (the Cultural Revolution). Many of the books they read were translations because in Deng Xiaoping's speech to the Fourth Congress of Writers and Artists in 1979, he had urged writers to modernize by learning from the West. There was no time to properly digest books; people "felt as if overnight, academia and the publishing industry introduced more than 200 years of Western aesthetics and literary and artistic thought into China" (Xiao, n.d.).

One of the earliest academic series was the *Chinese Translations of Academic Masterpieces* series (*Hanyi shijie xueshu mingzhu congshu*), introduced in 1982 on the eve of the eighty-fifth anniversary of the prominent Commercial Press, which invested a great deal in this publishing venture. This series was its response to the CCP's call to "bring order out of chaos" (*boluan fanzheng*). Editor Chen Yuan planned the series carefully with the long-term goal of translating a complete set of key foreign works in the fields of philosophy and social sciences (excluding Marxist works) (Xie and Ding 2008). Professor Chen Xiaoming, a well-known figure among China's new generation of scholars, asserts that his generation relied on the timely resources published in this series "as the foundation of our academic life." Though only twenty-one years old at the time, he was "gnawing on Hegel, Kant, and Fichte" (Chen 2010). Ben Gu, Director of the Foreign Acquisitions and Cataloguing Department of the National Library of China, recalls that during college, he lived frugally in order to buy books in the *Chinese Translations of Academic Masterpieces* series. His favourite genre was philosophy. Gu writes that "although I did not fully understand all that I read, these books laid a solid foundation for my future work" (Gu 2009). Later, he was not only a reader of Commercial Press books but also a translator for the publishing house.

Although the *Chinese Translations of Academic Masterpieces* series was an important one, most critics posit that "book series fever" began when the Sichuan People's Publishing House launched the *Towards the Future* (TF) series (*zouxiang weilai*) in 1984 (Keyser 2003). Jin Guantao, one of the editors, claims that it presented "an attractive alternative to bland, tasteless official fare. Students and intellectuals woke up to the fact that ideas could be sweet, stimulating and, what was really tantalizing, something plastic and responsive to individual creative energy, something belonging to themselves." This series had a great impact on Chinese society; it also sparked the "culture fever," "aesthetics fever," and "new methodology fever" (Chen and Jin 1997, 125).

The TF series was the forerunner of similar-themed series, edited mostly by enthusiastic young men in their early thirties, such as the *Culture: China and the World* (*Wenhua: Zhongguo yu shijie*) series, the *Three Aspects* (*Sange mianxiang*) series, and the *Tradition and Change* (*Chuantong yu bianqe*) series (Wang 2003). All of these aimed to provide an emporium of knowledge on Western philosophy, history, literary theory, and other disciplines. Some books in the series were direct translations, but most were original Chinese texts heavily influenced by foreign works (Wang 2003).

Xie Yong, an avid reader of the TF series who "bought almost every book in the series [he] came across," fondly recalls:

> Borrowing a popular saying, it was a feast of ideas ... Looking back, I cannot help but marvel at the boldness of the Editorial Board of the TF series for their attempts at encyclopedic coverage. They only had one purpose in mind when publishing these books that crossed disciplines and time: to help enlighten people, to promote the acceptance of universal values, and to push towards the modernization. Today's academically-successful middle-aged intellectuals more or less have read several books in this series. (Xie and Ding 2008)

These intellectuals read academic book series because they believed China needed to catch up with the rest of the world after the devastation of the Cultural Revolution and the way to do that was through reading and learning from Western modernization theories.

Nationwide, salons and reading groups were formed by intellectuals and students, who gathered to discuss aesthetics, modernity, existentialism, and various philosophical questions raised by the works of Michel Foucault, Roland Barthes, Fernand Braudel, the Russian formalists, and other writers introduced during the 1980s. Academic book series aimed to provide a systematic introduction to these foreign concepts, but readers did not necessarily approach the books methodically. Reading was frequently a rushed affair, and overly keen readers faced the challenge of trying to stay afloat in the torrent of information (Xiao n.d.).

Popular Series: *Fifty Cent* Series

The Shanghai Culture Publishing House's *Fifty Cent* series (*Wujiao congshu*), edited by He Chengwei under the slogan "little books, big business," was launched on 22 July 1986. It was targeted at mid- to lower-level readers who needed readable, affordable books of general knowledge. There were already many book series on the market at that time, but many were read only by more highly educated people who felt confident in engaging with academic language and specialized topics. He Chengwei commented that "during the early reform period, people were ignorant and needed to know what the world was like and how to live in it" (in Wu 2008). He believed that the *Fifty Cent* Series could cater to this need. The popularity of the series can be observed in a television news report documenting the day *Wujiao congshu* first appeared on the shelves of bookstores in Shanghai: huge crowds of customers grabbed as many books as they could without even stopping to read the titles *(Xingjing Bao* 2008). He Chengwei notes that during the initial "tryout sales," more than 2,000 books were purchased in two hours. In Shanghai alone, 28,000-plus books in the series were sold within the first ten days (*Xingjing Bao* 2008). By March 1988, it was being reported that 30 million copies of the *Fifty Cent* Series had already been printed.

"*Wujiao*" in the series title conveyed several meanings. Besides identifying the price of the books, it referred to the five categories of books (*wu* means five) that were being published in the series: literature, art, life, athletics, and entertainment. Five descriptions were attached to the series: "most new, most beautiful, most meaningful, most entertaining, and most attractive." These were later replaced with the following: "quality," "affordability" and "suitable for both refined and popular tastes." The editor wanted readers to feel that they were getting value for money. To that end, the Shanghai Culture Publishing House had improved its printing technology so that it could include higher-quality photographs in the books. Some titles, such as *Best of World Stamps*, featured up to one hundred photos. The series won the New National Bestsellers Award several times.

What distinguished the *Fifty Cent* series from other popular book series is that the publisher heavily promoted it. It had a close relationship with bookstores, and this helped spark readers' interest in the books. The series was so popular that the publisher issued a "best of" selection from them based on readers' recommendations and votes. This suggests that readers had a certain influence on editorial policies. Reader participation may well have improved sales.[4]

Appealing Factors

The *Fifty Cent* series has been described as "delicious cultural fast food" ("*Shanghai Shuzhan*" 2008). Readers found the books' low prices attractive. They were also concise enough to read quickly and small enough (130 mm by 184 mm) to carry easily. Because the books cost only fifty cents (compared to the average price of ninety-nine cents), even children could afford them out of their pocket money.[5] They ranged in length from 40,000 to 100,000 words (100 to 120 pages). Blogger Da Huzi (2009) finished reading *Discovering the Origins of Chinese Surnames* (*Zhongguo xingshi xungen*) in two days, as evidenced by the inscription on the first page of his book: "October 22–23, 1987, read."

According to Li Zhong (2011), "each of the books in the Fifty Cent Series is a thin booklet – short and pithy, with rich subject matter covering the humanities and history, astronomy, geography, as well as many topics closely related to people's lives." Books in the series ranged from abridged translations of Dale Carnegie's self-help manuals, to Doris Lessing's novels, to horror novels and thrillers such as *666* and *The Tower*, to the Guinness Book of World Records, to explorations of ghosts and death and a guide to interpreting body language. This eclectic variety of titles is not surprising, considering that books focusing on friendship, career, love, marriage, and practical problems were sought after in the 1980s.[6] Many of the books offered practical advice for everyday life – for example, how to cook well, how to dress well, and even how to grow taller. The 86,000-word *Family Kitchen Consultant* (1986) is one of blogger Kaoshan hanxue's favourite books. She has been using it for the past twenty years and declares that the book "has influenced me greatly and enhanced my life."[7] She claims that although this "little book is only 115 pages long, it is rich in content, informative, and very suitable for everyday common readers ... It has changed my habits, taught me many truths in life. It has affected me for 20 years, and will continue to do so in the future" (Kaoshan hanxue 2007). There are many glossy cookbooks available on the current book market, but she has stayed loyal to this book, which she bought on a summer day when she took her son out for a walk.

Even though the books in the series were not closely related thematically, readers found them collectable. Over the years, netizen Jimmy has accumulated more than one hundred books from the *Fifty Cent* Series on his bookshelf, ready for his children to enjoy when they are old enough to read them (in *"Wo jioushi"* 2011). Mei Chengding loved the *Fifty Cent* books because besides being cheap, they contained a great deal of information on various subjects. Whenever he came across a book in the series, he would buy it. He once purchased six books at once when he was out of town on business, cherishing them as precious treasures (Mei 2012). By 1988, he had already collected more than twenty volumes.

Many of the readers of this series were in primary school or high school when they first discovered them. A Gu, a member of the *Douban Book* website (similar to *Goodreads*), claims that he borrowed *49 Great Mysteries of the World* (*Shijie 49 dami*) from his classmate many times when he was in grade five or six. That book, which covers topics such as the Loch Ness Monster, UFOs, and aliens, influenced him so much that he later became a translator of science fiction (A Gu 2013). Netizen Senlin shuiche became interested in books when he was in high school and often hovered around discount bookstores and bookstalls that sold second-hand books. He acquired two dozen *Fifty Cent* series books when he was thirteen or fourteen years old. Titles in his collection include *49 Great Mysteries of the World*, *Discovering the Psychological Aspect of Human Habits* (*Renlei xiguan xinli tansuo*), *Foreign Celebrities and Detectives* (*Waiguo mingren yu tan'an*), *Ghost Culture* (*Gui wenhua*), and *Modern Family 184* (*Xiandai jiating 184*). Looking over these books again, he wonders why he was interested in Miriam Stoppard's *50 Plus Lifeguide* (*Nianguo wushi bi du*) as a teenager (*"Wo jioushi"* 2011). The fact that he bought the book attests to the success of the *Fifty Cent* series in impressing on readers a sense of collectability. It also demonstrates that young readers purchase books not originally targeted at their age group. Perhaps he was not as picky because he had fewer books to choose from at the time.

Li Zhong asserts that he began collecting books in the series when he was in high school: "In 1986, I was a high school student especially interested in collecting stamps and reading. The first time I saw *Best of World Stamps* (*Shijie youpiao zhi zui*) in a bookstore I could not put it down and bought it immediately. I still have it in my collection" (Li 2011). The *Fifty Cent* series was also the first set of books that Li bought with his wages after he graduated from university. He really liked *Contemporary Love Poems from Taiwan* (*Taiwan dangdai aiqing shixuan*), *Humour Power, The Best of Foreign Comics* (*Waiguo manhua jingxuan*), and *How to Develop the Right Hemisphere of Your Brain* (*Kaifa ren de youban nao*), but the book that influenced him most was Cao Minghua's *A Female University Student's Notes* (*Yige nu daxuesheng de shouji*). According to Li, "I read [it] over and over at least a dozen times.

In particular, I was deeply influenced by her definition of happiness written in the form of a formula: 'happiness = what you have / what you desire'" ("*Huainian yanshan*" 2007).

Prior to the Reform period (1978–), at a time when collective interests were supposed to take precedence over individual self-interest, the individual was expected to be subordinate to family, society, and nation, to be part of the masses, and to sacrifice for others (Schell 2010, 79). But after the Reform era was launched, it became possible to think about achieving individual happiness, success, and wealth. With new opportunities came increasing pressures and challenges, especially after 1986, when a new regulation declared that employees would be hired by state enterprises through open competition. Cao Minghua's formula warned readers that they should not desire more than they already had because doing so would lead to discontent and unhappiness. For a high school student like Li, Cao's message reassured him that despite his uncertainty about the future, he could find happiness if he tamed his desires. Another reader named Wang Dongqing was impressed by Cao Minghua's candour and admired her straightforward way of writing. Wang states that she changed her own journal-writing style after reading *A Female University Student's Notes* (Wang 2010).

But not all readers were adoring fans of the *Fifty Cent* series. For example, a reader wrote to the editors of the *China Book Review* that his son had been shamed by his schoolmates when he unknowingly repeated several mistakes in *Most of the 80s* (*Bashi zhi zui*). Examples include the sentence "Italy's Bologna University was a 20th-century university established in 1088." The capital of Saudi Arabia was identified as Jordan, while the total number of calories for a banana was listed at a staggering 7,800 calories (Yu 1989, 188). Adults easily recognize these blatantly obvious mistakes; child readers may be misled with incorrect information.

Modes of Reading

Readers of the *Fifty Cent* series appreciated the materiality of the books as well as their contents. To illustrate how much he cherished the books, one reader wrote to *Zhonghua dushu bao* (China Reading Weekly) to recount an incident from 1988. One day a female supervisor spotted him reading *Forbidden Books in China and Abroad* (*Zhongwai jinshu*) and asked to borrow it for a day. Because he was her subordinate, he agreed reluctantly but cautioned her to take good care of the book because it was brand new. She returned it three days later in such a wretched state that it looked as if it had been subjected to the "torture of the Kuomintang [Nationalist Party]:[8] some pages were ripped while others were stuck together because rice had been dropped in between them. Remnants of her meal had stained several other pages. Devastated, he wondered how a person who did not cherish books could become a government official (Mei 2012). After this experience, he did not want to lend his books to anyone. While Mei is very protective of his books, other readers feel that books are meant to be shared. That said, not having them returned can be painful. One blogger lamented: "I often discussed my reading experiences with colleagues and shared my reviews. It is a pity that after I lent out my books they were never returned" ("*Huainian yanshan*" 2007).

Mei's story reflects the different relationships that readers have with books. Some bibliophiles treasure their books and handle them gently (sometimes with gloves); others enjoy a book fully when they fold down pages, write notes in the margins, underline passages, and read while eating or drinking without worrying whether there will be stains or other damage done to the pages, spine, or cover. For example, Xiao Ying remembers that when he got carried away during his reading in the 1980s, he would highlight numerous sections of the books he borrowed from the library. The kindly librarian, who was slightly older than his mother, would fine him 13 yuan (his monthly stipend at the university was 22 yuan per month) and then blame him for causing trouble for his mother. He would proudly respond, "If my mom knew, she would be celebrating with me" (Xiao n.d.). Similarly, a Douban Book member from Shanghai read and reread *49 Great Mysteries of the World* until the book was in tatters: "Sticky tape was used to keep the cover together and the pages were full of notes made with a ballpoint pen" (Yag 2013). For these readers, these marks were a sign that the book was loved.

Nostalgic Memories

Many readers present nostalgic narratives of reading the *Fifty Cent* series as children. For example, netizen Jimmy still occasionally flips through two books on his bedside table: Jean-Henri Fabre's *The Insect World* (*Kunchong ji*) and the *Fifty Cent* series' *Animal Vignettes* (*Dongwu xiaopin jingcui*), which contains writings by the naturalist Comte de Buffon and the novelist Jules Renard. Reading these French authors in bed on a clear night, he is "transported back to his youth when he would read while lying on the grass by the Yi River" ("*Wo jioushi*" 2011). This idyllic image of childhood reading may be idealized in retrospect, but another reader has an even stronger emotional reaction to the *Fifty Cent* series:

> When I accidentally came across this discussion thread (on the Douban Books website) on the *Fifty Cent* series, I actually cried. Back in primary school, I was often home alone because my parents were too busy working. I would sit on the floor with my back against the bookshelf and read. At that

time, my family had a complete set of the *Fifty Cent* series. The book in the series that I read and reread was *49 Great Mysteries of the World* [*Shijie 49 dami*] ... Even though twenty years have passed in the blink of an eye, I still remember the contents of the book ... All my childhood fantasies began after reading this book; it was like opening an unknown door and seeing a different world. I miss the carefree and whimsical thoughts I had as a child; it would be so nice if people never have to grow up. (Yag 2013)

Memories of childhood reading lead the reader to express a deep longing for eternal youth, a time when the worries and pressures of adulthood do not exist and there is freedom to daydream and imagine all day long. The reader (screen name Yag) characterizes the thoughts he or she had as a child as "carefree," but these memories may be selective and affected by nostalgic hindsight. Susan Stewart contends that nostalgia "wears a distinctly utopian face, a face that turns toward a future-past, a past which has only ideological reality" (1993, 23). Yag's recollection of childhood reading may be romanticized and unreliable, but the fact that he chose *49 Great Mysteries of the World* over all the other books in the series suggests that children have strong agency in choosing their reading material.

Researching the reading experience is difficult because people may have trouble remembering the exact circumstances or cannot describe the experience clearly. Examining marginalia contributes to a better understanding of the reading experience. For example, Da Huzi (2009) used marginalia to help reconstruct the day he purchased *Discovering the Origins of Chinese Surnames* (*Zhongguo xingshi xungen*), which he found lying on his brother's desk. He had forgotten when he bought the book, but the words "87.10.21 Benxi" helped him remember how it came into his possession – that year, he was involved in the construction of a power station in the small city of Benxi. He had purchased the book while waiting for the train.

Conclusion

During the global financial crisis, memories of the *Fifty Cent* series resurfaced as journalists and essayists called for the lowering of book prices. Contemporary reporters and reviewers lament the current preference of many readers for thick, luxurious coffee table books, which are characterized by plenty of white space and not much content. Strong nostalgia can be found in recent publications such as *Returning to the 1980s* (*Chongfan bashi niandai*), *1980s and I* (*Wo he bashi niandai*), and *Interviews with Artists in the Eighties* (*Bashi niandai fangtanlu*). Many look back at this decade as "full of potential and freedom," as "an age of innocence, idealism, and enthusiasm" when the "youthful enthusiasm of a whole generation was released," as a time when the cultural aspirations of the Chinese people were broadened as a result of the "open door" policy (Cheng 2009; Ma 2010; Wang 1995). In these books, waves of nostalgia can be observed throughout recollections of 1980s reading. As many of the interviewees pointed out, books were a vital component of 1980s culture, a time when a single novel could inspire multiple debates (*Tiantian New News* 2009). Books have since lost their dominance in the culture industry in China; nowadays, the Internet, films, video games, social media, and other forms of entertainment vie for people's attention. Critic Xiao Ying (n.d.) has described contemporary reading in China as "fashionable reading" (*shishang yuedu*), "a reflection of consumer culture where readers are coerced to read certain books and urged to buy marketed books." According to Xiao, contemporary readers have little choice but to read whatever is currently popular because these are the heavily marketed books fed to them through the media.

In the 1980s, reading was more of a collective phenomenon. Because not many books were available at the time, everyone seemed to be reading the same titles. As one reader put it, "hundreds of millions of people" were paying attention "to the same book at the same time" (*Tiantian New News* 2009). So it was quite easy to generate a sense of community through reading, as Zhang Lixian's comment reveals: "There was so much time for reading, and so many people to share reading experiences with. Is there anything more blessed than that? No." (Zhang 2008). There was much more time for reading during the 1980s because many in China did not have a television.

The term *"re* (fever)" denotes a short-lived trend that fades after an unusual spike in activity. So it is not surprising that the "book series fever" gradually subsided after the early 1990s. After 1992, increasing commercialization influenced the book market and bestseller lists came to dictate publishing trends. As one production editor of a Beijing publishing house told me in an interview conducted in May 2012, the first step they take when deciding on a possible translation project is to look at the Amazon bestseller list. Based on forecasted profit, they begin negotiating translation rights with the author even before they have read the whole book. Not everyone is happy about this reliance on bestseller lists. Xie Xizhang states, "I look at the bestseller list now, and only feel sad. In my opinion, it reflects the process of the degradation of the national spirit" (Xie n.d.). Similarly, blogger Xinqing Kezhan writes that "in the face of the deprivation of 'spiritual content' in the cultural market today, I really want to cry: 'Come back, Fifty Cent Series.'" He feels that a book priced at 1,000 yuan does not contain the same "nutrients or rich content as the Fifty Cent series" (in *"Huainian yanshan"* 2007).

According to Wang Luxiang, the rise in management books suggests that people are now reading mostly for utilitarian purposes. He worries that nowadays, compared to the 1980s, there are very few debates about spiritual or philosophical matters. While acknowledging that reading on the "spiritual level" still exists, he feels that "it is no longer popular among the masses" (*Tiantian New News* 2009). Anxiety about the degradation of China's national spirit in the face of crass commercialisation and commodity culture underlies these narratives of reading. The case studies of readers of academic book series and popular book series demonstrate the diversity of reading after the end of the Cultural Revolution, which was a time when people were unable to access much reading material other than the works of socialist writers and thinkers. Although they were reading the same book series, the readers approached the books with different motives and expectations. For some, it was to learn how to cook or how to collect stamps. For others, it was to obtain historical knowledge, to learn how foreigners think, or to solve the great mysteries of the world. Some wanted to emulate the lives of celebrities or heroes or to live vicariously through fictional characters' adventures and love stories.

People at the time read across a very broad spectrum, whereas many contemporary intellectuals "are biased in favor of reading books related to their discipline only" (*Tiantian New News* 2009). Reading in the 1980s is viewed through a nostalgic lens because this decade has been idealized as an era when people were less cynical, materialistic, and pragmatic. Idealistic editors and publishers of the 1980s were not so profit-driven and wanted to introduce important ideas to the reading public. They were more willing to take risks on topics that were not necessarily going to have mass appeal but that would challenge readers' thinking and perspectives. As more and more readers reflect on their reading in the 1980s, a rich repository is growing for further research into this decade, which has so far received little scholarly attention.

Notes

Research for this chapter was made possible by a post-doctoral fellowship from the Australian Centre on China in the World, the Australian National University. Travel funding to attend the "Researching the Reading Experience" conference was provided by the College of Asia and the Pacific, the Australian National University. I would like to thank the editors for their feedback on earlier versions of this paper.

1 According to statistics, in June 1979 there were 450 million remaindered copies of works by these authors in storage (Barmé 1996, 9).
2 By the late 1980s, state-owned stores totalled about 9,000 while there were 11,000 collective bookstores and more than 40,000 small, privately owned bookstores (Pei 1994, 155).
3 The Academia Press (*Xuelin*) was founded in July 1981.
4 He, Chengwei. 2012. Interview with author, 17 May.

5   After 1988, book prices rose from 50 cents to 80, 90, and then 125 cents.
6   Zhou 1987. Other series, such as the *Efficiency* series (*Xiaolu congshu*), which were translations of Japanese works published in the 1970s and early 1980s, taught readers various skills for success in the workplace. Titles included *How to Improve Your Memory*, *How to Improve Your Leadership Skills*, *How to Think Creatively*, *How to Conduct Effective Meetings*, and *How to Raise Academically Successful Children*. The *Sisters* series (*Jiemei congshu*) claimed to be the first series catering to women that "genuinely" spoke on behalf of women. This series covered topics such as cooking, interior design, mothering, health and fitness, female mind and body, female emancipation, and laws to protect women.
7   The book was written by Qian Guosheng and edited by Chen Zhongchao, with cover design by Lu Zhenwei.
8   The Kuomintang was founded by Sun Yat-sen and Song Jiaoren after the Xinhai Revolution (1911). It ruled much of China from 1928 to 1949 under the leadership of Chiang Kai-shek, who was defeated by the CCP during the Chinese Civil War.

References

A Gu. 2013. "*Fangfu kandao tongnian de zhizi* [As If Seeing My Childhood Self]," Douban Book, 26 April 26. http://book.douban.com/subject/2032711/discussion/19021882

Barmé, Geremie R. 1996. *Shades of Mao: The Posthumous Cult of the Great Leader*. New York: M.E. Sharpe.

Chen, Fang-cheng, and Guantao Jin. 1997. *From Youthful Manuscripts to River Elegy: The Chinese Popular Cultural Movement and Political Transformation 1979–1989*. Hong Kong: Chinese University Press.

Chen, Xiaoming. 2010. "*Wo de bashi niandai yuedu jiyi*" [My Memories of Reading in the 80s]. *Dushi wencui* 1. http://lnlib.vip.qikan.com/Article.aspx?titleid=dswc20100117

Chen, Yi. 1992. "Publishing in China in the Post-Mao Era: The Case of *Lady Chatterley's Lover*." *Asian Survey* 32(6): 569–70.

Cheng, Guangwei, ed. 2009. *Chongfan bashi niandai* [Returning to the 1980s]. Beijing: Beijing University Press.

Da Huzi. 2009. "*22 nian qian de yiben shu*" [A Book from 22 Years Ago]. *Hubian luanzhao – Da Huzi yingxiang shenghuo* [blog], 9 August. http://blog.sina.com.cn/s/blog_57ffb6260100e7vt.html

Dong, Re. 1986. "*Chubanjia de zhi yu xing – zan qingnian xuezhe congshu*" [In Praise of the Young Scholars Series]. *Liaowang Magazine*, 20 June.

Fang, M., Chen Sha, and Yu Y. 1988. "*Congshu re sanrentan*" [Three People's Discussion of the Book Series Fever]." *Xinhua wenzhai* 10: 202–7.

Fang, M., M. Teng, and Chen Sha. 1988. "*Congshu jieshao: jinjinian congshu chuban zongshu*" [Introduction to Book Series: A General Report on the Recent Publication of Book Series]. In *Zhongguo chuban nianjian 1988* [China Publishing Yearbook 1988], 267–71. Shangwu yinshuguan.

Gu, Ben. 2009. "The Chinese Translations of Academic Masterpieces and Me." *Ben Gu* [blog], 16 August. http://www.bengu.cn/homepage/paper/sinablog089%2820090816%29.htm

"*Guoren 30 nian yuedu bianqian shi*" [A History of Change in Chinese People's Reading in the Last 30 years]." 2010. *TechCn* [blog], 20 October. http://www.techcn.com.cn/index.php?doc-view-150070.html

He, Xiaoju. 2000. "*Cong kafuka kaishi*" [Starting with Kafka]. *Nanfang Zhoumo (Southern Weekend)*, 15 September. http://edu.sina.com.cn/critique/2000-09-15/12241.shtml

"*Huainian yanshan yehua he wujiaocongshu*" [Missing Night talks on Yan Mountain and the Fifty Cent Series]." 2007. *Xinqing kezhan* [blog], 17 June. http://blog.sina.com.cn/s/blog_4d09a9ae01000amc.html

Hou, Jie. 2011. "*Bashi niandai de dushu shenghuo: Ji'e er fengkuang de yuedu niandai*" [Reading in the 1980s: An Era of Hungry and Crazy Reading]." *Culture China Web* [blog], November 21. http://cul.china.com.cn/2011-11/21/content_4638137.htm

Kaoshan hanxue. 2007. "*Yiben yingxiang le wo 20 nian de shu*" [A Book That Has Influenced Me for 20 Years]," *Kaoshan hanxue* [blog], 10 April. http://blog.sina.com.cn/s/blog_4b2b27b301000a0c.html

Keyser, Catherine H. 2003. *Professionalizing Research in Post-Mao China: The System Reform Institute and Policy Making*. Armonk: M.E. Sharpe.

Kong, Shuyu. 2005. *Consuming Literature: Best Sellers and the Commercialization of Literary Production in Contemporary China*. Stanford: Stanford University Press.

Lee, Gregory B. 2009. *China's Lost Decade: Cultural Politics and Poetics 1978–1990*. Lyon: Tigre de Papier.

Li, Zhong. 2011. "*Wujiaocongshu zhong de jiyou wenxian buyi*" [Addendum to the Stamp Collecting Book in the Fifty Cent Series]." *Huaishuiji xianke* [blog], 7 September. http://blog.sina.com.cn/s/blog_60bc93fe0100yclt.html

Link, Perry. 2000. *The Uses of Literature: Life in the Socialist Chinese Literary System*. Princeton: Princeton University Press.

Ma, Guochuan, ed. 2010. *Wo he bashi niandai* [1980s and I]. Hong Kong: SDX Hong Kong.

Mei, Chengding. 2012. "*Ai shu, suoyi buyuan bieren lai jieshu*" [Because I love Books, I Don't Want Others to Borrow Them]." *Zhonghua dushu bao* [China Reading Weekly], 11 January. http://epaper.gmw.cn/zhdsb/html/2012-01/11/nw.D110000zhdsb_20120111_1-08.htm?div=-1

Pei, Minxin. 1994. *From Reform to Revolution: The Demise of Communism in China and the Soviet Union*. Cambridge, MA: Harvard University Press.

"*Renwen chubande xianzhuang tiaozhan yu weilai: zhongre renwenchubanjia duihua*" [The Current State of Humanities Publishing and Future Challenges: Dialogue between Chinese and Japanese Humanities Publishers]. 2008. *Shuye guancha luntan* [Book Discussion Forum] 29. http://blog.sina.com.cn/s/blog_4dd46c0101008dy4.html

Schell, Orville. 2010. *Discos and Democracy: China in the Throes of Reform*. New York: Knopf Doubleday.

"*Shanghai shuzhan huigu gaigekaifang 30 nian chuban lichen*" [Reviewing 30 Years of Publishing after Reform and Opening Up at the Shanghai Book Fair]." 2008. *China Web* [blog], 16 August. http://big5.china.com.cn/book/txt/2008-08/16/content_16241661.htm

Shiao, Ling. 2010. "Culture, Commerce, and Connections: The Inner Dynamics of New Culture Publishing in the Post-May Fourth Era." In *From Woodblocks to the Internet: Chinese Publishing and Print Culture in Transition, circa 1800 to 2008*, edited by Cynthia Brokaw and Christopher Reed, 213–48. Leiden: Brill.

Stewart, Susan. 1993. *On Longing: Narratives of the Miniature, the Gigantic, the Souvenir, the Collection*. Durham: Duke University Press.

Tiantian New News. 2009. "*Mingjia siren yuedushi: Wang Luxiang*" [Personal Reading History of Wang Luxiang], 18 August. http://book.sina.com.cn/news/a/2009-08 18/ 1745259583_3.shtml

Wang, Dongqing. 2010. "*Shu, wumaoqian yi ben*" [Fifty Cents a Book]. *Wenzibao*, 27 May. http://wenxue.news365.com.cn/12b/201006/t20100601_2723657.htm

Wang, Edward Q. 2003. "Encountering the World: China and Its Other(s) in Historical Narratives, 1949–89." *Journal of World History* 14(3): 327–58.

Wang, Shaoguang. 1995. "The Politics of Private Time: Changing Leisure Patterns in Urban China." In *Urban Spaces in Contemporary China: The Potential for Autonomy and Community in Post-Mao China*, edited by Deborah S. Davis, Richard Kraus, Barry Naughton, and Elizabeth J. Perry, 149–72. Cambridge: Cambridge University Press.

"*Wo jioushi de wujiaocongshu (wangluo ganyan ban)*" [The Fifty Cent Series I Knew (Internet Reflections Edition)]. 2011. *Wangjuan Publishing House* [blog], 22 February. http://blog.sina.com.cn/s/ blog_6431f96d0100ojr5.html

Wu, Yunbo. 2008. "*Wujiao congshu: xiaocongshu qiaodong dashichang*" [Fifty Cent Series: Little Book Series Pry Open the Big Market]. *Xinjing Bao* (*The Beijing News*), 20 September. http://www.thebeijingnews.com/culture/spzk/2008/09-20/ 008@021833.htm

Xiao, Ying. n.d. "*Dushu, xuyao yi zhong jingjie*"[Reading Requires a Certain Atmosphere]. *Jilin shen renliziyuan he shehui baozhangting* [Human Resources, Jilin Province]. http://hrss.jl.gov.cn/jgjs/jswm/201004/t20100430_712969.html

Xie, Xizhang. n.d. "*Chongdu bashi niandai de liyou*" [Reasons to Re-Read the 80s]." *Xie Xizhang* [blog]. http://blog.sina.com.cn/xiexizhang

Xie, Yong, and Ding Dong. 2008. "*Huiwang 'Congshure'*" [Looking Back and the Book Series Fever]." *China Youth Daily*, 19 October.

Yag. 2013. "*Fangfu kandao tongnian de ziji*" [As if Seeing My Childhood Self]." Douban Book, 12 September. http://book.douban.com/subject/2032711/ discussion/19021882

Yu, Hesheng. 1989. "*Weile haizi, qing bianji tongzhi ...*" [For the Sake of Our Children, Would the Comrade Editors Please ...]." *China Book Review* 1: n.p.

Zhang, Lixian. 2008. *Shankai, rang wo gechang bashi niandai* [Move Over, Let me Serenade the 80s]. Peking: People's Literature Publishing House.

Zhao, Dingxin. 2001. *The Power of Tiananmen: State-Society Relations and the 1989 Beijing Student Movement*. Chicago: University of Chicago Press.

Zhao, Lanying, and Xiao Guangen. 1986. "Shanghai 'goushure' de 'redian' zainali?" [What are the Key Features of the Shanghai Book-Buying Fever]. *Renmin ri bao* [*People's Daily*], 2 September, 3.

Zhuang, Jian. 2010. "*Zailushang – xiezai hanyi shijiexueshu mingzhu congshu chuban zhiji*" [On the Road – Written for the Publication of *hanyi shijiexueshu mingzhu congshu*]." *Guangming Daily*, 15 January. http://www.chinamedhis.com/article .asp?articleid=593

Zhongguo tushu shangbao. 2009. "*Xinzhongguo 60 nian zuijuyingxiangli de 600 benshu mingdan jiexiao*." 29 September. [The List of the 600 Most Influential Books in China over the Past 60 Years Revealed]. http://book.sina.com.cn/news/ v/2009-09-29/1155260866.shtml

Zhou, Sha. 1987. "*Shenghuo Qishilu de qishi* [What We Can Learn from the Revelation of Life Series]." *Qingnian duwu* [Youth Reading]: 53–54.

Enabling Testimonies and Producing Witnesses   23
Exploring Readers' Responses to Two Norwegian Post-Terror Blogs

Tonje Vold

On 22 July 2011, two acts of terror killed seventy-seven people in Norway. Not since the Second World War had Norwegians been attacked on such a scale on their own soil. In a country of 5 million inhabitants, practically every Norwegian knew someone who lost someone or who was present at the sites of terror that day.

The facts of the terror have been laid down by the 22 July Commission and can be summarized as follows: a thirty-seven-year-old right-winger named Anders Behring Breivik parked a car containing a bomb outside the Government Building (22.juli-kommisjonen 2012, 14). When the bomb exploded at 15:26, Breivik was on his way to the Worker's Youth League camp on the small island of Utøya. He arrived at 17:17 and, dressed as a policeman, conducted a massacre among the 600 teenagers and young adults. Shelters were few, and many tried to escape in the cold water. Though people from the mainland launched their boats to help, 69 were killed and 158 injured. The police arrived at 18:25 and arrested Breivik ten minutes later.

In the years since, the story of that day has been written in a variety of documents and literary genres, many of them focusing on the terrorist. However, the contribution made by social media users to shaping the historiography of 22 July from the survivors' and bystanders' points of view should not be overlooked. The news of the Utøya massacre was first heard through social media as the people on the island phoned home and sent text messages while hiding, while friends and relatives used Twitter and Facebook to obtain information. Because the shootings at Utøya happened off-camera, without any media present, and journalists had to respect that the eyewitnesses were young people who had been severely traumatized, there was a distinct information gap in the nation. Social media again became a major source of information. A number of blogposts were published in which the survivors told their stories. These soon spread on social media and via online newspapers to other media. Some were translated by blog readers or editors. So these stories spread throughout the world – they went, as we say, viral.

Although little research has been conducted so far, these social media texts constitute a significant archive for anyone interested in how nations respond in the immediate aftermath of a terror attack as well as in the importance of online reading. It is my overall contention that the reading/writing processes I trace are practices of producing witnesses and enabling testimony through Internet interaction. Nowadays, as terror shocks the public repeatedly, one of the most important achievements of blogs is that they require readers to distinguish the unbelievable "real" story from other news stories and from fiction. In the readers' responses we may also trace how the reading experience comes to highlight certain aspects of their identity in ways that inform us with regard to how communities are constructed in response to a national crisis. For this background, this article explores the reading experience embedded in online testimonial practices and theorizes on the reading of the survivors' blogs in the contexts of terror and trauma.

Exploring the Experiences of Reading Post-Terror Blogs

The UK Reading Experience Database defines the reading experience as "a recorded engagement with a written or printed text" (http://www.open.ac.uk/Arts/RED/experience.htm). However, what constitutes this experience and what it means for the reader is far more difficult to pinpoint. Literary critic Derek Attridge (2004) underscores the emotional and ethical components of the experience of reading: "to experience something is to encounter or undergo it, to be exposed to and be transformed by it, without necessarily registering it – or all of it – as an emotional, physical or intellectual event" (19). Blog readers' online comments document reading experiences, but such comments are typically focused on the subject matter raised by the blogger and not on reading per se. Nevertheless, comments left on a blog may bear witness to a transformation that has taken place in the reader, though the larger implications may be unclear to him or her.

When exploring comments posted on a blog, we cannot trace the reasons for posting the comments. Those comments may be empathic or polite, or they may reflect nothing more than the blogosphere's conventions; therefore, the task of establishing their authenticity is not my concern. My interest is restricted to an analysis of the messages as short texts that are part of a social context and an online dialogue. Read against theories of testimonial practices, they do reveal certain patterns of response that I find suggestive not just of the post-terror sentiments in Norway, but of online reading as a social practice in a post-terror context.

So far I have found twenty-five blog posts from the days after 22 July, written by survivors who describe what took place on the island. The stories are often quite detailed accounts of young people being shot, shot at, or killed, or of hiding, escaping, and fearing for their lives. My readings of these blog posts and especially of the responses left by online readers constitute the empirical material for this chapter.

As these bloggers are young and have provided sensitive information, it is crucial that their privacy be respected. So the direct quotations from the Utøya survivors have been drawn from two published sources: Emma Martinovic's blogpost reprinted as a book, *Lever! (Alive!)* (2011), and Prableen Kaur's memoir *Jeg er Prableen (I am Prableen)* (2011). Quotes from comments have been selected from online replies to Martinovic's and Kaur's blogposts. Kaur's blog posts generated 467 replies, and there have been 1,156 to Martinovic's. These readers posted their comments anonymously, so it is difficult to trace any of those posts back to one specific person; even so, to further protect their identities, references other than to the blog they respond to have been left out. All translations are mine.

Readers Enabling the Testimony: "For God's Sake Write"

Blogs belong to a grey zone between private and public narrative. In keeping with this liminal position, the blogging survivors vary with regard to whether they perceive their posts as personal/private (diary) or public (news story). While the blogs by Utøya survivors are public, for those who wrote the initial blogposts, the existence of readers seems not to have been a premise for writing.

Utøya survivor Emma Martinovic created a blog and wrote in her first post: "I have chosen to put up this blog, mostly in fact for my own sake. I need to have a place to write. I will write from the minute the bastard ["jævelen," literally, the devil] started shooting until the minute I was safe. I will explain painful events that can be hard to read. The pictures in my head are still unclear; things have not yet fallen in place" (2011, 7).

By contrast, Utøya survivor Prableen Kaur already had a blog. In her memoir, she describes the process of blogging about the terror on the morning of 23 July as for her own sake: "I have to 'write it off me' before I begin to forget things. I start writing. I figure out a possible opening, write it down. The fingers move by themselves. I write page by page without stopping" (2011a, 132).

Their online activities suggest they have an urgent need to express themselves. These writers conceptualize writing as something they do "for their own sake." But at the same time, the warning from Martinovic shows that she has taken into account a reader to whom she will be explaining things, for she is addressing her text to someone, an addressee, "out there." The texts are, to some extent, premised on the existence of a reader, although these writers simultaneously stress writing as a private activity.

In contrast to an imagined reader of a published article or book, this imagined community almost immediately materializes as real people listening in on their stories, replying to the blogger and commenting on what they have read. So there are two questions: Do the readers interpret the situation as private or public? And how do they see their own role in the communication process?

The blog readers become the first audience for the Utøya story. The confused references to time in Martinovic's blog post and the use of the present tense in the quote from Kaur indicate the strength of their emotions when writing and the need to make things fall in place. Speaking in the context of interviewing traumatized Holocaust survivors, trauma specialist Dori Laub presents the first listeners to the trauma story as those who are enabling the testimony:

> The emergence of the narrative which is being listened to – and heard – is … the process and the place where the cognizance, the "knowing" of the event is given birth to. The listener, therefore, is a party to the creation of knowledge *de novo*. The testimony to the trauma thus includes its hearer, who is, so to speak, the blank screen on which the event comes to be inscribed for the first time. (1992, 57)

In the case of these blogs, the face-to-face listener, witness, or therapist is substituted for online readers who, to a greater or lesser degree, then involve themselves in communication with the blogger. As a very explicit example of how readers enable the continuation of writing and witnessing and how they become inscribed in the narrative, Martinovic, after a while, sets up a question-and-answer session, in effect allowing herself to be interviewed by the readers. The background is the many similar questions the readers ask her. As she answers the questions, she reflects that "there are many things I haven't thought about before you have asked here" (2011, 35). She provides the readers with information; in turn they help her shape her story.

But the readers are not always strongly aware that they are enabling her testimony, although many are concerned about the therapeutic aspects of writing. One reader tells Kaur to "write. For god's sake write. Use the words as your ventilation." Another of Kaur's readers comments:

> I have experienced war and believe that what you need most now is a hand to hold, a shoulder to cry on, many releasing hugs and someone you can talk,

talk, and talk to – or with. Might well be others from Utøya. Accept all the help you are offered to avoid life-long psychological problems, depressions etc. Big and warm hug to all of you who survived. My heart aches at the thought of the pain and sorrow you live in now. (Kaur's blog)

This reader's strong identification with Kaur's situation is based on recognizing her as a trauma victim. This commenter provides advice based on her own experiences. She stresses the importance of personal communication and of putting experiences into words, without considering either her own role as a reader in a social setting or whether blogging might also do Kaur some good.

Kaur seems to have positioned herself as a witness, in that her motivation for writing is to document the events, yet she also underscores her private reasons for writing. The need to remember may seem paradoxical, given what she has just gone through, but Kaur's imagined reader also includes herself, hence she narrates her story as both a private and a public writer.

In these blogs, self-narration is being conducted through a dialogue in which stories are constructed as both private confessions and testimonies (which might be used for private reasons). The online readers are contributing both to a therapeutic narration for a personal recovery process, and to a story of national significance that must not be forgotten. In the process, the reader becomes both a listener and a second witness.

Readers as Witnesses with Distance and Empathy in the "Grid of Trauma"

The survivors are first-hand witnesses, but what is the online readers' relation to the terror? Do they turn into witnesses as well?

Since the turn of this century, acts of terrorism have brought about a shift regarding who is to be considered a witness. According to literary critic Elizabeth Swanson Goldberg, with terrorism there has come an "expansion of the concept of witness from first-person or observer, which of necessity limits the number of witnesses for any given event, to a virtual explosion of witnesses all over the globe not only to the event of the 9/11 attacks, but also to the global shifts and cataclysms that have attended it" (2007, 23). In theorizing witnessing after the 9/11 attacks on the United States, the point has been made that the number of people who witnessed the event in real time through images of the acts far exceeded the number of witnesses to any other traumatic event. The entire global village tuned in, even if there was huge difference in intensity between watching the events on-screen and experiencing the terror (2007, 23).

In line with Goldberg's argument, cultural critic Ann Kaplan underscores the number of positions and different contexts a person may hold in relation to a traumatic event. She includes listening to a story to her examples on how people experience trauma:

> At one extreme there is a direct victim, while on the other we find a person geographically far away, having no personal connections to the victim. In between are a series of positions ... People experience trauma by being a bystander, by living near to where the catastrophe happened, or by hearing about a crisis from a friend. (2005, 2)

Kaplan emphasizes that the most common way by far to experience trauma is through the media. Most people nowadays experience trauma through reading, or watching TV, or (as in the case at hand) by reading blogposts. Terrorism's goal is to instil fear in a population by inflicting pain on part of it; it follows that when readers respond emotionally to terror, they have in a certain sense been made part of the terrorist project. Whether they open a blogpost for information, for a good read, or to comfort the survivors, do the blog visitors become witnesses to the mediatized terror story?

The difference between the experience of being shot at, and the experience of having someone narrating the story of having been shot at *to* you, cannot be too strongly emphasized. Indeed, a great number of readers underscore precisely this point by saying it is impossible for someone on the outside to ever understand what the survivors have gone through (thus implicitly disagreeing with the cultural critics). While thanking Kaur for sharing her story, one reader says, "I will not say it helps us understand, because we never will do, we who were not there" (Kaur's blog). The trauma belongs to the survivor. The blogs offer readers a safe position as *witnesses to narrated events*, not as *victims*. And furthermore, their positions as witnesses are inseparable from their position as readers – they are distanced, they look at the event through words.

Historian Dominick LaCapra emphasizes that trauma has a social aspect – that the "grid" of a traumatic event involves "the victim, perpetrators, bystanders, collaborators, resisters, those in the grey zone, and those born later" (2001, 175). LaCapra's research refers to the Shoah, but he writes that the concept is translatable to other contexts as well. The main point is that a trauma cannot be viewed solely as the damaging event itself; one must also consider the reactions to the event in social and historical space. Scholars have referred to this concept with reference to South Africa in order to make the point that the traumatic past was not just the private traumas of the perpetrators and victims, but something connected to a larger whole (van der Watt 2005). Similarly, Kai Eriksson considers it proper to speak of "traumatized communities" as "distinct from assemblies of traumatized persons"

(1995, 185). The readers underline their different positions relative to the events, but their distance does not imply indifference. As a reader of Martinovic puts it, "I will never be able to place myself within your feelings and experiences, but the reading is strong and touching" (Martinovic's blog). The readers often report how the reading is painful and makes them cry, and offer support.

Most of the responses to the blogs are very short, often just one phrase. The repetitive nature of the responses creates a discourse of gratitude and empathy. In the comments posted to Kaur's blog, the word "tears" is used 125 times, "thoughts" (as in "warm thoughts" or "my thoughts go out to you") 121 times, "thank you" 104, "cry" 95, and "warm" 84 times. "Sorrow" is mentioned 74 times, "God" 39, "understand" 23, "shock" 18, "suffer" 14, "strength" 18, and "support" 13. In Martinovic's blog, "thoughts" appears on 232 occasions, "warm" 199 times, "tears" 171, "cry" and "thank you" 150 and 71, respectively.

In the social media in the days after 22 July there was a lot of "holding hands," companionship, and care, according to reporter Espen Egil Hansen (Andenæs 2012, 64). The emotion-laden "empathy discourse" we see in the blogs corresponds to other sorrowful social practices in the public sphere at the time, such as laying of wreaths and lighting of candles in Oslo City Centre. The unity of the responses implies that online reading can be regarded as a similar social ritual through which the readers express their compassion in recognition of an unfathomable first-hand experience. This is not a time for analysis or for the expression of rage or hatred. Possibly, the blog form helps shape such responses. It has been noted that social media have the effect of enforcing drama.

The Virtual Community as "Me" and "We"

For LaCapra (2011) and Kaplan (2005), the experiences of the mediatized trauma may reach far beyond the immediate geographical environment. Perhaps reading the comments made by blog readers can suggest how far such a grid of terror can stretch geographically and how such a community is formed. This indicates that the experience of reading a survivor blog may involve shifting identifications.

There is great variety in the positions the readers conceptualize for the blogger and for themselves. Various personal, national, or international communities and relationships are created with the blogger. A very few relate to Kaur based on a previous relationship:

> Prableen!!! Thank god you are safe and sound J Daddy called me from India yesterday and told me that you were at that camp. I was so afraid for your sake. I watched the news all the time, prayed, cried, prayed more … (Kaur's blog)
>
> When I heard you were with your parents I was so relieved. I'm unable to put into words how relieved I was. (Kaur's blog)

A much larger number point out the *lack* of a previous relationship, and that their own reactions are very strong considering that they are responding to a stranger's personal narrative: "Hi! I don't know you, but I saw someone sharing your parts of your post on FB and went in to read. I now sit and cry. So horrible what you have been through" (Kaur's blog).

Some strangers enact a more personal, individual identification. One reader says she is responding to Kaur's text "as a mother," and another mentions having lived through a war. A number of readers reveal that they know someone who was at Utøya or someone who died in the attack.

A few of the commenters make themselves available for future contact. One writer says: "Best of luck, and don't hesitate to contact if you want to. but think first and foremost on yourself … I hope this can be a support for you. Hug from [full name]" (Kaur's blog). Another says: "Let me know if you ever come to Tunisia, I will be more than happy to show you around and please make sure you get some real sun and possibility to get rest, take good care and again – all my love) [reference to blog]" (Kaur's blog). Here, efforts are being made for direct interpersonal communication in Kaur's best interest in this specific situation.

Interestingly, there are many who, in their responses to Kaur's text, instead of positing themselves as individuals, stress that they are speaking on behalf of a "we" or "us," a certain collective, or they shift between the singular and the plural: "I don't know you, but you must be proud of yourself that you kept calm. Never stop working for what you believe in, keep being brave. Thank you for sharing this with us" (Kaur's blog). These readers often identify themselves with the Norwegian people: "I don't know you, words are poor, the media coverage and especially this blog burn soars in the soul of the whole Norwegian people." Also, readers from abroad speak on behalf of their nations: "The whole of Denmark suffers with you." Or indeed on behalf of the entire world: "I am English and live in the Caribbean. The whole world is shocked and stunned by these events." By alluding to a larger "we," the support for Kaur supposedly acquires more weight; the readers identify with the whole of a nation (or the world) and speak on its behalf.

As the story circulates in the broader world, Kaur's text is read metonymically, as a message from Norway itself: "Horrible! Sweden cries with you, things like this cannot happen ... Sweden suffers with you, Norway!" (Kaur's blog). Whereas some readers imagine themselves as speaking on behalf of the Norwegian nation, here it is Prableen Kaur who occupies the place of the nation – perhaps the reader is addressing the many Norwegian readers of the blog. For some of the commentators, what has happened indeed makes national borders irrelevant; one Swede says that "today it doesn't matter which side of the border we live on, today we are all Norwegians" (Kaur's blog). The identification is as humans towards other humans.

Reading Kaur's gruesome story has the effect that readers emphasize their togetherness and sameness. Readers stress their reading as an interpersonal communication between individuals but at the same time as transnational communication between peoples and nations. It is likely that the impersonal relation between blog owner and reader has led to the metonymical positions. The readers' comments document their reading of Kaur's personal story as a testimony of great national and international concern; this allows them to conceptualize themselves as individuals and as a world community.

The Mutual Needs of Sharing Experiences

For LaCapra, there is a significant difference between speaking directly to a witness – as, for instance, a therapist does – and working with mediated testimonies in the form of "reading texts, working on archival material, or viewing videos," where such contact is not paramount (2011, 98). Yet the blog reader constructs her position on a dynamic site, and she may do both; she may read the text in silence *and* speak directly.

Moreover, while there is an asymmetric situation, with one initial writer and a number of followers, there is no formal frame for interaction between the subjects, as there would be in a therapy session. There are outlets also for the readers to bear witness, given that the blogs enable the readers' testimony in a dialogue that is quite flexible.

Some readers, although they were not present at the camp, share with Kaur and Martinovic the experience of not knowing what has happened with family and close friends:

> This is BLOODY AWFUL! I really can't believe all this I sit and read. To think that one of my closest friends is still missing. Another one I know is at the hospital from being hit by two bullets in the stomach (lungs) and the arm. And my very best friend is luckily at home, sleeping. Just waiting for my best friend to wake up, so I can visit her and maybe give her good hugs and a little gift. Will maybe attend an open house thing for those who will not be alone. This is horrible, and I can't put into words what I have felt the last hour. To

> not know if your friend lives or not … Can't be put into words. Good luck. Wishing you the best. (Kaur's blog)

Another one states:

> Is maybe stupid of me to mention this, but I lost [deceased] at the [indicating place on Utøya]. It is difficult for me to read stories from [that place]. I really want to fight for everyone we have lost, and fight to get Norway together again and Utøya back. No-one shall take it away from us! I will fight from top to toe for [deceased] and I will fight for freedom … My brother also hid in the woods and he cried when he came home, felt nice to see him unharmed but not nice to see him scared to death and sorry. L (Kaur's blog)

In Laub's (1992) model, the listener represents the "blank screen" onto which the trauma is projected, but this is hardly the case with readers in social media in the immediate context of a terrorist attack, which produces fear in a larger population. There are many readers who, when writing, document their own need to place the event in time and place. In this context of emotions and confusion, the blog owners show an eagerness to listen to the readers' stories in detail and encourage them to narrate. For instance, Emma Martinovic says, "I also wish to hear your stories, or if you want to talk. Please contact me at [mail address] or scream it out in the comment field."

The material shows that blogs are a particularly useful venue for sharing impressions and emotions, one that enables testimonies from the blogger as well as from her readers. The experience of reading in the immediate aftermath of terror seems closely connected to the readers' need to work through their own situations and the stress and anxiety from which they reportedly suffer. The confessions may be minimal: "I am all in tears," "my heart is bleeding," "I cannot stop crying," "I am in shock." Or they may be more elaborate, as in the quotes above.

Hence, reading is sometimes much more than a way to gather information or to show support for the survivors; reading a blogpost is also a way for the readers themselves to put things in place. There seems to be a therapeutic aspect to reading the blogposts, corresponding to the therapeutic aspects of writing them, and a mutual need by reader and writer to share stories and to listen to them.

Confronting the Writer

However, the *distance* that the Internet provides is also something that readers make use of as they please. According to Laub, it is important that the listener also listen to himself and assert his own place in the narrative as separate from that of the trauma speaker. The listener must know her place and not intrude in the narrative too early, or to critically: "The listener has to feel the victim's victories, defeats and silences, know them from within, so that they can assume the form of testimony" (1992, 57–58).

But as hundreds of strangers responded to Martinovic, often anonymously, some of them clearly did not care about their role as the enablers of testimonies. While most readers were considerate, at times the information hunger threatened to rule out empathy. Some even behaved offensively. Nine days after the terrorist attack, a reader posted a harassing comment on Martinovic's blog under the name of Anders Behring Breivik.

Most of the readers comforted Martinovic, but some confronted her and challenged her reactions, for instance, by saying she should "get over it." The comment is omitted from her book, but her response was this: "Many ask why I am so emotionally unstable? I'm sorry once again, but isn't it comprehensible that I am emotionally unstable? That I cry and am scared of pretty much everything" (72).

In general, Martinovic is very appreciative of her readers, but there are times when she seems to need to regain control over the communication. She sets up the interview session partly to control the many questions she is asked, but she also admits, "I must say that there are also questions that are insanely 'harsh' that I wasn't prepared for" (35). Where distance from the readers may be experienced as creating a safer zone for communicating trauma than face-to-face communication, there is also evidence that the same distance opens the door at least partly to harassment, careless comments, and unwanted confrontations.

To the degree that testimonials are meant to chronicle personal experience, their truth-value is more or less inviolate. Yet blogposts are not universally conceived as testimonial practices to be handled with care and without challenge. A capable writer like Martinovic nevertheless negotiates this pressure:

> I have chosen to answer those that I can manage and those I know that you really want me to answer (35). I have chosen [to answer your questions] for so many reasons, but I want people to understand, and I wish for myself to "be finished" with media while I can, so that when I return to my "dark hole" I wish to be left in peace and use my time with friends, family, and my psychologist. (2011, 37–38)

The Janus face of the blog – it is a public statement that can also be edited to secure her privacy – is visible here. The two sides of testifying surface: private confession and public testimony.

Trauma emerges not just as something that needs to be aired, but as something to be debated: "How should one react?" And from this, a larger question surfaces: "Who owns these stories?" Put another way, and more deeply, "Who has the right to question trauma?" This is a public discussion worth having. The intimate yet staged performance of the blog, through the contributions of the readers and the writer, opens space room for a debate that is seldom staged so explicitly.

Defictionalizing the Events, or Looking for a Good "Reality"?

Judging from the responses to the blogposts, the process of comprehending acts of terror seemingly goes through stages where it is crucial to distinguish the new events from other similar events of terror, either in other countries or in fiction. A lot of gratitude is expressed in the comment field; the readers thank the writers repeatedly for giving them their stories "so that we can understand."

The blogs contribute necessary knowledge in personal and political terms. So very often, even when the readers are motivated by an urge to understand the acts of terror, it seems quite impossible to distinguish between the blogger's two roles – citizen-journalist and private person. One journalist commenting on the blogpost makes this point succinctly:

> Thank you Prableen, for making us understand the horrors and fear you experienced at Utøya. It is important that we know what happened. Only then can we support those of you who went through this. Only then can we understand the despair of those who have lost someone in the night-mare. Our common knowledge about the tragedy is also the best premises for fighting the feeling of powerlessness and the crippling fear in the times coming. You have impressed me before, also, Prableen, as on the Labour Party's national meeting this spring. [Full name], journalist in [newspaper]. (Kaur's blog)

The need for information is not limited to establishing the forensic facts and details; it includes the need to understand the social dimensions of the terror – what the victims went through and what families are currently coping with. The personal aspects of the acts are stressed, and again we see a reader expressing care towards the blogger. This need may have been influenced by the media coverage. At the time, the perpetrator gained almost unlimited attention, and his picture was disseminated repeatedly throughout all media channels. The blogs shift the focus from the mystery of the terrorist to the stories of those affected.

Many of the readers express a need to recognize that the terror really happened and that it was a unique event. One reader describes this as follows:

Dear you, Words are so poor, but yours hit hard and give this incomprehensible event a face. It is not just "images on TV." The fear, the anxiety, the sorrow ... the hope. You make it tangible, and I thank you for having written about your experiences, even though your words made my eyes fill with tears. I wish the best for you and yours. (Martinovic's blog)

Reading Kaur's blog gives the terror at Utøya "a face." Reading the blogs brings terror closer; the readers cannot externalize the acts as "just another news story," something that normally happens overseas. The story is individual, unique, and real. This reader recognizes the report's importance for her own understanding of the terror and for Kaur's continued well-being.

Other readers emphasize that the blogpost makes the terror lose its fictional character. For instance, one reader comments: "Thank you so very much that you want to share your story with us. It makes us understand that it is true. It was like watching a movie. Incredible, horribly tragic. Can't find other words" (Kaur's blog). The *defictionalizing* of the events is an important effect of the experience of reading the blogs. From the readers' responses, we see that an important aspect of reading involves making a well-known terror plot an individual experience and grounding the events as facts.

But we could also ask whether the movie-like plot of the terror story is what draws the readers to these blogs. Is there also an urge for a good story here? The Utøya narrative *is* unreal; in many of its aspects, is it almost *too* narrative-like – a terrorist camouflaged as a policeman takes a boat to an island after bombing government buildings, kills the skeptical adults who don't trust him, then tricks young people into thinking they are safe, before hunting them down. The truth aside, this story does contain some thrilling elements. The Twitter-stream and the blogs, in turn, create a new story; it is fascinating to dig into it all with a sense of "reality hunger" and taste for horror.

Readers may, of course, have their own private needs to have a "good cry." A reader may well turn to literature in order to question specific life dilemmas or difficult psychological issues. Fiction reading and therapy resemble each other in some ways, as Liz Burns (2009) points out. All the more so, perhaps, when the material is life writing – as is the case with the blogs – and when the exchange between reader and text takes place within a social space. Perhaps these blogs, like fiction, offer catharsis. We may well note, again, the way reader and blog owner share the same need to defictionalize the story. Martinovic herself writes that the whole thing was "like an episode of CSI" (2011, 38).

In traumatic memory, the injuring events are replayed and relived. To get it right, or to place the events for herself, Martinovic narrates three times the story of what happened to her at Utøya. She says she does so in order to be able to put her feelings in place within the story. When her testimony turns a generic story into a precise narrative of what happened, she presents a first step for writer and reader to relate to the terror as something that actually took place in a certain way.

An Archive of Living Memories

The reception of the first blogposts exposes the shifting conception of narrator and listener for writer and reader alike. In the post-terror situation, the survivors' blogs document in equal measure the desire to confess a personal story or trauma narrative and the desire to testify – to record a particular important historical event. This dual motivation is expressed in their often dual modes of writing. They combine confessional/therapeutic writing, where the writer tells the story of her own suffering and inner life and of her mourning, as if the blog was a diary. This is blurred with testimonial writing, where the writer documents the events that took place, either to herself or to others.

In the readers' comments we see this same duality. Some respond to the personal narration and encourage the writer to keep writing in order to heal; others respond to the narrative in terms of a story about the nation. In many comments these two responses are combined. Many comment on the reading experience as "tough" – as a transformation of an intellectual, emotional, or ethical kind, reflecting Derek Attridge's definition (2004, 19) of the reading experience.

When we focus mainly on the readers of the blogposts, we see a process whereby readers enable the testimonies. In turn, the blog owners help readers comprehend what happened. Even though the first-hand experience is impossible to share, the readers as first listeners respond to the events as they are told, emotionally and ethically. Also, the blogs function as social arenas for reconciliatory practices: comfort spreads towards the survivors but also towards the readers. This arena even provides an outlet for the readers' own confessions. The comments imply that the "grid of trauma" in the nation after 22 July spread across national borders as a result of the mediation of the terror events that bloggers provided. But we also see that the distance between narrator and listener opens the way for insensitive behaviour, and there is reason to believe that the readers do not convey every aspect of their motivations for reading in the comments.

Evidently, while the readers' lives moved on after a rather short while, the writers/survivors have needed more time. Quite rapidly, we see the readers' interest in the blogs drop, and the support is clearly coming from the readers towards the writers and not the other way around. As the blogs continue, the processes of mourning occupy more space; the writers are grieving their friends. These mourning processes are perhaps not as engaging for the readers; perhaps they seem less unique, or perhaps rather they seem too private. In the media, some of the victims chose to speak more freely with journalists, and the blogs quite soon lost their news value.

The blogs have now acquired a historical dimension. In the ensuing years there has been harsh criticism of the police and the government by an established commission; there has been a ten-week trial during which many of the survivors gave witness, and there have been heated public debates about the political intent of the terror – all of which make the blogs now seem dated.

The first post-terror election replaced the social democratic government and installed, for the first time, a government of the right-wing Populist Party to which Breivik once belonged (although he considered it too soft). Perhaps the nation moved too quickly from a state of shock to one of denial. The blogs have indeed become time witnesses, an archive of social memories.

For some of the writers today, their blogs still continue to be a place where they may "write it out," as in Emma Martinovic's case. Prableen Kaur now uses her blog for political reasons, to post her speeches and political articles. This blog testifies to a young life moving on, leaving this one particular story behind. If the wounds are not completely healed, the particular testimony is at least safely in place in the archive, filed under July 2011.

References

22.juli-kommisjonen. 2012. *Rapport fra 22.juli-kommisjonen*. NOU, 2012: 14.
Andenæs, Ivar. 2012. *Medier i sjokk og sorg. Pressens møte med terroren 22. juli 2011* [*Media in Shock and Sorrow: The Press's Encountering the 22 July 2011 Terror*]. Oslo: Cappelen Damm Høyskoleforlaget.
Attridge, David. 2004. *The Singularity of Literature*. London: Routledge.
Burns, Liz. 2009. *Literature and Therapy: A Systemic View*. London: Karnac Books.
Goldberg, Elizabeth Swanson. 2007. *Beyond Terror: Gender, Narrative, Human Rights*. New Brunswick, NJ: Rutgers University Press.
Kaplan, Ann E. 2005. *Trauma Culture: The Politics of Terror and Loss in Media and Literature*. New Brunswick: Rutgers University Press.
Kaur, Prableen. 2011a. *Jeg er Prableen* [*I am Prableen*]. Oslo: Gyldendal.
———. 2011b. "Helvete på Utøya [Hell at Utøya]" [blogpost]. http://prableen.origo.no/bulletin/show/672218_helvete-paa-utoeya?ref=checkpoint
LaCapra, Dominick. 2001. *Writing History, Writing Trauma*. Baltimore: Johns Hopkins University Press.
Laub, Dori. 1992. "Bearing Witness, or Vicissitudes of Listening." In *Testimony: Crises of Witnessing in Literature, Psychoanalysis, and History*, edited by Shoshana Felman and Dori Laub, 57–75. London: Routledge.
Martinovic, Emma. 2011. "Helvete på Utøya [Hell at Utøya]" [blogpost], http://utoyahelvette.blogg.no/1311527989_helvette_p_utya.html

———. 2011. *Lever!* [*Alive!*] Oslo: Portal.
The Reading Experience Database. 2014. "What Is a Reading Experience?" http://www.open.ac.uk/Arts/RED/experience.htm
van der Watt, Lise. 2005. "Witnessing Trauma in Post-Apartheid South Africa: The Question of Generational Responsibility." *African Arts* 38(3): 26–39.

Notes on Contributors

Gitte Balling holds a PhD in literary aesthetic experiences. She is an Associate Professor at the University of Copenhagen, Denmark, where she teaches primarily in audience development, literature, sociology, digital reading, and media culture. Among her research interests are cultural promotion, literature sociology, digital youth, and cultural policy.

Jenny Bergenmar is an Associate Professor in Comparative Literature and Senior Lecturer in the Department of Literature, History of Ideas and Religion, University of Gothenburg. Her research centres on the history of reading, reception history, and digital humanities. In collaboration with Maria Karlsson, Uppsala University, she has researched the large collection of letters to Selma Lagerlöf from her audience in the project "Reading Lagerlöf. Letters from the Public to Selma Lagerlöf 1891–1940." She is currently working on the project "Swedish Women Writers on Export in the 19th Century," investigating the transnational circulation and reception of Swedish literature written by women.

Marianne Novrup Børch is Professor of English Studies at the University of Southern Denmark, where she teaches literatures in English. She specializes in the early periods, but recent cultural developments have turned her attention to today's interest in "writing back" to older, often canonized works as well as to the contemporary upsurge of fantasy, a genre akin to the medieval romance. Forthcoming is a book on Arthurian literature as a corpus of legends that continues to be rewritten and reconceptualized.

Liz Brewster is a lecturer at Lancaster Medical School, Lancaster University, UK. In 2012, she was awarded her PhD from the Information School at the University of Sheffield. Previously, her master's research on bibliotherapy was awarded the SINTO/Bob Usherwood prize for the dissertation making the most significant contribution to improving professional practice. She has previously worked in public and academic libraries, including the John Rylands University Library, and as a researcher at the Universities of Sheffield and Leicester.

Shih-Wen Sue Chen is a Lecturer in Literary Studies in the School of Communication and Creative Arts at Deakin University. She was previously a post-doctoral fellow at the Australian Centre on China in the World, Australian National University, and Adjunct Assistant Professor in Tamkang University, Taiwan, and has lectured in National Tsing Hua University, Taiwan. She is the author of *Representations of China in British Children's Fiction, 1851–1911* (Ashgate, 2013).

Gabrielle Cliff Hodges is a Senior Lecturer in Education at the University of Cambridge Faculty of Education. She taught in three 11–18 comprehensive schools in Cambridgeshire, in the last as Head of the English department, before moving into teacher education in 1993. She co-ordinates and teaches on the secondary English PGCE course, and also supervises master's and PhD students. She has published many chapters and articles on reading, writing, and language in secondary English teaching. Her main area of research is reading, especially young people's development as readers within and beyond the classroom. She has recently published *Researching and Teaching Reading: Developing Pedagogy through Critical Enquiry* (Routledge, 2016).

Teresa Cremin is a Professor of Education at The Open University, UK, Past President of the UK Literacy Association, a Fellow of the English Association, and Board Member of Booktrust and The Poetry Archive. Her research explores teachers' literate identities and the impact of their habits and practices as literate individuals on the classroom community of readers and writers. She has also examined extracurricular reading and creative pedagogic practices such as storytelling, drama, and play. Teresa has written extensively on these issues, most recently *Writing Voices: Creating Communities of Writers* with D. Myhill (Routledge, 2012) and *Reading for Pleasure: Children and Teachers Together* (Routledge, 2014).

Elisabeth Davies teaches in the areas of information organization and information behaviour in the Faculty of Information and Media Studies, University of Western Ontario. Her research interests include temporality and documents, and the dynamics of social information practices.

Danielle Fuller is Reader in Canadian Studies and Cultures of Reading in the Department of English Literature at the University of Birmingham. She has always been fascinated by writing, publishing, and reading communities and the ways that knowledge and value are brokered within them. These interests informed her first book, *Writing the Everyday: Atlantic Canadian Women's Textual Communities* (McGill-Queen's, 2004). Originally trained in literary studies, she has spent the last decade using methods from cultural studies while working on interdisciplinary projects with DeNel Rehberg Sedo, including "Beyond the Book" www.//http://www.beyondthebookproject.org/. Their latest co-authored publication is the monograph *Reading Beyond the Book: The Social Practices of Contemporary Literary Culture* (Routledge, 2013).

Maria Karlsson is a Senior Lecturer at the Department of Literature, Uppsala University. Her research interests are the history of reading, Cultural Studies, gender, intersectionality, queer theory, and political narratives. In collaboration with Jenny Bergenmar, University of Gothenburg, she has researched the large collection of letters to Selma Lagerlöf from her audience in the project "Reading Lagerlöf: Letters from the Public to Selma Lagerlöf 1891–1940."

Eva Maria (Emy) Koopman is a PhD candidate at the department of Media and Communication at the Erasmus University Rotterdam, in the Netherlands. She has a background in both Literary Studies and Clinical Psychology and is currently combining both fields in her research on reader reactions to suffering (particularly grief and depression). She focuses on the reactions of empathy and reflection. She has published on empathic and reflective reader responses, the ethics of reading and writing about suffering, and the functions of reading literature during grief.

Arnold (A.) Lubbers holds a PhD in Book and Manuscript Studies from the University of Amsterdam in Amsterdam, the Netherlands. He has taught on Dutch institutional reading culture in the long nineteenth century, which is also the focus of his research. He has published on book clubs and their choice of literature in the context of rising nationalism. He is interested in institutional reading culture in the nineteenth century and colonial reading culture. He is employed as Policy Officer at the Dutch Organisation for Scientific Research (NWO) in the Humanities division, working on funding instruments for research on cultural heritage, among other things.

Marianne Martens is an Assistant Professor at the School of Library and Information Science (SLIS) at Kent State University. Previously, Martens served as vice-president at children's publisher North–South Books, in New York. Martens's interdisciplinary research is grounded in LIS and Media Studies and focuses on how books paired with technology are changing the reading experience for young people. She is the author of *Publishers, Readers, and Digital Engagement* (Palgrave Macmillan, 2016).

Lynne (E.F.) McKechnie is a Professor in the Faculty of Information and Media Studies at The University of Western Ontario in London, Ontario, where she teaches primarily in the Library and Information Science programs. Her research centres on the intersection of children, reading, and public libraries. Along with Catherine Ross and Paulette Rothbauer, she is co-author of *Reading Matters: What the Research Reveals about Reading, Libraries, and Community* (Libraries Unlimited, 2006).

Pamela McKenzie is an Associate Professor at the Faculty of Information and Media Studies at The University of Western Ontario. She is interested in temporal, textual, and interactional aspects of information seeking, sharing, and use, in the intersections of information work and caring work, and in gendered and embodied information practices and spaces. Her research focuses on the ways that individuals in local settings collaboratively construct information needs, seeking, and use, and on the discursive organization of document and library use.

Cecilie Naper is an Associate Professor (PhD) in the Institute of Archive, Library, and Information Science at Oslo and Akershus University College. She has published widely in the field of sociology of literature, including topics such as popular genres, reading and fascination, the mediation of literature in Norwegian public libraries, and the relationship between the politics of literature and reading habits. Her current research project centres on reading among inmates in women's prisons.

Knut Oterholm, cand., philol., is an Assistant Professor in the Department of Archivistics, Library, and Information Science, Oslo and Akershus University College of Applied Sciences. He has published articles on the concepts of literary quality and mediation. His latest publication is "Sense-Perception and Attention – Articulation and Voice: An Embodied Perspective on the Mediation of Literature" (together with Kjell Ivar Skjerdingstad). Since November 2013 he has been a PhD candidate at Oslo and Akershus University College.

Magnus Persson is a Professor in Comparative Literature in the Faculty of Education and Society at Malmö University, Sweden. He teaches and supervises students in mother tongue education on all levels. His research deals with reading from a media ecological perspective, reception theory, cultural studies, and popular culture. His latest book is from 2012 and is called *Den goda boken. Samtida föreställningar om litteratur och läsning [The Good Book: Contemporary Notions of Literature and Reading]*.

Joron Pihl is a Professor in Multicultural Education at the Department of International Studies and Interpreting, Oslo and Akershus University College, Norway. Pihl was head of the research project Multiplicity, Empowerment, Citizenship: Inclusion through Use of the Library as Learning Arena, 2007–2011 in Norway. Pihl is co-editing a forthcoming book about literacies, school and library partnership, and social justice (Sense Publishing). Pihl is a member of the management board of Nordic Centre of Excellence – Justice through Education in the Nordic Countries.

Paulette Rothbauer is an Associate Professor in the Faculty of Information and Media Studies at The University of Western Ontario. She has studied the everyday reading experiences of queer young women, rural and small-town youth, and has recently launched a project that examines the reading and library practices of adults seventy years of age and older. In her reading research she is primarily concerned with the ways in which reading practices constitute readerly identities for those people who may be marginalized from mainstream book and reading cultures. She also sustains an interest in the conditions in the publishing scene that saw the emergence of modern Canadian young adult literature.

DeNel Rehberg Sedo is a Professor in the Department of Communication Studies at Mount Saint Vincent University, Halifax, Nova Scotia. Along with Danielle Fuller, she co-authored *Reading beyond the Book: The Social Practices of Contemporary Literature* (Routledge) as a result of a five-year, international AHRC-funded project. DeNel is also editor of and a multiple contributor to *Reading Communities from Salons to Cyberspace* (Palgrave Macmillan). Her published and ongoing research includes work on cultural practices in historical and contemporary book groups. She is also interested in cultural production and literacy in non-traditional environments, including social networking sites.

Kerstin Rydbeck is a Professor in Library and Information Science at Uppsala University, Sweden. Her doctoral dissertation (1995) was a study in the sociology of literature about the use of literature within the Swedish temperance movement at the turn of the twentieth century. Her more recent research has focused on the history of popular education from a gender perspective, research circles as a method for evidence-based library and information practice (EBLIP), and reading group activities in contemporary Sweden.

Lucia Cedeira Serantes is an Assistant professor at the Graduate School of Library and Information Studies, Queens College (CUNY). She holds a PhD from the Faculty of Information and Media Studies, The University of Western Ontario, where she studied young adult readers of comics and their reading experience. Her general research interest focuses on young adults, media consumption, identity, culture, and social structures (such as libraries). Her research was awarded the John A. Lent Scholarship in Comics Studies (International Comics Arts Forum).

Kjell Ivar Skjerdingstad is a Professor of Library and Information Science at the University College of Oslo and Akershus, Norway. He holds a PhD in Scandinavian Literature and is a specialist on the twentieth Century Modernism of Tarjei Vesaas. His current work focuses on the theory and practice of the mediation of literature in libraries and other arenas as well as the phenomenology of reading and reading experiences.

Mette Steenberg is a post-doctoral fellow at the Interacting Minds Center, Aarhus University, Denmark. Steenberg's research focuses on the relationship between literary reading and mental health. She has recently conducted an explorative field study of the relationship between reading forms, modes of engagement, and mental health benefits in both affective and psychotic populations, presented in the present publication. Together with a group of Nordic researchers, she is currently engaged in developing a theoretical and methodological framework for the empirical study of affective and cognitive dimensions of experiential forms of literary reading.

Joan Swann is Emeritus Professor of English Language at the Open University. She is a sociolinguist whose main research interests lie in language and identity, creativity in language, and storytelling in educational and other settings. Current projects include the study of everyday literary discussion, with a particular focus on contemporary reading groups – both friendship groups and those meeting in schools and other institutions. Among her most recent publications are *Creativity, Language, Literature: The State of the Art*, edited with Rob Pope and Ronald Carter (Palgrave Macmillan, 2011), and *The Discourse of Reading Groups: Integrating Cognitive and Sociocultural Perspectives*, with David Peplow, Paola Trimarco, and Sara Whiteley (Routledge, 2016).

Kristin Skinstad van der Kooij is an Associate Professor in Multicultural Education at the Department of International Studies and Interpreting, Oslo and Akershus University College. She is a member of Nordic Centre of Excellence in Education – JustEd.

Tonje Vold is an Associate Professor at the Institute of Archive, Library, and Information Science at the University College of Oslo and Akershus, Norway. She has lately explored the cultural responses in Norway post–22 July; other than this her research centres on post-colonial and world literature, children's literature, feminist studies, and literature, ethics, and law. She holds a PhD in comparative literature on J. M. Coetzee's writing, and has co-edited anthologies on the topics of sociology of literature (2013), disability and media studies (2014), and mediation of literature and culture (2015).

Sara Whiteley is a Lecturer in Language and Literature at the University of Sheffield, England. Her research interests lie at the interface between language and literature, in the disciplines of stylistics, cognitive poetics, and discourse analysis. She is particularly interested in studying the experience of reading contemporary prose and poetry. She co-edited the *Cambridge Handbook of Stylistics* (Cambridge University Press, 2014) and along with David Peplow, Joan Swann, and Paola Trimarco, is co-author of *The Discourse of Reading Groups: Integrating Cognitive and Sociocultural Perspectives* (Routledge, 2016).

Index

Figures are indicated by page numbers in italics.

Aberdeen, Lady, 59–60
Academia Press (China), 352, 362n3
Accelerated Reader program, 256
acceleration, 218–20, 224
accountability discourses, 301
adults: role in children's reading, 56–57, 63–64, 68
advance review copies (ARCs), 264
Aerts, Remieg, 333
aesthetics, 11, 38. *See also* aesthetic experience; aesthetic texts; literary aesthetic experience
aesthetic experience, 38–40, 50. *See also* literary aesthetic experience
aesthetic texts, 264, 274
affect, Deleuzian, 305–6
affective criticism, 21
"The Affective Fallacy" (Beardsley and Wimsatt), 20–22
affective labour, 265–66
Allington, Daniel, 76, 84n1, 280
aloud, reading, 63, 193, 253
ALSC (Association for Library Service to Children), 254
Älvdalen, Sweden, 239, 240
Amanti, Cathy, 57–58
Amazon Mechanical Turk, 273
Ambjörnsson, Ronny, 234
American Association of School Librarians, 257
Anderson, Benedict, 334
Andrejevic, Mark, 265
"Answers to Correspondents" section, in journals, 77–78
The Anxiety of Influence (Bloom), 96n1, 96n11

ARCs (advance review copies), 264
Aristotle, 118, 200–201
Armitage, Simon, 103. *See also* "I'll Be There to Love and Comfort You" (Armitage)
Arnone, Marilyn P., 258
Aronsson, Karin, 280
articulated reading experience, 43, 47, 116, 117. *See also* reading experience
Art & Lies (Winterson), 96n7
assessment, reading, 301, 302, 311, 314. *See also* proficiency, in reading
Association for Library Service to Children (ALSC), 254
Atkinson, Paul, 227, 228
Atrophil and Stella (Sidney), 91
Attridge, Derek, 1, 368, 380
author events, 139–41, 145–46, 272. *See also* mass reading events
autobiographical selves, 151, 153, 163
autobiographies, 58–59, 199–200, 211. *See also Tonio* (Van der Heijden)

Baby Story Time study, 250–51
Bale, Kjersti, 128–29
Balling, Gitte, 3
Balukhaty, Sergej, 317
Balzac, Honoré de, 79
Bank, Jan, 332, 335
Bassett, Raewyn, 152
Baumgarten, Alexander, 38
Beagan, Brenda, 152
Beardsley, Monroe C.: "The Affective Fallacy," 20–22
"Becoming a Nation of Readers" (report), 253
Bei Dao, 351
"Bekjendelser" ["Confessions"] (Ingemanns), 193–95
Benwell, Bethan, 280

bestseller lists, 361
Beyond the Book study. *See* mass reading events
bibliotherapy, and mental health: approach to, 8–9, 167, 168; conclusions from, 178–80; demographics of study participants, 173–74; on diversity of books read, 174–75; emotive model, 169, 175–76; escapist model, 169–70, 176–77; informational model, 171, 178; life narratives approach to, 171–72; methodology for study of, 173; and reader response theory, 168–69; readers on, 167, 174; scholarship on, 167–68; service providers on, 167; social model, 170–71, 177. *See also* shared reading groups, and mental health
Bilderdijk, Willem, 341
Bildungsroman, 319, 328–29
Birkerts, Sven, 149, 150, 151
Black, Fiona, 79
Black, Malcolm W., 79
Blanchot, Maurice, 117
Blankets (Thompson), 217
blended-worlds, 111
Blixen, Karen: "The Ship-Boy's Tale," 188–89, 190
blogs, 368, 369, 375. *See also* blogs, on Norway mass shooting; social media
blogs, on Norway mass shooting: approach to, 13, 368; confrontational readers of, 376–77; and defictionalizing of events, 378–79; historical dimension of, 381; and mutual sharing of experiences, 375–76, 380; overview of shooting event, 367; and ownership of trauma, 377–78; public/private nature of, 369–70, 371, 377, 380; reader responses to, 370–71, 372, 373, 380; relationship of readers with authors, 373–75; sources for study of, 369; as therapy, 379–80; value of over time, 380–81
Bloom, Harold: *The Anxiety of Influence*, 96n1, 96n11; and Byatt on literary influence, 95; on encounters with literary precursors, 89, 90; and Freud, 89, 96n2; on imaginal, 87–88, 118; on judging his theory, 96n10; on Oedipus complex, 96n3; *Omens of the Millennium*, 87; use of terms by, 96nn4–6; *The Western Canon*, 89

Bokcirklar.se [*Bookcircles.se*], 238
Bokelskere.no [*Booklovers.no*], 318, 321, 325, 327
book circles. *See* reading groups, in Sweden
book clubs, 170. *See also* bibliotherapy, and mental health; book clubs, Dutch; mass reading events; reading groups, in schools; reading groups, in Sweden; shared reading groups, and mental health
book clubs, Dutch: approach to, 12–13, 332, 334; choice of reading material in, 339, 344; demographics in, 334, 338; and domesticity literature, 341; *Idle Hours Usefully Spent* (book club), 331, 336, 344; membership in, 336; and national civil society, 331–32, 335–36, 344–45; and nationalistic literature, 339–40; and national literary heritage, 340–41; objective of, 338; regulations of, 338–39; scope of, 337–38; and translations of foreign novels, 341–43, 343–44. *See also* Netherlands
book history. *See* history, of reading
Booklovers.no. See *Bokelskere.no*
book series fever: approach to, 13, 349, 350, 362; academic series, 353–55; appeal of *Fifty Cent* series, 356–57; and comprehension of content read, 350, 355; development of, 352, 354; end of, 361; introduction to *Fifty Cent* series, 350, 355–56; mistakes in *Fifty Cent* series, 358; nostalgic memories and *Fifty Cent* series, 359–60; other popular series, 363n6; quality of publications, 352; and reading in China in 1980s, 349, 350–51, 361; and reading practices, 358–59; scholarship on, 349–50. *See also* China
bookstores: and reading groups, 235
Børch, Marianne, 118
Botzakis, Stergios, 217
Bourdieu, Pierre, 266
boys, reading by, 252, 258, 265. *See also* men
Brabham, Edna Greene, 256
Brandhorst, Tim, 275
The Bride's Farewell (Rosoff), 291–92
British Council: Reader Development program, 238
Brône, Geert, 100
Brooks, Peter, 126, 318

Broom, Alex, 172
Bruner, Jerome, 57
Buijnsters, P.J., 343
"Building Dwelling Thinking" (Heidegger), 124
Burgess, Amy, 151, 153
Burns, Liz, 379
Butler, Dorothy, 250
Byatt, A.S., 95. See also *Possession* (Byatt)

calendars, 152, 154–55, 161–62. *See also* rereading, of ephemeral documents
Calinescu, Matei, 149, 150, 151
Canada Reads (radio program), 134, 136, 137
Cao Minghau, 358
Carle, Eric: *The Very Hungry Caterpillar*, 251
Carnegie Medal. *See* reading groups, in schools
catharsis, 169, 175, 200–201, 202–3, 212, 379
Chapman, Gwen E., 152
Chaucer, Geoffrey: *Troilus and Criseyde*, 90
Chen Dezhong, 351
Chen Pingyuan, 351
Chen Sha, 349–50
Chen Xiaoming, 353
Chen Yuan, 353
childhood reading experiences: approach to, 6, 55; adults' role in, 56–57, 63–64, 68; advantages of, 281; being read to, 63, 253; childhood memories of interviewees, 60–61; conclusions from, 68–69; importance of reading memories, 66; influences on, 63–64; keeping childhood books, 65–66; Lady Aberdeen example for using theoretical perspectives, 59–60; and libraries, 64–65; methodology for study on, 55–57; reading as escape, 67–68; reading in school memories, 62; secondary school memories, 61; similarities and differences across generations, 66–68; social and cultural perspectives on, 57–58; spatial and historical perspectives on, 58–59, 68–69; and teenage book market, 67, 68. *See also* comics, and time; early literacy; literary reviews, by teenagers; multilingual students, reading experiences of; online reading audiences; schools

China: academics and reading, 353; contemporary publishing and reading in, 361–62; nostalgia for 1980s, 360–61; publishing in 1980s, 351–52, 362n2; reading in 1980s, 349, 350–51, 361; Reform period, 358. *See also* book series fever
China National Publishing Administration (CNPA), 350, 351
Chinese Translations of Academic Masterpieces series, 353–54
Christensen, Lars Saabye: "Gensynet" [The Reunion], 188, 190
civil society, 334–35
Clark, Christina, 286
Clauren, Heinrich, 341
Clay, Marie, 250
close readings, 20, 34, 77, 129n1
CNPA (China National Publishing Administration), 350, 351
cognitive poetics, 7, 99–101, 113. *See also* "I'll Be There to Love and Comfort You" (Armitage); Text World Theory framework
Cohen, Laura J., 171
Colclough, Stephen, 76
Cole, David R., 302, 305–6
college students, 221
comics, and time: approach to, 9–10, 217–18, 222, 230; and college students, 221; and different types of comics, 226; and flow, 225–26; justifications for reading comics, 224–25; and malleability of time, 220, 227–29; perception of comics as light reading, 222–23; scholarship on, 221; and time scarcity, 223–24, 229–30
Commercial Press (China), 353–54
Consuming Literature (Kong), 350
cosmopolitanism, 342–43
Coté, Mark, 265
Crane, Mary Thomas, 30
crazy reading, 349. *See also* book series fever; China
creative reading, 258
creativity, 91, 95
Crewe, Louise, 152
crime fiction (detective stories), 33, 176
critical reading: approach to, 5–6, 19, 20, 34; and absence of pleasure, 28–29; construction of critical position, 24–25; crisis of, 34; critiques of, 20, 24, 25, 34;

Culler on, 23–24; and detective stories, 33; as dispassionate, 21–23, 23–24; for distancing reader from text, 25; exclusivity of, 26; in higher education, 24, 25; and immersive reading experiences, 29–30, 33; importance of, 34–35; Jameson on, 27–28, 30–31; by lay readers, 30; *vs.* lay reading, 19–20, 24–25, 26–27; as meta-reading, 28; and New Criticism, 20, 23; pleasures of, 29, 34; and political desire, 34; surface/depth metaphors in, 30–32, 33; suspicion in, 24, 29, 33; as sympathetic reading, 32–33; types of, 20. *See also* hooks, bell; Jameson, Fredric
Csikszentmihalyi, Mihaly, 225
Culler, Jonathan, 23–24, 126
cultural adaptability, 87
cultural criticism, 20

Da Huzi, 356, 360
Darnton, Robert, 59, 73
Davies, Elizabeth, 149–50
Davis, Philip: *Reading and the Reader*, 118
deceleration, 220. *See also* acceleration
de Certeau, Michel, 228
Deleuze, Gilles, 302, 304, 306, 310, 311, 313
Deng Xiaoping, 353
depression, 172, 195. *See also* bibliotherapy, and mental health; shared reading groups, and mental health
desire, 302, 304, 305, 313
detective stories (crime fiction), 33, 176
Dewey, John, 39–40
dialogic reading, 254–56
digital character extensions, 273–74
digital formats, 264, 274. *See also* blogs; online reading audiences; social media
discourse analytic approach, 280–81
discourse-world, 101, 107
distant reading, 74
Djuve, Maja Troberg, 324
Dong Xiuyu, 351
Do the Right Thing (film), 32
Douban Book (website), 357
Dowrick, Christopher, 184–85
The Drake Chronicles (Harvey) digital character extensions, 263, 264, 273–74
drama paradox, 200
Dr. Jekyll and Mr. Hyde (Stevenson), 89
Dufour, Dany-Robert, 127
Durkheim, Émile, 218

Dushu [*Reading*] (journal), 349
dwelling, 7, 118, 124–25

early literacy: approach to, 11, 250; Baby Story Time study, 250–51; book ownership study, 252; and dialogic reading, 254–56; and emergent literacy, 250; factors for fostering reading, 252–53; Genevieve example, 258–59; and levelled reading, 256–57; library visit study, 251–52; Marissa example, 249–50; and overemphasis on specific skills, 253–54; and readicide, 253, 257–58, 281. *See also* childhood reading experiences
education. *See* literacy education; multilingual students, reading experiences of; schools
efferent texts, 264, 274
Efficiency series, 363n6
Eliot, Simon, 74, 76
Eliot, T.S.: "Tradition and the Individual Talent," 88–89
emergent literacy, 250
emotions, 20–23, 29, 141. *See also* catharsis; critical reading; emotive bibliotherapy; empathy
emotive bibliotherapy, 169, 175–76
empathy, 175–76, 204, 373
enchantment, 143
Engelsing, Rolf, 82
ephemeral documents. *See* rereading, of ephemeral documents
equality, 10, 11
e-Readers, 275, 275n7
Eriksson, Kai, 372
Eriksson Barajas, Katarina, 280
escape, reading as, 67–68, 169–70, 176–77
The Ethics of Reading (Miller), 127
events. *See* mass reading events
"Every Child Ready to Read @ your library" (manual), 254
experience: aesthetic experience, 38–40, 50; *vs.* articulating experience, 3; definition of, 1; duality of, 37–38; Gadamer on, 38; literary aesthetic experience, 37, 41–43; psychological understanding of, 51n1; Stigel on, 38

fan mail. *See* Lagerlöf, Selma, letters to; letters, to authors
fantasy, 122, 176

Felski, Rita, 20, 24, 29, 33, 34, 143
feminism, 328–29. *See also* gender
Fifty Cent series, 350, 355–57, 358, 359–60, 362n5
Fifty Shades of Grey (James), 329n4
film, 28, 143
first-person introspection, 100
Fish, Stanley E., 170, 264, 274
Fister, Barbara, 221
Fjestad, Ellen: *Together We Shall Hold the Heavens*, 118–20
Fleming, Denise: *Lunch*, 249
Florida, Richard, 134
flow, 225–26
Ford, Jamie. *See The Hotel on the Corner of Bitter and Sweet* (Ford)
Fosse, Jon, 117
Foucault, Michel, 91
free voluntary reading (FVR), 258
Freud, Sigmund, 89, 90, 96n2, 127
Frid, Nina, 238
Fuck Off I Love You (Mæhle), 123–24
Fuller, Danielle, 235
fun. *See* pleasure
function-advancers, 106, 107
FVR (free voluntary reading), 258

Gadamer, Hans Georg, 2, 38–39
Galef, David, 149, 150, 151
Gallagher, Kelly: *Readicide*, 253. *See also* readicide
Gallik, Jude D., 220
gatekeeping, 264, 265
Gavins, Joanna, 111
gender: and creativity, 91, 95; and differences in reading choices, 68; in letters to Lagerlöf, 81–82; and literature, 328–29, 329n4; and reason, 26
genre, 152–53, 319, 327
genre fiction, 176
"Gensynet" [The Reunion] (Christensen), 188, 190
geographic information systems (GISs), 78–79
German Romanticism, 37–38
Gerrard, Teresa, 77–78
Get into Reading (GiR) program, 183. *See also* shared reading groups, and mental health
Ghost Hunters: Book One (Hovden), 120–22

Gilbert, Julie, 221
girls, 252, 265. *See also* feminism; gender
GiR (Get into Reading) program, 183. *See also* shared reading groups, and mental health
GISs (geographic information systems), 78–79
Global Infatuation (Wirtén), 329n3
Goldberg, Elizabeth Swanson, 371
González, Norma, 57–58
graphic novels. *See* comics, and time
grief. *See* suffering; *Tonio* (Van der Heijden); trauma
Grossman, David, 199, 211
Gu, Ben, 353–54
Guattari, Félix, 302, 306, 310, 311, 313
Guillory, John, 19

Habermas, Jürgen, 233
Hall, Geoff, 280
hallucination, affective theory of, 21
Hansen, Espen Egil, 373
Harlequin, 329n3
Hartley, Jenny, 241
Harvey, Alyxandra, 272–73. *See also The Drake Chronicles* (Harvey) digital character extensions
Hawthorne, Nathaniel: *The House of Seven Gables*, 88
Hayles, N. Katherine, 34
Heap, James L., 221
He Chengwei, 355
Heidegger, Martin, 118, 124, 125
Helmers, Jan Fredrik, 343
The Help (Stockett): introduction to, 317; amateur reviews on, 321–22, 326; as melodrama, 320–21; professional reviews on, 324, 326; protagonist's journey in, 319; recommendations of, 327; sense and sensibility reviewers of, 326; setting of, 317. *See also* social melodrama
Hidle, Mie, 324, 325, 326
Higashi, Chris, 134
Hislop, Victoria: *The Return*, 325. *See also The Island* (Hislop)
historical fiction, 177
historical perspective, 58–59. *See also* childhood reading experiences
history, of reading, 73–74, 83

Hodges, Gabrielle Cliff, 117
Hoggs, James, 84n1
holding-ground, 118
hooks, bell: approach to, 19, 27, 33; on absence of pleasure in critical reading, 28–29; and critical reading as sympathetic reading, 32–33; on critical reading by lay people, 30; and cultural criticism, 20; on *Do the Right Thing* (film), 32; on immersive reading experiences, 29–30, 33; on Julien's film on Langston Hughes, 32–33; and political desire and critical reading, 34; and surface/depth metaphor, 31–32; on *Wings of Desire* (film), 31–32; *Yearning*, 27, 28–29, 29–30. *See also* critical reading
Hope, A.D., 95
horizon of expectations, 318–19
The Hotel on the Corner of Bitter and Sweet (Ford): introduction to, 317; affective reviewers of, 327; amateur reviews on, 322–23, 326, 327; as melodrama, 320; professional reviews of, 324, 326; recommendations of, 327; sense and sensibility reviewers of, 326; setting of, 317. *See also* social melodrama
The House of Seven Gables (Hawthorne), 88
Hovden, Magne: *Ghost Hunters: Book One*, 120–22
Howard, Vivian, 138, 226
Huey, E.B.: *The Psychology and Pedagogy of Reading*, 1–2
Hughes, Langston, 32–33
Hughes-Hassel, Sandra, 220–21
humans: as subjects, 126–27
Hungary: *Moli.hu*, 325
Hunsberger, Margaret, 221–22, 229
Hurston, Zora Neal, 32
Hu Yaobang, 349

I Can Read series, 256
identification, 203–4
identity, 151, 159–61
ideology, 5
Idle Hours Usefully Spent (Dutch book club), 331, 336, 344
"I'll Be There to Love and Comfort You" (Armitage): approach to, 99, 113; methodology for study on reading, 101–2; participants in study, *102*; reader responses to, 102–3, 104–6, 109–10; summary of text, 103–4; Text World Theory reading of, 106–7, 108–11, 112. *See also* cognitive poetics
imaginal, 87–88, 118
imagined community, 334
implied reader, 263–64, 274
inference, 107
informational bibliotherapy, 171, 178
Ingemanns, B.S.: "Bekjendelser" ["Confessions"], 193–95
The Intellectual Life of the British Working Class (Rose), 59, 76
intensive/extensive reading, 82
intentionality and unintentionality, 41–42, 48–49
International Reading Association: "Leisure Reading," 253
Internet, 264, 265, 274. *See also* blogs; online reading audiences; social media
interpretation: and cognitive poetics, 100; and quantitative research, 74; as reading, 28. *See also* critical reading
interpretive community, 170, 264, 274
Iser, Wolfgang, 221, 263, 274
The Island (Hislop): introduction to, 317; affective reviewers of, 327; amateur reviews of, 323, 327; as melodrama, 320; professional reviews of, 324–25; recommendations of, 327; setting of, 317. *See also* social melodrama

Ivanič, Roz, 151, 153
James, E.L.: *Fifty Shades of Grey*, 329n4
Jameson, Fredric: approach to, 19, 27, 33; on critical reading, 27–28, 30; and cultural criticism, 20; and political desire and critical reading, 34; *The Political Unconscious*, 27–28, 30–31; *Signatures of the Visible*, 27, 28; on society, 34; spatial metaphors in works of, 30–31; writing style of, 27. *See also* critical reading
Jansen, Dick, 337
Jauss, Hans Robert, 318–19, 327, 328
Jeg er Prableen [*I am Prableen*] (Kaur), 369. *See also* blogs, on Norway mass shooting; Kaur, Prableen
Jensen, Lotte, 334, 339
"Jens Thorstensen" (Jørgensen), 195

Jin Guantao, 354
Johannes, G.J., 333
Johansen, Jørgen Dines, 50
Jørgensen, Hans Otto: "Jens Thorstensen," 195
journals: "Answers to Correspondents" section in, 77–78
Julien, Isaac, 32–33

Kant, Immanuel, 25–26, 126–27
Kaplan, Ann, 371–72, 373
Karr, Clarence, 76
Kate Greenaway Medal. *See* reading groups, in schools
Kaur, Prableen, 369, 371, 381. *See also* blogs, on Norway mass shooting
kenosis, 95
Kloek, J.J., 334
Kogawa, Joy, 141
Kong, Shuyu: *Consuming Literature*, 350
Koopman, Emy M., 200
Koopmans, Anske, 331
Krashen, Stephen D.: *The Power of Reading*, 253, 258
Kristeva, Julia, 89
Krøger, Catherine, 325
Krol, Ellen, 341
Kuomintang [Nationalist Party], 358, 363n8

Lacan, Jacques, 89, 94
LaCapra, Dominick, 372, 373, 375
Lafontaine, August, 341
Lagerlöf, Selma, 75, 79–80, 83. *See also* Lagerlöf, Selma, letters to
Lagerlöf, Selma, letters to: categories of, 79, 81; diversity of, 74–75, 78; emotional reading practices in, 82; and gender of readers, 81–82; from help-seekers, 75, 76; and influence of press, 83; and intensive reading practices, 82, 83; macro-analytical analysis of, 78–79; methodology in study of, 76, 81; and performance of reading, 81; religious, 82; and social class, 80–81; specific descriptions in, 77. *See also* Lagerlöf, Selma; letters, to authors
La lecture et la vie (Lyon-Caen), 79
language, 49–50, 57
Laub, Dori, 370, 376–77
Lazzarato, Maurizio, 265

Leccardi, Carmen, 219, 230
Lee, Spike: *Do the Right Thing*, 32
Leech, Geoffrey N., 100
Leerssen, Joep, 332, 333, 335, 341
Lefebvre, Henri, 218
"Leisure Reading" (International Reading Association), 253
letters, to authors: approach to, 6, 74, 83–84; Balzac and Sue study, 79; for history of reading, 83; interpretation of, 76–77; for macro-analytical analysis, 77, 78; truthfulness in, 76; writers of as minority, 76. *See also* Lagerlöf, Selma, letters to
levelled reading, 256–57, 312, 313
Lever! (Alive!) (Martinovic), 369. *See also* blogs, on Norway mass shooting; Martinovic, Emma
Levy, Andrea: *Small Island*, 144–45
Lexile Framework for Reading, 256
libraries: in China in 1980s, 351; and dialogic reading, 255; in Haarlem, Netherlands, 343; influence of, 64–65, 250. *See also* reading groups, in Sweden
Li Honglin: "No Forbidden Zones in Reading," 349
lines of flight, 311
lists, 152, 156. *See also* rereading, of ephemeral documents
literacy, early. *See* early literacy
literacy education, 313–14
literary aesthetic experience, 37, 41–43. *See also* aesthetic experience
literary criticism. *See* critical reading; literary reviews, by teenagers; new criticism; social melodrama
literary influence, 88–89, 90–92, 95, 96n1
literary reviews, by teenagers: approach to, 7, 115, 116; and close readings, 129n1; on construction of literature, 123–24; and dwelling, 118, 119–20, 124–25; focus on quality of reading experience, 115–16, 117–18; and invisibility of reading experience, 116; and patronizing attitudes, 123–24; and readers' working through subjectivization, 125–26, 127–28; reviews as emblematic of reading experiences, 117; reviews of *Fuck Off I Love You* (Mæhle), 123–24; reviews of *Ghost Hunters: Book One* (Hovden),

120–22; reviews of *Together We Shall Hold the Heavens* (Fjestad), 118–20; tangible connections for entering literary world, 120, 122; and tempering, 128–29
literary scholars, 19. *See also* critical reading
literature: and connections to other people, 120; emotional effects of, 169; as place to be, 118, 120; as social practice, 280. *See also* reading; reading experience
Littau, Karin, 20, 24
Liverpool Reads, 144, 145
Lives of the Saints (Ricci), 143
Li Zhong, 356, 357, 358
Loots, Cornelis, 343
love, 94, 95
Lunch (Fleming), 249
Lyon-Caen, Judith: *La lecture et la vie*, 79

Mæhle, Lars: *Fuck Off I Love You*, 123–24
magazines, 65, 220, 221
Mai, Anne-Marie, 124
Markless, Sharon, 168
Martinovic, Emma, 369, 370, 376, 377, 379–80, 381. *See also* blogs, on Norway mass shooting
Marvell, Andrew, 90, 96n6
Marx, Karl, 35
Masny, Diana, 302
Massey, Doreen, 58, 68–69
mass reading events (MREs): approach to, 8, 134, 135, 146–47; author events, 139–41, 145–46; in Canada, 141–42; *Canada Reads* (radio program), 134, 136, 137; community experienced through, 143–45; goals for, 133–34; growing prevalence of, 134; local made social through, 141–43; and mass media, 135, 136–37, 138, 146; methodology for study on, 133; multiple connections created by, 138–39; One Book, One Community programs, 133, 134–35, 140–41; pleasure from, 137–39, 146–47; public spaces for hosting, 135; Richard & Judy Book Club (TV book club), 134, 135–36, 137; and self-improvement goals, 145; spectacle aspects of, 145–46; and technological change, 146; types of activities in, 138
Mathijsen, Marita, 334, 339, 344

McChesney, Robert, 263
McDonald, Bertrum H., 79
McKechnie, Lynne (E.F.): *Reading Matters*, 2–3, 253–54
media: and mass reading events, 135, 136–37, 138, 146; and suffering, 201; and trauma, 372. *See also* blogs; social media
melodrama, 317–18. *See also* social melodrama
memoirs. *See* autobiographies
men: in letters to Lagerlöf, 81–82; and mental health problems, 173; reading by, 203, 237. *See also* boys, reading by
mental health, 172, 173, 179, 183–84. *See also* bibliotherapy, and mental health; shared reading groups, and mental health
Merleau-Ponty, Maurice, 120
metaphors: for rereading, 158–59, 163; and Text World Theory, 111–12
Mijnhardt, W.W., 334
Miller, Carolyn R., 152–53
Miller, John Hillis, 20, 127
Milton, John: *Paradise Lost*, 90, 91, 96n6
MLT (multiple literacies theory), 301, 302, 305, 313–14
modal-worlds, 108–9
Moli.hu, 325
Moll, Luis, 57–58
Montaigne, Michel de, 128
Moretti, Franco, 74
MREs. *See* mass reading events
Mukařovský, Jan, 41–42, 50–51. *See also* intentionality and unintentionality
multilingual students, reading experiences of: approach to, 12, 301, 314; and access to books, 313; Anzor example, 306–8; comparisons of self to characters, 309–10; desire to read generated from, 304–5; impacts of reading experiences, 311, 312; and individual choice of books, 309, 311–12; and language of instruction, 311; and levelled reading, 312, 313; methodology for study on, 303, 311; and multiple literacies theory, 302, 305, 307, 313–14; overview of project on, 303–4; and process of becoming, 306–7, 308, 312–13; and reading proficiency, 312; and rhizo-analysis, 302–3, 312; and

social dimension of reading, 305–6; and typical reading assessments, 311; underestimation of, 314; and views of community and school, 310
multiple literacies theory (MLT), 301, 302, 305, 313–14
Multiplicity project. *See* multilingual students, reading experiences of
My Sister Lives on the Mantelpiece (Pitcher), 283, 292–94
myth, 5

Nabokov, Vladimir, 150
National Early Literacy Panel, 253–54
national literature, 334
nation-building, 332–33
Neopets (virtual pet website), 265
NetGalley, 264
Netherlands, United Kingdom of the, 331, 332–34, 335, 340, 343. *See also* book clubs, Dutch
NetSlaves, 265
New Criticism, 20–21, 22, 23
Nietzsche, Friedrich, 95
9/11 attacks, 371
"No Forbidden Zones in Reading" (Li), 349
Norberg-Schulz, Christian, 124, 125
Norheim, Marta, 324, 325
Norway. *See* blogs, on Norway mass shooting; *Bokelskere.no*; literary reviews, by teenagers; multilingual students, reading experiences of
Norway mass shooting, 367. *See also* blogs, on Norway mass shooting
nostalgia, 360
NoveList K-8 Plus, 256
Nussbaum, Martha C., 201

OBOCs (One Book, One Community programs), 133–34, 134–35, 140–41. *See also* mass reading events
Ødegård, Knut, 324–25
Oedipus complex, 96n3
OlderWomanGroup (*TwilightSaga.com*), 270, *271*, 272
Oliver, Mary Beth, 201
Omens of the Millennium (Bloom), 87
Ommundsen, Wenche, 139
One Book, One Community programs (OBOCs), 133–34, 134–35, 140–41. *See also* mass reading events

online reading audiences: approach to, 11–12, 263; and affective labour, 265, 266–67; aggregation of, 266; community formed among, 270, 272; development of, 268–69, 274; digital character extensions for *The Drake Chronicles* (Harvey), 263, 264, 273–74; and e-reading platforms, 275; and girls, 265; Older WomanGroup (*TwilightSaga.com*), 270, *271*, 272; peer-to-peer interactions on, 267, 269; proprietary sites for, 266, 267, 268, 269; publishers' benefits from, 274; *RandomBuzzers.com*, 263, 266–68, 275n2; and reader–author interactions, 267–68, 272–73; and removal of gatekeepers, 265, 267; and romance readers study, 264; *TwilightSaga.com*, 263, 266, 268–70, *271*, 272; and Web analytics, 274
Opening the Book project, 238, 243n3
Oprah's Book Club, 134
originality, 88, 95. *See also* literary influence

Paradise Lost (Milton), 90, 91, 96n6
participant observation, 173
past, 88
Pattee, Amy, 266
Pawley, Christine, 81
Pearl, Nancy, 134
PEER sequence, 255
peer-to-peer sites, 264. *See also* online reading audiences; *RandomBuzzers.com*
Peeters, Frederik, 227
Peplow, David, 280
Petiet, Francien, 340
Pitcher, Annabel: *My Sister Lives on the Mantelpiece*, 283, 292–94
PLA (Public Library Association), 254
pleasure: of critical reading, 29, 34; from mass reading events, 137–39, 146–47; reading for, 220, 225, 281; and reading groups, 185, 282, 285, 295
The Political Unconscious (Jameson), 27–28, 30–31
politics, 4, 10–11, 69. *See also* blogs, on Norway mass shooting; book clubs, Dutch; book series fever; China; early literacy; multilingual students, reading experiences of; online reading audiences; reading groups, in schools; social melodrama

Possession (Byatt): approach to, 6, 88; on encounter with literary precursor, 92, 94, 95, 96n8; letters in, 93–94; summary of, 93–94; theory in, 96n9

Poulet, Georges, 221

The Power of Reading (Krashen), 253, 258

practical criticism, 96n1

Practical Criticism (Richards), 22–23

practice, 4, 7–8. *See also* bibliotherapy, and mental health; comics, and time; mass reading events; reading groups, in Sweden; rereading, of ephemeral documents; shared reading groups, and mental health; *Tonio* (Van der Heijden)

Prinos, Anne Merethe K., 325

proficiency, in reading, 311, 312, 313. *See also* reading assessment

psychology, 22

The Psychology and Pedagogy of Reading (Huey), 1–2

Public Library Association (PLA), 254

publishing industry, 263, 266, 275n1. *See also* online reading audiences

Pybus, Jennifer, 265

quality, 117–18

Radway, Janice: *Reading the Romance*, 227, 264, 267, 269, 270, 272

Raising a Reader Massachusetts, 255–56

Rancière, Jacques, 10–11

RandomBuzzers.com, 263, 266–68, 275n2

Reader Development program (British Council), 238

reader response theory, 59, 116, 168–69, 170, 221, 263–64

readers: negative perceptions of, 285–86; as subjects, 126–27

readicide, 253, 257–58, 281

Readicide (Gallagher), 253

reading: as being embedded in contexts that can't be fully understood, 2; as enchantments, 143; as escape, 67–68, 169–70, 176–77; as flow activity, 225; as focal practice, 229; Gadamer on, 2; in Germanic languages, 5; history of, 73–74, 83; Huey on, 1–2; as interpretation, 28; as open and uncertain phenomenon, 1–2; for pleasure, 220, 225, 281; reasons for, 138; as seeing, 5; and theory, 5; and time, 220–22; transactional process of, 57–58, 168–69, 187–88, 217, 264. *See also* readers; reading experience; reading groups; rereading

reading aloud, 63, 193, 253

Reading and the Reader (Davis), 118

reading assessment, 301, 302, 311, 314. *See also* proficiency, in reading

Reading Don't Fix No Chevys (Smith and Willhelm), 258

reading events. *See* mass reading events

reading experience: approach to, 1, 2, 3, 4, 6, 13, 37; and aesthetic experience, 37, 38–40, 50; articulated, 43, 47, 116, 117; and book as aesthetic and literary object, 45; challenges to, 48–49; characteristics of good, 45–46; and classroom, 117; commonplace notions of, 37; definition of, 3, 368; as difficult to articulate, 49–50; dual role of for entertainment and knowledge, 44–45; emotional and ethical components of, 368; enjoyment in, 48; and expectations and motivations, 47–48; and independent reading, 301; as individual, 43; as invisible, 116; Jauss on, 318–19; and literary aesthetic experience, 37, 41–43; methodology for study of, 43–44, 51; on plotting the, 3; reception theory approach to, 41–43, 50–51; and shared reading, 185; as spatial phenomenon, 51; as temporal phenomenon, 47, 49, 51. *See also* experience

Reading Experience Database (RED), 3, 73, 368

reading groups: for adults, 294–95; and bookstores, 235. *See also* bibliotherapy, and mental health; book clubs, Dutch; mass reading events; reading groups, in schools; reading groups, in Sweden; shared reading groups, and mental health

reading groups, in schools: approach to, 12, 279–80, 282; case study groups, 296–97; as countercultural, 286–87, 290–91; differentiated from English class, 279, 284–85, 295; and discourse analytic approach, 281, 292; discussion of texts in, 291–94; as extracurricular, 279; focus on good quality literature in,

283–84; and food and drink, 290; and humour, 291; methodology for shadowing study, 282–83, 288, 297n2; motives for study on, 281; and negative perceptions of reading, 285–86; non-hierarchical nature of, 287, 288, 289, 290, 291, 297n4; pleasure as focus of, 285; as safe space for readers, 286; and school reading policies, 281–82, 295–96; teachers in, 287–88

reading groups, in Sweden: approach to, 10; contemporary, 236, 237; future work needed on, 242, 243; history of, 233–35, 236; in libraries, 238, 239, 240–41, 242–43; and low price of books, 237–38; methodology for study on, 237, 239; and minority culture, 239; participants in library circles, 240–41; participation rates in, 235–36, 237; regional variations in, 238–39; study associations in, 243n2; study on in Uppsala, 243n4; terminology for, 236; types of literature read by library circles, 242

Reading Matters (Ross, McKechnie, and Rothbauer), 2–3, 253–54

reading revolution, 82

reading studies, 3

Reading the Romance (Radway), 227, 264, 267, 269, 270, 272

reason, 25–26

reception theory, 41–42, 50–51, 59. *See also* intentionality and unintentionality

RED (*Reading Experience Database*), 3, 73, 368

Rehberg Sedo, DeNel, 235, 241

requiem novels. See *Tonio* (Van der Heijden)

rereading: as encounter with past self, 150; and identity as writer, 151; for mastery over text, 149–50; by readers of Selma Lagerlöf, 82. *See also* rereading, of ephemeral documents

rereading, of ephemeral documents: approach to, 8, 149, 151–52; and absences in texts, 155–56; calendars, 152, 154–55, 161–62; conclusions from, 162–63; as contingent, 159; and failure of note systems, 160–61; and future reading and editing, 155; and identity, 159–61; lists, 152, 156; and meaningfulness of tools for writing, 154–55; metaphors for, 158–59, 163; methodology in study on, 152–53; and performative rereading in study, 154, 163; and relationships, 161–62; and revision of texts, 156–57; shopping lists, 152; and writing as memory aid, 157. *See also* rereading

"Researching the Reading Experience" conference, 14n1

The Return (Hislop), 325

rhetorical reading, 20

rhizo-analysis, 302–3

Ricci, Nino: *Lives of the Saints*, 143

Richard & Judy Book Club (TV book club), 134, 135–36, 137

Richards, I.A.: *Practical Criticism*, 22–23

Ringgaard, Dan, 124

Roback, Diane, 269

Rock, Jan, 341

Rodge, Pradnya, 220–21

romance novels, 329n3

romance readers, 227, 264, 267, 269, 270, 272

Rosa, Hartmut, 218–20, 224, 229

Rose, Jonathan, 59, 73, 76

Rosenblatt, Louise, 57, 116, 187, 217, 264, 274

Rosoff, Meg: *The Bride's Farewell*, 291–92

Ross, Amanda, 137

Ross, Catherine Sheldrick, 2–3, 171, 252–53

Rothbauer, Paulette: *Reading Matters*, 2–3, 253–54

Sabeti, Shari, 217

scarcity of time, 219

Scheele, Brigitte, 200, 212

Scheuerman, William E., 218

Schneider, Greice, 228

scholars, literary, 19. *See also* critical reading

Scholes, Robert, 58

schools: English classes in, 279, 284–85; language of instruction in, 311; and levelled reading, 312; political intervention in, 69; and reading experiences, 116, 117; reading policies in, 281–82, 301. *See also* literacy education; multilingual students, reading experiences of;

reading assessment; reading groups, in schools
Schopenhauer, Arthur, 5
science fiction, 176
Sedgwick, Eve Kosofsky, 31, 34
Seeing Stars (Armitage), 103
Seen Reading (Wilson), 14n4
Serlen, Rachel, 74
shadowing, 279, 297n1. *See also* reading groups, in schools
Shakespeare, William, 89, 96n2
Shanghai Culture Publishing House, 355. *See also Fifty Cent* series
shared reading. *See* bibliotherapy, and mental health; book clubs, Dutch; mass reading events; reading groups, in schools; reading groups, in Sweden; shared reading groups, and mental health
shared reading groups, and mental health: approach to, 9, 183; clinical group for, 191–92, 193; community seniors group for, 191, 192, 193; conclusions from, 195–96; discussions on depression in, 195; embodiment in reading experience, 188–89, 194–95; facilitation of, 184; and framing of activity, 192–93; as "free space," 187; group processes in, 184–85; and literal interpretations of text, 188, 189; and mental health, 183–84; mental health hospital groups for, 186–87; methodology for study of, 185–86; participation of staff in, 187; and reading experience research, 185; and recovery from mental health problems, 189; schedule of, 184; and sitting quietly, 189–90; and social interactions, 187–88, 190–91, 193, 194–95; therapeutic effects of, 184–85; types of literature read in, 184; and unintended consequences, 185. *See also* bibliotherapy, and mental health
"The Ship-Boy's Tale" (Blixen), 188–89, 190
shopping lists, 152. *See also* rereading, of ephemeral documents
Short, Mick, 100, 103
Shrodes, Caroline, 169
Shusterman, Richard, 40
Sichuan People's Publishing House, 354
Sidney, Philip: *Atrophil and Stella*, 91

Signatures of the Visible (Jameson), 27, 28
Silfverstolpe, Malla, 233
Sisters series, 363n6
Skei, Hans H., 324, 325, 326
Small, Ruth, 258
Small Island (Levy), 144–45
Smith, Michael W.: *Reading Don't Fix No Chevys*, 258
social acceleration, 219, 224
social bibliotherapy, 170–71, 177
social interactions, 187–88, 190–91
social media, 265, 272, 273, 373. *See also* blogs; blogs, on Norway mass shooting
social melodrama: introduction to, 12, 317–18; affective reading responses to, 326–27; analysis of reviewers, 325–27; appeal of, 327–28; characteristics of, 319, 327; differences among, 320; historical development of, 328–29; literary critics on, 318; methodology for study on, 318, 321; popularity of, 318; reviews by amateurs on *Bokelskere.no*, 321–23; reviews by professionals, 324–25; sense and sensibility reviewers, 325–26. *See also The Help* (Stockett); *The Hotel on the Corner of Bitter and Sweet* (Ford); *The Island* (Hislop)
social networks, 265. *See also* blogs; social media
socio-cultural theory, 69
spatial perspective, 58. *See also* childhood reading experiences
Squires, Clare, 235
St. Clair, William, 83
Stevenson, Robert Louis: *Dr. Jekyll and Mr. Hyde*, 89
Stewart, Susan, 360
Stigel, Jørgen, 38
Stockett, Kathryn. *See The Help* (Stockett)
Stockwell, Peter, 99
The Stone Carvers (Urquhart), 137, 142
Stony Brook Reading and Language Project, 254
Streatfield, David, 168
Street, Brian, 280
study circles. *See* reading groups, in Sweden
subjects, 126–27
Sue, Eugène, 79
suffering, 199–200, 200–201, 210, 212. *See also Tonio* (Van der Heijden); trauma

Sulzby, Elizabeth, 250
Swann, Joan, 280
Sweden, 233–34, 237–38. *See also Bokcirklar.se* [Bookcircles.se]; reading groups, in Sweden
sympathy, 204

Teal, William, 250
technological acceleration, 219
teenage book market, 67, 68, 275n8
teenagers. *See* literary reviews, by teenagers
Television Without Pity (TWoP), 265–66
tempering, 7, 128–29
Terranova, Tiziana, 265
terrorism, 371, 372
text-worlds, 101, 106, 107–8
Text World Theory framework: overview of, 99, 101, 112; blended-worlds, 111; discourse-world, 101, 107; function-advancers, 106, 107; and inference, 107; and metaphor, 111–12; modal-worlds, 108–9; text-world, 101, 106, 107; world-builders, 106, 107; world-repair, 109–10; world-replacement, 110. *See also* cognitive poetics; "I'll Be There to Love and Comfort You" (Armitage)
TF series (*Towards the Future* series), 354
theatre professionals, 149–50
theory, 4, 5. *See also* childhood reading experiences; cognitive poetics; critical reading; Lagerlöf, Selma, letters to; letters, to authors; literary influence; *Possession* (Byatt); reader response theory; reading experience; reception theory; Text World Theory framework
third-person observation, 100
Thompson, Craig: *Blankets*, 217
Thompson, John B., 263
"Thoughts on Education" (Kant), 126–27
time, 218–19, 220–22. *See also* acceleration; comics, and time
time-use studies, 219, 220
Together We Shall Hold the Heavens (Fjestad), 118–20
Tollens, Hendrik, 343
Tonio (Van der Heijden): approach to, 9, 199; and catharsis, 202–3, 205–6, 209, 210, 212; clarification and insight gained from, 209–10, 211–12; content of, 202; emotional responses provoked by, 206–7, 211–12; methodology for study on, 203–4; motives for reading, 204–6, 210–11; narrative style of, 202; responses to narrative style of, 207–9; success of, 202; and suffering, 199, 202, 212
Towards the Future series, 354
Toyne, Jackie, 170, 171
tracked reading. *See* levelled reading
"Tradition and the Individual Talent" (Eliot), 88–89
transactional process of reading, 57–58, 168–69, 187–88, 217, 264
translations, 342–43, 343–44
trauma, 370, 372–73, 377–78. *See also* suffering
Troilus and Criseyde (Chaucer), 90
TwilightSaga.com, 263, 266, 268–70, 271, 272
Twilight series, 268–69, 329n4
TWoP (*Television Without Pity*), 265–66

unintentionality and intentionality, 41–42, 48–49
Urquhart, Jane: *The Stone Carvers*, 137, 142
Usherwood, Bob, 170, 171

Vandaele, Jeroen, 100
Van der Heijden, A.F.Th., 202–3. *See also Tonio* (Van der Heijden)
Vartanian, Talin, 137
The Very Hungry Caterpillar (Carle), 251
Villaume, Susan Kidd, 256
Vold, Tonje, 126
voyeurism, 211
Vygotsky, Lev, 57

Wang Dongqing, 358
Wang Luxiang, 351, 361
Wang Zizhou, 349
Warner, Michael, 20, 24, 25–26
Web analytics, 274
Weil, Simone, 5
Wells, Gordon, 250
Wenders, Wim: *Wings of Desire* (film), 31–32
Wenger, Etienne, 288
The Western Canon (Bloom), 89
Whitehurst, Grover J., 254–55
Whiteley, Sara, 280
Willhelm, Jeffrey D.: *Reading Don't Fix No Chevies*, 258

Wilson, Julie: *Seen Reading*, 14n4
Wimsatt, William K.: "The Affective Fallacy," 20–22
Wings of Desire (film), 31–32
Winterson, Jeanette, 91, 96n7
Wirtén, Eva Hemmungs: *Global Infatuation*, 329n3
witnesses, 371
Wittgenstein, Ludwig, 2
women, 265. *See also* feminism; gender; girls
Woolf, Fergus, 96n8
Woolf, Virginia, 90, 91
world-builders, 106, 107
world-repair, 109–10
world-replacement, 110
writing: as memory aid, 157

Xiao Ying, 359, 361
Xie Xizhang, 361
Xie Yong, 354

YA book market, 67, 68, 275n8
Yearning (hooks), 27, 28–29, 29–30

Zhang Lixian, 361
Zhang Yiwu, 351
Zhao, Dingxin, 352
Ziolkowska, Sarah, 226

www.ingramcontent.com/pod-product-compliance
Lightning Source LLC
Chambersburg PA
CBHW072141100526
44589CB00015B/2029